C0-AWO-096

THE BEHAVIOR OF INCOME SHARES

Selected Theoretical and Empirical Issues

NATIONAL BUREAU OF ECONOMIC RESEARCH

CONFERENCE ON RESEARCH IN INCOME AND WEALTH

The Behavior of Income Shares

Selected Theoretical and Empirical Issues

STUDIES IN INCOME AND WEALTH
VOLUME TWENTY-SEVEN
BY THE CONFERENCE ON RESEARCH
IN INCOME AND WEALTH

A REPORT OF THE
NATIONAL BUREAU OF ECONOMIC RESEARCH, INC.

PUBLISHED BY
PRINCETON UNIVERSITY PRESS, PRINCETON
1964

L. C. CARD: 63-20662

Printed in the United States of America

Relation of National Bureau Directors to Publications Reporting Conference Proceedings

Since the present volume is a record of conference proceedings, it has been exempted from the rules governing submission of manuscripts to, and critical review by, the Board of Directors of the National Bureau. It has, however, been reviewed and accepted for publication by the Director of Research.

(*Resolution adopted July 6, 1948, as revised November 21, 1949*)

Prefatory Note

This volume of *Studies in Income and Wealth* is the outcome of the Conference on Income Shares held in April 1961 at the Carnegie Endowment International Center in New York City. The Program Committee consisted of Charles F. Schwartz (chairman), Charles L. Schultze, and Louis Weiner; the latter two served as coeditors for this proceedings volume, ably assisted by Stephen P. Taylor. Joan Tron prepared the manuscript for press and H. Irving Forman drew the charts.

Contents

THE BEHAVIOR OF INCOME SHARES

Selected Theoretical and Empirical Issues

Introduction

CHARLES L. SCHULTZE AND LOUIS WEINER

THE Conference on the Behavior of Income Shares held in New York in April 1961 covered a wide range of issues and approaches. The first three papers by Scitovsky, Lebergott, and Solow are devoted to a general consideration of the determinants of factor shares in the long run. The first paper is primarily a survey of current theory; the latter two include considerable empirical material as well. The paper by Schultze is also a theoretical and empirical paper, but it deals with short-run movements in shares and emphasizes the impact of cyclical changes in shares on the movement of output. In the fifth paper, Simon Goldberg provides a comprehensive study of long-run income shares for the Canadian economy, and a supplement by Frank Leacy analyzes the short-run fluctuations. The final two papers take up special problems: Michael Gort is concerned with the conceptual and measurement problems of factor shares by industry and George Borts copes with the difficult issues involved in estimating income produced on a state and regional basis. A number of positive contributions were made by the discussants, many of whom went beyond a critique of the main papers, introducing new approaches and in some cases new data. In summary, the conference made much progress in particular areas, but many basic problems of theory, of concept, and of data adequacy remain unresolved.

In the opening paper of the Conference, Scitovsky surveys the major competing theories of income distribution. As he points out, there are four possible subjects that theories of income distribution could deal with: the distribution of income by occupations, by size, by factor shares, and by the income categories of the official personal income accounts. It is with the third classification, functional distribution, that Scitovsky is mainly concerned. Two different streams of theory can be distinguished in the literature dealing with functional income distribution. The first concentrates on the individual decision processes of business firms and factor suppliers. It is consequently microeconomic in orientation, and usually, although not universally, oriented towards a marginal productivity approach. The second major stream of theory, currently represented by

NOTE: We wish to acknowledge here the substantial contribution made by Stephen P. Taylor.

the work of Phelps-Brown and Kaldor, is macroeconomic in character, and is based upon an aggregate, Keynesian-type framework.

Scitovsky further subdivides income distribution theories into those which treat the short-run change in factor shares and those which attempt to explain the (alleged) long-run constancy of shares. After examining the various reasons given in the literature for the countercyclical movement of labor's share in national income, Scitovsky devotes his major attention to the theories which attempt to deal with the relative constancy of shares in the long run.

The first of these is the marginal productivity theory. The chief feature of this approach is its reliance upon factor substitution and downward sloping demand curves as an explanation of relative stability of shares. Since prices and quantities are assumed to move in opposite directions, some stability in shares is guaranteed. Indeed Bronfenbrenner has shown that constant elasticities of substitution substantially different from one are consistent with relatively moderate changes in shares. Further, the direct impact of relative prices on factor substitution is reinforced, indirectly, in the goods market; as relative factor prices change, the relative prices of goods change, inducing substitution towards those goods employing relatively more of the cheapened factor. The mutual interaction of relative prices and factor quantities may be expected to operate in the assumed manner, however, only in periods of full utilization of resources. Scitovsky further points out that the occurrence of technological progress of a nonneutral character can result in changing factor shares, even if all the other assumptions of the marginal productivity theory are met.

The basic characteristic of macroeconomic theories is that they utilize the identity, $P/O = (P/K) \cdot (K/O)$ (where P = property income, K = capital stock, and O = output) to explain the stability of factor shares. If any two of these ratios can be shown to be constant, the remaining one is, by necessity, constant. The theories of Kaldor, and Phelps-Brown and Weber, each of whom uses some variant of this approach, are examined in turn. The chief problem of course is the determination of which ratios are fundamental, and which derived. Further, it is indeed possible that one or more of the above ratios may be more appropriately explained by the combined effect of factor substitution and technological change, as in the microeconomic theories.

In commenting on Scitovsky's paper, Edward Denison raises the point that the venerable "constants" so often cited in the literature, P/O, P/K, and K/O must refer to the same conceptual framework. Each time one of the above numbers appears in the ratios, it must be the same number. However, the first two ratios are customarily in current dollar terms, whereas the final ratio, the capital-output ratio, is usually cited in constant dollar terms. To preserve consistency, a fourth ratio—the price of capital goods divided by the price of national product—must therefore be introduced. Denison then goes on to point out that there is no set of definitions of the various numbers, which uniformly applied, will allow all three ratios to show long-term stability in the United States. Hence, says Denison, these arguments which purport to explain long-run constancy of the various ratios, are attempting to explain a nonexistent phenomenon.

As if in reply to Denison, Modigliani opens his comment on Scitovsky's paper with the observation that "the task of explaining the stability [of factor shares] is such a fascinating and challenging game that it is hard to resist, even if the stability is after all a figment of somebody's imagination." Modigliani calls on his own theory of saving, as a major aid in the explanation of long-run share stability. As he points out, any explanation of factor shares must involve capital-output relationships, which in turn cannot be explained in the absence of a theory of saving. The Modigliani-Brumberg saving hypothesis embodies a relationship between the saving rate and the ratio of wealth to income. This relationship is such that a constant exponential growth rate of income and a constant interest rate produces a rate of wealth accumulation equal to the rate of growth in income; i.e., K/O, looked at from the supply of capital side, will be constant. Similarly, on the demand side of the market for capital, if technological progress is neutral and occurs at a relatively constant rate, then a stable interest rate implies a constant K/O ratio, and a constant exponential rate of growth in income. But with the market cleared at a constant capital-output ratio and a constant rate of return to capital, factor shares will also be constant. This is indeed a fascinating explanation of what both Denison asserts and the data in Kuznets' *Capital Formation* show to be a "figment of somebody's imagination."

Stanley Lebergott's paper on "Factor Shares in the Long Term" approaches the problem of the constancy of shares from a completely different viewpoint. The share of national income flowing to wages or against capital is a function of the quantity and price ratios of the two factors. But, says Lebergott, the quantity ratios are themselves a function of price ratios in an earlier period. Lebergott then proceeds to cite the reasons why the price of capital service must "bear a constant long-term proportionality to that of labor."

In a competitive economy, long-run changes in wage rates will be approximately equal in both capital goods producing and capital goods using industries. Moreover, historical experience suggests that productivity gains in the two groups of industries have not been so different as to make their wage costs diverge significantly. Hence the capital service prices and unit wage costs have maintained a more or less unchanged relationship. This is the chief reason, says Lebergott, to expect that share ratios should not have changed drastically.

Unit labor costs, however, as Jack Alterman points out in his discussion of Lebergott's paper are not the "price of labor"; hence the constancy of the relationship between capital goods prices and unit labor costs does not reflect a constant relationship between the prices of the two factors. Waiving this point, proportional movements in the price of capital goods and unit labor costs will not result in constancy of labor shares unless the capital-output ratio and the rate of return on capital remain unchanged (or change in opposite directions by proportionately equal amounts). But given continuing changes in production functions and steady increases in the capital-labor ratio, what factors explain constancy of the capital output ratio and the marginal product of capital? These questions drive us back once again to consideration of "neutrality" of innovations, the elasticity of substitution, and shifts in product mix—precisely the kinds of considerations which Lebergott set out to avoid in his approach to the problems of factor shares.

In the second and empirical part of his paper Lebergott carefully examines the nature of the factor share data during the period prior to 1919, and concludes that we have little evidence on which to base any firm conclusion about the constancy of shares during that period. Many of the techniques used to construct income data during these early years almost guarantee stability in shares. Moreover the frequently cited conclusion, based on studies of Simon Kuznets and Gale Johnson, that the labor share has increased since these earlier years is found by Lebergott to be without substantial foundation. Most of the rise comes in the single year between 1919 and 1920, and Lebergott points out that the particular assumptions used in constructing entrepreneurial income—whose decline explains most of the change—appear to be unreasonable. Using alternative techniques, Lebergott produces a series which shows little change in share between the two years. Since 1919 is used as a link year between earlier and later time series, this revision largely eliminates the long-run increase in labor shares.

Lebergott concludes that the problem of factor shares is almost hopelessly complicated by the problem of disentangling the labor and capital components of entrepreneurial income. Neither of the two commonly used techniques for making this split provides realistic answers. We can neither assume that the rate of return on capital in the unincorporated sector is equal to that in the corporate sector, nor that the return to entrepreneurial labor is equal to that of employees. Hence, analyses of factor shares might be more appropriately confined to those sectors, like manufacturing and public utilities, where the unincorporated business component is small.

One promising step in this direction is taken by Alterman who develops an analysis of factor shares for the corporate sector of the economy. Here the problem of allocating entrepreneurial income does not arise. After adjusting corporate profits for the effect of accelerated amortization and changing methods of depreciation, Alterman finds that factor shares on net corporate income were almost exactly the same in 1922–29 as in the period 1947–59. If adjustments were made to place depreciation on a replacement cost basis, however, the property share would presumably have fallen.

Further refinement of data for the corporate sector, including the development of longer-term historical series on corporate capital stocks, output, and labor productivity, may furnish insights into the determinants of factor shares which cannot be gained by working with aggregate national income data, complicated as the latter are by the problem of allocating entrepreneurial income.

With Robert Solow's paper "Capital, Labor and Income in Manufacturing," the focus shifts from statistical description of income distribution to an attempt to measure the long-run underpinnings of factor shares as stated in production functions. His emphasis is on substitutability among factors in production; if factors are paid according to their marginal productivities, long-run distribution of total income hinges on the degree to which one type of input can be substituted for another to equalize marginal gains. As Solow points out, production functions do not determine income distribution by themselves, since structure of demand acts on the other side of the market to influence product mix and hence the mix of production functions actually used. Nonetheless, he chooses to look at production functions alone. The paper is an extension of his earlier work with Arrow, Chenery, and Minhas on a form of production function more general than the Cobb-Douglas form. Both forms assume constant elasticity of substitution among factors, but Solow's allows that elasticity to be of any value, whereas Cobb-Douglas implies that it be always unity; the Cobb-Douglas form is, in the algebra, a special case of the broader function used by Solow.

Using both cross-sectional data for U.S. regions and time-series information, Solow undertakes to measure all of the parameters of his model for manufacturing industries, basing the calculation on a sequence of assumptions concisely listed by Eisner in his comment on the Solow paper. The results of the calculation are far from conclusive, however, since the regional material yields a wide scatter of estimates of substitution elasticities that tends well above others found in international comparisons. Eisner's comment is itself a real contribution in its discussion of the reasons why Solow's estimates of elasticity should be expected to be biased upward to the extent that short-run disturbances are reflected in the figures. Terleckyj points out that Solow's assumption of constant elasticity of substitution across time is not an essential ingredient of the calculation and that the procedure can in fact be used to estimate movements or trends in substitution elasticity.

In another comment, Kendrick offers an alternative set of estimates for elasticity of substitution in manufacturing. Using two points in time—1953 and 1957—rather than cross-sectional data, he produces a set of figures that are in general well below Solow's and more consistent with one another.

Charles L. Schultze's paper on "Short-Run Movements of

Income Shares," like the Solow one, is very much in the contemporary econometric fashion. Throughout the paper the underlying concern is with the short-term stabilizing effects of cyclical shifts in corporate profits and corporate saving, so that attention is directed mainly to corporate profits, defined as before tax and inclusive of depreciation allowances. Schultze "attempts to provide a set of functional relationships which illuminate the factors affecting cyclical shifts in income distribution. The orientation, however, is not mainly towards an explanation of short-run shifts in the distribution of income for its own sake. Rather it concentrates on those aspects of the income distribution process which themselves affect the level and rate of change in income and output."

The share of retained profits in private nonfarm GNP is viewed as equal to the product of three independent ratios: (1) gross retained profits to gross profits; (2) gross profits to profits originating in corporations; and (3) gross product originating in corporations to private nonfarm product.

Basically, Schultze accepts the Lintner hypothesis on retained profits relative to total profits; i.e., dividends are essentially a function of a weighted moving average of past profits, with the current profits term receiving only a small weight.

With respect to gross profits as a share of corporate gross product, Schultze's hypothesis is that it is composed of a trend (time) component and a "cyclical component, which responds to deviations in corporate product from its full capacity 'norm.' This component has zero value when corporate product is at its normal full capacity level." Conceptually, Schultze views "normal full capacity" as the point of minimum average unit costs. In practice he necessarily settles for something different. An equation incorporating a time trend and deviations from "normal full capacity" was fitted to data for the years 1922–41 and, on a quarterly basis, for relevant subperiods from 1948–59.

On the corporate share of total private nonfarm product, Schultze tests the hypothesis that "as output falls below capacity (estimated similarly to corporate capacity) the proportion of output originating in the corporate sector tends to decline; the opposite occurs as output rises relative to capacity." Here, in contrast to the coefficients for the relationship between the corporate profits share and deviations from normal full capacity, which was fairly stable among cycles, "the coefficient seems to be smaller, the larger the amplitude of cyclical fluctuation," suggesting to Schultze the probability that the true relationship is nonlinear.

With this basic approach, Schultze comes up with a great variety of correlation coefficients, slopes, and elasticities and a wealth of comment on his various hypotheses and their relevance for short-run changes in output and incomes.

Bert G. Hickman, in a penetrating and constructive discussion, raises some questions about the basic Schultze hypothesis that the profits share is positively related to the level of capacity utilization. Thus, why should the profit share fall below normal for output deviations on either side of normal capacity, since normal capacity has been defined as that level of output for which average unit cost is a minimum. Hickman discusses the conceptual issues and reviews a variety of possible explanations for the high positive correlations which Schultze actually obtained. A number of cogent comments are made on the empirical measurement of capacity and its effects on numerical estimates of the marginal response of profit to output.

The paper by S. A. Goldberg on "Long-Run Changes in the Distribution of Income by Factor Shares in Canada" represents the first comprehensive study of factor shares for Canada. The paper is distinguished by the meticulous care with which the available data are handled and by the careful manner in which the main conclusions are formulated. The main long-term comparison is between the average of the years 1926–30 and 1954–58, but data are presented for all intervening years. In addition, new data on domestic income and wages have been compiled and are presented for the period 1919–25.

The main emphasis is on the wage share. The wage share of domestic income increased from 56.7 per cent of domestic income in 1926–30 to 66.2 per cent in 1954–58, a rise of 17 per cent—mostly since 1953. The shift was largely at the expense of unincorporated income, a fact which raises the difficult question of the labor share of such income. The stability of the investment share reflects a rise in corporate profits and a decline in other investment income.

A more detailed analysis is made of factor shares, particularly the wage share, in private business product. Here, the important finding is that the rise in the wage share is greatly reduced when allowance is made (1) for interindustry shifts (of which the declining importance of agriculture is the most important); and (2) for the shift from the unincorporated to the incorporated form of business organization. According to Goldberg, "the most reasonable conclusion perhaps is that the rise in the standardized (i.e., adjusted for interindustry shifts) wage ratio in the corporate portion of the economy from 1926–30 to 1954–58 was positive but considerably smaller than the 8.7 per cent (from 61.2 to 66.5 per cent) of the total nonfarm private business product." Analysis of the new data for 1919–25 provides "further doubt that trend significance can be attached to the increase in the wage ratio from 1926–30 to 1954–58 after removal of the effect of the changing relative importance of constituent industries." This finding is quite similar to that of Lebergott in his discussion of the U.S. data for the same period.

F. H. Leacy contributes a "Supplement on Short-Term Fluctuations" to the Goldberg paper. On the whole, both annual and quarterly data (for the postwar period) indicate that wages and salaries show less cyclical variation in percentage terms than does total product, while corporate profits after I.V.A. vary more. In general, but subject to differences among industries and to differences among cycles, the wage share tends to move opposite to the cyclical movement of total product.

M. C. Urquhart in his discussion of the Goldberg paper stresses that "while there is some presumption that the share of labor income in the economy as a whole may have risen very moderately in the last forty years, it is not yet clearly evident that this is so." In part, this conclusion is based on an interpretation of the evidence Goldberg has presented. In addition, Urquhart raises questions about the possible importance of the fact that prices were falling in 1926–30 and rising in 1954–58 and about reliability of the estimates of capital consumption allowances. E. C. Budd's discussion provides an extended comparison of Goldberg's conclusions for Canada with comparable data for the United States. He finds a very close correspondence between the two countries in the rise in the wage share since 1926, but important differences in behavior of the other shares. Budd extends his comparative analysis to make allowances for interindustry shifts and to the shift from noncorporate to corporate.

He concludes that for both countries "a substantial part of the rise in the wage share was due to the relative decline in agriculture"; he attributes relatively minor influence to other output shifts or to the shift from the noncorporate to the corporate form of business organization.

Michael Gort's paper takes up the problems of measuring factor shares from production in individual manufacturing industries. After reviewing the main conceptual ambiguities he considers the ubiquitous problem of multiple-product lines within single establishments and the extent to which these might blur the estimates for the primary products of each industry. On the basis of simple but plausible assumptions he is able to indicate the possibility of sizable influences of secondary products on the over-all distribution of industry income. Isolation of earnings associated with separate products significantly broadens the variation of calculated capital returns among products.

Robert Williams points out two problems in Gort's form of calculation. First, Gort's results require an explanation of why manufacturers earning high returns on primary products would be engaging in lower-yield secondary products at all. Second, perhaps part of the explanation of the first, is that the wide variation among firms in earning power within industries probably occurs in secondary as well as primary product lines, leading to the conclusion that over-all returns for an industry may be more indicative for primary products than Gort's adjusted yields.

George H. Borts' paper on "The Estimation of Produced Income by State and Region" represents a pioneer study, and, as such, it deserves and receives praise from Daniel Creamer, Robert E. Graham, Jr., and Werner Z. Hirsch who discuss it. However, as is often true of pioneer studies, heroic assumptions are involved in piecing together the results, and a number of these assumptions are criticized.

Borts creates, for the first time, state estimates of income produced, as distinct from income received, for nine major industry divisions. (State estimates of income received are regularly compiled by the National Income Division of the Department of Commerce.) His estimates are made for two years, 1929 and 1953. The major problem in measuring "produced" income on a state basis is to estimate the returns to capital and entrepreneurs; available estimates of compensation of employees, which constitutes the remaining (roughly 70 per cent) income, are taken as appropriate for his income concept.

Creamer, Graham, and Hirsch are all critical of the methods used to estimate what Borts calls net entrepreneurial income (N.E.I.). Borts himself, of course, acknowledges the data limitations for such an effort and suggests some changes in current methods of data collection in order to provide current estimates of produced income on a state and regional basis.

Creamer makes a rather devasting criticism of the methods used to estimate N.E.I. in manufacturing industries by states, revealing an apparent flaw in Borts' use of *Statistics of Income* (Internal Revenue Service) data to adjust Census value added data. Since Borts states that his estimates for manufacturing are among his most reliable, the reliability of his estimates for other industry sectors is clearly brought into question.

Graham raises some rather cogent questions about the measurement of N.E.I. "produced" on a regional basis: do profits originate where a company's capital equipment is located, where its sales are made, or where entrepreneurial decisions are formulated? Graham comments that "much thinking along definitional lines remains to be done in order to formulate a satisfactory set of concepts before we get into the measurement phase of the geographic distribution of income produced."

Borts finds that produced N.E.I. is distributed more equally and far differently than received N.E.I., and he shows that extraordinary shifts in the relationship of produced to received N.E.I. took place between 1929 and 1953. Hirsch properly complains that Borts provides few answers as to the reason for the differences in the ratios in either year and for the shifts between 1929 and 1953. Hirsch in fact questions whether certain of these differences can be accepted in the light of what appear to him to be reasonable hypotheses.

Altogether, Borts' contributions to the subject is indeed impressive, both in terms of its evidence of painstaking labor in evolving his estimates and in suggesting some of the imaginative analytical uses to which such estimates could be put. Clearly, however, much needs to be done, along both conceptual and statistical lines, to promote reliable regional estimates of income produced.

A Survey of Some Theories of Income Distribution

TIBOR SCITOVSKY

UNIVERSITY OF CALIFORNIA AT BERKELEY

The theory of income distribution is in a highly unsatisfactory and controversial state. Further thinking on the subject can be facilitated by a survey that does the tedious but necessary preliminary work of reviewing the field, putting it into some kind of order, and pointing out the more obvious strengths and flaws, connections and inconsistencies. It is in this spirit that the following comments are offered.

There are at least four possible subjects that a theory of income distribution could cover: first, the level and changes in the level of incomes earned in particular occupations; second, the distribution and changes in the distribution of personal incomes by size; third, the functional distribution of income among the owners of the different productive factors; and fourth, the relative size and changes in the relative size of the various components of the official personal income accounts.

The first, being the least ambitious, is probably also the most promising, but so little work has been done in this area that there is virtually nothing to review. On the second subject, the most important work, Champernowne's,[1] is beyond my grasp, and apart from that very little has been done. The available data cover too short a period of time to base theories on, and we have not yet progressed beyond the simple notions of the classical economists who looked to death duties and increasing education to diminish inequalities of income. The effectiveness of this last factor has recently been questioned,[2] but there is still plenty of scope for more work on this subject. Another equally obvious influence on income distribution by size has never been mentioned and may well be worth looking into. There is evidence of a secular trend toward increasing centralization and an increasingly large-scale organization of economic, social, and political life; this means a changing pattern of demand for people, with fewer positions available in the higher and more in the lower echelons. The demand for skilled people has declined relative

[1] D. G. Champernowne, "The Graduation of Income Distributions," *Econometrica*, October 1952, and "A Model of Income Distribution," *Economic Journal*, June 1953.

[2] H. P. Miller, "Income in Relation to Education," *American Economic Review*, December 1960.

to that for the unskilled, as has the demand for executives relative to that for clerks and for generals relative to privates. Automation may well arrest or reverse this trend in the future, but in the past such changes in the pattern of demand may well have exerted on income distribution an equalizing force no less important than the influences exerted on the supply side. The rising interest in the economic returns to education, viewed as investment in human resources, is likely to stimulate work on this aspect of income distribution; but so far there is little or nothing to report on.

Whereas on the first two subjects there has been too little theorizing, on the third—the functional distribution of income—there are a large number of theories, using a variety of approaches and explaining a variety of phenomena; and hence it is in this area that there is the greatest scope as well as the greatest need for a survey. Almost all of this work is concerned with the twofold division between the share of labor in national income and the share of all other factors, loosely called capital. The classical system of three factors of production has been abandoned, largely because such categories as rent, interest, and profit in the national income accounts bear little relation and cannot easily be made to bear a meaningful relation to the factors land and capital. This is also the reason why the fourth subject—distribution by components of the national income accounts—has received little attention and tends to merge with the third subject.

The numerous theories of the division of income between labor and capital can be classified according to their approach and according to what they are trying to explain. As to the former, the distributive shares depend partly on the behavior of individual decision-makers, entrepreneurs, and consumers, and partly on the magnitude and pattern of demand and the relative supply of the different factors. The theories that center attention on the individual decision-maker's behavior are known as microeconomic theories; those that explain shifts in the distributive shares by changes in demand, supply, or institutional factors we shall call macroeconomic explanations. Those that treat demand and the supplies of factors as endogenous variables, both determined by and determining the distributive shares, we propose to call macroeconomic theories.

As to the second method of classification, we shall distinguish between theories that explain the constancy and those that account for changes in the share of labor in national income. This, obviously, is not an exhaustive classification, but it covers most theories and all those we propose to deal with. Our discussion begins with the second group of theories, all of which happen to be macroeconomic explanations.

Short-Run Macroeconomic Explanations

The U.S. data show a pronounced anticyclical movement in labor's share of national income according to almost any of the customary U.S. definitions of labor's share—i.e., wages and salaries, employee compensation, or this plus some part of the earnings of the self-employed.[3] The U.K. data show less regularity, primarily, I believe, because labor's share traditionally means wages only; and whereas the share of wages in wages and profits moves *against* the cycle, the share in total income (which also comprises salaries, rent, and interest) of wages and profits combined moves *with* the cycle, and these two contrary tendencies are mutually offsetting in their influence on the share of wages in national income.[4]

The main explanation of the anticyclical behavior of labor's share (according to the U.S. definition) is, I believe, what Burkhead calls the capacity effect.[5] The greater the utilization of capacity, the larger the output over which fixed costs are spread and the smaller therefore the fixed costs per unit of output. The importance of this effect is probably increasing with the secularly increasing share of fixed in total costs and of supervisory and administrative workers in the total labor force.[6]

A second explanation of this anticyclical behavior is what some writers call the lag effect,[7] i.e., the alleged lag of wages behind price increases in times of prosperity and inflationary pressures.

[3] James C. Beck, "Labor's Share and the Degree of Utilization of Capacity," *Southern Economic Journal*, April 1956; Jesse Burkhead, "Changes in the Functional Distribution of Income," *Journal of the American Statistical Association*, June 1953; Edward F. Denison, "Distribution of National Income since 1929," *Survey of Current Business*, June 1952; Joseph Phillips, "Labor's Share and 'Wage Parity,'" *Review of Economics and Statistics*, May 1960.

[4] E. H. Phelps Brown and P. E. Hart, "The Share of Wages in National Income," *Economic Journal*, June 1952, pp. 253–277.

[5] Burkhead, *JASA*, June 1953, p. 209.

[6] Charles Schultze, *Recent Inflation in the United States*, Chap. 4, Study Paper No. 1, Joint Economic Committee, 86th Congress, 2nd Session, Washington, 1959.

[7] Burkhead, *JASA*, June 1953, pp. 209–210.

That such a lag exists has for a long time been assumed by most economists, on the basis partly of a priori reasoning and partly of the evidence of the more spectacular hyperinflations of history.[8] All the recent evidence, however, seems to go counter to this notion and to show that prolonged inflation other than hyperinflation does not diminish labor's share in the national income, except in some cases of repressed inflation.[9] This need not imply that a wage lag and consequent income redistribution cannot and do not exist in the short run, at the peak of cyclical prosperity, during temporary bottlenecks and inflationary pressures. This subject, however, needs further investigation and one must keep an open mind in the interim.

A third explanation given by Burkhead is the compounding effect:[10] the cyclical shift to profits is also a shift to saving, and the capitalists' higher savings give rise to higher incomes. I find this explanation unconvincing, since the earnings of capital move presumably with the stock of capital rather than its rate of accumulation.

A fourth explanation, which seems rather obvious but is not mentioned anywhere, might have to do with the composition of output. Cyclical fluctuations in demand and hence output are fluctuations not only in magnitude but also in composition. In times of prosperity, demand and output are not only higher but also different in composition, with investment goods and consumer durables and luxuries accounting for a larger share of the total. If labor's share in the income generated by these industries is different from what it is in the rest of the economy, then their increased importance will also lead to a redistribution of income.[11]

We must also mention here the so-called Keynesian theory

[8] C. Bresciani-Turroni, *The Economics of Inflation,* London, 1937, especially Chap. 8.

[9] G. L. Bach and A. Ando, "The Redistributional Effects of Inflation," *Review of Economics and Statistics,* February 1957; *Economic Survey of Europe in 1956,* Geneva, United Nations, 1957, Chaps. 8 and 9; E. H. Phelps Brown and M. H. Browne, "Distribution and Productivity under Inflation, 1947–57," *Economic Journal,* December 1960.

[10] Burkhead, *JASA,* June 1953, pp. 209–210.

[11] This factor, however, may well pull in the opposite direction. A rough calculation based on recent U.S. data shows that in investment goods industries (construction and producer durables) the share of employee compensation in total income generated was 75 per cent, higher than the 69 per cent average for the economy as a whole. The inclusion of consumer durables and luxuries is likely to diminish the disparity but not to reverse it.

of distribution, the rudiments of which are contained in the *Treatise on Money* and which has been further developed by Boulding, Hahn, Kaldor, Kalecki, and Robinson.[12] This is an implicit theory, which links investment and income distribution by analyzing the latter's effect on the community's propensity to save, postulating the equality of saving and investment as an equilibrium condition, and tacitly taking for granted that a rise in investment will somehow redistribute income in favor of capital. It has been criticized, even ridiculed, for taking for granted what a proper theory of income distribution ought to explain explicitly;[13] it may be fairer, however, and more fruitful to inquire into the causal factors that it takes for granted. The theory is supposed to apply equally to underemployment and full-employment situations (though Kaldor and Robinson would restrict it to the latter); at least as far as the former are concerned, the U.S. data certainly bear out the theory, and the macroeconomic explanations just discussed can serve as the causal factors implicit in it. If labor's share in national income is inversely correlated with the level of national income within the business cycle, it must be similarly correlated—*and for the same reasons*—with the share of net investment in net national income, which we know to be directly correlated with the level of income. One thinks first of the capacity effect as the most obvious reason why a rise in investment should, through its stimulating effect on the level of income and capacity utilization, reduce the relative share of labor; and the lag effect seems a possible further explanation too.

As to the validity of the theory in full-employment situations, I know of no statistical evidence; but if the capacity effect and the lag effect adequately explain a fall in labor's share during cyclical upswings of falling unemployment, they should also explain a fall in labor's share resulting from rising investment at times when the labor force is fully employed. This is certainly so when a rise in investment at a time of full employment implies

[12] K. E. Boulding, *A Reconstruction of Economics*, New York, 1950, Chap. 14; F. Hahn, "The Share of Wages in the National Income," *Oxford Economic Papers*, June 1951; N. Kaldor, "Alternative Theories of Distribution," *Review of Economic Studies*, No. 61, 1955–56; M. Kalecki, "A Theory of Profits," *Economic Journal*, June-September, 1942, pp. 258–261; J. Robinson, *The Accumulation of Capital*, London, 1956.

[13] J. Tobin, "Towards a General Kaldorian Theory of Distribution," *Review of Economics and Statistics*, February 1960.

an increase in hours worked and an expansion of the labor force. The argument becomes more complex when the rise in investment involves a transfer of resources from other sectors of the economy; but the capacity effect and the lag effect are operative and may exert the dominant influence even then. Some adherents of the Keynesian theory seem aware of its limitations (Robinson's "inflation barrier" and Kaldor's "subsistence minimum" indicate some distrust of the lag effect), and within such limits its validity should not be denied merely because one is annoyed by the way in which it is stated.

Long-Run Macroeconomic Explanations

In addition to countercyclical changes, the U.S. data also show a secular increase in labor's share of the national income; all the economists who have worked with these data have sought and found special explanations to account for this trend.[14] One of these is the increasing importance of the government contribution to the national product, since, according to present accounting practice, this consists solely of employee compensation. Another explanation is the secularly diminishing importance of agriculture, where labor's share in value added is especially low and where, in addition, labor's real income is understated in view of the lower-than-average prices paid by farm workers. A third explanation is the secularly rising proportion of wage and salary earners and the diminishing proportion of small (i.e., unincorporated) businessmen in the total labor force.

It is to isolate and eliminate the effect of this last factor that it has become customary in the United States to define the labor share or service share as employee compensation plus all or part of the earnings of unincorporated business, regarded as "entrepreneurial labor income."[15] The effect of the diminishing importance of agriculture is isolated by comparing the actual share of labor to what it would be if the weights of the different sectors had remained constant;[16] the effect of government's in-

[14] Denison, *Survey of Current Business*, June 1952; Phillips, *RES*, May 1960; Dale H. Johnson, "The Functional Distribution of Income in the United States, 1850–1952," *Review of Economics and Statistics*, May 1954, pp. 175–182; I. B. Kravis, "Relative Income Shares in Fact and Theory," *American Economic Review*, December 1959, pp. 917–949.

[15] Johnson, *RES*, May 1954; Kravis, *AER*, December 1959; Burkhead, *JASA*, June 1953; Edward C. Budd, "Factor Shares, 1850–1910," in *Trends in the American Economy in the Nineteenth Century*, Studies in Income and Wealth, 24, Princeton for NBER, 1960.

[16] Johnson, *RES*, May 1954, p. 180; Kravis, *AER*, December 1959, pp. 934–935.

creasing importance is eliminated by excluding the government contribution from both national income and labor's share.[17]

There are a number of other factors as well, such as the influence of war and the great depression on the decade estimates and the change in the source and nature of the data at the very date (1929) when they seem to show the greatest change in labor's share. We shall pay no more attention to these factors, however, because the first three explanations between them deal, to the satisfaction of most writers on the subject, with just about all the secular change in labor's share of the national income in the United States.[18]

These conclusions are at least as interesting for what they imply as for what they actually say. Economists who try to explain changes in distributive shares by invoking special factors and particular trends seem to believe in the constancy of distributive shares, which would obtain if it were not for these special factors. And if they succeed in explaining fully the changes in relative factor shares by these special factors, then they have come close to proving indirectly the existence of other factors at work which tend to maintain the stability of distributive shares. Further support for this line of reasoning comes from a comparison of the American and the British data. The latter show that the share in the national income of wages alone was virtually constant over the period 1870–1950, with swings no greater than 8 per cent away from the average.[19] When one recalls that in Britain agriculture was much less important throughout this period, and that the other two factors—the increasing importance of government and the rising proportion of employees—both affect salaries and not wages, then the British findings appear to confirm rather than to contradict the U.S. data; and they strengthen the feeling that there must be other factors making for the constancy of distributive shares.[20] Some people may also wish to attach importance to the fact that all the factors invoked to explain the secular change in

[17] Denison, *Survey of Current Business,* June 1952; Phillips, *RES,* May 1960, pp. 177 ff.; Kravis, *AER,* December 1959, p. 927; George J. Schuller, "The Secular Trend in Income Distribution by Type, 1869–1948: A Preliminary Estimate," *Review of Economics and Statistics,* November 1953; Johnson, *RES,* May 1954, pp. 179–180.

[18] Kravis alone feels differently and, for an earlier period, Budd. Unfortunately, the latter's paper reached me too late for more than a cursory glance.

[19] Phelps Brown and Hart, *Economic Journal,* June 1952.

[20] It is worth noting in this connection that Budd, dealing with U.S. data for 1850–1910, finds a greater stability in the share of wages than in that of wages and salaries or of services.

distributive shares in the United States are macroeconomic. While this proves nothing, it might rule out *some* macroeconomic explanations of constancy and suggest that we should at least begin our search for the explanation of the constancy of distributive shares among the microeconomic factors.

Microeconomic Theories

The first of these is the marginal productivity theory of distribution. It is worth recalling that parts of this theory were, to some extent, originally developed to provide a rebuttal of Marx's theory of exploitation and an ethical basis for the distribution of income in a free enterprise economy. This explains the argument, on the assumption of perfect competition, that each factor's rate of remuneration equals the value of its marginal contribution to output, and the related argument, based on the assumption of long-run competitive equilibrium, that the capitalist gains nothing from being in the seemingly advantageous bargaining position of the entrepreneur who does the hiring and firing.[21]

Today, we no longer seek ethical content in economic theories, and many of us have become reluctant to assume perfect competition and long-run equilibrium; nevertheless, most people still adhere to the marginal productivity theory. For one thing, its generality and elegance has considerable appeal; for another, it fits in best with our marginalist approach to economics; for a third, the acceptance of the marginal productivity theory of income distribution is closely bound up with the assumption of an aggregate production function whose analytic convenience has enticed many economists to slur over or disregard the objections to it. Its modern form, however, is a very much watered-down version of the neoclassical marginal productivity theory and amounts to little more than a market theory of income distribution. By this we mean a theory that stresses merely that the rates of remuneration of productive factors are market prices determined by supply and demand, and influencing in turn the quantities and proportions in which individual entrepreneurs demand the services of the productive factors.

The main purpose to which the theory is put nowadays is to explain the relative stability of factor shares. Given a market the-

[21] I am here referring, of course, to the use of Euler's theorem for solving the adding-up problem.

ory of income distribution, it is enough for demand curves to slope downward and for the main disturbances to come from the supply side in order to assure contrary and hence offsetting movements in factor supplies and factor prices. These, in turn, assure the relative stability of factor shares, in the sense that factor shares in total income fluctuate relatively less than either factor supplies or factor prices. That such stability exists becomes obvious on considering that the supply of reproducible capital has increased twice as fast as the supply of labor;[22] and there is no need at this stage to enter the controversy over how constant something must be to be called constant. Those who believe in the constancy of relative factor shares have further assumed unit or near-unit elasticity of substitution between labor and capital, and also neutral technical progress—this latter to explain the constancy of shares even in the face of some disturbances (technical progress) coming from the demand side. These assumptions, however, are not an integral part of the marginal productivity or market theory of income distribution and may be left aside while we analyze the theory.

The theory that rates of factor remuneration are and behave like market prices implies the assertions, first, that the quantities and proportions in which the services of the productive factors are demanded depend on relative prices; and second, that total demand for productive services influences their prices. We propose to offer some critical comments on both these assertions.

As to the first, factor substitution in response to a change in relative factor prices can be direct and indirect. Direct substitution is made by entrepreneurs; and it is well known, though not stressed often enough, that the scope for this is extremely limited. The proportions in which the entrepreneur combines labor and capital in his day-to-day production decisions are largely determined by the nature of his productive equipment and methods, which have been fixed for the useful lifetime of his plant at the time when he built his factory and bought his equipment. Changing relative prices influence the entrepreneur's factor proportions mainly through their impact on his investment decisions; and these affect factor proportions only in a small fraction of the total productive system.[23] The manufacturing capacity created

[22] Kravis, *AER*, December 1959, p. 918.

[23] The fact that disused capacity can be brought back into production does not really modify this statement. For the change in factor proportions that

by gross investment in the average year is only about one-tenth of total manufacturing capacity.

It is also worth asking exactly how a change in prices influences the proportions in which labor and capital are combined in investment projects. The standard argument is that a rise in wages relative to product prices will lower the profitability of investment on *all investment projects*, but to a lesser extent on the more capital-intensive ones, which is why demand will shift toward capital. The tacit assumption underlying the argument is that the total volume of investment remains unchanged despite the reduced profitability of all investment (and despite the higher wage level, which may affect total consumption), and that total income and employment also remain unchanged. When this assumption is false, the effects of changed levels of investment and income on the nature of investment and on income distribution must also be taken into account; and these effects may modify or change the argument. Because the scope for direct factor substitution by entrepreneurs is so limited, economists have stressed the importance of indirect factor substitution by consumers. A rise in the relative price of labor raises the prices of labor-intensive goods relative to those of capital-intensive goods; this prompts consumers to shift their demand from the former to the latter, thereby indirectly bringing about a shift in demand from labor to capital. The argument is impeccable, but its importance must be judged by empirical results. For indirect factor substitution by consumers, in contrast to direct factor substitution by entrepreneurs, exerts its influence on factor shares through interindustry shifts, and these should be separable from the forces that operate within an industry. Suggestive in this connection is Solow's finding that interindustry and intersector shifts in demand and output have had no stabilizing effect on labor's share in aggregate income;[24] but it

---

this implies is usually incidental and comes about in response to a rise in demand, whichever way relative factor prices have shifted. With demand unchanged, relative factor prices would have to change drastically indeed to bring disused capacity back into use.

[24] Robert M. Solow, "A Skeptical Note on the Constancy of Relative Shares," *American Economic Review,* September 1958, pp. 618–631. Solow presents his findings as an argument against relying on macroeconomic explanations of the stability of factor shares. I am not familiar, however, with any macroeconomic theory that would invoke interindustry shifts as a stabilizing factor, except for the argument of this paragraph, which is an integral part of the marginal productivity or market theory of income distribution.

is only suggestive, partly because his data relate to industries and sectors too broadly defined to have too much bearing on the present argument, and partly also because his conclusions, even if based on a finer industry classification, would prove the unimportance of indirect factor substitution by consumers only in the (to my mind likely) case that the elasticity of direct and indirect substitution combined should be nearer unity than the elasticity of direct substitution alone.[25]

We can now proceed to examine the second assertion, which is that the change in factor proportions wrought by individual decision-makers in response to a change in relative prices will change total market demand for the different factors and thus influence, in its turn, relative factor prices. Two observations need to be made in this connection. One is that this part of the mechanism will operate only at high activity levels, for it is difficult to imagine the forces of demand and supply in factor markets influencing prices at times when the labor force, existing plant capacity, and the potential supply of savings are all underutilized.

Our other observation is that to analyze the effectiveness of this part of the mechanism would require a detailed comparative study of price and wage behavior both between the capital goods and other sectors and between periods when plant capacity is more fully utilized than the labor force and periods when the reverse is true. Some such studies are being made as part of the current analysis of inflation, an important by-product of which may well be additional information on and insight into the workings of factor markets.

To sum up, our criticism of the market theory of income distribution is that it is based too little on direct evidence about how factor markets operate and too much on analogy with the very much simpler operation of market supply and demand and substitution in markets for consumer goods. We do not deny that market forces operate in factor markets; but they may be much weaker and much more sluggish than is generally supposed; and for all we know they may, in some respects, operate quite differently from those that operate in the market for bread.

At best the market theory explains not constancy but merely

[25] I am indebted to Professor M. Reder for cautioning me against reading too much into Solow's elegant argument.

a fair degree of stability in factor shares, and even that only in the face of disturbances coming from the supply side. To explain the constancy of relative factor shares would require unit elasticity of factor substitution. There is quite a literature, to which we can only refer here, to warn against accepting unit elasticity on the evidence that the Cobb-Douglas function gives a good fit to time-series data.[26] On the other hand, several people have pointed out recently that what constancy there is in relative factor shares in the United States is compatible not only with unit elasticity but also with a whole range of values of the elasticity of substitution if this is not too far removed from unity, and especially if it is above unity.[27] The first reaction to this argument is to point out that the elasticity of substitution would be expected to be below rather than above unity,[28] and to ask what is "not too far removed." We have neither statistical estimates of the elasticity of substitution nor intuition to tell us what are reasonable or likely values.

As to disturbances emanating from the demand side, the discussion in the previous two sections has shown that factor shares *are* affected by quite a variety of changes that emanate from the demand side; there is only one such change, though a major one, that seems to have left relative shares unaffected—technological progress. The kind of progress that leaves relative factor shares unchanged has been defined as neutral; and the fact that progress in our economy has been so close to neutral needs an explanation and can hardly be regarded as an accident of history. No satisfactory explanation has been offered as yet by the upholders of the marginal productivity theory; some tentative explanations offered by others will be discussed in the next section.

A second microeconomic theory of income distribution is Kalecki's theory.[29] This is a first cousin of the marginal pro-

[26] E. H. Phelps Brown, "The Meaning of the Fitted Cobb-Douglas Function," *Quarterly Journal of Economics,* November 1957; and some of the literature referred to there.

[27] M. Bronfenbrenner, "A Note on Relative Shares and the Elasticity of Substitution," *Journal of Political Economy,* June 1960; also Solow, *AER,* September 1958, p. 629; and Kravis, *AER,* December 1959, p. 940.

[28] After all, the relative supply of labor has been diminishing and its relative share has, if anything, increased.

[29] M. Kalecki, "The Determinants of Distribution of the National Income," *Econometrica,* April 1938, reprinted with significant changes in his *Essays in the Theory of Economic Fluctuations,* London, 1939, and also in his *Theory of Economic Dynamics,* London, 1954.

ductivity theory, from which it differs, in a formal sense, by dropping the assumptions of perfect competition and long-run equilibrium, and making instead the simplifying assumption of constant returns to scale (horizontal marginal and average direct cost curves)—at least within the range of underemployment, which is Kalecki's sole concern. The main determinant of income distribution in his theory is the percentage gross profit margin entrepreneurs add to marginal or average direct cost in setting their prices, and Kalecki regards this as an index of the degree of monopoly. In early versions of his theory, this is determined by (and stands in a definite relation to) the price elasticity of demand facing the entrepreneur; in the last version, the degree of monopoly is more generally defined in order to include oligopoly as well.

The great merit of Kalecki's theory is that it relates income distribution to the entrepreneur's pricing policy and makes the stability of distributive shares partly dependent on the stability of entrepreneurial profit margins. This means that it is a short-run theory, which has to do with the firm's day-to-day pricing decisions. Thus it contrasts with (and perhaps complements) the market theory, which is a long-run theory and mainly has to do with the entrepreneur's investment decisions and very little with his day-to-day decisions on the relation of prices to wages and the determination of output in the face of given prices and wages. Kalecki's theory suffers from the lack of a satisfactory and integrated theory of monopolistic and oligopolistic competition; and it may well be that a fully satisfactory explanation of distributive shares will have to await the development of such a theory. His simplifying assumption of horizontal marginal cost curves has been justly criticized;[30] but its abandonment only complicates without destroying his theory. It should also be stressed that the theory explains distributive shares in the gross product, not in net income, and hence allows for cyclical fluctuations in the *income* shares; that labor's share in the theory means the share of wages only and excludes salaries that do not enter prime costs; and that vertical differentiation also plays an important role. Kalecki himself believes in a secular increase in the degree of concentration and monopoly and provides a somewhat unconvincing

[30] Melvin W. Reder, "Rehabilitation of Partial Equilibrium Theory," *American Economic Review,* May 1952, pp. 191–192.

argument for reconciling this with the constancy of distributive shares; but others, testing his model, have found the degree of monopoly to be constant.[31] Further testing of his model should investigate the importance and implications of the alleged secular shift from wage-earning production workers to salaried supervisory and administrative employees. With Kalecki's theory linking distributive shares to the firm's pricing policy and the market theory linking it to the firm's investment decisions, one should hope that future work on the theory of investment by the firm, and on the influence of the firm's monopoly power and pricing policy on its investment decisions, will provide the means to integrate these two microeconomic theories of income distribution.

Macroeconomic Theories

The classical example of this group of theories is Ricardo's subsistence theory of wages. This asserts that the wage rate always tends toward the subsistence level, because a higher wage will raise the birth rate and a lower one will raise the death rate of workers, thereby increasing or diminishing the supply of labor and thus depressing or raising wages until they return to the subsistence level and equilibrium in the supply of labor is restored.

The beginnings of a modern macroeconomic theory of income distribution can be found in—or read into—Hicks' *Theory of Wages,* where he introduces the idea of induced technical change in an attempt to account for the stability of factor shares. He knew that the market theory of distribution explains the relative stability of factor shares only in the face of disturbances emanating from the supply side, and even then only when the elasticity of substitution is near unity. This accounts for his attempt to make the nature of innovation depend on economic factors, but his argument is hard to follow and incomplete. It is similar, however, to part of the theory to be discussed presently and will be referred to below in that connection.

Another macroeconomic theory, and perhaps the most satisfactory one, can be pieced together from an article by E. H. Phelps Brown and B. Weber and from several papers by N. Kaldor.[32] The first two authors have shown that in England not

[31] Ashok Mitra, *The Share of Wages in National Income,* The Hague, 1954.

[32] E. H. Phelps Brown and Bernard Weber, "Accumulation, Productivity and Distribution in the British Economy, 1870–1938," *Economic Journal,* June 1953,

only the share of capital in income but also the rate of return on capital invested and the level of output per unit of capital have all shown a remarkable constancy over time. Any two of these imply a third, so that if the constancy of two is explained, the constancy of the third follows. Accordingly, Phelps Brown and Weber, in a tentative theoretical explanation of their findings, argue the existence of economic forces that keep stable the first and the third relations mentioned above. Kaldor, in his turn, explains the same findings in terms of economic forces stabilizing the first and second relations and obtains the stability of the third as a consequence. We shall argue presently that while neither approach is fully convincing, the two combined provide a better theory than either of them singly.

Phelps Brown and Weber explain the stability of the first relation—the share of capital in total income—by a propensity of businessmen to maintain, at least in the short run, a fixed proportional relation between prices and direct costs. In other words, they accept Kalecki's theory in its simplest form, finding statistical confirmation of this constancy by Phelps Brown and Hart.[33] Kaldor relies on essentially the same argument, although his explanation is very differently worded.

The existence of forces stabilizing the second relation—the rate of return on capital invested—is developed in detail by Kaldor along lines reminiscent of Ricardo's subsistence theory of wages.[34] He argues that the expected rate of earnings on capital must exceed the market rate of interest by a minimum margin in order to repay the entrepreneur for his risk and trouble; that when expected margins exceed this minimum, the resulting faster rate of capital accumulation will soon depress rates of return and bring expected margins closer to the minimum; whereas if expected margins fall below the minimum, the consequent choking off of capital accumulation will soon raise the margin again if population continues to grow and technology to progress. Kaldor's argument explains

pp. 263–288; N. Kaldor, "A Model of Economic Growth," *Economic Journal*, December 1957, pp. 591–624; Kaldor, "Economic Growth and the Problem of Inflation," *Economica*, August 1959, pp. 212–226 and 287–298; Kaldor, "Capital Accumulation and Economic Growth," in *The Theory of Capital*, New York, 1961.

[33] Phelps Brown and Hart, *Economic Journal*, June 1952, pp. 267–268.

[34] Phelps Brown and Weber also mention this as a possibility but do not elaborate it.

a long-run stability not so much of the rate of return on capital as of the margin between this rate and the market rate of interest on riskless securities; but in view of the latter's historical behavior, Kaldor's theorem fits Phelps Brown's data very well. It might be added that there is nothing marginal about Kaldor's expected future rate of profit on capital invested, since this is based on the past actual rate of profit, which in turn is the ratio of profit per output (the net profit margin) to capital per output.

The long-run stability of the third relation, the capital-output ratio, is again argued by Phelps Brown and Weber, or rather they outline and refer to an argument found in more detail elsewhere. As is well known, when the return on capital is constant, a proportional rise in output and the stock of capital means neutral technical progress. And neutral technical progress can be equated, as a rough first approximation, to parallel productivity increases in consumer goods and capital goods industries; for productivity increases in the former are labor-saving, those in the latter capital-saving improvements. Phelps Brown and Weber expect the neutrality of technical progress to be assured by the forces that tend to keep productivity increases in these two groups of industries parallel. These forces have been better described in the literature on economic development, especially by the critics of the doctrine of balanced growth.[35] A productivity increase in one industry generates pressures on other industries to raise their productivity too. These pressures take a variety of forms: the squeezing of profits in competing and the creation of bottlenecks in related and complementary industries. An earlier generation of theorists would have concluded that a change in relative prices would lead to a gradual shrinking of the former and expansion of the latter industries; but a closer look at the historical evidence (and perhaps also a new fashion in theorizing) suggests that this will only happen as a last resort. Established firms will do their utmost to improve productivity and lower costs before accepting the death sentence of dwindling profits; and bottlenecks are usually broken not by a gradual expansion of the factor in short supply but by a technical breakthrough that dispenses with or greatly reduces the need for this factor. There

[35] Albert O. Hirschman, *The Strategy of Economic Development,* New Haven, 1958, especially Chap. 4; also my "Growth—Balanced or Unbalanced?" in M. Abramovitz *et al., The Allocation of Economic Resources,* Stanford, 1959.

is mounting evidence that one innovation leads to another through economic pressure as much as through the similarity of technical conditions and problems; and if all this leads to parallel increases in labor productivity, it also assures neutral technical progress. Needless to say, this is no exact equilibrating mechanism but a very rough and approximate equalizing force.

As already mentioned, Phelps Brown and Weber rely on this last and on the first equilibrating force to account for the stability of the three relations; Kaldor relies on the first two and deduces the neutrality of technical progress as an indirect consequence.[36] There is no need, however, to choose between these two explanations. If any two of the three equilibrating forces were strong, the third would indeed be unnecessary for explaining the stability of the three relations; but this is not the case. Parallel increases of productivity in different industries are at best a very long-run and approximate tendency; and equally long run is the tendency of capital accumulation to influence the profitability of capital. By contrast, the entrepreneur's tendency to maintain a stable relation between prices and direct costs is a short-run stabilizing influence, which may be subject to secular change. The three stabilizing forces therefore should be recognized as mutually reinforcing, and the theories of Kaldor and Phelps Brown and Weber as complementary. They need to be developed further and restated more carefully but are nevertheless the most, perhaps the only, satisfactory macroeconomic theory of income distribution. It should be noted in closing that this theory does not hinge on interindustry shifts, is therefore not subject to Solow's criticism,[37] and can accommodate the changes in income distribution brought about by interindustry shifts, which are discussed among the macroeconomic explanations.

COMMENT

Edward F. Denison, Brookings Institute

Professor Scitovsky provides a short survey of distribution theories that I found useful, enlightening, thought-provoking, and,

[36] The most nearly complete and satisfactory statement of Kaldor's theory is contained in the unpublished paper mentioned in footnote 32. His presentation is more suggestive and persuasive than this account, owing primarily to the use of his "investment function" as an explanatory device.

[37] Cf. footnote 24.

happily, presented without a single mathematical symbol. For this I salute him.

Insofar as Scitovsky is simply reporting the views of others, he must, in all fairness, be considered immune to criticism. However, he also classifies the various theories, and points out their most important strengths and flaws, connections and inconsistencies. Here he is fair game and if we can use the pretext of his comments to strike a blow at any of the authors he cites, so much the better. In the latter part of my comment I shall attempt to do so.

Scitovsky devotes almost all of his paper to the functional distribution of income. However, he gives only the barest mention to the distribution of national income by type of income, as published by the Commerce Department. This series reports the form in which income initially accrues to suppliers of the factors of production, before government steps in to take and give via taxes and transfer payments. This is one of the most interesting distributions, and not only because we have some data that we can try to explain. It is, after all, the distribution that most of the shouting is about. The public outcry is not over the functional distribution as economists define it but about how the income of farm proprietors is too low, or corporate profits have been squeezed, or are too big, and so on. Work by Charles Schultze, among others, has shown how illuminating analysis based on this classification can be in examining business fluctuations. I suspect it would also be useful to try to bring the tools of economic theory and empirical investigation to bear upon the reasons that this distribution is what it is, and has changed as it has over longer periods. Those who think the division of income between corporations and persons has something to do with the saving rate, and this includes most economists, should be interested in such a study. Some work has been done for individual shares, such as the income of farm proprietors and independent professionals, but not, I think, comprehensively. Any general theory would have to include both the determinants of the various legal forms of organization and the composition of the resources going into the mixed shares in terms of the classifications used in economic theory.

The theories that Scitovsky does discuss, insofar as they rely on data at all, reverse this process. Instead of trying to develop a theory to explain the data, they try to adjust the data to a classification that theory can explain, or restrict themselves to only a portion of the economy where statistics and the shares of theory correspond, or else slur over the differences. Only infrequently do they seriously try to go beyond a simple two-way division between labor income and all other income.

For the study of such a classification, the economy can be broken down into three parts. In one—private corporations organized for profit—the actual shares correspond tolerably well to those of theory. In a second part—proprietorships and partnerships—any division of income into the categories of economic theory is simply a reflection of the assumption on which it is based. In the rest of the economy—government, households and institutions, noncorporate ownership of real property, etc.—each economic unit gives rise almost entirely to either labor or nonlabor income so that within it there is little problem of the distribution of income. But this does not mean these economic units can be ignored, nor that theory can simply deal with the rest of the economy as if they didn't exist. In 1957 they contributed one-fifth of labor income. They contributed almost one-third of nonlabor income if corporate profits are measured before tax and almost one-half of nonlabor income if corporate profits are measured after tax,[1] as would seem appropriate for those theories relying on the rate of return or some relation between saving and after-tax labor and nonlabor incomes. They absorb labor or capital, as the case may be, and create income that is spent or saved. Most of the theoretical models, as distinguished from the statistical studies, that Scitovsky discusses seem incapable of accommodating these entities.

Scitovsky's classification of theories by what they are trying to explain seems to me inadvertently to bias and limit the subsequent discussion in a way that is very much to the disadvantage of the marginal productivity theory. He says, "we shall distinguish between theories that explain the constancy and those that account for changes in the share of labor in national income." That is to say, he deals with theories that will explain why, if labor income is 70 per cent, it will remain at 70 per cent or will grow to 75 per cent. But he does not consider why it was 70 per cent rather than 10 or 100 per cent in the first place.

It does not seem to me that this question can be answered with-

[1] This calculation divides national income originating in proprietorships and partnerships between labor and property income in the same proportion as income originating in corporations.

out reference to marginal productivity. The marginal productivity theory also purports to explain occupational differentials, which the other theories he discusses do not. The marginal productivity theory itself is consistent with any statistical division of national income between labor and other income, until the quantities, functions, etc., needed to arrive at some numerical division are introduced. Von Thünen was the first to try to take this theory as a point of departure to use observed data to derive a formula that would yield a numerical answer for the statistical distribution of income. Acceptance of the marginal productivity theory did not rest on the validity of von Thünen's formula, and I doubt that it will or should rest on anyone else's formula. Scitovsky asserts that the main purpose to which the theory is put nowadays is to explain the relative stability of factor shares. But the theory cannot itself be tested by seeing whether or not the distribution is stable.

The exclusive focus on changes or stability in the labor share of income, as distinct from its level, avoids any discussion of whether the macroeconomic theories Scitovsky describes can explain, or even are consistent with, equilibrium for individual economic units. I wish Scitovsky had indicated, in each case, whether the theorist was trying to explain why economic forces, operating through the marginal productivity process, lead to some particular change or lack of change in the distribution of national income, or whether he has some other concept of equilibrium or none at all.

I am particularly interested in the part of Scitovsky's paper where he pieces together what he calls "perhaps the most satisfactory macroeconomic theory." I shall try to show that it is not satisfactory at all, and indeed is completely untenable for the United States from the late twenties to the present. In this section, if we follow Scitovsky, we need be concerned with only three numbers, although two more are hiding under the table: (1) nonlabor income, which sometimes gets called income from capital and which I shall therefore call C; (2) total national income or product, which I shall call Y; and (3) total capital input or capital stock, which I shall call K. If we set down the ratio of each of these three numbers to the other two, we get three ratios, and any two ratios determine the third. We can write the equation: C/Y (the nonlabor share of national income) equals C/K (the rate of return on capital) times K/Y, the ratio of capital input to national product. If two of these ratios happen to be constant over time, the constancy of the third follows automatically. Scitovsky notes that Phelps Brown and Weber argue that economic forces keep the nonlabor share of national income and the capital-output ratio constant, and this makes the rate of return constant. Kaldor thinks that economic forces keep the nonlabor share of national income and the rate of return on capital constant, and this explains constancy in the capital-output ratio. Finally, Scitovsky himself suggests that all three ratios have some tendency toward stability and these three stabilities mutually reinforce one another.

The important thing to note is that the equation holds only if the same numbers are used for nonlabor income, national income, and capital input each time they appear in the ratios. I concede that, taking each ratio separately, there is some definition of the numerator and denominator that will yield a ratio that evidences no clear and pronounced upward or downward long-term trend. This is not a very stringent statistical test of stability, since any series that fluctuates at random will meet it, but I shall waive the question of what stability means. The point I wish to develop is that there is no set of definitions which, if uniformly applied, will allow all three ratios to show long-term stability in the United States by even the loosest definition of stability. If this is so, the whole argument collapses.

Let me note first that, to use only three series and three ratios in the equation, it is necessary to use prices of the same date in all three ratios. Actually, it is customary to use *current* prices in the first two ratios and *constant* prices in the capital-output ratio. In fact, the theoretical rationale for stability in each requires that this be done. On this basis, balance requires that the right side of the equation be multiplied by another ratio, that of capital stock prices to national product prices. Our theorists get around this difficulty by assuming that productivity increases at the same rate in the production of capital goods as in that of consumption goods, and hence that prices will increase at the same rate, so this ratio too is stable. But actually, the ratio of prices of capital goods output to other prices has risen hugely—by about one-third since 1929, implying that productivity has increased vastly less in capital goods production than elsewhere. Maybe the price indexes are no good and this did not really happen, but in the absence of alternative data there can be no empirical support for the assumption of equal productivity and price changes in capital goods industries and elsewhere. And these are the same price data used in measuring real capital stock.

Second, the ratios must refer to the same part of the economy—either all of it or some clearly defined sector. Most favorable to the argument—since it is the only way a tolerably constant income distribution can be obtained—is to deal with corporations alone, or else with what I have called elsewhere the ordinary business sector, consisting of corporations, proprietorships, and partnerships. This is pretty awkward for the theoretical argument, as I have already suggested, but let us waive that too. For what I really want to stress is the definition of *nonlabor income*, *C*, and of *capital input*, *K*. Nonlabor income enters into two ratios. It is absolutely necessary to *include* corporate income taxes to make nonlabor income a constant fraction of national income in corporate or ordinary business. Even then the data for the last few years suggest a downward movement in the nonlabor share but let us waive that.

But to get a stable rate of return on capital it is necessary, and the theoretical argument seems to require, that corporate profits be measured *after* deduction of corporate income taxes. The Machinery and Allied Products Institute (MAPI) estimates for corporations make the point very clearly.[2] With their adjustments, profits *before* tax averaged 19.2 per cent of corporate income produced in 1923–29 and 21.4 per cent from 1950 to 1959. Inclusion of interest would largely eliminate any change. Profits *after* tax dropped from 16.0 to 9.6 per cent of corporate national income, or by two-fifths, and inclusion of interest would further accentuate the change. On the other hand, profits *after* tax were 5.6 per cent of net worth from 1923 to 1929 and 5.5 per cent from 1950 to 1959. But on a *before*-tax basis, the rate of return increased from 6.5 to 11.1 per cent, or by seven-tenths.[3] This general characteristic of the profits record is well known. It pops up particularly in discussions of the incidence of the corporation

[2] Data cited in the following paragraphs are those underlying charts presented in the *Capital Goods Review*, May 1959.

[3] Other estimates do not yield so clear-cut a result as the MAPI estimates. Comparison of Office of Business Economics profits estimates with Raymond W. Goldsmith's net stock figures suggest the before-tax rate of return has risen while the after-tax rate has fallen. On this basis, there is *no* stable ratio to be explained.

income tax. The stability of *before*-tax corporate income in the corporate national income total suggests the tax is not shifted, while the stability of the rate of return computed *after* tax suggests it is shifted.

For the first two ratios, C/Y and C/K, both to be constant when nonlabor income, C, is defined in the same way, total income, the denominator of the first ratio, would have to rise by the same amount as the net capital stock, the denominator of the second ratio. MAPI estimates show the ratio of income produced in corporations to corporate net worth increased from 27.2 per cent in 1923–29 to 47.6 per cent in 1950–59, or by three-fourths. Under these conditions there *cannot* be *any* definition of nonlabor or property income that will yield stability in both the nonlabor share of national income and the rate of return.

This brings me to the measure of capital, K, which appears in the second and third ratios. In the second, the rate of return calculation, the denominator is the net capital stock, and it *must* be the net capital stock if the ratio is to be stable statistically or if the theoretical argument for stability is to be sensible. But as we have just seen, if the net capital stock is used in the third ratio, the capital-output ratio, and it is computed in current dollars, that ratio drops drastically.

Even when we measure the capital-output ratio in constant prices, if we use the net capital stock to measure capital input the ratio drops dramatically from the twenties to the recent period. I supposed this to be well-known from the work of Kendrick, Kuznets, and Goldsmith, and surely so since Arthur Smithies' attempt to explain this change appeared in the *Quarterly Journal of Economics* last May.

The stable constant-dollar capital-output ratio can still be salvaged, or nearly so, if capital input is measured by constant-dollar depreciation on structures and equipment rather than by capital stock. This works out with both the Kendrick and the MAPI estimates for, say, the years 1909, 1929, and 1957. A case can be made that this is the way capital input of structures and equipment ought to be measured, and that the ratio of depreciation to net output is the one that could be expected to be stable on a priori grounds. But if stability in the capital-output ratio is achieved by the use of depreciation to measure capital input, depreciation would also have to be substituted for net stock in the *second* ratio, and this would make the "rate of return" drop drastically. Nor would there be any theoretical reason to expect stability.

I do not think that changes of two-fifths to seven-tenths in a ratio meet even the most tolerant ideas of stability. They seem to me sufficient to dispose of any notion that stability in two of the ratios can explain stability in the third, or that, as Scitovsky suggests, stability in all three can be mutually reinforcing.

It is true, of course, that the English authors cited in this section have relied on English as well as United States statistics. But only the article by Phelps Brown and Weber tries to deal simultaneously with the three ratios. And they say that in the 1924–38 period one of the ratios, that of capital to output, was about the same as from 1870 to 1914, while the other two ratios were both very different. Within the 1924–38 period they find that the ratio of real output to real capital rises sharply, while the other two ratios are supposed not to have shown a trend, although this is not very clear from their charts. Neither within nor between periods is stability of all three ratios really claimed. The three ratios are not given for individual years. Nor are any data subsequent to 1938 provided.

One might suggest that the model builders, in particular, would do well to look a little more carefully at the numbers before they set out to rationalize them. But even to the extent they do, it sometimes seems to matter but little. Thus Kaldor, in one of the articles cited by Scitovsky, appends a footnote that Phelps Brown and Weber indicate a rising capital-output ratio in England from 1900 to 1914 and a falling ratio for 1924–38, and that in the United States the ratio rose from the 1880's to 1909–18, ignoring the depression period, has shown a falling trend since, and is not significantly different now from what it was sixty years ago. In other words, I interject, the ratio has behaved in a perfectly random fashion. But not to Kaldor. Returning to the text, he criticizes existing theories because they cannot explain such constancies except (and I quote) as the result of "some coincidence—as, e.g., that 'capital saving' and 'labour saving' inventions happened (historically) to have *precisely* offset one another."[4] In a similar vein, Scitovsky remarks in his present paper that the marginal

[4] Nicholas Kaldor, "A Model of Economic Growth," *Economic Journal*, December 1957, pp. 592–593 (my italics).

productivity theory "at best explains not constancy but merely a fair degree of stability in factor shares." One can only wonder how any theory can be criticized on this ground!

FRANCO MODIGLIANI, Northwestern University

1. Scitovsky's valuable and stimulating survey offers quite a tempting range of topics to pick from for a discussant. But to keep this comment within bearable limits, I shall have to confine myself to a criticism of the last section of his survey, in which he reviews and elaborates upon various "macroeconomic theories" designed to provide an explanation for the "observed" long-run stability of the three ratios. These are: (1) the share of property (i.e., nonlabor) income P in total income Y, or P/Y; (2) the ratio of the stock of capital K to income, or capital coefficient, K/Y; (3) the rate of return on capital, $r = P/K$. As Scitovsky reminds us, these three ratios are not independent so that the constancy of any two implies the constancy of the third.

I shall pass by the issue of whether the empirical evidence adequately supports the long-run stability of these ratios. For one thing, even if these ratios have not remained absolutely constant, it would seem at the very least that their long-run fluctuations have been quite moderate by comparison with the very large changes which have occurred in each of the numerators and denominators separately, as well as in such ratios as output per employed or capital per employed. Besides, the task of explaining the stability is such a fascinating and challenging game that it is hard to resist, even if the stability is after all a figment of somebody's imagination!

My comments fall into two parts. First, I should like to offer some criticism of Scitovsky's largely favorable review of the theories advanced by Kaldor and by Phelps Brown and Weber. I propose to argue that neither of these models, at least as interpreted by Scitovsky, is satisfactory, and more specifically that the first, though logically correct, is unconvincing, while the second is neither convincing nor logically correct. Having thus cleared the ground of opponents, I shall proceed to summarize an alternative explanation which has been advanced in some earlier work of mine, and which Scitovsky did not include in his survey.

2. Kaldor's theory, as interpreted by Scitovsky, is an exceedingly simple and ingenious one. Also, contrary to most other ex-

planations, it succeeds in explaining the stability of the capital-output ratio with no explicit reference to, or reliance on, the nature of technological progress, or, for that matter, on marginal productivity and the price mechanism. Stated very simply, it relies on the identity between the ratio of capital to output and the ratio of the rate of return on sales to the rate of return on capital, or,

$$K/Y \equiv (P/Y)/(P/K), \tag{1}$$

and on two mechanisms accounting respectively for the long-run stability of the numerator and the denominator ratio.

The stability of the numerator, according to Scitovsky, is explained by the hypothesis that producers set prices by adding a constant percentage mark-up, say, $m/(1 - m)$ to unit labor cost. As is well known, such a constant mark-up policy implies that total labor cost, or labor income, will tend to represent a constant fraction $(1 - m)$ of total product Y, and therefore the rate of return on sales P/Y will tend to be m—a result of which Weintraub[1] has made a good deal.

This mechanism is supplemented by a second one which Scitovsky hardly discusses and which insures that the rate of return on capital r will gravitate toward a long-run equilibrium value r, pulling in turn the capital output ratio toward an "equilibrium" value $\bar{k} = m/\bar{r}$. The essential ingredient of this mechanism is the hypothesis that the rate of investment depends both on the rate of growth of income (the conventional acceleration principle) and on the rate of return on capital. The postulated relation is such that when $r = \bar{r}$, and hence $k = \bar{k}$, the rate of growth of capital just equals the rate of growth of income, with the result that K/Y stays put at $\bar{k}$ and hence also r at $\bar{r}$.

If, however, at any point K/Y should happen to fall short of $\bar{k}$, say, because of technical change or other disturbance, then as a result of the unchanged mark-up m, the rate of return on capital would rise above $\bar{r}$. The increase in r in turn leads to a step-up in the rate of investment, which causes capital to grow faster than income, so that K/Y will rise back toward $\bar{k}$, thereby also pulling r back toward r.

I should add at this point that my interpretation of Kaldor's model, based on his published work,[2] is somewhat different in the

[1] S. Weintraub, *A General Theory of the Price Level, Output, Income Distribution and Economic Growth*, Philadelphia, 1959.

[2] I am referring in particular to "A Model of Economic Growth," *Economic Journal*, December 1957, pp. 591–624.

details, if not in the broad outline. As I see it, the constancy of the capital-output ratio is based on the interaction of his investment function with his "technical progress function" (stating that the rate of change of output is a function of the lagged rate of growth of capital). These two functions insure that the rate of growth of *both* income *and* capital must gravitate toward an equilibrium rate G, and hence income and capital must tend to become proportional. Given this rate of growth, the share of property income P/Y and the capital coefficient are simultaneously determined with the help of the investment function and by relying on Kaldor's peculiar theory of distribution, according to which the factor shares are determined, of all things, by the ratio of investment to income.

However, these differences of interpretation are perhaps a matter of detail. What is essential is that, in either interpretation, the cornerstone of Kaldor's model is the assumption that, even at full employment, the rate of investment is completely determined by the investment demand; whatever this demand, the level of saving and consumption passively adjusts to it through the intermediary of Kaldor's amazing theory of distribution. Hence, even without criticizing other aspects of his model, such as his nondescript "technical progress function," anyone who, like myself, is inclined to share Tobin's dim view of Kaldor's theory of distribution and saving behavior must regard his whole explanation as unconvincing, in spite of its undeniable ingenuity.

3. The Phelps Brown and Weber model again accounts for the stability of the labor share in terms of a stable mark-up on labor costs; but, in contrast to the Kaldor model, it endeavors to explain directly the stability of the capital coefficient—the stability of the rate of return being thus accounted for as a necessary consequence of the other two. Unfortunately, just how Phelps Brown and Weber propose to explain the stability of the capital coefficient is not very clear, either in their original work or in Scitovsky's interpretation. Scitovsky seems to suggest that this stability is derived from the constancy of the shares plus the hypothesis that technological change has been neutral on balance, which is itself explained by a variety of forces. There are unfortunately two serious difficulties with the passage in which Scitovsky advances this proposition. In the first place, neutral technical change has been defined in a variety of ways, and Scitovsky fails to make clear which concept he is adopting, although from the context

one must conclude that he refers to Harrod's definition.[3] Second, and more important, it is in general *not* true that constancy of the shares and Harrod-neutral technical change imply constancy of the capital-output ratio.

In order to establish this point, let us recall that Harrod's definition can be paraphrased as follows: technical change between some initial date 0 and some later date t is neutral if, the rate of interest being unchanged between the two dates, the most economical

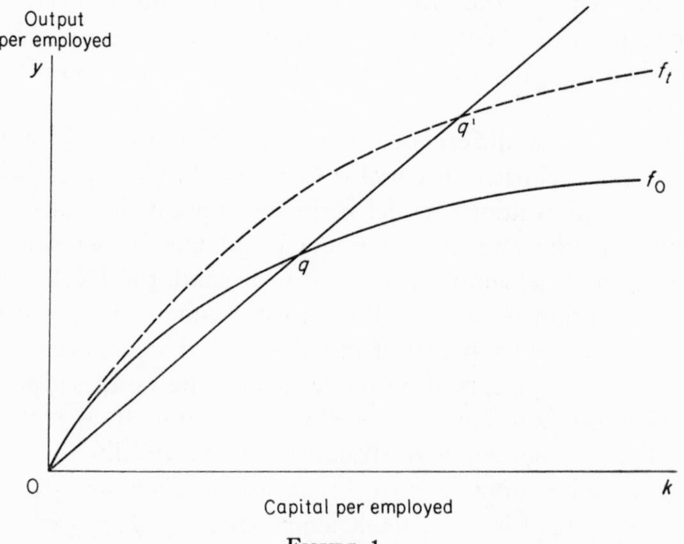

FIGURE 1.

(least-cost) input combination implies an unchanged capital output ratio, i.e., if $r_0 = r_t$ implies $K_t/Y_t = K_0/Y_0$ (it being assumed that the least-cost combination in fact prevails). It will be useful, for later reference, to exhibit analytically and graphically just what Harrod-neutral technical change implies with respect to the shift in time of the production function. Let $Y = F_0(K,E)$ denote the production function (homogeneous of first degree) at the initial date, E standing for total employment. Making use of the homogeneity properties, it can be rewritten as: $y = f(k)$, where $y = Y/E$ and $k = K/E$ denote respectively output per employed and capital per employed. This function can be represented by a curve in the (y,k) plane, such as the solid curve of Figure 1.

[3] R. Harrod, *Towards a Dynamic Economics*, London, 1948, p. 23.

It should be noted that the slope $f'_0(k)$ of this curve for any given value of k represents the marginal productivity of capital for the given input combinations, and therefore also the rate of interest for which k is the least-cost combination.

Now, let $X = F_t(K,E)$ denote the production function at date t. It can be readily established that if the shift in the production between 0 and t is Harrod-neutral throughout, F_t must be related to F_0 by the equation

$$F_t(K,E) = F_0[K,H(t)E], \tag{2}$$

where $H(t) > 1$ if in fact technology has improved. In other words, for any given combination of inputs, the output with the new production function will be the same as if the production function had remained unchanged but labor input had been increased by a factor $H(t)$, or each worker had become the equivalent of $H(t)$ workers. Because of the homogeneity, the new production function at time t can be restated in the form

$$Y/[H(t)E] = f_0[K/H(t)E], \text{ or } y = f_t(k) = H(t)f_0[k/H(t)]. \tag{3}$$

In terms of Figure 1, the new production function f_t is represented by a curve such as the dotted one, which can be derived from the f_0 curve as follows: through any point q of the old function, draw the radius vector $0q$ and extend it to the point q', such that $0q'/0q = H(t)$. Then q' is on f_t, and f_t itself is the locus of such points obtained by sliding q along f_0. To verify that this locus represents a Harrod-neutral shift of the locus f_0, we need only to observe that, by construction, the slope of f_t at q' is the same as the slope of f_0 at q. In general, therefore, for any given rate of interest or slope, the point chosen on f_t and that chosen on f_0 will lie on the same radius vector. But this in turn implies that these two points will be characterized by the same capital coefficient, since along any radius vector we have $y/k = (Y/E)/(K/E) = Y/K =$ constant. In fact, the slope of the radius vector through any point q, when referred to the y axis, represents precisely the capital coefficient at q. It should be noted that the shift in the production function between 0 and t might be Harrod-neutral in a neighborhood without being so throughout.

We may add in passing that Harrod's definition of neutral change is quite different from the most common or "classical" one, according to which a change is neutral if, and only if, for every combination of inputs, the ratio of the marginal product of any two inputs is the same for F_t as for F_0; that is, the marginal productivity of all factors rises in the same proportion. This definition implies that, if the shift between 0 and t is classical-neutral, then F_t is related to F_0 by the equation $F_t(K,E) = C(t)F_0(K,E)$, with $C(t) > 1$. Similarly f_t is related to f_0 by the relation $x = f_t(k) = C(t)f_0(k)$. Thus f_t can be obtained graphically from f_0 by multiplying the ordinate of each point on f_0 by the factor $C(t)$.

Now it is immediately apparent from the definition and from our graph that, if technical change is Harrod-neutral, constancy of the capital output ratio implies constancy of the shares. For, in this case, we know we are moving from a point such as q on f_0 to a point q' on f_t lying on the radius vector $0q$, and since the slopes at q' and q are the same, we must have $r_t = r_0$. But this condition, together with the relation $K_t/Y_t = K_0/Y_0$, assumed *ex hypothesis*, implies $r_tK_t/Y_t = r_0K_0/Y_0$, i.e., constancy of the shares. Unfortunately the converse proposition, on which Scitovsky seems to rely, is *not* true: that is, constancy of the shares does *not* necessarily imply constancy of the capital-output ratio. The easiest way of disproving Scitovsky's inference is to provide a counter example. Suppose, then, that the production function F_0 is of the Cobb-Douglas variety, or, say, $X = F_0(K,E) = AK^aE^{1-a}$. Suppose next that F_t is another Cobb-Douglas function of the form

$$Y = F_t(K,E) = AK^a[H(t)E]^{1-a} = F_0[K,H(t)E] = AH(t)^{1-a}K^aE^{1-a}. \quad (4)$$

By comparing equation (4) with equation (2), we see that the shift from 0 to t satisfies the definition of Harrod-neutrality. At the same time, from a well-known property of the Cobb-Douglas function we know that, if factors are paid their marginal product, the share of capital is given by a, the exponent of K, independently of the input combination chosen. Since the exponent of K does not change between 0 and t, we must have $r_0K_0/Y_0 = P_0/Y_0 = a = P_t/Y_t$, i.e., the shares are constant. And yet from this information, we can make no inference whatever about the capital-output ratios which are respectively $K_0/Y_0 = (1/A)(K_0/E_0)^{1-a}$ and $K_t/Y_t = (1/A)(K_t/H(t)E_t)^{1-a}$, and will be equal if, and only if, $K_t/E_t = H(t)(K_0/E_0)$. In other words, at least in this particular example, the constancy of the shares, plus Harrod-neutrality, does not entitle us to draw any conclusion about the behavior of the capital-output ratio.

The shortcoming in Scitovsky's argument which we have just brought out could no doubt be remedied by imposing some further specifications on the nature of the production function and/or technical progress. But even if this were done, another and more fundamental flaw would remain in the proposed explanation of the constancies. To see that this must indeed be the case, we need only observe that in the model under discussion we find no reference, explicit or implicit, to the supply side of the capital market, i.e., to the set of forces or mechanisms controlling the community's willingness to accumulate capital through the process of saving. This is an important departure from the Kaldor model, in which, at least, such a mechanism was provided for, even if not very convincingly. Surely there must be something wrong with a line of reasoning that purports to draw conclusions about the stock of capital and its behavior in time merely from information about technical knowledge and pricing behavior. Fortunately, the flaw is not too difficult to ferret out: the root of the difficulty lies in an unholy marriage of a marginalistic model of factor remuneration, with a mark-up—and hence nonmarginalistic—model of price determination. To be more specific, in order to make inferences about factor shares from the hypothesis of Harrod-neutral technical change, we must conceive of the capital share or rate of return on sales P/Y as determined by r and by the capital-labor ratio chosen by producers in response to r, which in turn implies a unique value for the capital-output ratio K/Y, and hence finally for $rK/Y = P/Y$. But then we cannot simultaneously postulate that P/Y is determined independently by an exogenously given "customary" mark-up on labor costs. In brief, the explanations used to establish the constancy of P/Y and that of K/Y are inconsistent with each other!

4. Let me now move on to the more constructive task of outlining an alternative model which can also account for the historical constancies and which, at the same time, meets Scitovsky's challenge of accomplishing this task within the framework of the marginal productivity approach. The argument developed below is to some extent a summary of parts of a recent paper by Albert

Ando and myself,[4] although it places much greater stress on the role of technical progress (which was treated only in passing in our paper) and relies on less restrictive assumptions.

The point of departure of the model is a theory of saving behavior, the main elements of which were first presented in my joint paper with R. Brumberg, "Utility Analysis and the Consumption Function: An Interpretation of Cross-Section Data."[5] As shown in the essay I wrote with Ando, cited above, and in other papers,[6] this model implies an aggregate consumption function of the form $C_t = cY^*_t + bW_t$, where C_t denotes the current rate of consumption at time t and Y^*_t the (anticipated) rate of nonproperty income, both measured in terms of current prices, and W_t represents the aggregate current market value of households' net worth. It has also been shown that the coefficient c (a pure number) and b (with dimension 1/time) will tend to be roughly constant in time, at least as long as the rate of return on capital, r, and the growth trend of Y^* are roughly constant. For purposes of long-run analysis, which is our present concern, we can identify Y^*_t with current labor income, to be denoted by X_t. In the interest of brevity, we may also ignore here the existence of nonreproducible tangible wealth and of government operations (including the national debt). Under these conditions W can be identified with reproducible tangible wealth, or K, and private income, $X + rK$ coincides with net output, Y.[7] The long-run aggregate consumption function thus becomes:

$$C_t = cX_t + bK_t = c(X_t + r_tK_t) + (b - r_tc)K_t = cY_t + (b - r_tc)K_t. \quad (5)$$

[4] "Growth, Fluctuations and Stability," *American Economic Review*, May 1959, pp. 501–524.

[5] In *Post-Keynesian Economics*, K. Kurihara, editor, New Brunswick, N.J., 1954.

[6] F. Modigliani and R. Brumberg, "Utility Analysis and the Aggregate Consumption Function," mimeographed; A. K. Ando, "*A Contribution to the Theory of Economic Fluctuations and Growth*," Ph.D. thesis, Graduate School of Industrial Administration, Carnegie Institute of Technology, 1959; A. K. Ando and F. Modigliani, "The 'Life Cycle' Hypothesis of Saving: Aggregative Implications and Tests," *American Economic Review*, March 1963, pp. 55–84.

[7] For an analysis of the economic implications of the national debt within this framework, see my recent paper, "Long-Run Implications of Alternative Fiscal Policies and the Burden of the National Debt," *Economic Journal*, December 1961. The effect of nonreproducible tangible wealth and of the discrepancy between private net income and output will be examined in a forthcoming paper.

Now it can be readily shown that this consumption function has the following basic implication: if Y_t fluctuates around an exponential growth trend with a stable rate of growth of, say, n per cent per year, and if r_t fluctuates similarly in the neighborhood of a constant level r, then the ratio of wealth to income K/Y will gravitate around a stable "equilibrium" value, say, a. This equilibrium value is related to the parameters of the consumption function by the equation:

$$a = (1 - c)/(n + b - rc). \qquad (6)$$

To prove this proposition, let us note that eq. (5) implies the saving function $S_t = Y_t - C_t = (1 - c)Y_t - (b - rc)K_t$, i.e., saving is an increasing linear function of income and a decreasing function of the stock of wealth (since the model itself, as well as empirical verifications thereof, indicate that $b > r$ and $c < 1$). But S_t is simply the rate of growth of wealth, or $dK/dt \equiv \dot{K}_t$. Making the substitution, dividing by K_t, rearranging terms, and using eq. (6), we get:

$$\dot{K}_t/K_t = (1 - c)(Y_t/K_t) - (b - rc) = n - \frac{n + b - rc}{K_t}$$

$$\left[K_t - \frac{1 - c}{n + b - rc} Y_t\right] = n - \frac{n + b - rc}{K_t} [K_t - aY_t]. \qquad (7)$$

From this equation, we can immediately infer that K_t/Y_t must gravitate toward the value a given by eq. (6). For if K_t/Y_t exceeds this value, i.e., $K_t > aY_t$, then we see from eq. (7) that $\dot{K}_t/K_t$ will be smaller than n, the rate of growth of Y_t. But then Y_t must be rising faster than K_t, and hence, K_t/Y_t must be decreasing in time and approaching a. Conversely, if at any point K_t/Y_t falls short of the equilibrium value, then the rate of accumulation will become sufficiently brisk to cause K_t to rise faster than Y_t, until equilibrium is re-established.

We can thus conclude that, *if* income exhibits an exponential growth trend and r is stable in time, then the stability over time of the ratio of wealth to income, or capital coefficient K/Y, can be accounted for by the supply side of the capital markets, as an implication of the consumption function (5). In order to complete our explanation of the "constancies," we need to introduce some further hypothesis on the nature of technical progress and the demand side of the capital markets, which insure an exponential growth trend and the stability of r. In particular, the following two assumptions can be shown to be sufficient: (a) that technical progress, for the reasons mentioned by Scitovsky and related mechanisms stressed by Fellner,[8] tends on balance to be Harrod-neutral, thus satisfying equation (2); and (b) that technical progress tends to shift the production function outward at a roughly constant proportional rate, or more precisely, that the time path of the quantity $H(t)$ of equation (2) tends to follow an exponential trend of the form $H(0)e^{pt}$.

To show that assumptions (a) and (b), together with the consumption function (5), imply the three constancies, it is convenient to proceed in two steps. Let us suppose at first that the labor force is constant and equal to E. Then $Y_t = Ey_t$ is proportional to y_t, and its growth is entirely due to rising output per capita, or productivity. Now assumption (a) (Harrod-neutral change) implies that, if the available capital is proportional to income, i.e., K/Y is constant, then the rate of return r needed to clear the capital markets will tend to remain constant; and the consumption function insures that, with a constant r, the capital-output ratio will be constant, *provided* Y grows exponentially. To complete the argument, it is therefore sufficient to show that if the capital-output ratio is constant, i.e.,

$$K = aY \text{ or } k = ay, \tag{8}$$

then assumption (b) insures that income will in fact follow an exponential growth trend. To verify this last conclusion, we only need to substitute eq. (8) into eq. (3), obtaining

$$y = H(t)f_0[ay/H(t)].$$

The value of y satisfying this equation, say, y_t, can be written in the form

$$y_t = y_0H(t) = y_0H(0)e^{pt},$$

where y_0 is a constant satisfying the condition $y_0 = f_0(ay_0)$. Thus y, and hence Y, will tend to grow at the rate p, and hence also eq. (8) will hold, with the constant a given by eq. (6), after setting $n = p$.

This result can be illustrated in terms of Figure 1. We can think of y_0 as the y coordinate of the point q at the intersection of

[8] See, e.g., William Fellner, *Trends and Cycles in Economic Activity*, New York, 1956, Chs. 7, 8, and 9.

the "initial" production function f_0 with the radius vector $0q$, having equation $k = ay$. Then y_t is represented by points at the intersection of this radius vector with a succession of outward shifting production functions f_t. These successive points of intersection are moving outward on the radius vector at the exponential rate p.

The reasoning is essentially unchanged if we drop the assumption that population is constant and assume instead that the labor force is itself growing at the exponential rate p'—that is, $E = E_0e^{p't}$. The only difference is that now total income, $Y_t = y_tE_t = y_0e^{pt}E_0e^{p't} = y_0E_0e^{(p+p')t}$, will grow at the rate $p + p'$, and hence, the equilibrium value of the capital coefficient a will be given by eq. (6) with $n = p + p'$.

We have thus shown that the three constancies can be explained by the $M - B$ consumption function, plus the hypothesis that technical progress has tended, on balance, to be of the Harrod-neutral variety and to take place at a roughly exponential rate. One significant implication of this model is that the rate of growth of income is completely determined by the rate of technical progress p and the rate of population growth p'—although it reflects in part also the growth of capital per employee, which is brought about by the consumption function, and occurs at the same rate as the growth in productivity.[9] Hence, the growth trend of income is independent of the marginal propensity to consume c or, for that matter, of the saving ratio S/Y; these quantities determine only the equilibrium capital output ratio and hence the ray on which we move, but not the speed of movement.

Unfortunately, it is not possible to expatiate here on this implication of the model, nor to bring out other interesting properties and possible generalizations, including the adaptability of the model

[9] In other words, the growth p in per capita output is due only partly to the outward shift in the production function, the remaining part being due to the growth of k, or in capital per man. It is this increase in capital per man which enables output to grow along the ray $0q$ of Figure 1. If instead k were to remain constant, we would not be moving along the ray $0q$, but instead along a vertical line through q, and the growth of output would be smaller, and might not even be exponential. To illustrate, if the production function were of the Cobb-Douglas type (4), we would have $Y_t = AK^a[H(t)E]^{1-a}$, or $y_t = [H(t)]^{1-a}k^a$. Hence, if k were constant and $H(t) = H(0)e^{pt}$, the rate of growth of y_t would be only $p(1-a)$. We might also note that the constancy of the three ratios requires only the constancy of the *over-all* rate of growth of income n; we can therefore relax the assumption that p and p' are individually constant as long as their sum is reasonably stable.

to an explanation of cycles as well as long-run trends.[10] There are, however, two brief concluding comments I should like to indulge in. First, the alternative model I have presented does not imply that the historical constancies will necessarily be maintained in the future. I can see no strong ground for confidence that technical progress will forever remain Harrod-neutral on balance, or that it will continue to occur at a roughly constant rate (or that the sum of p and p' will remain constant); and a change in any one of these conditions will in turn tend to disturb the constancy of the capital-output ratio. However, partly on intuitive grounds and partly for reasons too complex to report here, I would be inclined to expect that the (full-employment) rate of growth n and the capital-output ratio are likely to change at best very slowly. My second remark is that whether or not I have persuaded the reader of the usefulness of the specific model reported here, I hope at least to have made a convincing case for the central importance of the much-neglected supply side of the capital market for an understanding of the behavior of the capital-output and the capital-labor ratios, and more generally, of the phenomena associated with growth.

In summary, I have tried to bring to light some shortcomings of the macroeconomic theories reviewed by Scitovsky. I have also presented an alternative model in the hope of undermining his contention that "no satisfactory explanation [of the constancies] has been offered as yet by the upholders of the marginal productivity theory." Whether or not I have been successful in this last respect is left for the reader to decide.

Reply by Tibor Scitovsky

Let me say first of all how pleased I am that my survey should have called forth such interesting and constructive comments. I feel apologetic toward Modigliani for having missed his and Ando's very relevant and interesting paper, especially because I quite

[10] Some of these implications are spelled out in Ando and Modigliani, *American Economic Review*, May 1959, and in "Long-Run Implications of Alternative Fiscal Policies and the Burden of the National Debt," *Economic Journal*, December 1961. It should also be noted that the model can be generalized to allow for monopolistic and oligopolistic market structures, provided the ratio of price to (long-run) average cost remains reasonably constant in time.

agree that the role of the supply side of capital needs and deserves to be more fully explored.

As to the critical comments on my survey, let me begin by defending myself against Denison's charge of my having been unduly critical of the marginal productivity theory. I am sorry if I have created that impression, because I fully agree that marginal productivity is the basic building block for explaining both income distribution and many other things in economics; and my criticism was only aimed at too exclusive and too naive a reliance on it.

The other criticisms of both Denison and Modigliani have to do with the tail end of my survey, concerned with Kaldor's contribution and that of Phelps Brown and Weber. I was impressed more with their approach than with their arguments, and with the general proposition that when economic forces tend to stabilize each of several interdependent variables, they mutually reinforce each other. This seemed and still seems to me an idea worth exploring further, especially in the area under discussion, where so much remains yet to be explained. Denison's point that changes in tax rates and prices make it impossible for all the interdependent variables stabilized by market forces to be stabilized simultaneously is perfectly correct; but instead of destroying the original argument, it merely introduces a range of indeterminacy into it. I stand corrected by Modigliani's criticism of my understanding of Phelps Brown and Weber's argument, but find unconvincing his objection to Kaldor's argument as a complete and even more as a partial explanation. Modigliani's main objection seems to be "the assumption that, even at full employment, the rate of investment is completely determined by the investment demand"; and I should like to remind him that all Kaldor does is to shift the limit, up to which he assumes this, from full employment to what Joan Robinson calls the inflation barrier.

Factor Shares in the Long Term: Some Theoretical and Statistical Aspects

STANLEY LEBERGOTT

WESLEYAN UNIVERSITY

> All generous minds have a horror of what are commonly called "facts." They are the brute beasts of the intellectual domain. Who does not know fellows that always have an ill-conditioned fact or two that they lead after them into decent company like so many bull-dogs, ready to let them slip at every ingenious suggestion, or convenient generalization or pleasant fancy?—HOLMES, *The Autocrat of the Breakfast Table*

RATIONAL regularities pervade economic theory. But how rarely are they revealed in empirical records. And how resigned economists have become to it all, knowing full well that any constancy—whether of theory or the real world—will be hidden by the coarse irregularities of the published statistics. So well have they learned this depressing lesson, however, that they are quite unprepared on the rare occasions when a rigid constancy is reported. The share of wages in the national income seems to be such a constant, and a particularly dubious one—for it appears not only to lack a basis in theory, but even to be in conflict with it. Not surprisingly some of the most distinguished economists have been bemused by this. Keynes, with Anglo-Saxon understatement, spoke of the constancy as "a bit of a miracle." Schumpeter decided that it was "a mystery"—as did Joan Robinson. Solow has found that the miracle "may be an optical illusion," but still ranks it as "an interesting problem."[1] And Reder's recent review of the problem concludes that we are still in the dark.[2]

We consider here both some theoretical and statistical aspects

NOTE: I am deeply indebted to Bert Hickman for raising more penetrating questions on an earlier draft than are answered in this one.

[1] J. M. Keynes, "Relative Movements of Real Wages and Output," *Economic Journal*, March 1939, p. 48. J. A. Schumpeter, *Business Cycles; a Theoretical, Historical, and Statistical Analysis of the Capitalist Process*, Vol. II, 1939, pp. 575–76. R. M. Solow, "A Skeptical Note on the Constancy of Relative Shares," *American Economic Review*, September 1958, pp. 618, 628. The longer term stability in manufacturing was indicated by data for 1914–26 in an odd little study by Jurgen Kuczynski and Margaret Steinfeld, *Wages and Labor's Share*, 1927, pp. 54–55, but no analysis was really made of the results.

[2] Melvin W. Reder, in a perceptive (unpublished) paper read at the 1960 Annual Meeting of the American Economic Association.

of the question explicitly raised by Keynes: why, over so long a period in which the relative amounts of labor and capital changed so drastically, did the share of labor and capital in the national income remain relatively so stable? In Part I we discuss the forces determining factor shares, and conclude that "relative constancy" should exist, given the market mechanisms that determine the shape of the underlying production functions.

In Part II we consider how apt have been the previous statistical series used for studying changes in the U.S. ratio of labor income to national income from 1850 or 1900 to date. We find that these data, while suitable for a great many other purposes, were originally estimated with so many constancies stipulated in the estimation procedure that we can safely conclude nothing from them about the constancy of labor's share.

In Part III we consider the difficulty of the entrepreneurial share—compounded as it is of earnings on capital and earnings by labor. We conclude that the conceptual problem of disentangling capital from labor returns to entrepreneurs makes useless a discussion of labor's share in total national income—as well as in any industry dominated by entrepreneurial activity, such as agriculture, construction, and trade and service.

PART I

The Medusa-like fascination of the constant share of labor income to national income springs from an apparently glaring contrast between the patterns of neoclassical distribution theory and the brute statistics on distributive shares.[3] Theory begins from the reasonable stipulation that the respective returns to capital and labor are fixed by the relative prices and quantities of each. But since the past century has witnessed phenomenal changes in "the techniques of production, in the accumulation of capital relative to

[3] We do not consider interests beyond distribution theory. A number of authors have, however, reviewed the data with the thought that such numbers cast light on "the significance of union power . . . economic development, egalitarian movements." (The quotation is from an admirable review by Paul Davidson, *Theories of Aggregate Income Distribution*, 1960, p. 1. See too, Allan Cartter, *Theory of Wages and Employment*, 1959, Ch. 11.) Simon Kuznets has some concise and conclusive remarks on the limitations of the data for any such discussions. See his "Quantitative Aspects of the Economic Growth of Nations," *Economic Development and Cultural Change*, April 1959, p. 56.

labor and in real income per head,"[4] should we not expect marked changes in the ratio of labor to capital returns? Most writers at this point have gone on to contrast the statistics with this apparent implication of theory. Solow, however, has properly raised the question: can one skip so simply from one to the other? What a gulf separates the individual firm as described in neoclassical theory from the compiled numbers on factor shares for the economy. Between the two, writes Solow, lie "a whole string of intermediate variables: elasticities of substitution, commodity demand and factor supply conditions, markets of different degrees of competitiveness and monopoly, far from neutral taxes" and so on.[5] Without necessarily agreeing that a look at these complicating forces leads to "an expectation of 'relative stability' if anything,"[6] we take his perceptive caution to mark precisely the point for initial inquiry—well before the statistics themselves are reviewed.

Let us begin with a definition: The ratio of wages to property income (R) is a function of the price and quantity ratios for labor services (w) and capital service (k):

$$R = f\left(\frac{P_w}{P_k}, \frac{Q_w}{Q_k}\right) \tag{1}$$

A constancy in the wage ratio must follow inexorably if every movement in the price ratio is neatly offset by a contrary change in the quantity ratio. Solow has demonstrated that such an offset is virtually assured if only we assume a reasonable figure of one-third for the elasticity of substitution.[7] Kravis finds, similarly, that a fairly constant share did appear for the U.S. because "under conditions of rapid expansion in production labor was relatively

[4] N. Kaldor, "Alternative Theories of Distribution," *Review of Economic Studies*, February 1956, p. 84. The recent discussion of excessive stability appears to stem from Keynes' 1939 article. In an earlier look at the same U.K. figures from Bowley—though not the U.S. figures—Hicks (*Theory of Wages*, 1948, pp. 130–133) concluded that the capital share fell significantly from 1880 to 1913 (34 to 31 per cent) because the elasticity of substitution fell. His frame of reference was the rise in the share from medieval times.

[5] Solow, "A Skeptical Note," p. 620. Martin Bronfenbrenner, in "A Contribution to the Aggregate Theory of Wages," *Journal of Political Economy* (December 1956) systematically reviews the most important of these factors in his study of the question of whether in recent American history wage rate increases have added to real demand.

[6] Solow, "A Skeptical Note," pp. 620–621.

[7] *Ibid.*, p. 629. See also Irving B. Kravis, "Relative Income Shares in Fact and Theory," in *American Economic Review*, December 1959, p. 940.

inelastic in supply and rising rapidly in price" while "capital was apparently much more elastic or at any rate rapidly growing in supply."[8] But we only push the question back a stage, if we thus demonstrate that a palatable figure for the elasticity of substitution will yield numbers within the bounds of our historical measures of labor's share.

Why this particular substitution rate? The elasticity of substitution that may be hypothesized—whether one-third, one-fourth or any other figure—is surely not a mysterious new constant, given by forces outside the market economy. Why this proportion, and why this elasticity, rather than any other?[9] Should we not hesitate to rely on a particular number as an explanation?

Kaldor premises stability as a result of a constant saving—output ratio, his corollary being that changes in the propensity to save out of profits compensate for changes in the propensity to save out of wages.[10] This question has been examined carefully by Melvin Reder who concludes that historical data are consistent with this theory—but likewise with quite different ones.[11] In a recent telling essay, Kaldor stipulates that "a capitalist economy, after a certain period of adaptation, will tend to settle down to a rate of economic growth and accumulation where the growth rate of capital is the same as the growth rate of output, since at this point the . . . rate of profit on capital will be neither rising nor falling. The historical constancy of the capital output ratio, of the share of profit in income . . . in advanced capitalist economies is thus explicable in terms of forces which tend to bring these two growth rates (of capital and output) into equality with

[8] *Ibid.*, pp. 943–944. Sidney Weintraub (*An Approach to the Theory of Income Distribution*, 1958, p. 82) finds that "either the *M/A* ratios (marginal to average physical product) and the *Ed* magnitudes (price elasticity of demand for specific products) must have remained constant or they must have operated systematically and fortuitously to neutralize each other's variation when the stock of equipment, the level of employment, and the nature of the product-mix underwent change."

[9] Premising a constant elasticity, in turn, implies that the historical curve relating the quantity to the price ratio must have been a straight line. But it is difficult to see an a priori reason why the line should be straight throughout time, or why a curvilinear relationship would not be equally reasonable.

[10] N. Kaldor, "Alternative Theories," p. 84. Allan Cartter (*Theory of Wages*, Ch. 11) presents a theory similar to Kaldor's in emphasizing the marginal propensities to save of laborers and capitalists, but does not premise stability of each, nor compensating movements.

[11] Melvin W. Reder, "Alternative Theories of Labor's Share," *The Allocation of Economic Resources*, 1959, Moses Abramovitz, ed.

one another." He goes on to state that "wages and profits form a constant proportion of output" in "any steadily growing economy where the proportion of output devoted to investment is constant" provided "the propensities to save out of profits and wages are assumed to be given."[12] But why these propensities need be stable through time is another matter, and requires some further demonstration. Indeed in a subsequent discussion of laggard growth he points out that "if the savings propensities were halved, the share of profit in income would be doubled at any given ratio of investment to output," and then goes on to discuss how "the process of accumulation and growth is periodically interrupted."[13] This surely implies that the saving propensities are not necessarily fixed.

We believe it possible to seek a solution in the theory of distribution; and suggest that a market mechanism does exist which works in the direction of long-run constancy—quite apart from any specific ratio of wages to national income, or elasticity of substitution, that may seem most reasonable to us. Agreeing with the emphasis placed on the elasticity of substitution by Solow and Kravis, we go on to consider the forces that determine the level of that elasticity over long periods, constant or not. Let us consider the quantity ratio in equation (1) above. What determines the size of this ratio? The answer, for a broadly competitive economy, is that the ratio is a function of two variables—the price ratio in the present period, and the quantity ratio in the previous period:

$$\frac{Q_w}{Q_k} = f\left(\frac{P_w}{P_k}, \frac{Q_{w_o}}{Q_{k_o}}\right) \tag{2}$$

That the price ratio in the current period is one forceful determinant we can hardly doubt: where entrepreneurs have free access to capital and labor markets we should expect shifts in the ratio of prices to induce shifts in the quantity of each used.

However, only limited substitution possibilities can be grasped within the short term. The production coefficients are therefore destined to appear invariant to many price changes. It is for this reason that we include the quantity ratios of the prior period as a

[12] N. Kaldor, "Economic Growth and the Problem of Inflation," *Economica*, August 1959, pp. 223, 225.

[13] N. Kaldor, "Economic Growth and the Problem of Inflation, Part II," *Economica*, November 1959, p. 290.

second variable—for they reflect the coefficients in being. (Thus, once a bank of machines has been installed, as Johansen has recently emphasized, it will require a fixed complement of manpower throughout the life of the machines.[14] While there are some qualifications to this generalization, they do not warrant ignoring this variable.[15])

But the fixed-complement technology itself is not really a given: for the ratio of manpower to machine inputs at time zero is in turn a function of relative prices in the previous period(s), when the machine-man ratio was adopted from a spectrum of alternatives. Substituting this earlier price ratio for the quantity ratio in the second equation gives us:

$$\frac{Q_w}{Q_k} = f\left(\frac{P_w}{P_k}, \frac{P_{w_o}}{P_{k_o}}\right) \tag{3}$$

Substituting (3) in (1) we get:

$$R = f\left(\frac{P_w}{P_k}, \frac{P_{w_o}}{P_{k_o}}\right) \tag{4}$$

The ratio of wage to property income is therefore a function of the price ratio of labor to capital in the current and preceding period(s).[16]

If this sequence of price ratios could vary randomly we would have precious little reason to anticipate any great stability of the wage-property income proportion. And if the ratios systematically rose or fell, we would expect that proportion to move remorselessly up or down. Only if basic forces made for a stability in the price ratios would we anticipate a stability in the income

[14] Lief Johansen, "Substitution versus Fixed Production Coefficients in the Theory of Economic Growth: a Synthesis," *Econometrica*, April 1959, p. 158.

[15] Should there occur a marked variation in the ratio of the price of labor to that of capital, marginal equipment can be sold in the market and new equipment bought—and bought until a point is reached where the technical ratio has actually changed. Over a longer period technical substitution is, of course, still more likely to take place as old equipment is fully written off.

[16] Since the entrepreneurial choice is really made with respect to price trends over the useful life of the capital investment under consideration, it is the expected price ratio that is relevant. We assume that to be some function of the past and present ratios. This is probably insufficient. An allowance should also be made for the change in these ratios: entrepreneurs would recognize the forces in this country making for a long-run rise in wage rates, the long-run accumulation of capital, and the decline in the risk component of capital cost. Such an allowance would lead to a bias in favor of a higher capital-labor ratio. However, this bias, if steadily exercised, would tend to bring back the relative price of capital.

ratio. At first sight we have no reason to expect such stability. (Indeed, if we attached the same importance to monopolistic elements as Kalecki and Mitra did when explaining the wage proportion, we would premise so solid a stability in the price trend for one factor as could only result in greater instability in the ratio of that price series to the other.[17])

True, if we assumed a fixed elasticity of substitution all would be magically simplified. For Bronfenbrenner's analysis demonstrates that any one in a wide choice of elasticities would all tend to give us factor shares that varied within only a narrow range.[18] But what warrant do we have for creating any such *numerus ex machina*, a new constant—unwavering and unyielding amid all the forces of economic change? Furthermore, a look at the Creamer-Kendrick data for manufacturing suggests that in this major sector the capital-labor ratio went in one direction from 1899 to 1919, and in the other from 1919 to 1953. Meanwhile (according to our estimates), factor shares remained almost unchanged. Hence, the elasticity of substitution must have changed significantly through time. It is, therefore, not by any arbitrary positing of a fixed elasticity that we can achieve a satisfying explanation of the relative constancy in the sequence of price ratios discussed above.

What can be said about the determinants of the price ratio? We simplify our problem by taking the price of labor as given in all periods. (Its determinants do not matter here: they are fixed as part of a general equilibrium solution. We need only deal with changes in the price of capital vis-à-vis that of labor.) What, then, fixes the price of capital used in production relative to those forces that determine the price of labor?

DEMAND FOR CAPITAL

Consider a manufacturing company: its demand for capital reflects the uses to which the capital will be put—investment in machinery, inventories, land, etc. Now while machinery, for example, is often treated as technically complementary to labor in the production of most goods (on terms set by the engineers) this basically

[17] Michal Kalecki, *Theory of Economic Dynamics*, 1954. Ashok Mitra, *The Share of Wages in National Income*, The Hague, 1954. Keynes, in "Relative Movements," speculated on the role of monopolistic elements, but did not accept them as a real explanatory force.

[18] Bronfenbrenner, "A Contribution to the Aggregate Theory."

reflects the underlying price relationship.[19] Were labor to become a free good while machinery continued to command a price, then over time one would expect a marked increase in the ratio of labor to machinery as capital saving methods were introduced. "Technical" requirements might still forbid complete substitution; sociological ones would certainly do so. But, within the limits set by these constraints, there would still be ample room for wide variation determined by the relative profitability of using one factor instead of another. But that profitability would be set by the changing price ratio of one to the other—assuming an initial long-run competitive equilibrium position in which the marginal revenues from each were equal.

SUPPLY OF CAPITAL

The supply forces that work to fix the cost of capital include the interest rate and the price of a physical unit of capital. Variations in the former appear to have had small impact on the long-period share of return to capital in the national income—small not in terms of economic importance, but as compared to the much greater effects of variation in the prices of machinery and plant. Over the past sixty years producers' durable equipment has risen about 300 per cent in price, while ten-year bond yields have changed about 10 per cent, from 3.2 to 2.9 per cent.[20] Moreover, the ratio of interest to total costs of machinery service is relatively small over the life of most equipment. Thus, while variations of high economic significance have occurred in interest rates, their contribution to changing the numbers on factor shares has been feeble in comparison with the effect of variations in the prices of machinery and other capital items.

Let us look to the determinants of the price of these services.[21]

[19] Variations in the demand for capital as a purely technical complement to labor will not tend to change the relative price of one to the other and hence can be ignored here. To simplify discussion we convert the problem to a two-factor one, treating land costs henceforth as commutable into machinery and construction costs. We label the latter as machinery for convenience.

[20] Kuznets' implicit price index for producers' durables just about doubles from 1897–1901 to 1927–31, and the Department of Commerce series more than double from 1929 to 1957. See Bureau of the Census, *Historical Statistics of the United States, Colonial Times to 1957*, pp. 142–144. Bond yield data from *ibid.*, p. 657.

[21] We consider first the unit price of equipment assuming no change in its productive capacity. But in the real world, of course, the manufacturer may cheapen machinery service either by cutting price, raising productive capacity or a combination of the two.

The supply forces which fix the price of machinery are those involved in: the cost of labor; the cost of materials; "normal profits"; and rents, advertising and other costs.

In 1957 the machinery industries sold something like $26 billion worth of goods,[22] of which: $10.0 billion was used for wages and salaries; $8.0 billion was used for materials purchases; $0.3 billion was used for rent and interest; $1.1 billion was used for net profit (after tax); and $1.7 billion was used for taxes.

We assume that variations in rent, taxes and corporate dividend policy are numerically unimportant in determining price variation, given their small share in total cost, a generally competitive industry, and their limited dollar range. Hence, it is the fluctuating level of wage and of material costs that dominates the change of final product charges by machinery industries.

Material (and component) costs are determined on the demand side first by variations in total production; but these, involving technical complementaries, do not alter the capital-labor price ratio.[23] Secondly, these costs are determined by the buyer's option of producing in a different fashion, using a different level of fabrication as a partial substitute for raw materials or components. The use of the latter option, of course, is influenced by the supply schedules for the industries that provide materials to the components and materials industries *per se*, and by the wages in the latter industries. On the supply side, these will reflect, to an important extent, wage costs in steel, hand tools, coal, railroads, and other industries that directly or ultimately provide materials to the machinery industries.

[22] For machinery except transport and electrical, data on sales, rent, interest, profit, and taxes from IRS, *Statistics of Income, Corporation Income Tax Returns, 1957–58*, p. 27. For compensation of employees we use *U.S. Income and Output*, p. 200. For materials, we take the IRS total for cost of goods sold, deduct wages, and round the figures. The major problem in this simple procedure is a possible significant change in inventory holdings. From IRS, *Business Statistics*, 1959, p. 20, we see that inventory change over the taxable year was in fact quite small, assuming most tax years to end June through January.

[23] This statement is something of an exaggeration: at markedly different levels of output there could be economies of scale greater for one factor than another. (Eric Schiff's penetrating discussion in his paper "Factor Substitution and the Composition of Input" in *Output, Input, and Productivity Measurement*, Studies in Income and Wealth 25, Princeton for NBER, 1961, emphasized the scale effect and pointed out that production processes are not necessarily so "input homogeneous" as to permit easy substitution throughout the scale range.) We would expect that, in the long run, changes in size of production run (and possible plant) consequent upon scale economies would be explicable for present purposes by the mechanism discussed below.

Hence, it is wage costs in the machinery industries, and in the suppliers to these industries, that substantially shape the supply price of machinery.[24]

If changes in wage costs to the machinery industries bore no necessary relationship to changes in other industries this would not get us forward; but in fact they do. Wage rates for unskilled labor in the machinery industry, for example, must broadly move together with those for unskilled labor in steel. If machinery industries begin paying more, then the steel industry and others must match the rate change for the same quality of labor, or begin to lose labor.[25] The same is true for cranemen, machinists, carpenters, truck drivers, etc. And there must be a similar correspondence even for jobs that seem peculiar to one industry: were machinery industries to double the rate paid on a simple assembly operation characteristic of these industries, the steel industry and others must begin to raise their rates for broadly similar skills or see their expert semiskilled people begin moving out to jobs in machinery (and vice versa if steel or coal moves first). In a competitive labor market over the long term, therefore, we expect to see wage rates for major occupations change similarly in machinery industries and in their supplying industries.[26]

There remains one step. If productivity advances in the machinery industries had been negatively correlated with those in the supplying industries, the broad correspondence of wage *rate* trends might have been so nullified as to make each wage *cost* series take a different path. We see no reason to assume so unlikely a negative relationship. Because of the endless problems of measuring deflated output in the machinery industries, we have little empirical

[24] I am indebted to Bert Hickman for calling my attention to the similar point made by Robert Grosse in his valuable "The Structure of Capital" in *Studies in the Structure of the American Economy*, edited by W. W. Leontief, 1953, p. 186. Grosse finds that "substitution occurs chiefly when there are technical improvements in capital goods production which result in a fall in the ratio of the price of capital goods to the price of labor. But with a given technique, there will be relatively little price substitution." Since the choice of technique itself is determined by relative prices and returns there is no need for the latter assertion.

[25] We are speaking here of correspondence of movement, not identity of level.

[26] We assume that the role of union and government intervention, however great, does not require significant modification of this statement. In a recent review of the considerable literature on the role of the union, and an extended analysis of his own, Gregg Lewis concluded that the absolute influence of unions was relatively small. See H. Gregg Lewis, "The Effects of Unions on Industrial Wage Differentials," in *Aspects of Labor Economics*, Princeton for NBER, 1962. A fortiori, the differential effect as between industries using the same type of labor is likely to be still less.

material. But if we may take such other metal manipulating industries as transport equipment to give us a suggestion and relevant indication, we find that their productivity advanced over the decades in the same direction as that for steel, coal mining, lumber manufacturing, etc.[27]

Surely the thrust of productivity advance was also at work in the machinery industry. If so, one would expect the price of machinery services to fall in relation to wage rates.[28] This result, however, would depend on the source from which this productivity advance derived. If it involved the use of machinery, then the machine-producing industry must needs be defined as, in this respect, a machine-using industry. In that event, however, we are promptly returned to the original question on the forces that make for the substitution between capital and labor.

But suppose the productivity advance in machinery occurred in the industry *qua* producer. It would then have had to result from the other modes by which the entrepreneurial function is exercised. For example, highly skilled tasks would be broken down to use less skilled labor. Noncompeting groups in the labor market (immigrants, women, nonwhites) would be hired in increasing measure to replace higher cost groups. Maintenance, stand-by, finishing, clerical operations would be cut out or cut down. Each of these steps would cut wage *costs* without touching wage *rate* trends. New plants would be established in states with lower labor costs, and in areas closer to the optimum location between new market concentrations and factor sources. New control systems and revised layouts would make more efficient use of existing stocks and input flow patterns. In general, this range of procedures could induce productivity advances, and in significant volume, without proportionate increases of capital or labor inputs. Many would require no increase of inputs.[29]

[27] Solomon Fabricant, *Employment in Manufacturing, 1899–1939: An Analysis of its Relation to the Volume of Production*, New York, NBER, 1942. Harold Barger and Sam H. Schurr, *The Mining Industries, 1899–1939: A Study of Output, Employment and Productivity*, New York, NBER, 1944.

[28] We consider here factors making for a decline in the price of machinery services. Producers may pass on the decrease in their costs either by reducing machinery prices, by improving the output capacity of machinery while keeping prices rigid, or by a combination of the two. Hence, reported machinery price series without an adequate allowance for changes in machinery productivity do not measure changes in the price of machinery services.

[29] Summarizing data in John W. Kendrick, *Productivity Trends in the United States*, Princeton for NBER, 1961, Fabricant estimates that the physical output of

But each of these entrepreneurial gambits is available to machine-using as well as to machine-producing industries. And at any time they have an equal incentive to reduce costs by adopting such alternatives. It is, of course, unnecessary and unreasonable to presume that more efficient techniques would be seized upon at precisely equal rates in machine-using and machine-producing industries. We do assume, however, that (apart from input increases) the long term forces making for productivity advance in the machinery industries, and thereby making for lower machinery service prices, will find their parallel in similar forces that lower labor costs in the machine-using industries. Hence, the obvious fact of productivity advance in the machinery industries does not *per se* imply any changing ratio of capital to labor price—that ratio whose approximate long-term stability we have inferred above as confronting the machine-using industries.

A second component of capital costs, beyond that for machinery and equipment, is for buildings. By the same line of reasoning as that used above, the bulk of building service price variation will be determined by wage rate variation in the building industry and those industries (cement, steel, mechanical items) that supply the construction industry—with a lesser contribution from variations in profit margins and productivity differentials.

A third component of capital costs is that for financing inventories. The price of inventories will vary with the price of the final product which, in turn, is largely dominated by the course of wage costs in the given industry and those preceding it in the production sequence.

Finally, the decision to hold funds in working capital—whether currency, deposits, securities, or receivables—must be made in terms of the opportunity cost of using such funds for actual investment in inventories or productive equipment, and hence be relatable to the same factors as determine the cost of such investment.

A significant qualification to the above would appear to be the fact that contracts are made at one point in time for the acquisi-

---

the economy rose by 3.5 per cent a year from 1889 to 1957, whereas man-hours and tangible capital inputs jointly rose by only 1.7 per cent (Solomon Fabricant, *Basic Facts on Productivity Change*, New York, NBER, 1959, p. 19). From the numbers we infer a significant contribution by forces other than these tangible inputs—among which we give pride of place to the entrepreneurial function.

tion of capital, while their terms are constant for years afterwards despite subsequent variations in the wage cost figures. In one respect this argues for a distributed lag function, recognizing not merely current trends in wages but previous trends—with a diminishing distribution of weights through time. But a substantial link to current trends is still maintained for most contracts by virtue of the fact that the contracts can be broken by refinancing. The opportunity cost involved in continuing old financing is largely set by the cost of breaking old contracts and the cost of borrowing under current terms. Because of the costs and difficulties of refinancing, there will be no instant and proportionate response in contractual changes as current changes in investment opportunity occur. And the increasing reliance on internal financing for capital expansion and replacement, rather than resort to borrowing or the use of senior equity securities, tends to diminish further the scope for such response. However such response as does occur through refinancing has a clear bias: since it occurs at the option of the borrower, it will take place only when current costs of new capital are below those for which he has contracted. Old borrowings bring a bias to the capital-labor price ratio since old contracts are broken at the option of the borrower (i.e., via paying off and refinancing), and that option is exercised more when the price of capital is declining relative to that of labor than when the ratio is going the other way.

It must be noted that not all data on the comparative trend of the price of capital and labor in the U.S. would be suited to the question as we have posed it. The required measure of the price of capital is one that has meaning only for those industries in which the entrepreneur can, in principle, substitute between his capital and labor inputs. Hence, the valuable Kendrick series, which includes imputed rent of owner-occupied houses and an entreprenurial allocation of a kind not suited to our immediate concern, is unfortunately not usable here.[30]

[30] His series includes the imputed rent of owner-occupied residences in the capital return. Variations in the "price" of such capital, which will reflect variations in property taxation and building maintenance costs, will not cause owner occupiers to change the proportions of labor to capital in their occupancy activity. No more suitable, are series where no market measure of the capital input to the sector existed—as, for example, those computed by deducting an arbitrarily estimated "labor compensation" of proprietors from their total return. (The residual estimate of capital compensation to proprietors is then divided by a capital input series to get a price of capital series.) Such a pro-

The above model is intended to describe only longer-term changes in relative prices and factor shares for individual industries, or more accurately for those constellations of products in which sets of firms tend to specialize and, by virtue of that specialization, tend to be termed industries. The shifting of the boundaries for these product groups over time surely tends to blur the boundaries of what is defined as an industry. But even if individual industries continue clearly delimitable through time, the combination of these industries into a grand total for the economy is another matter. The changing weight of products and "industries" in that total over the years involves a significant aggregation problem. In theory we would expect a nation to shift toward those industries that use its most abundant resources and away from those using scarcer resources; i.e., to change a specialization whenever what was once a high cost resource becomes a low cost one, and vice versa. The unsettled controversy over the Leontief paradox suggests, however, that empirical verification in this area is still significantly incomplete.[31]

In summary, we define the share of national income flowing to wages as against capital as a function of the quantity and price ratios of each factor. We find that in the long run the quantity ratio is in turn a function of the changing price ratios. Taking the price of labor service as given, we contend that the changing price of capital service must bear a constant long-term proportionality to that of labor. This proportionality derives from the fact that the supply forces working to fix the price of capital are dominantly wage costs in the capital-producing industries and those that supply them. In a competitive market these wage costs parallel wage-cost changes in capital-using industries because wage changes for identical occupations must bear a parity to one another in all employing industries; while historical experience suggests that productivity trends in the supplying and using industries are not so negatively related as to make costs take a different course from rates.

---

cedure does not deal with measures separately available to the proprietor, as would be necessary if his substitution between capital and labor inputs were a function of price ratios.

[31] We refer to Leontief's conclusion that the U.S. tends to export goods using relatively greater amounts of labor, to import those using relatively greater amounts of capital, and to the extensive literature by Diab, Swerling, Hoffmeyer, *et al.*, on this proposition.

PART II

What basis do we have for asserting that the share of wages in the national income prior to 1919 was in fact stable?[32] The answer, in brief, is: very little. Most of the studies in the field rely on the estimates of R. F. Martin, W. I. King and Gale Johnson (Martin relies largely on King for the period 1909–19).[33] We consider each before turning to the data since 1919.

KING'S ESTIMATES FOR 1850–1900[34]

To assess the adequacy of King's data for the study of factor share changes prior to 1900, we review some of the ratios and averages implicit in his figures. The result of that review is not one to encourage our use of his totals for reaching any conclusion as to the stability of factor shares. We infer this from a consideration of data for three sectors—agriculture, government, and commerce—which together account for well over half of his income totals in these decades.[35]

Agriculture

King's figures show an unreasonably high share of farm product going to wages for 1870 and 1880 (his data imply almost 50 per cent of product in wages), then decline to nearly 20 per cent by

[32] We do not discuss the variety of data available for other countries: to understand the derivation of their estimates is a major project in itself. The interested reader will find a variety of comparisons for several countries, with data adjusted as best may be for comparability, in Livio Livi, *Primo Computo Del Reddito Distributto al Fattori Della Produzione*, 1958, Ch. 11, especially p. 172. Professor Livi's data show great stability for some nations, great change for others, over the period from 1938 to about 1954.

[33] R. F. Martin, *National Income in the United States, 1799–1938*, 1939; W. I. King, *The Wealth and Income of the People of the United States*, 1915; and D. Gale Johnson, "The Functional Distribution of Income in the United States, 1850–1952," in *Review of Economics and Statistics*, May 1954. A well known extensive study is E. C. Budd, "Factor Shares, 1850–1910," in *Trends in the American Economy in the Nineteenth Century*, Income and Wealth 24, Princeton for NBER, 1960. Among the significant briefer studies is the discussion in William Fellner, *Trends and Cycles in Economic Activity*, 1956, Appendix to Part 3, Parts 7 and 5; Simon Kuznets, *National Income: A Summary of Findings*, New York, NBER, 1946, p. 50, and Kuznets' review, more in accord with the conclusion of stability, in his "Long Term Changes in the National Income of the United States of America Since 1870" in *Income and Wealth of the United States* (International Association for Research in Income and Wealth, 1952, p. 85).

[34] I am most grateful to Elizabeth Jenks for comments on my interpretation of King's procedures, and for unpublished data from his "data books."

[35] King, *Wealth and Income*, p. 140.

1910.[36] The latter ratio is reasonably close to the Department of Agriculture estimates for that year,[37] but the ratios in the early decades are startlingly high. The enormous 1870–1910 decline is difficult to credit for a period during which the ratio of hired labor to entrepreneurs actually rose.

A second, no less disturbing aspect of King's figures is their implication that earnings per farmer (including imputed value of food and home) were less than those per farm employee.[38] Contemporary materials, as well as most data for later years, suggests quite the reverse.

Commercial and Professional Services

King estimated the total product of trade, service, finance, insurance and real estate—accounting for 30 per cent of the national product in 1910—"on the basis of a constant ratio to the product of urban population and average income."[39] What is important for present purpose is not that this large sector was estimated in this quite arbitrary, if reasonable, fashion. Rather our concern is that the wage component is likely to have been estimated with equal (or greater) arbitrariness: King gives no information from which his procedure could be deduced. Hence, we have little basis for using the trend in the factor-share ratio for total national income (including as it does a large allowance for wages) to deduce yeasty conclusions about the trend in factor shares.[40]

[36] *Ibid.*, pp. 138, 260.

[37] U.S. Department of Agriculture, *Major Statistical Series of the U.S. Department of Agriculture*, Vol. 3, p. 46, 1957.

[38] King, *Wealth and Income*, p. 150, refers to the Census of 1900, *Occupations* (p. 1), as his source for persons employed in agriculture. Referring to that volume we see, e.g., that his six million for 1870 is identical with the reported Census total for farmers and employees in agricultural pursuits. We therefore divide the Census 3.0 million farmers into King's entrepreneurial earnings (p. 263); then divide the residual 2.9 millions (for employees) into King's wage total for farming employees (p. 260). The result is about $240 per employee, $190 per entrepreneur. If, moreover, we assume that no money wage should have been set down for unpaid family workers, this $50 gap—in the wrong direction—would have been still greater.

[39] King, *Wealth and Income*, p. 138.

[40] King reports money earnings per employee for all industries combined (*ibid.*, p. 168). If we divide that average into his wage aggregates for the trade, service, finance group (p. 260), the result shows no rise in the number of employees in this group from 1850 to 1910. In other words, his implicit trend for earnings per employee in this category would have had to decline substantially over the decades, or to have risen significantly less than that for all employees, to give a reasonable employment trend for the group.

Government

King's description of how he estimated the product total for this group reads in its entirety, "The services of the government were assumed to be worth the amount paid for running the government."[41] We follow this thin lead by comparing, e.g., his $437 million for government product in 1870 with the $588 million total for federal expenditures plus state and local taxes.[42] Hence, a state and local surplus carry-over of about $150 millions—more than half again as great as the $280 millions of taxes they raised—would have had to exist if King's totals were to be reconciled with these expenditure figures.

No information is given on how the wage component of this government was estimated. If we refer to the same population census source that King cites as the basis for his employment estimates, add up the occupations shown there as associated with government employment, and divide the total into his wage bill, we get an average of $5,000 per employee in 1870.[43] This figure is over twelve times the reasonable average ($397) that he estimates for all nonfarm employees.[44] But since most government employees prior to 1900 were wage earners and lower salaried personnel, an average of at most $500 would be more like the true figure than $5,000.

MARTIN'S ESTIMATES, 1900–20[45]

Entrepreneurial income plus salaries and wages account for nearly 90 per cent of Martin's income totals in these years.[46] Hence, to assess the constancy of factor share ratios from these data must largely require that his estimates for the two shares have been independent of one another.

[41] *Ibid.*, p. 129.

[42] State and local taxes from a Census source cited in some of King's notes: 1870 Census, Part III, *The Wealth and Industry of the People of the United States*, p. 11. Federal expenditures are from Bureau of the Census, *Historical Statistics*, p. 710.

[43] 1900 Census, *Occupations* (p. 1) checked against 1870 Census, *The Statistics of the Population of the United States*, 1872, pp. 764–765. We add: employees of government, clerks, officials of government, army officers and soldiers. (Excluding the military would make matters worse.) The government employee average in 1900 was much the same as that for all employees.

[44] King, *Wealth and Income*, p. 168.

[45] Martin, *National Income*.

[46] *Ibid.*, p. 22.

Mining

Since Martin relies largely on King, the latter's lack of notes means that one cannot assert too flatly how the Martin estimates were derived. We believe, however, that the King-Martin procedure for these decades amounts to assuming that the trend of average wage per employee was identical with that for average earnings per entrepreneur.[47] Hence, no matter how great the actual variations in the relative earnings of each, these estimates would not show any change in the ratio of entrepreneurial earnings to wages and salaries.

Manufacturing and Trade

Martin assumed that the trend of earnings per employee and per entrepreneur were the same for 1899–1919. Indeed, for manufacturing, he used the same figures.[48]

Construction, Transportation, Service

For each of these industries Martin used the trend in the wage-salary bill to extrapolate that of entrepreneurial earnings, implicitly assuming (1) a constant ratio of average wage-salary to average entrepreneurial earnings, and (2) a constant ratio of employees to entrepreneurs.[49]

[47] Martin, *ibid.*, p. 119, adopts King's average entrepreneurial income for the years, 1909–19, and uses Douglas' earnings in coal mining to run back to 1899. King, of course, gives no description but his average wage in all mining (Martin, p. 93) appears to be much the same as his coal mining wage (Martin, p. 319—weighting anthracite and bituminous together). For employees, Martin uses Douglas' average earnings in coal mining also, to interpolate between 1902 and 1909 Census earnings figures. But, since Douglas interpolated between Census benchmarks to begin with, this means that Martin used the same average earnings trend for employees and entrepreneurs. (Martin actually uses coal plus oil mining, stipulating that oil wages varied with the value of petroleum production. But since oil wages account for 10 per cent or less of the combined total this variation makes little difference.)

[48] Martin, *National Income*, pp. 120, 121. For trade, he implicitly assumed a constant ratio of entrepreneurs to employees in the Census of Population occupation category "wholesale and retail merchants and dealers." However, in actual Census reporting a proportion of that category was actually employees—i.e., salesmen and store managers. See Alba Edwards, *Comparative Occupation Statistics*, 1943, p. 110.

[49] Martin, *National Income*, pp. 120, 121. He may have implicitly assumed a downward (or variable) trend in one set of ratios that was precisely offset by an upward (or variable) trend in the other. This seems most unlikely.

Conclusion

For industries which (in 1910) accounted for approximately two-thirds of Martin's total for realized private production income, he estimates 1900–20 trends in entrepreneurial income by assuming a constant ratio of employee earnings to earnings by entrepreneurs. For a substantial group, he assumed a constant ratio of employees to entrepreneurs as well. His method of estimate thus precludes variation in a large area. Within this area, variations in the ratio of entrepreneurial earnings to wages and salaries, and hence, in the ratio of wages and salaries to national income, could occur. We conclude that the use of such data for discussing stability in the ratio of labor income to national income is futile, adding little to our knowledge of the subject.

JOHNSON'S ESTIMATES, 1900 AND LATER

In his well known study, Gale Johnson has developed a series for factor income distribution from 1900 on. "As is generally known," he summarizes, "employee compensation has increased in relative significance since 1900—from about 53–55 per cent of the total in the first two decades to about 64 per cent in recent years . . . the total share of labor (i.e., including entrepreneurial labor) increased consistently for each overlapping decade beginning in 1915 . . ."[50] The overlapping decade figures, however, hide what the annual data show: that this basic advance to a new level was largely achieved in two jumps, from 1917 to 1918, and again from 1919 to 1920 (see Table 1 in which we summarize some of Johnson's results, utilizing unpublished annual data kindly provided by him). A look at the underlying data indicates the sources of this gain—decline in corporate profits, decline in entrepreneurial earnings, and a marked rise in wages.[51] How reasonable are such declines and the changing ratio that they produce?

1. For 1917–18 Johnson relies on a series published as "Department of Commerce" but concerning whose method of estimate we have no information.[52] That series shows a 25 per cent fall in

[50] D. Gale Johnson, "Functional Distribution," pp. 177–178.

[51] We rely on unpublished data kindly provided by Professor Johnson.

[52] The series was taken from the NICB, *The Economic Almanac 1951–1952* (page 208). Though labeled there as "Department of Commerce" it has apparently never appeared in any Department of Commerce publication and that Department has no information on its source.

TABLE 1
SHARE OF EMPLOYEE COMPENSATION IN NATIONAL INCOME

Year	Per Cent
1900–09	55.0
1910–14	55.4
1915–19	51.8
1920–24	61.7
1925–29	59.6
1915	53.5
1916	52.3
1917	46.7
1918	54.2
1919	52.6
1920	60.9
1921	66.9
1922	59.9
1923	60.4
1924	61.5

SOURCE: Johnson, "Functional Distribution."

nonfarm entrepreneurial income from 1917 to 1918—an almost incredible change under wartime conditions, particularly when the available estimates show no decline in the number of these entrepreneurs. King's estimates, as well as the Martin estimates based largely on them, show a mild gain over the period.[53] Until there is some basis for knowing how this "Department of Commerce" series was derived we find little plausibility in these particular figures. They imply that a sizable decline of average entrepreneurial earnings in trade, service, and manufacturing occurred at a time when the wage rates and annual earnings of employees in these sectors were rising significantly. It is most improbable, however, that the earnings of self-employed carpenters were declining while those of hired carpenters were soaring, or that the incomes of store owners were falling while those of store managers were rising. *A fortiori,* the labor component of nonfarm entrepreneurial income should certainly not be assumed to have declined (as is implicitly done in Johnson's computation of the service share, which takes that component as a flat percentage of the total).

2. It is for 1919–20, however, that the major problem arises. The ratio in 1918–19 did not differ significantly from that pre-

[53] Martin, *National Income*, p. 39; King, *Wealth and Income*, p. 108; and Kuznets, *National Income*, p. 463.

TABLE 2
FACTOR INCOMES AND SHARES, 1919 AND 1920
(dollar figures in billions)

	Johnson Data	Revised Data
Nonfarm entrepreneurial		
1919	9.4	7.8
1920	7.2	7.2
Farm entrepreneurial		
1919	8.8	9.5
1920	7.4	7.1
Corporate profits		
1919	7.7	8.4
1920	5.5	9.4
Interest and rent		
1919	7.5	7.5
1920	8.2	8.2
Employee compensation		
1919	37.1	37.7
1920	43.9	43.9
National income		
1919	70.5	70.9
1920	72.1	78.1
Share of wages in national income (per cent)		
1919	52.6	53.2
1920	60.9	56.2
Share of wages in nonfarm income (per cent)		
1919		60.1
1920		60.1

vailing over the first decade of the century. The real jump—to the level for the 1920's as a whole—came from 1919 to 1920. An explanation involves several elements. In Table 2, we show the Johnson estimates for major income categories for these two years, and also show our own revised estimates. We turn now to a description of the basis for our revision.

For nonfarm entrepreneurial income the Kuznets total (which Johnson uses without change) falls by $2.2 billion from 1919 to 1920. Of that decline, $1.6 billion is in trade alone.[54] Kuznets actually estimates a rise for the earnings withdrawn by trade entrepreneurs, for he assumes they gained as did the average earn-

[54] Withdrawal and savings data from Kuznets, *National Income*, pp. 312, 316.

ings of trade employees. The decline in trade income that he reports derives from his estimate of a still greater decline in the net savings of trade entrepreneurs.[55] The latter is computed on the assumption that the profit rate on sales of trade entrepreneurs paralleled that of trade corporations.[56] The following is a summary of the implicit averages from Kuznets, and our estimate of King's implicit figures.[57]

		1919	*1920*	*1921*	*Change, 1919 to 1920*
Average annual entrepreneurial income:	Kuznets	$4,023	$2,556	$1,420	−$1,477
	King	2,535	2,460		− 75
Average annual wage-salary:	Kuznets A	1,399	1,418	1,354	+ 19
	Kuznets B	1,506	1,664	1,451	+ 158

King's entrepreneurial income series declines trivially, while his wage-salary figures, and both Kuznets' wage-salary averages, show rises from 1919 to 1920. Kuznets' entrepreneurial average, however, shows a marked decline. If we follow the procedure used in later years of national income estimation we would expect a rough concordance of change between the total income of the average entrepreneur in trade and the income of the average employee. Had Kuznets followed this procedure for his trade (and manufacturing) estimate no marked change would appear in his

[55] The procedure for estimating the trade withdrawals is outlined in *ibid.*, p. 724.

[56] *Ibid.*, pp. 628, 726. Kuznets outlines a more complex procedure which we here define roughly as "profit rate on sales."

[57] Kuznets data from *ibid.*, pp. 718–719. The implicit King figures were derived as follows. Realized income drawn by entrepreneurs and other property owners is given in King (*Wealth and Income*, p. 108). From this total we deduct dividends, interest and rent to derive his implicit entrepreneurial income. King's dividend and interest figures appear in Simon Kuznets, *National Product in Wartime*, New York, NBER, 1945, p. 141. His rent total can be computed by deducting from his realized income total (W. I. King, *The National Income and its Purchasing Power*, New York, NBER, 1930, p. 94) Kuznets' estimates of the same total minus rent (*Simon Kuznets, National Income and Its Composition 1919–1938*, New York, NBER, 1941, Table 86). We then divided this total by King's estimate for the number of entrepreneurs (*King, National Income*, p. 62). The results will differ from those appearing in Kuznets' *National Product*, p. 141, because of adjustments made by the latter in the King data (*ibid.*, p. 144).

implicit, or in Johnson's explicit, figures on the U.S. total wage share from 1919 to 1920.

Alternatively one can do as Kuznets did, and stipulate that the withdrawn portion of entrepreneurial earnings did move with wages and salaries, but that, in addition, net savings of the enterprise moved in relationship to sales, as did the corporate profit ratio. Our only empirical evidence is from a different period: since the middle 1930's, when independent data begin, there appears to be a rough relationship between the trend in total income per entrepreneur in trade and the average employee in trade.[58]

We prefer to assume that the alternative incomes that link the entrepreneurial and labor market, and that affect the flow of manpower from one to the other, are total incomes in each category, rather than that one component of entrepreneurial income parallels wages while the other may pursue its separate path. We estimate a revised figure for nonfarm entrepreneurial income by assuming that the average income of trade entrepreneurs remained unchanged from 1919 to 1920, while wages rose.[59]

For farm entrepreneurial income we use the latest Department of Agriculture estimates[60] rather than earlier ones. These figures show a greater decline than those embodied in the Kuznets figures—apparently because of a far greater fall in cotton marketings.

For corporate profits we take the recent estimates of Goldsmith.[61] The gain shown would be even more marked if the basic Ebersole data on corporate profits were superseded by the NBER corporate sample for these years.[62]

[58] Department of Commerce estimates prior to the Bureau of Internal Revenue figures for entrepreneurial earnings in the late 1930's cannot be considered independent evidence on this point. The two move in the same direction in 1945–46 as well. They do not do so for 1946–48, as was pointed out in a comment by Selma Goldsmith. We attribute the entrepreneurial income decline in 1946–48 to the rise of about 10 per cent a year in the number of trade entrepreneurs, largely under the stimulus of GI loans, etc. No equal pressure on entrepreneurial earnings, however, is suggested for 1919–20, when the count of entrepreneurs rises only 3 per cent according to King. (Cyclical forces predominate in 1920–21 and 1948–49 and overwhelm the factors we are distinguishing here.)

[59] Kuznets (*National Income*, p. 718) shows a fall of $1.6 billion, with essentially no change in the count of entrepreneurs. We take 1920 as given and deduct $1.6 billion from Johnson's 1919 figure for nonfarm entrepreneurs, so that the implicit component for trade stays constant.

[60] *USDA Agriculture Handbook* No. 118, Vol. 3, p. 43.

[61] Raymond W. Goldsmith, *A Study of Saving in the United States*, Princeton University Press, Vol. III, 1956, p. 435 for tax liability and inventory valuation adjustment; Vol. I, 1955, p. 939 for net earnings.

[62] Goldsmith, *ibid.*, used the original estimates of J. F. Ebersole, S. S. Burr, and

For interest and rent we use the Johnson figures.

For employee compensation we adopt, with only one change, the Kuznets figures used by Johnson. The construction sector shows a marked rise; we believe a decline to be more reasonable.[63] The reported rise was estimated as follows: Ohio and Pennsylvania ratios of wages and salaries to gross construction totals were applied to U.S. gross construction activity totals. The results were then divided by an average wage-salary whose 1919–20 change is given by that for Ohio and Pennsylvania.[64] As thus estimated, the activity per person engaged falls slightly from 1919 to 1920 in current dollars, and a 20 per cent decline in constant dollars is implied.[65] We prefer here to assume that the constant dollar volume of work per employee did not decline from 1919 to 1920.[66] Working from employment and earnings data that we have derived elsewhere, we deduce a 1919–20 rise of $50 million instead of the $650 million rise implicit in Johnson's figures.[67]

To summarize, our revisions of Johnson's estimates of the share of wages in national income (see Table 2) are the result of: our revision of Kuznets' trade entrepreneurial total; the adoption of the latest revision of the USDA figures for farm entrepreneurial incomes rather than the earlier one available to Johnson; the use of corporate profits data derived from Goldsmith's recent study

---

G. M. Peterson, "Income Forecasting by the Use of Statistics of Income Data," *Review of Economic Statistics,* November 1929. The NBER data appear in *Historical Statistics,* p. 591. Because they relate only to large corporations it seems inappropriate to use them. However, examination of the Ebersole estimates indicates that $15.7 billion was added to the reported *Statistics of Income* figures for 1919, largely on the basis of fitting trends to the number of returns, total depreciation reported, etc., for various sets of years. With a profit rate of 8.7 per cent implicit in the reported figures this comes to a fairly arbitrary implicit correction of the reported figures by the addition of $1.4 billion to the 1919 net income total, leading to a greater 1919–20 decline.

[63] For the rise see Kuznets, *National Income,* p. 641.

[64] *Ibid.,* pp. 646, 653.

[65] For gross per person engaged, we use data from *ibid.,* pp. 641, 643. The gross per employee, while not directly estimated, should, we assume, have moved in the same way. The implicit deflator is that derived from the constant and current price construction totals in Simon Kuznets, *Capital in the American Economy, Its Formation and Financing,* Princeton for NBER, 1961, Vol. II, Tables 4 and 5.

[66] Our only independent evidence on this point relates to the period since 1940, when our construction employment figures are derived independently of the volume totals. For these years, a rise in the real output per employee takes place even when the rate of gain in construction is checked.

[67] We work essentially from the same activity figures as used by Kuznets, but deflate somewhat differently. Most important, however, we have an employment benchmark prior to 1929, and also interpolate between a 1900 and 1929 benchmark for activity per employee in constant dollars.

rather than those in the quasi "Department of Commerce" series; and a minor change in the employee compensation figures of Kuznets that underlie Johnson's figures. As can be seen from Table 2, the gain in the share of wages as shown in Johnson's original figures was 8.3 percentage points, and in our revised figures, 3 percentage points. The gain in the revised figures is thus half as great. Johnson links his series for the years 1900–19 by a ratio link in 1919. But the level of these earlier years would be much closer to that of the 1920's if the revised data were used for 1919.

One further comment must be made. If one takes the revised figures, which reflect a marked fall in farm entrepreneurial earnings, and computes the wage share only for nonfarm income, the result is the following:

	1919	*1920*	*Gain*
Wage ratio in nonfarm income	60.0	60.1	0.1

The gain for the nonfarm economy was trivial. Hence, the massive upward shift shown in the original estimates diminishes considerably in the revised figures. Of the gain that does appear, virtually all reflects a shift within the farm sector.

KING'S ESTIMATES, 1909 AND LATER

For 1909 and subsequent years, King provides annual estimates that constitute the ultimate basis of most of the later work in the field.[68] They have been used by the Department of Agriculture to extrapolate national income back to 1909. They appear to be the most likely source for the "Department of Commerce" series published in the *Economic Almanac*, and were also used by Johnson to run his data back to 1909. These estimates likewise constitute the basis for Martin's extrapolation of most of his components back to 1909 from 1919. Since King's post-1919 figures have been clearly superseded by Kuznets' work, only their use for 1909–19 extrapolation remains to be considered.

King's results can be summarized simply. From 1909 to 1917 he notes little change in the ratio of wages and salaries to the national income, while for 1918 he estimates a gain.[69] Hence the rise he shows in labor's share from 1909 to 1919 derives from his

[68] King, *National Income.*

[69] King's data as summarized and adjusted in Kuznets, *National Income*, Table 94. If we relate King's employee compensation to his realized income (Kuznets, *National Income*, p. 471) we arrive at the same trend.

estimate that a marked gain took place in 1917–18. How does this gain arise? It comes rather simply from his estimate that entrepreneurial withdrawals rose a trivial 5 per cent, while employee compensation rose by 25 per cent.[70] Since he shows virtually no change in the number of entrepreneurs over this period, and a decline in the number of employees, he implies an even greater discrepancy on a per-earner basis. Moreover, he assumes a $2 billion rise in realized income drawn from farming. Therefore he implicitly estimates no rise (or an actual decline) in income per nonfarm entrepreneur during a period when wages were skyrocketing.[71]

Labor's share, in consequence, jumps. Such a change is wholly unreasonable. First, had such a differential developed, a substantial movement from entrepreneurial pursuits into wage work should have taken place—as it did in 1941–42. But King stipulates no change in the number of entrepreneurs. Second, experience in World War II (for which we have data rather than reasoned surmise to guide us) indicates that entrepreneurial income rose by as much as, or more than, wages. From 1940 to 1941, for example, wages and salaries rose by about 30 per cent—or much the same as from 1917 to 1918—but income per entrepreneur rose by nearly 40 per cent.[72] If the wage worker were buying cotton shirts in 1917 and silk ones in 1918, something must have happened to the income of the trade entrepreneur selling him the shirts. And with construction wage rates rising (according to King) and construction booming, would the incomes of the independent construction entrepreneur have remained unchanged?

ESTIMATES SINCE 1919

For the period since 1919, estimates derivable by known procedures become available. The Kuznets figures for 1919–38 have already been considered in connection with Johnson's estimates. We concluded that the gain from 1919 to later years (and by extension, from 1919–20 or 1919–24 to later years) reflects a significant 1919–20 rise in the estimates. After reducing this estimated rise by adopting alternative estimating techniques, we con-

[70] Data summarized in Kuznets, *National Income*, Table 93.

[71] King's count of entrepreneurs appears in his *National Income*, p. 62; his realized income figures from *ibid.*, p. 108.

[72] U.S. Department of Commerce, *National Income*, 1954 edition, Tables 14, 17, 25 and 28.

cluded that the remainder is equivalent to the decline in farm entrepreneurial earnings. Hence, the share of wages in nonfarm income originating did not change in the 1919–29 period. Given the tremendous impact of the depression on the data for the 1930's, they are not very useful in considering long-term trends.[73] We therefore show no rise in the share of labor in nonfarm income originating.

For the period since 1929 the Department of Commerce figures have been precisely and comprehensively analyzed by Edward Denison.[74] After excluding household and government sectors (presumably because of the lack of a property income counterpart to wages for these sectors), Denison finds that a small gain in the employee percentage in the ordinary business sector took place from 1929 to 1950.[75] The well known sizable rise of the employee share in over-all national income over this period, therefore, proves to be primarily a reflection of changes in imputed rent on owned homes, profits on investments abroad, and other flows that are irrelevant to an interest in the substitution of one productive factor for another in the process of economic change.

It would be pleasant to conclude that the brief run of these two sets of data, for 1919–29 and 1929–50, are fortunate confirmations of the economic process outlined in Part I above. However, it is necessary to pursue one further analytic issue—that concerning the entrepreneurial share. Unless we do so, we shall not be clear about precisely what the empirical data on factor shares can actually tell us concerning changes in the production function, the elasticity of substitution, and the relative flows of capital and labor.

PART III

What basis is there for judging how closely the real world conforms to the pattern outlined in Part I of this paper? The obvious source—national income statistics—is subject to a number of deci-

[73] "The relative share of income from work in national income as a whole shows, of course, appreciable short-run variations in the course of the business cycle . . . . Consequently, when we engage in long-run analysis it is essential to select for comparison periods during which the cyclical factor may be assumed to have canceled out." Fellner, *Trends and Cycles*, p. 264.

[74] "Distribution of National Income," *Survey of Current Business*, June 1952.

[75] Denison (*ibid.*) reports a gain of under 1 per cent. If we use revised data from *U.S. Income and Output* (p. 134), the figure is 1.4 per cent. Hence there seems to be no basis for the 5 per cent figure referred to in conference discussions.

sive qualifications. Many of these, fortunately, have recently been canvassed by Irving Kravis, who demonstrates that varying treatment of these elements, numerous and significant though they are, would distort our reading of final results by very little.[76] However, a single major factor remains, and it makes inappropriate any extended attention to the statistics on labor's share in total national income, its share of income originating in agriculture, trade and service, or any combination that includes these sectors.

The problem here is the entrepreneurial puzzle. At the end of the year the entrepreneur finds in his till a sum—or sustains a loss—reflecting the return on his personal abilities as well as return on his capital invested. To discuss the relative return to the capital and to the labor which he uses in his activities, we must disentangle the contributions made by each. If we cannot do so, we must eschew the apparently relevant data for those industry sectors dominated by entrepreneurs. What are our choices? (1) We may ask the farmer, or businessman, but even if he could give us reliable figures, one may doubt whether a rational entrepreneur would attempt to do so: what the market has joined together he does not separate. (2) We might make some guesses from an analysis of the production function. But theory tells us nothing about how to allocate the joint product of two or more factors so as to reveal the average contributions of each factor. (Deductions as to the contribution of marginal increments of each factor to marginal changes in product do not help much for allocating the entire output.) (3) We might see what indications the market gives us—but the market does not operate in these terms and provides us with no information.

Failing all else, most analysts have made different types of arbitrary allocations. One is to stipulate a rate of return to entrepreneurial labor, with the balance of the entrepreneur's income considered the return to his capital.[77] Conversely, others have

[76] See Kravis' lucid discussion of market-nonmarket activity shifts, the role of government debt and of historical cost depreciation, etc., in "Relative Income," pp. 926–930.

[77] This procedure has been widely used, by W. J. Spillman, the Department of Agriculture and others. Its most recent important use is in the study by John W. Kendrick, *Productivity Trends: Capital and Labor*, New York, NBER 1956. Kendrick estimates labor input by weighting manhours in each major industry group, inclusive of those worked by proprietors and unpaid family workers, by base period average hourly employee compensation.

stipulated a rate of return to his capital and thence inferred the return to his labor. These procedures, of course, give significantly different results—but neither has any better theoretical justification than the other. A more thoughtful proposal allocates entrepreneurial income between capital and labor in accordance with the ratio of property to wage income in the portion of the economy outside the entrepreneurial sector, changing when that ratio changes.[78] While more precise, it does not seem to solve the problem.

1. How can we agree on what rate of return to stipulate for entrepreneurial capital—since this must be done, implicitly or explicitly? The risk may be greater, or less, than that which prevails for capital in, say, the corporate sector. Perhaps we could agree that an entrepreneur investing in his own store, or farm, must surely be more confident of earning a return than if he invested randomly in any other store or farm. (Would the typical entrepreneur go into business if he lacked such confidence?) But if so, his risks (as he perceives them) are smaller than those for investors generally in the same industry. To assume that his capital earns the full market rate of return would therefore overstate the rate for an equivalent risk as the entrepreneur himself saw it. But even if there were full agreement on this—which is doubtful—could we agree on the proper reduction to be made in the market rate to give a truer measure of his earnings on capital?

2. Can we proceed any more successfully by first intuiting the labor earnings of the entrepreneur? The massive decline of self-employment in trade, service and agriculture during 1941–42 suggests that much disguised unemployment existed in those industries—with many a self-employed person whose capacities were below the average for employees in the same industries. The market value of the labor services of such entrepreneurs may be zero, but so long as they can pay themselves (out of capital) they will receive more than the market would pay them. (Data showing a short work year for certain categories of entrepreneurs, and the high failure rate for firms in trade and service suggest that this

[78] Kravis, "Relative Income," p. 925. Denison suggests: "if one *must* allocate, a preferable procedure would be to assume the division between labor and property inputs and income to be the same in noncorporate as in corporate firms." See the comment by Edward F. Denison on paper by Edward Budd in *Trends in the American Economy*, p. 402.

is not merely hypothetical.[79]) Conversely, there will unquestionably be many entrepreneurs whose talents reach far above the level for employees in the same industry. How do we rationally estimate the proportion in each category? Surely not by using the simple 50-50 proportion implied when we estimate their average labor income as equal to the average for all employees.

3. The advantages of being one's own master surely exist and are surely positive. If they operated as other equalizing advantages do, they should work to keep down the dollar returns from self-employment. But by how much? And if some mystic with a Monte Carlo method gave us a figure, how much should we deduct from the labor share and how much from the property share? If one economist makes such an assignment, on what basis can he contend his assignment ratio is preferable to any other?

4. But away with these qualifications. Suppose we make an allocation at a point in time. On what basis can we choose the true allocation for the next point in time? The shifting tide of hopefuls that enter, and failures that leave, self-employment suggests that the net returns to self-employment are ever changing relative to the returns to capital and labor elsewhere. But how much of this net change occurs in the return to capital and how much in the return to labor? Without light in this apparently impenetrable maze we cannot know how the relative returns to each change over time. Kravis' solution is surely in the right direction: he stipulates that for the self-employed, the ratio of capital to labor returns will run parallel with that for the rest of the economy. But our present problem still remains—the regress is apparently an infinite one. If the ratio of one to the other is assumed to vary with the rest of the economy, then its assumed variation over time adds nothing to our knowledge of true variation over time: we are simply iterating the changes in the non-self-employ-

[79] In a typically incisive discussion of the allocation of entrepreneurial income between labor and property, Kuznets suggests different markets for entrepreneurial and other capital, as for entrepreneurial and other labor, noting that "a direct estimate of the return on the property component" for U.S. agriculture "leaves a return on labor that is below the going wages of hired labor; and a direct estimate of the return on labor leaves a return on property distinctly below any comparable return rate." Simon Kuznets, "Quantitative Aspects of the Economic Growth of Nations," IV, *Economic Development and Cultural Change*, April 1959, p. 26. Compare Simon Rottenberg, "Note on Economic Progress and Occupational Distribution," *Review of Economics and Statistics*, May 1953, for general comments on the level of entrepreneurial abilities in underdeveloped countries.

ment sector.[80] With the evidence from our competitive economy of flows of men (and money) into and out of enterprise, we have no basis for assuming that the rate of return to men (or money) in entrepreneurial pursuits remains stolidly constant relative to the return in corporate enterprise, or government bonds (or enlistment in the army).[81]

5. We conclude that nothing useful can be learned by dealing with relative shares for: (a) the economy as a whole, (b) the nonfarm economy, (c) agriculture, distribution or any industry (or combination of industries) in which entrepreneurial income plays a significant part. If we stipulate an unchanged ratio of labor to capital income for entrepreneurs within the entrepreneurial industries, we clearly add nothing to our knowledge of the changing rate of return to each factor. If we stipulate that the returns moved parallel to those in the rest of economy or industry, we simply iterate what we know already. If we are free to stipulate a changing ratio—and in the mobile, competitive real world changes surely must take place—we can discover empirical relationships of any type, largely given by our initial arbitrary stipulation of how these changes took place. Hence such limited bits of information on total entrepreneurial income as exist are of little service in our quest.

GOVERNMENT

Without descending to modern instances there is clearly no basis for distinguishing what portion of the ancient Roman Senator's salary derived from his florid oratory (labor) and what from the shining toga and elegant ivory chairs (capital) in which he reposed. Nor would one want to deduce, even with data, that the man with the larger desk received a higher income because he had a larger desk (more capital): his commanding presence alone might account for that income. Moreover, our income estimates include no allowance for the services of government capital. As estimates have been made hitherto, a rising level of government

[80] Kravis does not suggest that the absolute level of return here adds to our knowledge, seeking only to deal with the central issue of changing relative income shares. He notes the desirability of allocation not in proportion to economy-wide shares but those within the same industry (see "Relative Income," p. 926). But even if this were done, it would not meet the point we raise.

[81] And without identical changes of capital stock-labor ratios in entrepreneurial and those in non-entrepreneurial sectors we would have still not solved the problem.

employment automatically worked to bring an increase in labor's share—whether government assets quintupled over the same period, were reduced to zero, or remained unchanged.[82]

We conclude that for measuring long-term trends in relative shares there is little to be learned about changes in relative shares resulting even from massive changes in the production functions, if we concentrate our view on changes in total national income, or income inclusive of any significant entrepreneurial components. For the U.S., this leaves as industries not so dominated primarily manufacturing, and individual industries in transport, communications, and mining.[83]

Conclusion

In Section I we proposed a long-term mechanism of factor substitution that would work to bring an approximate stability in factor shares. In Section II we rejected existing long-term national income estimates as a basis for asserting that empirical data do demonstrate that such stability was in fact achieved in the U.S. during the past half century or so. Future work with empirical data, it would appear, must relate to the direct process of factor use and reward where it takes place—within individual industries. It is this process rather than any pretty constancy that is of substantial analytic interest.

We have asserted in Section III that the entrepreneurial puzzle makes it meaningless to consider trends for any sector where the entrepreneurial share is a great one—agriculture, trade, service. And a variety of authors have demonstrated the signal effects of changing industrial composition on any gross aggregates.[84] We

[82] Solow excludes the government from his detailed analysis for this reason ("A Skeptical Note," p. 623). Kravis ("Relative Income," p. 928) and Denison ("Distribution of National Income," p. 17) each note the lack of a property component in government income originating. The difficulty of estimating the current value and return on government assets, particularly military assets, is, of course, the reason why we have no such data.

[83] We exclude government for reasons noted above. Construction, even without the great role of self-employment, has little reliable data on shares prior to 1939. The existing estimates are sensible reconstructions and do not rely on any independent measure.

[84] One of the earlier studies, albeit only for the period since 1929, was the lucid review by Edward Denison, "Distribution of National Income," in *Survey of Current Business*. Recently Cartter (*Theory of Wages*, pp. 161–167) noted that intersector shifts in large measure account for the change from the 1920's to the 1950's in the share for the private business sector. See too, Budd's detailed study ("Factor Shares," pp. 381–391); his more recent comments (U.S. Congress, Joint

conclude that the relevant U.S. data for studying factor substitution and return relate primarily to manufacturing, mining, the utilities, and railroads.[85]

Examination of some of these data at an aggregative level suggests, as one would expect, both constancy and variation. For example, adjusted data for manufacturing show that payrolls as a percentage of value added did show a long-term stability:[86]

1889–99	54.0
1919–29	51.5
1947–54	53.9

(Even the lower figure for the 1920's may reflect only the inclusion of contract work in these data, unlike those for the other periods.) A more precise measurement, using direct estimates of property income (incorporating an allowance for current value depreciation) can be made from the data of Wooden and Wasson,[87] who show an approximate constancy over the shorter period from 1929 to the early 1950's.[88] But an examination of data for

---

Economic Committee, *Employment, Growth, and Price Levels*, Part 8, 1959, pp. 2520, 2524); and Jesse Burkhead, "Changes in the Functional Distribution of Income," *Journal of the American Statistical Association*, June 1953.

[85] Conceptual and empirical problems make it useless to consider long-term trends for most components of finance and transportation.

[86] For 1899, the 1900 Census of Manufactures, I:59, provides data from which we can adjust to exclude contract work, hand trades, and firms grossing under $500. For the 1889–99 average, we compute ratios from the 1954 Census of Manufactures, Part I, pp. 2–3; then use the ratio of the 1899 average to the average of the two to raise the adjusted 1899 estimate. (1919–29 data on contract work for smaller firms are not available.) Data for later years are from the 1954 Census, Part I, pp. 2–3. Data prior to 1889 are not used because of major differences in coverage of small firms.

Solow ("A Skeptical Note," p. 627) notes a small increase after 1899 which he considers may be due to the changing character of output. Our data show no rise. The difference may stem from the fact that reliance on unadjusted Census data, as reported, involves the use of an 1899 figure inclusive of railroad car construction, while later censuses exclude this high wage-sales ratio industry.

[87] Donald Wooden and Robert Wasson, "Manufacturing Investment Since 1929," *Survey of Current Business*, December 1956, p. 20.

[88] An admirable, succinct study by Martin Bronfenbrenner, "A Note on Relative Shares and the Elasticity of Substitution," *Journal of Political Economy*, June 1960, emphasizes how wide a range of substitution elasticities and changes in capital-labor ratios are compatible with what appear to be "small" changes in labor's share. His review on this ground alone throws out much discussion about long-term stability. On the other hand, if we credit the Creamer-Kendrick data on the changes in the capital-labor ratio in manufacturing from 1899 to 1919, and the reversal from 1919 to 1953, then by the use of Bronfenbrenner's formula we can see that the labor-share ratios shown above imply striking changes in the elasticity of substitution from one period to the next. (See John Kendrick,

individual industries is really the area for investigation, and here preliminary study shows both striking regularity and striking variation. With the recent issuance of the long awaited study by Creamer, Dobrovolsky and Borenstein,[89] together with other volumes in the broad study of capital formation and financing it is possible to begin such work. The prospect for an extension of Department of Commerce work on manufacturing investment gives us hope of data carefully adjusted for the complexities of recent changes in depreciation allowances. Given such materials, economists ought to be able to say something more useful about the process of long-term factor substitution in the American economy.

COMMENT

JACK ALTERMAN, Bureau of Labor Statistics

Lebergott has provided us with an interesting and provocative paper to start the Conference. He has also succeeded in presenting his discussants with something of a dilemma. On the one hand, he proposes a theory based on the operation of certain market forces to explain the stability of factor shares. On the other, the paper implies that because of inadequacies in the data and, more important, the insuperable problem of allocating proprietors' income into labor and capital components, we cannot determine at present whether his particular theory, or for that matter, any general theory of factor shares is supported by empirical evidence. The paper implies that economists will have to await future work on individual sectors and industries, not affected by the "proprietor problem," before being able to say anything useful about changes in factor shares, factor substitution, and relative prices.

I should like to comment on both the theoretical and statistical

NOTE: The comments on Lebergott's paper represent my own views and are not to be considered as reflecting the official position of the Bureau of Labor Statistics, U.S. Department of Labor, on the topics under discussion.

EDITOR'S NOTE: Based on original version of the Lebergott paper (see the Lebergott reply).

Productivity Trends in the United States, Princeton for NBER, 1961, Table D-3.) Hence, the reported lack of change in labor's share for manufacturing would appear to be of economic significance.

[89] Daniel Creamer, Sergei P. Dobrovolsky, and Israel Borenstein, *Capital in Manufacturing and Mining*, Princeton for NBER, 1960.

aspects of the paper and indicate some reservations regarding the findings. Briefly stated, Lebergott's theory, considered as theory and without regard to empirical verification, is incomplete and can be considered an explanation of stability in factor shares only if certain other conditions are stipulated. Second, I would disagree with his finding that at present economists can say little that is useful regarding factor shares, even for areas of the economy not particularly affected by the proprietor allocation problem. I have attempted to provide some analysis of the change in factor shares in the corporate sector of the economy.

Lebergott's attempt to provide an explanation for stability in factor shares stems from his reluctance to accept the proposition that "reasonable" figures for elasticity of substitution or of propensities to save will yield numbers assuring relative stability in shares. As Lebergott asks, what is reasonable and why choose a particular figure? The theory developed in the paper suggests that a market mechanism exists which works to produce long-run constancy, apart from any estimate of elasticity of substitution that may seem reasonable.

Lebergott's theoretical explanation for expecting stability in factor shares is as follows:

> In summary, we define the share of national income flowing to wages as against capital as a function of the quantity and price ratios of each factor. We find that in the long run the quantity ratio is in turn a function of the changing price ratios. Taking the price of labor as given, we contend that the changing price of capital must bear a constant long-term proportionality to that of labor. This proportionality derives from the fact that the supply forces working to fix the price of capital are dominantly wage costs in the capital-producing industries and those that supply them. In a competitive market these wage costs parallel wage-cost changes in capital-using industries because wage changes for identical occupations must bear a parity to one another in all employing industries. On the other hand, historical experience does not suggest that productivity trends in the supplying and using industries are so negatively related as to make costs take a different course from rates.

It seems to me that the explanation for stability of income shares in terms of the general "proportionality" of changes in wage rates and in productivity for capital producing and using industries is incomplete. It is incomplete in that it does not really explain how the assumed correspondence in movement of over-all unit labor costs and capital goods prices is supposed to result in stability of income shares. The gap in the theory is due to the fact that the initial explanation of stability of income shares in terms of the relationship of the price of labor and capital, in which the price of labor is defined as wage rate and the price of capital may be defined as property income per unit of capital services, becomes an analysis of the relationship of the price of labor and the price of capital goods, primarily machinery. The price of capital goods is not the same as the price of capital and until Mr. Lebergott's thesis is expanded to explain the relationship between unit labor costs, the price of capital goods, and the price of capital, we do not know whether the theory does provide an explanation for stability in factor shares or perhaps only a tendency towards stability.

It may be useful as background for further discussion and clarification to indicate the conditions under which proportionate changes in over-all unit labor costs and the price of capital goods would result in stability in factor shares.

The conditions for stability in factor shares can be stated in the following set of propositions, in which the various items are to be interpreted as indexes of change.

Indexes of Change

W = total labor income (current dollars)
R = total property income (current dollars)
O = total output (constant dollars)
K = capital stock (constant dollars)
C = capital stock (current dollars)
$\frac{C}{K}$ = price of capital goods
$\frac{R}{C}$ = rate of return on capital

Factor shares will remain stable if labor and property income increase in the same proportion.

$$\frac{W}{R} = 1 \tag{1}$$

$$W = R \tag{2}$$

It follows that factor shares will also remain stable if labor income per unit and property income per unit increase in the same proportion.

$$\frac{W}{O} = \frac{R}{O} \tag{3}$$

Under what conditions will the change in unit labor and unit property costs be equal?

Property income per unit of output is equal to property income per unit of capital input, times the amount of capital per unit of output (the reciprocal of the capital productivity ratio).

$$\frac{R}{O} = \frac{R}{K} \times \frac{K}{O} \tag{4}$$

What is the relationship between the price of capital (R/K) and the price of capital goods (C/K), a relationship which is not explicitly stated in the Lebergott theory?

$$\frac{R}{K} = \frac{C}{K} \times \frac{R}{C} \tag{5}$$

The change in the price of capital is equal to the change in the price of capital goods times the change in the rate of return on capital.

We can now substitute step (5) in (4)

$$\frac{R}{O} = \frac{C}{K} \times \frac{R}{C} \times \frac{K}{O} \tag{6}$$

There is one further step needed to complete the statement of relationships. That is to introduce into the equation Lebergott's proposition regarding the parallelism in unit labor costs and the price of capital goods.

$$\frac{W}{O} = \frac{C}{K} \tag{7}$$

$$\frac{R}{O} = \frac{W}{O} \times \frac{R}{C} \times \frac{K}{O} \tag{8}$$

It follows that if the rate of return in capital (R/C) and the productivity of capital (O/K) are constant, or if they change by the same proportion, then the change in unit property income will equal the change in unit labor income and income shares will be stable.

$$\frac{R}{C} \times \frac{K}{O} = 1 \text{ or } \frac{R}{C} \div \frac{O}{K} = 1 \tag{9}$$

$$\frac{R}{O} = \frac{W}{O} \times 1 \tag{10}$$

$$R = W \tag{11}$$

To summarize, income shares will remain constant if the price of capital goods increases in proportion to the unit labor costs, only on the condition that the rate of return on capital changes in proportion to the average change in the productivity of capital. It follows from the above that before Lebergott's thesis regarding similar changes in unit labor costs and capital goods prices can be considered a complete explanation, even in a formal sense, of stability in factor shares, it needs to be expanded to provide an explanation of why the real rate of return on capital should be expected to increase in proportion to the increase in output per unit of capital.

There still remains the question of the extent to which the data and empirical research support the general notion of stability in factor shares and, more specifically, the validity of Lebergott's explanation. The paper indicates that the question of stability in factor shares cannot be answered at the level of the total economy because the particular method or assumption used to allocate the income of proprietors into labor and property components would determine the result. The paper concludes that we must await further work in those sectors of the economy where proprietors are not a major factor, e.g., mining, manufacturing, utilities, before we can provide useful answers to questions regarding long-run trends in factor shares.

Presumably because of the negative findings regarding the relevance of over-all data to the question of factor shares, the paper does not even attempt to determine whether there is any empirical evidence which supports some of the propositions developed in the theoretical section, particularly the relationship of changes in wage rates, output per man-hour, unit labor costs, and capital goods prices.

I would agree with Lebergott that we need more research on factor shares, factor substitution, and price at the sector and industry level, but I do not agree with the implication that pending further research in the sectors not affected by the "proprietor allocation problem," we can say little that is useful regarding changes in factor shares. A considerable amount of work has already been done by those who have, in a sense, anticipated Lebergott and argued that because over-all factor shares reflect varying labor-property relationships in substantially different types of legal and institutional organizations, the analysis of factor shares for the economy as a whole has relatively little meaning. Meaningful analysis, therefore, involves an attempt to determine what has happened to the various categories of factor income within relatively homogeneous groupings in the economy and also how much of the change in shares may be due to shifts within these homogeneous groupings. Denison's work in analyzing changes in factor shares in terms of homogeneous sectors and the further decomposition of changes in factor shares into inter- and intraindustry changes is well known and need not be elaborated upon here.[1] This analysis has been further refined by the work of Osborne and Epstein[2] for the corporate sector, and by Fitzwilliams[3] for the nonfarm-noncorporate sector to determine how much of the change in income, by type of income, has been due to interindustry shifts within the two major types of business. These studies have indicated that interindustry shifts within the homogeneous sectors mentioned above have had little effect on secular distribution of factor shares.

In terms of Lebergott's basic question: whether we can say anything useful regarding factor shares which is not subject to the criticism of being dependent on the method used to allocate proprietors' income, we must turn to the data for the corporate sector of the economy.

The estimates developed by the National Income Division, Department of Commerce, of factor shares originating in the domestic corporate sector of the economy represent a basic source of information for such an analysis. These estimates are available for the entire period since 1922—almost forty years. In order to

[1] Edward F. Denison, "Distribution of National Income," *Survey of Current Business*, June 1952. Also, "Income Types and the Size Distribution," *American Economic Review*, May 1954.

[2] Harlowe Osborne and Joseph Epstein, "Corporate Profits Since World War II," *Survey of Current Business*, January 1956.

[3] Jeannette Fitzwilliams, "Employment in Corporate and Noncorporate Production," *Survey of Current Business*, November 1959.

obtain an indication of the secular trend in factor shares over the period, a comparison of the percentage distribution in 1922–29 and 1947–59 has been made, omitting the abnormal years of the depression and World War II.

These estimates need to be adjusted to exclude the effect on corporate income originating and property income of the accelerated amortization program which started in 1950 and the changing methods of depreciation permitted under the 1954 Internal Revenue Code. The adjustments are necessary in order to provide comparability over time and to indicate what the corporate income and the property share would have been if straight-line depreciation had been used throughout the period. Estimates of the Machinery and Allied Products Institute were used to make the adjustments.[4] These adjustments yield results which seem to be roughly in line with similar estimates given in general terms in various articles in the *Survey of Current Business.* It should be noted that these adjustments are quite substantial (about $4 billion in 1959) and may become larger and, therefore, more important in the analysis of factor shares as the amount of depreciation under the 1954 Internal Revenue Code begins to cumulate, although this will be offset for a while by the decline in depreciation resulting from the 1950 accelerated amortization program.

Another adjustment to the estimates probably should be made in order to reflect replacement-cost depreciation rather than the book-value depreciation actually used. Here, it is not clear whether replacement-cost depreciation should reflect the increase in the productivity of capital goods as well as the increase in the price of capital goods or merely the latter. Pending clarification of this point, I have taken the figures as published except for the adjustments previously mentioned.

The percentage distribution of factor shares for subperiods, shown in Table 1, indicates relative stability between the two terminal periods, with some indication of a slight upward drift in the labor share during the postwar period, although this is moderated after adjustments for accelerated amortization and changing methods of depreciation.

How does the estimated change in factor shares for the corporate sector compare with the change for the total domestic economy? Estimates for the total domestic economy have been developed by

[4] Machinery and Allied Products Institute, *Capital Goods Review No. 38.*

TABLE 1
FACTOR SHARES IN CORPORATE SECTOR,[a] PERCENTAGE DISTRIBUTION

Year	Unadjusted		Adjusted	
	Labor[b]	Property[c]	Labor[b]	Property[c]
1922–29	77.0	23.0	77.0	23.0
1925–29	75.7	24.3	75.7	24.3
1947–59	77.9	22.1	76.8	23.2
1950–54	76.5	23.5	76.1	23.9
1955–59	79.4	20.6	77.9	22.1

[a] Excludes income from abroad.
[b] Compensation of all employees includes supplements, wages, and salaries.
[c] Profits (before Federal corporate income tax) and net interest.

John W. Kendrick in his book on productivity trends in the United States.[5] Kendrick allocated income of proprietors by assuming that they received the same compensation per hour as employees in the same industry. Kendrick's figures are available for selected years only. The comparison of the change between 1929 and 1957 indicates a substantially greater decline in the property share for the total domestic economy than that shown for the corporate sector (Table 2).

TABLE 2
CHANGE IN FACTOR SHARES, CORPORATE VERSUS TOTAL DOMESTIC ECONOMY

Year	Corporate		Total Domestic Economy	
	Labor	Property	Labor	Property
1929	74.6	25.4	72.3	27.7
1957	78.5	21.5	81.4	18.6
Per cent change	5.2	−15.4	12.6	−32.9

The change in factor shares for the corporate sector are less than half that indicated by Kendrick's figures for the total domestic economy. This underscores the need to analyze changes of factor shares in terms of homogeneous categories within the economy.

Having provided some indication of what the change in factor shares has been for the sector of the economy not affected by the proprietor allocation problem, we can turn to the question of whether there is any empirical basis for Lebergott's explanation

[5] John W. Kendrick, *Productivity Trends in the United States*, Princeton for NBER, 1961.

of stability in factor shares. Lebergott's theory assumes that increases in wage rates will be relatively evenly distributed throughout the economy, and that the resulting attempt to offset these wage increases by increased output per man-hour will produce an increase in unit labor costs for capital goods and supplying industries in about the same proportion as unit labor costs of capital using industries. This is a rather big assumption.

It would be difficult to determine this empirically. We can only approach the problem by trying to ascertain, following Lebergott's theory, whether prices of capital goods have moved in proportion to the change in unit labor costs. Here, we must also keep in mind Lebergott's admonition that for this type of comparison, unit labor costs cannot be based on any assumption as to the allocation of proprietors' income to labor and property components.

We have, therefore, used the data for the corporate sector of the economy, supplemented by other information, to try to fill in some of the numbers in the formulation developed as an expansion of Lebergott's theory.

Estimates of the change in labor income per unit of output and property income per unit of output for the corporate sector of the economy can be derived by dividing indexes of labor income and property income by an index of corporate output. Corporate output, in turn, can be derived by dividing estimated corporate gross product by the implicit price deflator for the private nonfarm business sector of the economy.

The variables underlying the change in property income per unit of output can be derived if we can fill in two missing pieces, the change in price of capital goods (an essential element in Lebergott's theory) and the increase in the physical quantity of capital inputs. Estimates for these items are not available for the total corporate sector so we have used the available estimates for total manufacturing as an indicator of the change in capital goods, prices, and capital inputs for the corporate sector. It should be noted that the estimates of capital input cover the depreciated value of plant and equipment, plus inventories. The stock of net plant and equipment refers to capital available rather than capital used. It can reasonably be argued that for some purposes the capital estimate should be adjusted to refer to capital used rather than available.

The labor percentage of corporate income changed from 74.6 per cent in 1929 to 77.7 per cent in 1959. The changes between

1929 and 1959 in factor shares and related variables are shown in the following indexes (1929 = 100).

Unit labor cost	194
Unit property cost	163
Capital goods prices	252
Equipment	243
Structures	318
Equipment and structures	287
Inventories	186

Unit property cost (163) equals price of capital goods (252) times rate of return (97) divided by capital productivity (151).

The relationships indicated by these figures do not seem to be consistent with Lebergott's explanation for relative secular stability in factor shares. The period covered is thirty years, and the increase in the labor share is relatively modest—3 percentage points. The price of capital goods, however, increased substantially more than unit labor costs. The rate of return did not increase in proportion to the increase in the productivity of capital but instead was relatively constant. The relative stability in factor shares was due largely to the offsetting changes among the variables rather than stability in the relationships as suggested by Lebergott's theory.

The results for the 1929–59 comparison are puzzling in at least one respect; the relative stability in the rate of return on the net value of capital available is quite inconsistent with a similar estimate for the corporate sector developed by the Machinery and Allied Products Institute. The MAPI figures indicate an increase of about 60 per cent between 1923–29 and 1959 in corporate profits, including intercorporate dividends, as a percentage of corporate net worth. The increase between 1923–29 and 1950–59 was 70 per cent. The MAPI estimates of net worth are based primarily on *Statistics of Income* data, adjusted to convert book value of plant and equipment to current cost, and further adjusted to reflect what net worth would be if straight-line depreciation had been used throughout. The MAPI figures have an additional adjustment to profits, not included in my estimate, to reflect current cost valuation of depreciation rather than book value depreciation. A similar adjustment to my estimate would have widened the gap rather than narrowed it. Recognizing all these differences, it seems difficult to believe that both estimates are "correct" and the big disparity between the estimates of rate of return can be attributed primarily to differences in basic data or methodology. This major disparity in findings needs to be clarified before we can describe, in empirical terms, the process by which stability in factor shares for the corporate sector of the economy has been achieved.[6]

GEORGE GARVY

The first part of Lebergott's paper suggests an explanation for the relative stability of the labor share in national income, which has been the subject of a good deal of research and theorizing ever since Keynes called it "a bit of a miracle." Lebergott's reasoning is simple and elegant. In ultimate analysis, the cost of capital goods can be reduced in essence to wage costs incurred in previous periods. Therefore, in the long run, the price of capital goods must bear a constant long-term relation to that of labor. Lebergott's theory includes a number of simplified assumptions which, however, do not diminish its usefulness in providing quite a satisfactory rationalization of the relative long-term stability of factor shares. I find it more realistic and therefore more appealing than reliance on the fact that, given the ratio in which labor and capital are typically combined in advanced economies, quite a wide range of elasticities of substitution are consistent with observed ratios of the labor share in national income.

The second part of the paper deals with several statistical series on which much of the analysis on long-run changes in factor shares rests; it is a skillful and imaginative contribution in the much neglected area of statistical criticism. Indeed, economists are always on the lookout for time series and cross sectional data that seem appropriate for testing theories. Statisticians are continuously striving to widen the scope of statistical data and to improve and refine current series. Perhaps not enough effort is devoted by either economists or statisticians to a critical review of synthetic

[6] Estimates of capital stock, which have been published since these comments were made (Simon Kuznets, *Capital in the American Economy*, Princeton for NBER, 1961; John W. Kendrick, *Productivity Trends*), would indicate that part of the disparity regarding the change in the rate of return may be due to the fact that the use of the change in manufacturing capital stock as an indicator of movement in total corporate capital stock probably overstated the increase in capital stock and correspondingly understated the increase in the rate of return. Preliminary calculations based on the new estimates indicate, however, that this would explain only part of the disparity, and that further research in this area is still required.

time series which have been constructed for earlier periods for which no data derived from records or estimates prepared by qualified statistical agencies are available. Lebergott's critical analysis casts considerable doubt on the validity of several widely accepted generalizations as to long-run changes in factor shares.

I find myself in complete agreement with Lebergott on the two main conclusions of the final section. One is his strong strictures against any attempts to split entrepreneurial income into a labor income and a return on capital component. I have made very similar points in commenting on a paper by Irving B. Kravis[1] (since they have been published in the meantime, I need not repeat them). I concur, in particular, with Lebergott that allocation of entrepreneurial income on the assumption that relative shares of labor and capital in this component move in the same way as in the non-entrepreneurial part of national income, does not add anything of analytical significance. I, therefore, fully agree with his second and related conclusion that an analysis of the labor share should be limited to the sector of the economy where both labor and property income originate; this limitation excludes by definition the government and the household sectors, and also suggests that sectors dominated by entrepreneurial activity, such as agriculture, retail trade and service industry, should be excluded.

While I find Lebergott's general position and conclusions very congenial to my own views, I remain unconvinced that the effort spent in recent years to measure and explain long-term changes in factor shares has yielded significant insights into the dynamics of our economy. The tenuous and changing relationship which exists between theoretical concepts of factors of production and the income streams actually measured in national accounts, precludes establishing a firm link between statistical findings based on the sort of data we have to work with and theoretical generalizations which they are supposed to support or to question. In recent studies of long-run changes in factor shares, a variety of statistical results have been obtained, depending largely on the assumptions made to narrow the gap between theoretical categories of factors of production and the type distribution of income. Empirical and theoretical work has been almost entirely concentrated—as again attested to by Lebergott's paper—

[1] *Proceedings of the Conference on Consumption and Saving* (University of Pennsylvania, 1960), Vol. II, p. 477 ff.

on the relative shares of labor and capital; little effort has been made to estimate the share of land. There is, furthermore, still little recognition of the fact that wages and salaries include a return on investment in human capital. Yet, the importance of human capital has been so clearly demonstrated by many recent economic developments, including the rapid resumption by Germany of its place as a leading industrial nation after a widespread destruction of its physical capital in World War II.

It is perhaps possible, following Lebergott's excellent suggestions, to make further progress towards a conceptually more satisfactory and statistically more reliable allocation of a large segment of national income between labor and capital for the period since 1900. But what questions will such a two-way breakdown help us to answer? Suppose that it will be possible to establish beyond statistical doubt that, over half a century, the share of labor compensation in the private sector has risen (fallen) by two percentage points; given the structural changes in our economy since the beginning of the century, what would be, precisely, the analytical value or the policy implications of such a finding?

PAUL STUDENSKI

Stanley Lebergott has ably analyzed some of the conceptual and statistical difficulties involved in the attempts to break down the national income total for the United States into its capital and labor shares and to measure the changes occurring over time in their relative magnitudes. He has emphasized particularly those difficulties which are due to the presence in our national income figures of a large amount of entrepreneurial income which contains both capital and labor shares. But he has not mentioned another difficulty, which, though of much smaller dimensions, is none the less material. I refer to the fact that the remuneration of corporate officers, which in our national income estimates is classified as labor income, contains within it a substantial amount of capital income.

It is a well known fact that due to the high rates of our federal corporation income tax and also the highly graduated rates of our federal personal income tax, corporate officers today prefer to take their shares of the company's income in the form of large salaries, bonuses and pension rights rather than in the form of ownership of stock and receipt of dividends. They prefer this form of remuneration because its payment is deductible from the company's taxable income and is, therefore, generally provided very liberally to them. In fact, this type of remuneration is generally set at amounts which would insure to the officers substantial net incomes after payment of personal income taxes—a result which cannot be readily obtained by the officers under a stock ownership type of reward. The incomes received by corporate officers in that form, however, are only in part derived from their personal efforts. In large part, they are earned by the company's capital and are paid to the corporate officers just as if these officers were owners of some of this capital except that the payments are made in a different form. These payments contain, therefore, substantial elements of capital income. They are in effect a mixed capital-labor income, rather than pure labor income. Their classification as labor income in our national income estimates, or analyses thereof, is not completely correct and tends somewhat to overstate the labor share and understate the capital share in the total.

This distortion of the relative sizes of the two shares is probably not very large, but its existence none the less cannot be ignored. It must be accounted for particularly, inasmuch as its importance seems to be increasing over time. The Soviet critics of our national income estimates are placing considerable emphasis on this flaw in our national income classification. In fact, they are attributing to it greater importance than is warranted by the facts; and they tend to discredit our estimates in part on this account. It seems to me imperative, therefore, that in all our estimates of the capital and labor shares in our national income total, we should clearly indicate that our figures of labor income contain this particular admixture of capital income and that we should even try to measure the probable extent of this admixture.

I should, therefore, like to ask Lebergott whether in the course of his analysis he has taken account of this particular overstatement of the labor share and understatement of the capital share and has attempted to estimate the magnitude of the resulting errors.

Reply by Stanley Lebergott

Alterman makes two major points. (1) He asserts that useful conclusions can be drawn concerning factor shares for the corporate universe, and backs this up with an excellent empirical discussion. My own analysis concentrated on the shortcomings of discussing constancy in the aggregate income share simply because that was the focus of much speculation in recent years. Although I find distribution and the process of factor substitution most comprehensible at an industry level, Alterman's fine positive contribution leads one to hope that he will further illuminate this intermediate level of aggregation. (2) The bulk of his comments derive from an unpardonable laxity in my original phrasing, which stipulated that the machinery producing industries passed the gains of their productivity advance on in the form of lower "machinery prices." It should have read "machinery service prices"—both as being more correct, and because it was irrelevant for my analysis whether these gains were passed on by lower unit machine prices, an increase in productive capacity per unit, or both. Alterman's equation (7) picks up this error, and most of his subsequent extended analysis and computations drive its sorry consequences home. (I take some consolation in having thereby elicited his elegant and equable analysis.)

Mr. Studenski questions the reported figures on labor's share, noting how elements of return to capital are really embedded in the figures for salaries of corporate officials. One might go further to note that some salary receipt is in the form of stock and other property, the return from which appears in the accounts as a return to capital rather than labor. And, of course, stock options are a salary equivalent that does not even appear in our accounts at all. The use of the reported data, after they have passed the purview of tax officials and tax lawyers, unquestionably poses problems as to their precision for settling issues of interest to economists.

Capital, Labor, and Income in Manufacturing

ROBERT M. SOLOW
MASSACHUSETTS INSTITUTE OF TECHNOLOGY

Introduction

The beginning student of general equilibrium economics soon reaches the saddening conclusion that "everything depends on everything else." Later on, with advanced study and maturity, comes the more sophisticated realization that "everything depends on everything else in two ways." Thus, for instance, income and output are produced with inputs of labor and capital goods and this provides one way in which they are interdependent. Reciprocally, (final) output must eventually be sold to recipients of wages or profits and this provides a second source of interdependence. How, then, on reading the title of this paper did you know which of the two relations it was going to be about? I think the probability is high that you assumed (correctly) that it would be about production relations and the reason is that papers on income distribution almost always are. Why?

The neoclassical theory of distribution is usually pigeonholed under the heading "marginal productivity" and marginal productivities derive from production functions. This is true enough; but the subset of Walrasian equilibrium equations having to do with marginal productivity does not constitute a complete theory of income distribution. This has been obscured by the custom of fitting aggregate production functions. To see the point it is only necessary to think of a two-product economy in which each of the products has a production function of Cobb-Douglas type, but with different elasticities. Then the relative shares of wages and profits in the net output of each industry are indeed determined solely by the marginal productivity conditions; but the macroeconomic distribution of income depends on the size of the two industries, hence ultimately on the demand of different classes of income-receivers for the two products. Therefore, when modern economists like Nicholas Kaldor and Joan Robinson claim that neoclassical distribution theory is all wrong because even in equilibrium relative shares depend on the rate of investment and propensities to save, they demonstrate only an imperfect under-

NOTE: I must acknowledge my debt to Henry Y. Wan, Jr., of M.I.T. for his careful and alert assistance.

standing of general equilibrium theory and the maxim that "everything depends on everything else in two ways."[1]

I say all this to make it quite clear that this paper does not pretend to offer a complete neoclassical account of the determination of distributive shares in the economy as a whole. In the first place, that is a general equilibrium problem, while this paper is limited to a few two-digit manufacturing industries. In the second place, I shall be concerned only with the production function half of the determinants of distributive shares; my object is to estimate production functions, elasticities of substitution between labor and capital, rates of technical progress, and perhaps some other interesting parameters descriptive of technical conditions in some branches of manufacturing. Naturally, I believe that information of this kind is vital to an understanding of distribution (and of other things), but I do not believe it to be the whole story.[2]

Fitting production functions for manufacturing industries together or separately is old stuff. The methods I shall use, however, are fairly new. The are put together from some recent papers of mine and my colleagues.[3] The main differences from standard practice are the following. First is the choice of a production function. About the only classes of production functions used in empirical work are the Leontief and Cobb-Douglas type. Thus elasticities of substitution are from the very beginning assumed to be either zero or one. Recently Arrow, Chenery, Minhas and I introduced a broader class of production functions characterized by a constant elasticity of substitution but permitting that elasticity to have any value. We discussed the fitting of such

[1] See Nicholas Kaldor: "Alternative Theories of Distribution," *Review of Economic Statistics*, Vol. XXIII(2), 1955–56, pp. 83–100, reprinted in *Essays in Value and Distribution*, London, 1960; and Joan Robinson: "Letter to the Editor," *Econometrica*, Vol. 27(3), 1959, p. 490. Also R. Solow: "Notes Toward a Wicksellian Model of Distributive Shares," in *The Theory of Capital*, ed. Lutz and Hague, London, 1961; and R. Findlay: "Economic Growth and the Distributive Shares," *Review of Economic Studies*, Vol. XXVII(3), 1960, pp. 167–178.

[2] Perhaps I should make a detailed apology for violating my neoclassical boy scout's oath and talking about rough indexes of "capital" instead of about precisely defined vectors of capital goods. But that would take me away from my real business; and besides, a clear statement of a view to which I subscribe is to be found in my friend Paul Samuelson's contribution to the Festschrift for Gustav Åkerman. I intend to meet that problem directly in a later paper.

[3] Particularly R. Solow: "Investment and Technical Progress," in *Mathematical Methods in the Social Sciences, 1959*. Stanford, 1960, and K. Arrow, H. Chenery, B. Minhas and R. Solow: "Capital-Labor Substitution and Economic Efficiency," *Review of Economics and Statistics*, Aug. 1961, pp. 225–50.

production functions to several mixtures of data. A second novelty in this paper is that I use a cross-section analysis (in which observations represent different regions of the United States in 1956) mainly for the purpose of estimating the elasticities of substitution; time-series analyses of the whole of each United States industry for 1949–58 then yield estimates of the other parameters. In the time-series analysis—this is a third difference from the usual approach—I allow for technological progress of a kind which requires up-to-date capital to be adopted. In fact the kind of technological change admitted is a pure and simple improvement in the efficiency of capital goods (which is *not* the same thing as capital-saving innovations). I confess that my motivation for sticking to this kind of technical change is about 60 per cent convenience and 40 per cent curiosity about the consequences of such an assumption.

I shall begin by setting out the theoretical foundations of the analysis; then comes a straight report of the empirical results, together with some brief interpretive notes.

The Representation of Technical Change

Consider a constant-returns-to-scale production function $Q = F(K, L)$. The most general way of indicating that technological limitations are shifting with the acquisition of new knowledge is simply to recognize that the production function shifts arbitrarily through time; we could write $Q = F(K, L; t)$ with the function homogeneous of degree one in K and L. A very restrictive (but the most commonly made) specification is that the effects of technical progress are neutral (or uniform, to choose a word not already encrusted with old meanings) in the sense that marginal rates of substitution do not change when innovation occurs; in that case the shifting production function can be written $Q = A(t)F(K, L)$. An intermediate assumption—more general than uniformity but less than perfectly general—is that technical advance takes the form of making labor and capital goods more productive in the precise sense that anything one man-hour or one machine-hour could do last year can now be done by 0.9 man-hour or 0.8 machine-hours. Formally, one can write $Q = F(\mu(t)K, \lambda(t)L)$.[4] If μ and λ are simply proportional, this is

[4] It should be obvious that, given constant returns to scale, nothing further is added by putting an extra multiplicative uniform factor out front.

nothing but uniform technical change all over again. Otherwise, homogeneity implies that

$$F[\mu(t)K,\ \lambda(t)L] = \lambda(t)F\left[\frac{\mu(t)}{\lambda(t)}K,\ L\right],$$

which is the same thing as uniform technical progress like $\lambda(t)$ accompanied by a change in the productivity of capital goods like $\mu(t)/\lambda(t)$ and no change in the specific productivity of labor.

Now suppose $\lambda(t)$ is constant (that is, equals 1, with no loss of generality) so that the only technical change is an increased productivity of capital goods. Notice that this kind of technical progress is not necessarily capital saving (in the usual sense of decreasing the marginal productivity of capital goods relative to that of labor at any specified K/L ratio). It is in fact capital saving, uniform, or labor saving according as the elasticity of substitution between K and L is less than, equal to, or greater than one. To see this, just write down the expressions involving marginal products for the share of rentals divided by the share of wages; an increase in μ works exactly like an increase in K; hence if the elasticity of substitution is less than one, an increase in μ lowers the share of rentals relative to wages; but since the K/L ratio is really unchanged, this must mean that the rental rate has fallen relative to the wage, and the change is capital saving; etc. Note also that the argument does not require λ to be constant; one simply thinks about μ/λ. In the empirical work, however, I shall mostly make the strong assumption that $\lambda = 1$.

The nice thing about this assumption is that it gives clear effect to the belief that technical progress is indissolubly bound up with investment and permits this case[5] to be handled in a particularly simple way. Suppose that, *with capital of vintage v* (i.e., produced at time v), output can be produced according to the production function:

$$Q_v(t) = F[\mu(v)K_v(t),\ L_v(t)] = L_v(t)F[\mu(v)K_v(t)/L_v(t),\ 1] \quad (1)$$

where

$Q_v(t)$ is output at time t produced with capital of vintage v;
$K_v(t)$ is the stock of vintage v capital surviving at time t;
$L_v(t)$ is the labor force assigned to operate it.

Of course $\mu(v)$ is the productivity factor attached to vintage v

[5] Analyzed from a less general point of view in my "Investment and Technical Progress."

capital and the whole point is that it is fixed forever once the act of investment takes place. The market will shuffle the homogeneous labor force $L(t)$ over the existing stock of capital of various vintages in such a way that

$$L(t) = \sum_{v=-\infty}^{t} L_v(t)$$

and the real wage (in terms of the product of this industry) is equal to the marginal product of labor which will have to be the same for all vintages of capital. Letting $W(t)$ be the product wage in this industry at time t, this means that

$$W(t) = F_2[\mu(v)K_v(t), L_v(t)] = F_2[\mu(v)K_v(t)/L_v(t), 1] \quad (2)$$

since partial derivatives of F are homogeneous of degree zero. It follows that $\mu(v)K_v(t)/L_v(t)$ depends *only* on the product wage and may be written $\varphi[W(t)]$. Now returning to (1) we see

$$\begin{aligned} Q(t) &= \sum_{v=-\infty}^{t} Q_v(t) = \sum_{v} L_v(t)F(\varphi[W(t)], 1) \\ &= F(\varphi[W(t)], 1)\sum_{v} L_v(t) \qquad (3) \\ &= F(\varphi[W(t)], 1)L(t) \\ &= F(\varphi L, L) \end{aligned}$$

But since $\varphi[W(t)] = \mu(v)K_v(t)/L_v(t)$, it follows that

$$L(t) = \sum_{v} L_v(t) = \frac{1}{\varphi}\sum_{v} \mu(v)K_v(t) = \frac{1}{\varphi}J(t) \quad (4)$$

where $J(t) = \sum_{v=-\infty}^{t} \mu(v)K_v(t)$ is a kind of "productivity-corrected" stock of capital at time t. Combining (3) and (4), we have

$$Q(t) = F(\varphi L, L) = F[J(t), L(t)] = F\left[\sum_{v=-\infty}^{t} \mu(v)K_v(t), L(t)\right], \quad (5)$$

which says that we can read off total output by inserting in the single-vintage production function the total input of labor and a suitably weighted sum of surviving capital inputs of various vintages.[6] (The weights are just the productivity factors.)

[6] This simple result depends crucially on the assumption that the full substitution possibilities of capital remain unimpaired even after it has been built. I propose to take up the opposite case in a later paper.

The CES Production Function

For statistical purposes it is necessary to specialize the production function to some particular functional form. The three-parameter family of production functions with constant but arbitrary elasticity of substitution can be written

$$Q = \gamma[\delta K^{-\rho} + (1 - \delta)L^{-\rho}]^{-1/\rho} \tag{6}$$

We have dubbed this the class of CES production functions. The constants γ, δ, and ρ may be called the efficiency, distribution and substitution parameters, respectively. As has been shown, the elasticity of substitution between capital and labor along the production functions (6) is given by $\sigma = (1 + \rho)^{-1}$.[7] Thus the Cobb-Douglas function is the special case with $\rho = 0$, in which case the exponents are δ and $(1 - \delta)$; this accounts for calling δ the distribution parameter.

Since (6) is nonlinear in its parameters, direct estimation from time series of Q, K and L, would be a complicated job. If, however, (6) is written

$$Q^{-\rho} = \gamma^{-\rho}[\delta K^{-\rho} + (1 - \delta)L^{-\rho}],$$

it is seen that an outside estimate of ρ will permit the other two parameters to be estimated by straightforward methods. The problem then is to find a convenient estimate of the elasticity of substitution. Now it has been shown[8] that for observations along any production function, the elasticity of Q/L with respect to W at any point will be equal to σ, provided the observations were generated by profit maximization in competitive labor and product markets, and provided the "price" of value-added is the same in all markets—which implies that the cost of capital varies, since the wage does. Since σ is constant along (6), it follows that an estimate of σ can be obtained as the slope of a regression of $\log Q/L$ on $\log W$ from observations generated under the circumstances described.

In fact, putting the product-wage W equal to the marginal productivity of labor from (6), one easily calculates

$$\log \frac{Q}{L} = \frac{1}{1 + \rho} \log W + \log [\gamma\rho(1 - \delta)^{-1}]^{\frac{1}{1+\rho}} \tag{7}$$

[7] See K. Arrow *et al.* in *RES*, August 1961.
[8] *Ibid.*

In our article on capital-labor substitution,[9] we took the leap of applying (7) to observations arising from the same manufacturing industry at about the same time in different countries. We were forced to conclude, on the basis of other data not used in (7) that the same industry in different countries could not honestly be treated as operating along the same production function, but that it is a fair working hypothesis that international differences in production functions are concentrated in the (uniform!) efficiency parameter γ. In this paper I propose to estimate (7) from observations pertaining to the same two-digit manufacturing industry in the same year in the nine different census regions of the United States. Since I do not have the additional information (mainly regional stocks of capital) necessary to test the hypothesis that observations thus generated come from a common production function, I am simply assuming that they do. This is risky, of course; but I hope I am justified in assuming that technological conditions among regions of the United States are substantially more homogeneous than among countries of the world in widely different phases of economic development.

It is to be noted that, because of the reduction (5), I am entitled to ignore the differing vintage structures of the capital stock in a given industry across regions at a single point of time.

I can hope, then, from the interregional cross-section analysis of a given industry, to estimate the parameter $\sigma = 1/(1+\rho)$, and therefore $\rho = 1 - (\sigma/\sigma)$, along with the constant $[\gamma\rho(1-\delta)^{-1}]^{\frac{1}{1+\rho}}$. Next, in another fit of recklessness, I propose to use the estimate of ρ thus obtained in a time series analysis of data for the same industry, aggregated across regions for the whole United States.

Specializing (5) to the CES production function (6), we have

$$Q(t) = \gamma[\delta J(t)^{-\rho} + (1-\delta)L(t)^{-\rho}]^{-1/\rho} \tag{8}$$

whence, as before,

$$Q(t)^{-\rho} = \gamma^{-\rho}[\delta J(t)^{-\rho} + (1-\delta)L(t)^{-\rho}]. \tag{9}$$

Here $J(t) = \sum_{\infty v = -}^{t} \mu(v)K_v(t)$ as in (5). From (9) we note:

$$Q(t)^{-\rho} - \gamma^{-\rho}(1-\delta)L(t)^{-\rho} = \gamma^{-\rho}\delta J(t)^{-\rho}. \tag{10}$$

[9] *Ibid.*

Call the left-hand side of (10) $R(t)$. The critical thing is that, given time series for $Q(t)$ and $L(t)$, we can "produce" a time series for $R(t)$. This is because the cross-section analysis has provided an estimate of ρ, so we can generate $Q^{-\rho}$ and $L^{-\rho}$ from Q and L. In addition, from an estimate of the constant term in (7), together with an estimate of ρ we can compute an estimate of $\gamma^{-\rho}(1 - \delta)$. Thus if we rewrite (10)

$$R(t) = \gamma^{-\rho}\delta J(t)^{-\rho} \tag{10'}$$

we can create an estimated time series for $R(t)$. With $J(t)$ we are not so lucky, since it depends on the unknown productivity-increase function μ. But a final burst of assumptions will do the trick.[10]

Write out (10′) in detail:

$$R(t) = \gamma^{-\rho}\delta\left[\sum_{v=-\infty}^{t} \mu(v)K_v(t)\right]^{-\rho} \tag{10''}$$

From (10″) we have

$$R(t)^{-1/\rho} = \gamma\delta^{-1/\rho} \sum_{v=-\infty}^{t} \mu(v)K_v(t) \tag{10'''}$$

and put the left-hand side, a time series which we can also estimate, equal to $Z(t)$. It will be recalled that $K_v(t)$ stands for the stock of capital of vintage v surviving in year t. Suppose that the survival curve for capital in this industry is exponential so that

$$K_v(t) = (1 - \theta)^{t-v}K_v(v) = (1 - \theta)^{t-v}I(v)$$

where $I(v)$ is gross investment in year v. This amounts to the assumption of a constant rate of mortality θ for capital, so that the average length of life[11] is $1/\theta$. Assume also that $\mu(v) = (1 + \mu)^v$, so that the productivity of capital increases geometrically at rate 100 μ per cent per year. Inserting all these assumptions in (10′′′) yields:

$$Z(t) = \gamma\delta^{-1/\rho}(1 - \theta)^t \sum_{v=-\infty}^{t} \left(\frac{1 + \mu}{1 - \theta}\right)^v I(v)$$

[10] From here on the reasoning is very much like that in my "Investment and Technical Progress."

[11] It is a weakness that the durability of capital is assumed to be technically fixed and unaffected by the process of technical change.

Finally

$$\Delta Z(t) = Z(t) - Z(t-1) = \gamma\delta^{-1/\rho}(1-\theta)^{-1}(1+\mu)^t I(t) - \frac{\theta}{1-\theta} Z(t) \qquad (11)$$

whence

$$\frac{\Delta Z(t) + \dfrac{\theta}{1-\theta} Z(t)}{I(t)} = \gamma\delta^{-1/\rho}(1-\theta)^{-1}(1+\mu)^t$$

or

$$\frac{Z(t) - (1-\theta)Z(t-1)}{I(t)} = \gamma\delta^{-1/\rho}(1+\mu)^t \qquad (12)$$

Once again, given a trial value of θ, the left-hand side of (12), say $Y(t)$, can be estimated as a time series from what has gone before and a time series of gross investment in the industry. A linear regression of the logarithm of $Y(t)$ on t should then yield:

$$\log Y(t) = \log(\gamma\delta^{-1/\rho}) + t\log(1+\mu), \qquad (13)$$

and the estimated constants of this line (together with the assumed value of θ and all the previous by-products) make it possible to wind up with estimates of γ, δ and μ which are the only outstanding parameters.[12]

Cross-Section Analysis: Data

For the cross-section estimate of equation (7) I have used data extracted from the 1956 *Annual Survey of Manufactures* (see Table 1). The year 1956 was chosen as a year of relatively high employment with little excess capacity; because it followed a similar year, one might hope the data would not represent a period of rapid transition. Of course (7) is an equilibrium relation and one can never hope to have observed an economy in full equilibrium. Relative tranquillity is the most one can ask for. As a measure of output for each industry, I have used value added. The labor input figures represent the total number of employees. These are not corrected for hours worked, since this information is avail-

[12] In principle one could repeat this process for different trial values of θ, and the best-fitting version of (13) taken as giving final estimates of the other parameters *and* θ. My assistant Henry Wan is of the opinion that θ ought to be estimated exogenously, since it is not integral to the model being studied and should not be used to absorb error. This seems to me to be a strong argument and, were data available, worth following up.

TABLE 1
VALUE ADDED AND TOTAL PAYROLLS PER EMPLOYEE, BY INDUSTRY AND REGION, 1956

Industry (Two-digit Census Categories)		Census Regions[a] NE	MA	ENC	WNC	SA	ESC	WSC	M	P
20 Food	A.	8,081	9,444	9,844	9,567	7,722	9,752	8,425	8,772	10,798
	B.	3,814	4,294	4,403	4,348	3,253	3,557	3,418	3,858	4,448
21 Tobacco	A.	5,802	6,318	10,221		14,732	16,399	2,999		
	B.	2,198	2,638	2,981		3,110	3,463	1,459		
22 Textile	A.	5,562	5,920	6,960	6,012	4,786	4,568	4,188		7,424
	B.	3,475	3,620	3,835	3,242	2,895	2,773	2,632		3,953
23 Apparel	A.	4,508	5,102	4,739	4,301	3,832	3,495	3,792	4,592	5,430
	B.	2,615	3,042	3,117	2,742	2,406	2,147	2,352	2,618	3,190
24 Lumber	A.	4,484	5,175	5,534	5,417	3,690	3,880	4,064	6,839	7,979
	B.	3,122	3,300	3,397	3,276	2,193	2,215	2,456	3,879	4,670
25 Furn. and fixtures	A.	6,273	7,127	7,380	6,903	5,732	5,022	5,616		7,432
	B.	3,595	3,957	4,204	4,019	3,185	3,079	3,197		4,054
26 Paper	A.	8,815	8,639	9,399	10,572	11,343	10,067	11,940	12,696	12,547
	B.	4,528	4,541	4,824	4,488	4,418	4,615	4,749	4,978	5,011
27 Printing, publ.	A.	7,700	9,977	8,773	7,634	8,039	7,744	7,481	7,120	8,479
	B.	4,519	5,117	5,087	4,274	4,611	4,361	3,992	4,223	4,939
28 Chemicals	A.	12,945	16,025	15,370	15,231	15,174	13,289	23,501	12,086	14,870
	B.	4,863	5,181	5,335	4,501	4,794	4,904	5,358	5,762	5,391

29	Petroleum	A.	12,817	14,249	20,616	17,386	10,709	16,846	19,938	18,110	16,486
		B.	5,492	5,836	6,134	5,403	4,770	4,875	6,003	5,543	5,946
30	Rubber	A.	7,933	9,389	8,621	12,456	7,803	13,274	13,721	13,719	9,450
		B.	4,405	4,631	5,000	4,668	3,803	5,000	4,609	4,965	4,863
31	Leather	A.	4,717	4,868	5,908	5,530	4,643	5,725	4,305	8,807	6,457
		B.	3,168	3,123	3,480	2,828	2,901	2,644	2,393	4,551	3,329
32	Stone, clay, glass	A.	8,053	8,986	9,688	10,140	7,645	8,449	10,608	10,311	8,610
		B.	4,427	4,565	4,656	4,326	3,714	3,571	3,953	4,149	4,419
33	Primary metals	A.	9,545	9,817	10,584	9,384	10,101	10,674	11,697	17,160	11,749
		B.	5,110	5,131	5,409	4,760	5,158	4,824	4,807	5,370	5,277
34	Fabricated metals	A.	7,759	7,967	8,866	8,925	8,258	7,489	7,818		9,181
		B.	4,409	4,518	4,923	4,549	4,104	4,027	4,448		4,838
35	Machinery, nonelec.	A.	8,641	9,083	9,730	8,705	7,775	9,590	10,617	9,491	9,080
		B.	4,906	5,169	5,424	4,667	4,449	4,510	4,974	4,856	5,126
36	Elec. machinery	A.	7,699	8,647	8,576	7,854	8,365	9,286	8,453	5,796	8,230
		B.	4,038	4,658	4,679	4,356	4,351	3,638	4,132	3,868	4,734
37	Transportation equip.	A.	8,740	8,880	10,015	9,155	9,383	9,115	6,156	8,301	9,050
		B.	5,290	5,468	5,374	5,073	5,139	4,592	5,178	5,399	5,796
38	Instruments	A.	7,814	9,599	8,821	9,568	5,596	6,690		6,069	9,141
		B.	4,319	5,212	4,774	4,935	3,718	4,199		3,832	5,152

SOURCE: *Annual Survey of Manufacturers*, 1956.

[a] The regions are: New England (NE), Middle Atlantic (MA), East North Central (ENC), West North Central (WNC), South Atlantic (SA), East South Central (ESC), West South Central (WSC), Mountain (M), and Pacific (P).

A = Value added per employee.

B = Payroll per employee.

able only for production workers; it would have been possible to use the production-workers manhours and payrolls, but the more inclusive data seemed to give a better fit. Finally, as a wage indicator I have used total payrolls per employee. Thus for each census region in each industry, the first row gives value added per employee and the second gives total payrolls per employee. Most of the industries have observations for each of the nine census regions. In a few cases one or more regions are missing because not all two-digit manufacturing industries are sufficiently dispersed.[13]

Cross-Section Analysis: Results

We can rewrite (7) simply as

$$\log \frac{Q}{L} = a \log W + b; \qquad (7')$$

a and b were estimated for each industry by a regression of value added per employee on payrolls per employee across regions. Table 2 summarizes the results.

In reading Table 2 one must remember that each regression line is based on nine or fewer observations so the usual "two-standard-error" rule does not hold. To give some idea of the sampling properties of the statistics, it is enough to know that the 95 and 97.5 percentiles of the t distribution with 7 degrees of freedom are 1.895 and 2.365 respectively. Thus, for instance, in testing a hypothesis on the slope of one of the regressions the acceptance region is about 1.895 or 2.365 standard errors on either side of the hypothetical regression slope, depending on whether the level of significance is 10 per cent or 5 per cent. Another useful critical value to keep in mind is this: for 9 observations, the 95 and 97.5 percentiles of the sampling distribution of the correlation coefficient (when the true parent correlation is zero) are .582 and .666. To reject the hypothesis that value added per employee and payrolls per employee are uncorrelated takes a sample correlation coefficient of .582 or .666 at the 10 per cent and 5 per cent levels, if the test is against a symmetrical alternative. In the present context, where the only plausible alternative to zero correlation would

[13] In many respects it would have been better to conduct the analysis on a state-by-state basis. I chose the larger geographical unit both because I was hurried and wished to save hand computation time and because on a state basis there would presumably be more variation among observations in product-mix within the broad two-digit industries.

TABLE 2

REGRESSIONS: VALUE ADDED PER EMPLOYEE ON PAYROLLS PER EMPLOYEE[a]

	Industry	(1)	(2)	(3)	(4)	(5)	(6)	(7)	(8)	(9)
20	Food	7	.6905	.2221	1.2680	.5799	.0702	0.4482	0.1594	.1118
21	Tobacco	4	1.9633	.2950	.2514	.9172	.1889	−0.4906	0.8799	.2865
22	Textile	6	1.2668	.1466	.2180	.9256	.0556	−0.2106	0.8419	.1434
23	Apparel	7	1.0075	.1308	.4877	.8944	.0476	−0.0074	0.6163	.1285
24	Lumber	7	.9928	.0930	.5070	.9421	.0633	0.0073	0.6001	.2404
25	Furniture & fixtures	6	1.1216	.1050	.4049	.9500	.0329	−0.1084	0.6970	.1183
26	Paper	7	1.7736	1.0058	−.3790	.3076	.1232	−0.4362	1.2383	.0433
27	Printing, publ.	7	1.0237	.2061	.5359	.7789	.0482	−0.0232	0.5924	.0827
28	Chemicals	7	.1410	.9476	2.4862	.0032	.1914	6.0922	0.0000	.0714
29	Petroleum	7	1.4536	.7121	.2876	.3731	.1698	−0.3121	0.8205	.0843
30	Rubber	7	1.4773	.8769	.0767	.2885	.2030	−0.3231	0.9494	.0819
31	Leather	7	.8911	.2657	.6708	.6164	.1362	0.1222	0.4710	.1813
32	Stone, clay, glass	7	.3200	.4592	1.7516	.0649	.1136	2.1250	0.0043	.0875
33	Primary metals	7	1.8697	1.2475	−.6537	.2429	.1611	−0.4652	1.4185	.0457
34	Fabricated metals	6	.8009	.2950	.9130	.5512	.0512	0.2486	0.3198	.0656
35	Machinery, nonelectrical	7	.6348	.4492	1.2074	.2219	.0782	0.5753	0.1493	.0615
36	Machinery, electrical	7	.3735	.5371	1.5434	.0646	.1310	1.6774	0.0160	.0862
37	Transportation equipment	7	.0586	.8217	2.0646	.0007	.1398	16.0649	0.0000	.0602
38	Instruments	6	1.5945	.1452	−.3437	.9526	.0471	−0.3728	8.6322	.1227

SOURCE: Calculated from Table I.

[a] Col. 1 equals the number of degrees of freedom (two less than the number of regions present); col. 2, the estimated value of a; col. 3, its standard error; col. 4, the estimated value of b; col. 5, the squared correlation coefficient; col. 6, the standard error of estimate; col. 7, the value of ρ corresponding to the estimated a; col. 8, the value of $\gamma^{-\rho}(1 - \delta)$ corresponding to the estimated a and b (see equation (10)); and col. 9, the sample standard deviation of the independent variable, in this case the annual wage or payroll per employee. The reason for presenting this last statistic is made clear in the text.

seem to be positive correlation, the same critical values for r give 5 per cent and 2.5 per cent levels of significance instead.

With these benchmarks before us, we can look at the goodness of fit of the cross-section regressions. Remember that column (5) of Table 2 gives r^2, not r. Of the nineteen two-digit industries, we can classify six (Nos. 21–25, and 38) as giving excellent fits. Another four (Nos. 20, 27, 31, and 34) fit less well, but with correlations which are clearly statistically significant. There are four complete failures (Nos. 28, 32, 36, 37). This leaves five industries (Nos. 29, 26, 30, 33, 35 in descending order of goodness of fit) with correlations like .6108, .5546, .5371, .4929, .4711, which are just on the borderline of statistical significance. With due skepticism of the results, it seems worthwhile to carry this last batch of industries on through the next stage of the analysis. So for the later time-series calculations there will be fifteen interesting industries left.

It is in general bad policy to seek good excuses for poor results. The hardy econometrician must learn to take his lickings in the conscious realization that "you can't win 'em all." That is surely the proper attitude in the present case. The model is after all a pretty bold simplification. Two-digit manufacturing industries are heterogeneous enough so that interregional differences in product-mix may still be important. I am fitting an equilibrium relation to data generated in the midst of an investment boom. There are very few observations. And besides, the results are not so bad. Still I am tempted to produce one possible excuse for those industries which give low correlations.

Note that my whole method depends on the existence of interregional differences in wage levels. If wage rates were approximately the same in all regions, then the theory maintains that value added per employee ought also to be the same in all regions. There would surely be minor differences in value added per head, if only on account of weather, product-mix and error of measurement. But if there were no wage differentials (or very small ones), I would get approximately zero correlations. It is interesting, then, that the industries with low correlations are almost uniformly those for which the sample standard deviation of the (log) wage variable is lowest. The eight industries for which that standard deviation is greater than .1000 are all among the satisfactory cases; the eight worst-fitting industries have with one or two exceptions the least variation in wages. I am curious about what distinguishes the industries with little interregional wage variation from those with much. One's first inclination is to check the prevalence of industry-wide collective bargaining, or especially mobile labor forces. It is true that the little-wage-variation group does include some industries with strong national trade unions (such as primary metals, transportation equipment, nonelectrical machinery, electrical machinery, and rubber). But this is a subject for more than casual observation.[14]

[14] I note that a simple rank correlation of the interregional standard deviation of wages with the fraction of production workers organized in each industry yields a rank correlation coefficient of —.75, clearly significant.

Cross-Section Analysis: Interpretation

If the cross-section data of Table 1 are generated under ideal conditions—that is, if they represent an approximation to competitive profit-maximizing equilibrium along a common production function—then the regression slopes given in column 2 of Table 2 ought to be estimates of the elasticity of substitution between labor and (efficiency-corrected) capital in each industry. That is quite an "if," and I would not wish this investigation to be thought of as more than a reconnaissance (or maybe a raid!). I must warn the reader that even a very good fit in Table 2 is not powerful evidence in favor of the intended interpretation. I have already mentioned one reason: even if the interpretation were right, the absence of interregional wage variation would make the statistical analysis meaningless. There is a more obvious reason: my argument runs in terms of the observed figures for net output per head being a response to a market-given wage, but a strong positive correlation might alternatively be interpreted as a wage differential which arises because of intrinsic interregional productivity differentials. The source of the productivity differentials might be almost anything—differences in effective production functions, differences in product-mix, differences in the age, sex or educational composition of the labor force. The only way in which I could hope to clinch my (hoped-for) interpretation would be to produce some kind of regional data on stocks of real capital and to show that the output, labor, and capital observations actually fall along a production function with the appropriate elasticity of substitution. Of course, no such capital data exist; and even if the usual sort of stock data were available, they might not measure the productivity-corrected concept I have used at the end of Section 2 of this paper.

Nor is it easy to test the estimated elasticities of substitution for consistency with the observed pattern of distributive shares in each industry over time. In theory, the more rapidly growing input ought to be imputed a decreasing or increasing relative share of the net output of an industry according as the elasticity of substitution between inputs is less than or greater than one. The case of unit elasticity of substitution is the famous Cobb-Douglas case of constant relative shares. The ratio of total payrolls to value added is easily obtainable for each industry in the period 1947, 1949–58, from the Censuses and Annual Surveys of Manufactures, and these are reproduced in Table 3. It may not be certain in every case which was the rapidly growing input—labor services or the services of a productivity-corrected stock of capital. Still it is probably a safe bet that over this decade of investment boom the capital factor increased more rapidly than the labor factor; this would be true without the correction for technological progress and even more strongly with it. Even so, it is not all clear sailing. Given the intrinsic sluggishness of a time series of relative shares and the fact that its business-cycle variation is likely to be as great as or even greater than the long-term component of its decade movement, I would hesitate to read anything out of Table 3.

It is interesting that the two industries for which Table 2 makes the strongest claim of a greater-than-unit elasticity of substitution, namely tobacco and instruments, do turn out in Table 3 to give evidence of a *declining* wage share. On the face of it, this is in conformity with the interpretation of the cross-section slopes as elasticities of substitution. The situation with less-than-unit estimates for the elasticity of substitution is, if possible, even less definite, mainly because columns 2 and 3 of Table 2 do not exhibit any slopes which are significantly less than unity. But I must strongly emphasize that I am not arguing, nor do I believe, that short-run distributive phenomena are to be explained in terms of long-run equilibrium behavior along neoclassical lines. I conclude then that Table 3 can provide no strong evidence either for or against the neoclassical interpretation of the cross-section results.

If, for the sake of the argument, we interpret the cross-section regression slopes as estimates of elasticities of substitution, they turn out sharply to contradict the empirical results obtained in our earlier study.[15] In that paper most of the estimates proved to be significantly less than unity, and none of the elasticities of substitution gave any indication of being greater than one. Also, the statistical fits (to approximately contemporaneous census data from eleven to nineteen different countries) were all very good. By contrast, in Table 2 at most ten of the nineteen regressions have a good fit. Even more surprisingly, the interregional cross-sections are not characterized by uniformly less-than-unit elasticities of substitution. Of the ten good fits in Table 2, three give point estimates of the elasticity of substitution which are less than one,

[15] Arrow *et al.* in *RES*, August 1961.

TABLE 3
WAGES AS PERCENTAGE OF VALUE ADDED

	Industry	1947	1949	1950	1951	1952	1953	1954	1955	1956	1957	1958
20	Food	41.98	44.54	43.70	45.55	44.96	44.11	46.28	45.56	45.30	44.58	44.70
21	Tobacco	32.09	26.69	26.36	26.88	27.74	25.67	26.29	25.11	23.73	23.04	20.85
22	Textile	53.10	62.71	59.61	63.42	63.59	63.84	63.86	61.25	62.19	61.44	59.14
23	Apparel	56.89	64.00	66.21	62.89	63.50	62.02	62.21	62.27	62.20	61.38	59.93
24	Lumber	53.56	62.24	55.21	57.20	60.06	59.61	60.64	59.91	62.26	64.02	64.08
25	Furniture and fixtures	59.81	61.07	60.76	59.70	58.96	61.53	60.89	59.41	57.78	58.05	59.85
26	Paper	44.55	51.12	46.76	43.60	48.35	48.85	48.41	47.86	47.72	48.46	49.24
27	Printing and publishing	53.34	58.90	59.28	58.01	57.72	57.24	57.87	56.67	55.73	55.68	57.16
28	Chemicals	35.61	35.78	32.36	34.10	36.50	36.48	36.08	32.90	33.73	33.76	32.93
29	Petroleum[a]											
30	Rubber	60.13	59.71	52.49	55.66	59.75	56.40	55.65	55.65	54.92	55.03	52.92
31	Leather	56.99	64.31	63.33	64.02	63.58	64.22	62.74	62.43	62.11	61.87	61.16
32	Stone, clay, glass	52.49	53.99	48.74	51.33	52.15	51.93	50.71	48.05	48.02	48.95	46.83
33	Primary metals	62.35	60.67	52.29	52.59	53.38	54.54	53.82	50.20	49.58	53.73	54.92
34	Fabricated metals	57.56	59.65	54.81	55.87	57.53	58.52	57.89	57.87	57.38	57.70	57.86
35	Machinery, nonelec.	61.50	59.30	57.77	59.98	57.62	58.86	58.28	59.49	59.47	58.60	57.52
36	Machinery, elec.	58.32	54.87	52.60	55.50	54.56	56.18	53.37	55.74	56.42	54.62	54.53
37	Transportation equipment	53.37	58.10	54.75	61.98	61.64	61.83	59.57	56.56	59.99	57.50	58.70
38	Instruments	61.59	60.82	58.50	62.66	59.15	56.81	56.39	56.79	57.34	57.64	55.31

[a] Not calculated.

three or four, are greater than one, and three or four are essentially equal to one. Only three of the estimated elasticities are significantly different from one at the 90 per cent level (two-sided test) and all three of these are on the greater-than-one side.

I cannot now give a completely satisfactory reconciliation of the two sets of empirical results, but I can suggest lines along which I think an explanation might be found. In the first place, so far as goodness of fit is concerned, the earlier observations come from a list of countries which included the United States and Canada at the high-wage end and Ceylon, India and Iraq at the low-wage end. Within any one industry the range of wage rates was always very wide, the highest running at least ten or twenty times the lowest. Within my interregional samples, the wage variation is much smaller; never in any industry is the highest wage as much as twice the lowest and almost always the range is much narrower. I have already mentioned that the lowest-wage-differential industries tend to be the ones for which the regression results are poorest. The point of analyzing interregional cross-sections is the chance that technology is much more homogeneous across such regions than across countries at widely different levels of development.[16]

Another difference between the earlier and the present results may cast some light on the size of the estimated elasticities. In the "capital-labor substitution" paper, we analyzed selected three-digit manufacturing industries (in the International Standard Industrial Classification); I have dealt with two-digit industries here. It seems plausible that, in general, elasticities of substitution should be smaller the more narrowly defined the industrial classification, and larger the higher the degree of aggregation. The reason is fairly obvious: one can imagine subindustries each of which has zero elasticity of substitution but which when aggregated exhibit highly variable factor proportions because the mix of subindustries is different in different regions. One would expect to find highly labor-intensive (low value added per employee) subindustries concentrated in low-wage regions, and conversely. Another way to

[16] It probably bears repeating that in ACMS it turned out that the data could be explained on the hypothesis of neutral differences in technology among countries. I would not even go so far as to believe that census regions of the U.S. share an identical technology within any industry. But I believe it is important to know how much of observed interregional differences are differences in technology and how much are adaptation to differing price structures.

see this point is to recognize that shifting the product mix is one way in which substitutions between labor and capital takes place; hence the more aggregated the industry the more plentiful the opportunities for substitution. Since the industrial classification in the earlier paper was finer than the one I have used here, it is perhaps natural that the elasticities of substitutions should have been systematically smaller.

This proposition could be checked in the obvious way: by replicating the cross-section regressions for each of the three-digit subindustries within a two-digit industry. It should turn out that the two-digit elasticity of substitution exceeds an average of the three-digit components. I have not had the time to perform such a check; but inspection of a few scatter diagrams suggests that it may indeed work that way. Further research is required before one can say how consistent the present results are with the earlier ones, but I think they might actually make a sensible pattern.

Here is perhaps the place to mention two other directions in which the analysis might conceivably be pushed—neither one led to anything in preliminary trials. First, the cross-section analysis could be done on a state-by-state basis. This would have two advantages: it would increase the number of observations in each regression, and it would increase the variability of the independent variable, the annual wage. There is a disadvantage too: the differences between one state and another are more likely to reflect simple product-mix differences than those between one census region and another. In any case, a few scatter diagrams were drawn up on the state basis; there is only a slight increase in interregional wage variability (not surprising, since census regions are fairly homogeneous blocks of states) and the promised improvement in fit was not great enough to justify rerunning the regressions.

Secondly, one of the serious weaknesses in the theoretical justification of this method is the assumption that observations represent situations of equilibrium. In the hope of dodging this difficulty, the previous year's wage was introduced as a second independent variable in each regression. But the intercorrelation between 1955 and 1956 wages across regions was in nearly all cases so high that the results were uninterpretable. There were cases in which using the 1955 wage (either alone or in combination with 1956) gave a noticeably higher fit than when only the 1956 wage was used. It seems entirely too *ad hoc* to do anything under the circumstances but discard the results using 1955 wages. Still, a more careful attack on this problem ought to consider some of the standard ways of formulating a disequilibrium model.[17]

Time Series Analysis: Data

To carry out the time series analysis suggested in equations (8) to (13), I need statistical counterparts of $Q(t)$, $L(t)$ and $I(t)$ for each industry. At first I intended to use the Commerce series for income originating, equivalent full-time employees, and capital expenditures, with appropriate deflation where necessary. But the published figures for capital expenditures group together a number of the two-digit industries into an other durables and an other nondurables category, and I was refused access to the disaggregated breakdowns. So I returned to Census data. They have the advantage of being on an establishment basis, which is probably best for an attempt to estimate production functions. But continuous series are available only for the decade 1949–58 and this is a very short period. Production functions for industries cannot be expected to describe short-run behavior faithfully, because year-to-year variations may be dominated by cyclical considerations—shortness of time, idle capacity, unexpected changes in output and other disequilibrium phenomena. So long as technological change is given an explicit place in the analysis, it would seem that long time series are more likely to give sensible results. This analysis of a single postwar decade must be thought of as a pilot study.

For $Q(t)$ I have taken, from the Annual Surveys and Censuses of Manufactures, value added deflated by an index prepared by Charles Schultze.[18] The Schultze index is designed for deflating income originating rather than value added, but I did not attempt to make the necessary adjustments.

For $L(t)$, corresponding to the cross-section analyses, I have

[17] There is another aspect of the situation which has become clearer to me since this paper was written. As mentioned earlier, the model assumes that price is uniform across regions while wage and capital costs vary. For some commodities it may be more plausible to assume that capital costs are the same, while both price and wage vary. Then the results require a quite different interpretation, and it may be necessary to deflate by an interregional price index.

[18] See Charles L. Schultze and J. Tryon: *Prices and Costs in Manufacturing Industries*, Study Paper 17, U.S. Congress, Joint Economic Committee, Washington, 1960. For present purposes the index was shifted to 1954 = 100.

used the Census figure for total employees. This series is no doubt deficient for several reasons. Presumably it does not correctly reflect inputs of labor services because of short-run fluctuations in hours worked. And it is further distorted by the grouping together of production workers and supervisory workers, subject as these classes are to sharply divergent trends. I use total employees rather than production worker man-hours for two reasons: greater inclusiveness, because to omit nonproduction workers altogether would be to omit an important input and component of value added; and comparability with the cross-section analyses.

Finally, a statistical counterpart of $I(t)$ has been put together out of the annually reported estimates of expenditures on plant and equipment in the Annual Surveys and Censuses of Manufactures. The plant expenditures and equipment expenditures were deflated separately, using the corresponding implicit deflators from the GNP accounts, and the deflated figures were added together to give $I(t)$.[19]

These three time series are reproduced for each two-digit industry in Table 4. For carrying out the analysis described in the third section of this paper, the only other inputs required are estimated values of the parameters ρ, $\gamma^{-\rho}$ $(1 - \delta)$, and θ. The first two of these are taken from the cross-section analysis and have already been recorded in columns 7 and 8 of Table 2. As for θ, the mortality rate on plant and equipment combined, trials were made with $\theta = .10$ and $.05$; that is, with average lifetimes of ten and twenty years for capital equipment.

Time Series Analysis: Results

Figure 1 shows scatter diagrams of log Y_t against time (see equation (13)) for fifteen of the nineteen industries. The remaining four comprise two in which computational difficulties could not be overcome, and two in which the results were negative. In principle, the slope of the regression line should be for each industry an estimate of $\log_e (1 + \mu)$. (And since μ is a small number, the slope should be approximately μ or a bit higher.)

One major difficulty appears immediately: in every instance, the

[19] The capital expenditures for 1958 are not yet available in the two-category breakdown. For that year, the total was deflated by an index combined of the two implicit deflators with weights obtained from interpolation between 1957 and 1959.

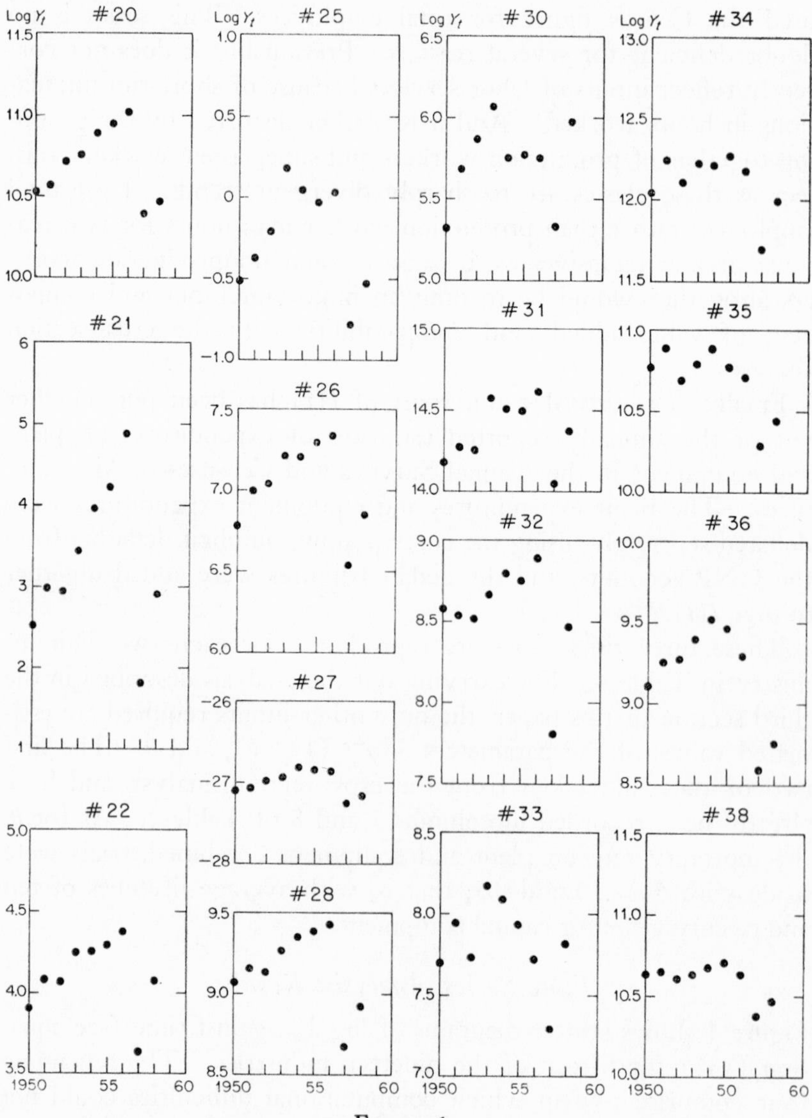

FIGURE 1.

last two points fall far below the rest of the scatter and completely spoil the picture. The reason for this is easy to find. The last two observations cover the period 1957–58. In most manufacturing industries these were recession years in which output increased only weakly (1957) or decreased (1958), while investment remained strong (1957) or at least positive (1958). The kind of model I am using can only explain this as a kind of sudden negative technological change. Of course we know better. We know that there is such a thing as idle capital. But the model, built on the assumption of free substitutability between hired labor and concrete capital goods, has no room for idle capital. The model thinks that labor is the variable factor, capital is an overhead, and let the quasi rents fall where they may. Much current speculation has it the other way: labor in fact being converted to an overhead while capital lies idle.

This is a difficulty faced by all models using a neoclassical production function, but it is troublesome only in the short run. If I had thirty or forty years of data, the business cycle dips would appear less substantial. It seems possible to construct a simple model which faces this problem squarely and is yet in the neoclassical spirit and I hope to describe how in a subsequent paper.[20]

Within the framework of this essay there are two possible ways to handle the situation. It would probably be preferable to try to adjust the last two (or indeed all) outputs in each time series to measure capacity rather than current output, and then to recompute. Lacking the time and facilities to do that, I must simply ignore the last two observations. And, rather than calculate linear regressions based on five degrees of freedom, I report in Table 5 the slope of a line drawn through the first and seventh observation in each scatter. These numbers are estimates of the annual rate of technological progress in each industry. They tend to be larger than we normally expect, but that is because they are not rates of increase of "output per unit of input." They are rates of "purely capital-augmenting" technical change, and would have to be divided in half or thirds to be converted into an approximate rate of uniform technical change.

It would be possible, from an estimate of the intercept of each line, to produce estimates of the other parameters of the production functions, γ and δ. Then, in turn, one could go back to the distributive facts and compare observed relative shares with those read off from the estimated production function. But it would be misleading to attempt this deeper analysis and interpretation without much longer time series, and I shall not try.

I report one puzzling fact. The whole procedure seems to be

[20] Since published as "Substitution and Fixed Coefficients in the Theory of Capital," *Review of Economic Studies,* June 1962.

TABLE 4

DEFLATED VALUE ADDED, NUMBER OF EMPLOYEES, AND EXPENDITURES ON PLANT AND EQUIPMENT, BY INDUSTRY

Industry[a]	1949	1950	1951	1952	1953	1954	1955	1956	1957	1958
20 Food										
Q	10,544	11,094	11,341	11,431	11,627	13,400	13,791	14,974	15,445	15,977
L	1,463	1,493	1,474	1,480	1,455	1,647	1,675	1,707	1,688	1,667
I	860	736	729	544	551	789	776	811	799	779
21 Tobacco										
Q	919	958	985	919	996	988	1,077	1,156	1,180	1,373
L	101	92	94	93	95	95	96	93	88	84
I	27	20	19	23	30	28	26	43	36	32
22 Textile										
Q	4,305	5,275	4,326	4,667	5,060	4,749	5,111	5,080	4,999	4,962
L	1,170	1,245	1,195	1,135	1,158	1,037	1,059	1,044	989	919
I	502	490	432	334	258	226	254	270	250	186
23 Apparel										
Q	4,589	4,694	4,643	4,902	5,382	5,147	5,632	5,650	5,802	5,798
L	1,161	1,151	1,123	1,143	1,227	1,190	1,248	1,271	1,264	1,168
I	64	73	74	56	61	77	83	80	92	90
24 Lumber										
Q	2,391	3,150	3,100	3,173	3,395	3,188	3,438	3,308	3,144	3,056
L	649	750	770	743	720	646	693	698	646	583
I	176	223	254	184	185	217	293	267	177	276
25 Furniture and fixtures										
Q	1,464	1,739	1,631	1,701	1,895	1,966	2,421	2,318	2,247	2,238
L	310	346	336	332	361	341	366	376	375	358
I	49	67	59	57	60	62	77	86	75	74

26 Paper										
Q	3,269	3,933	4,046	3,825	4,499	4,581	5,112	5,162	5,411	5,507
L	447	478	495	482	533	530	549	565	566	556
I	378	348	414	383	402	533	539	684	663	522
27 Printing and publ.										
Q	5,381	5,618	5,780	5,807	5,845	6,265	6,510	6,985	6,958	6,911
L	756	763	765	773	760	804	823	854	867	861
I	304	284	259	195	197	237	247	264	283	351
28 Chemicals										
Q	5,947	7,635	8,018	8,855	9,628	9,443	10,744	11,713	12,122	12,608
L	612	642	703	739	768	739	747	760	764	730
I	714	701	1,043	1,053	954	927	739	987	1,094	971
29 Petroleum	Not calculated									
30 Rubber										
Q	1,361	1,983	1,496	1,451	1,797	1,904	2,196	1,852	1,849	1,741
L	222	239	253	255	270	247	265	265	260	232
I	76	93	121	131	128	128	123	139	129	110
31 Leather										
Q	1,538	1,797	1,380	1,594	1,699	1,637	1,850	1,848	1,832	1,864
L	375	385	354	361	375	357	366	367	362	342
I	35	30	24	19	25	28	36	34	27	26
32 Stone, clay, glass										
Q	2,196	3,697	4,045	4,015	3,922	3,822	4,292	4,653	4,512	4,946
L	453	491	529	510	506	492	525	536	526	552
I	228	259	343	259	282	301	447	662	567	376
33 Primary metals										
Q	7,400	10,058	10,589	9,974	11,477	9,747	12,837	12,492	11,352	9,360
L	1,016	1,129	1,244	1,240	1,288	1,150	1,204	1,319	1,272	1,073
I	678	637	1,195	1,655	1,184	910	949	1,507	1,988	1,171

(continued)

TABLE 4 (concluded)

Industry[a]	1949	1950	1951	1952	1953	1954	1955	1956	1957	1958
34 Fabricated metals										
Q	5,772	7,105	7,374	7,348	8,535	7,596	8,337	8,291	8,359	7,939
L	872	989	1,035	1,008	1,118	1,019	1,093	1,102	1,114	1,038
I	276	368	376	338	428	432	444	454	456	391
35 Machinery, nonelectrical										
Q	9,226	10,272	11,847	13,281	14,251	12,339	13,217	14,354	13,589	12,485
L	1,295	1,368	1,604	1,651	1,691	1,542	1,605	1,718	1,707	1,549
I	418	392	669	637	691	714	634	810	858	645
36 Machinery, electrical										
Q	4,264	4,984	5,437	6,734	7,766	7,403	8,041	8,873	8,656	7,675
L	663	766	877	957	1,096	959	1,001	1,080	1,084	1,005
I	223	227	314	392	374	341	325	434	453	354
37 Transportation equipment										
Q	8,007	8,812	10,210	11,946	14,955	13,926	15,860	16,466	18,217	14,650
L	1,140	1,218	1,469	1,650	1,912	1,705	1,812	1,792	1,900	1,480
I	316	400	636	696	673	925	823	1,311	988	494
38 Instruments										
Q	1,325	1,529	1,571	2,091	2,234	2,129	2,264	2,403	2,516	2,492
L	205	226	253	279	285	273	283	297	307	291
I	69	75	90	74	91	94	103	132	126	105

SOURCE: Calculated from Annual Surveys of Manufacture and Censuses of Manufactures.

[a] Q = deflated value added.
L = number of employees.
I = deflated expenditures on plant and equipment.

TABLE 5
Rough Estimate of Rate of Technological Progress, by Industry

Industry Number		Crude Estimate of $\log_e (1 + \mu)$
20	Food	.0823
21	Tobacco	.3921
22	Textile	.0787
24	Lumber	essentially zero[a]
25	Furniture and fixtures	.0905
26	Paper	.0831
27	Printing and publ.	.0434
28	Chemicals	.0589
30	Rubber	.0736 (but see scatter)
31	Leather	.0730
32	Stone, clay, and glass	.0521
33	Primary metals	too irregular
34	Fabricated metals	.0325 (sixth observation, see scatter)
35	Machinery, nonelectrical	essentially zero
36	Machinery, electrical	.0389 (sixth observation, see scatter)
38	Instruments	essentially zero

[a] Omitted from Figure 1 since scatter is practically horizontal.

extremely insensitive to changes in the hypothetical rate of depreciation. The calculations were carried out on the alternative assumptions $\theta = .05$ and $\theta = .10$. The resulting figures for $\log_e Y_t$ differed only by one or two digits in the fourth decimal place.

Conclusion

I think it would be unwise to overinterpret these statistical results. It will take further research—and, most especially, longer time series—before one can know whether the figures in column 2 of Table 2 can be thought of as estimates of elasticities of substitution between labor and capital, and whether the figures in Table 5 have any merit at all as estimated rates of capital-augmenting technological progress. On the theoretical side, it would be interesting to see whether different and more satisfactory results could be obtained if it were not assumed that prices are uniform across regions. I would also like to state my complete agreement with a point raised several times in the discussion of this paper: that interregional differences reflect to an unknown extent differences in the quality of labor and the input of "social capital."

Despite these qualifications, all of which seem to be remediable,

I believe that the method illustrated here holds some promise of elucidating the characteristics of production relations and their (partial) implications for distribution.

COMMENT

ROBERT EISNER, Northwestern University

At one point in this paper Mr. Solow suggests that his investigation be thought of as no "more than a reconnaissance (or maybe a raid!)." In either event it is a heroic effort; Solow is an able, as well as an intrepid scout, and the remarks that follow are not meant to suggest that had I been on the mission I would have fared better. But with the advantage of hindsight, we may be able to raise some useful points with regard to the role of the mission as well as the limitations of the intelligence it has brought back.

Solow is appropriately modest. He recognizes that "everything depends upon everything else," but he hopes, with data of "a few two-digit manufacturing industries" and a particular kind of production function, to estimate parameters which will indicate "elasticities of substitution between labor and capital, rates of technical progress, real rates of return on capital, and perhaps some other interesting parameters descriptive of technical conditions in some branches of manufacturing." "*Naturally*," Solow writes (the underscoring is mine), "I believe that information of this kind is vital to an understanding of distribution (and of other things) but I do not believe it to be the whole story." Not the "whole story" but, Solow suggests, it relates to the "production function *half* of the determinants of distributive shares." (Italics mine.)

I seem to recall that Marx used to inveigh against the view, attributed to "bourgeois economists," that the laws of economics which they discovered (and the laws of distribution in particular) were "natural." There is after all nothing in nature that suggests that individuals (or corporations) should "own" or have title to the services of factors of production and should then receive returns equal to the marginal product of these factor services times the quantity of such services that they supply. I indeed have some very serious doubts that there is much in modern capitalism, as we know it, to determine distributive shares on this basis.

NOTE: I am indebted to my colleague, Robert H. Strotz, for helpful reactions to a draft of this comment.

It is easy to develop an illusion (as a scout or an economist) that a function that looms large in a particular market, or under specific assumptions including certain parametric assumptions, explains something as well in a wider or more general equilibrium or under the particular parametric assumptions which apply to actual behavior. Most of us recall, from histories of economic thought if not personal experience, the fate of seemingly irrefutable views that the amount saved depended positively on the rate of interest or the propensity of individuals to abstain from consumption. The Keynesian revolution led to the conclusion not only that this depends on the "everything else" encompassed by the marginal efficiency of investment schedule and liquidity preference, but that for certain not unreasonable parameters of these latter functions saving might not depend at all upon abstinence or interest rates—or might even depend on them only in perverse fashion. With a cynicism born of these confusions—of another era, of course—I would not, as does Solow, so quickly dismiss Kaldor and Mrs. Robinson for ignorance of elementary economics in denigrating or denying the role of the production function in the determination of relative shares. Everything depends on everything else in the sense that the world must mesh, but perhaps it is production functions themselves, quantities and values of inputs, and the product-mix that adjust so that the distribution of output conforms to a system fully determined without the information with which Solow is concerned—just as our abstinence has been found to adjust to income as determined by investment demand and a common floor to all marginal efficiencies.

My own hunch is that much more will be learned about distributive shares by investigations that deal with indifference surfaces and "production functions" involving *probability distributions* of outputs and returns, so that equilibria refer to combinations of expected returns and magnitudes of risk. Our economic and political institutions would determine in large part the risks facing individuals in their choices of actions leading to income; preference functions, themselves perhaps socially conditioned, would then determine, jointly with the supply conditions of risk and expected income, the equilibrium shares of final output. Such investigations would leave full scope to roles for monopolistic imperfections, lack of perfect information, disequilibria made chronic by immobilities (bred in part by uncertainty and ignorance) of specific and heterogeneous factors in a world of change. But if these are the critical elements—in nations, regions and industries—technologies and inputs of factors are among the determined rather than the determinants of distributive shares.

But all this is to question the priorities to be established to this kind of reconnaissance. It will perhaps also constrain us sharply in our evaluation of the results, but to see these constraints we shall have to get down to particulars.

Solow has on another occasion referred aptly to the role of "crucial" assumptions. It will be sobering to note the assumptions underlying the present analysis.

1. Constant returns to scale (production function homogeneous of degree one).
2. Constant elasticity of substitution.
3. Neutral or "uniform" technological advance.
4. Homogeneous labor, equally adapted to all vintages of capital. (There is no technological unemployment in this model!)
5. The rate of technological advance varying only with the rate of addition of new capital.
6. The productivity of new capital independent of the quantities of old capital ($Q = \Sigma Qv(t) = \Sigma F_v[u(v)K(t), Lv(t)]$).
7. The same production function within each two digit manufacturing industry for all vintages of capital and for all regions.
8. Perfect competition in labor and product markets.
9. Observations representing points of equilibrium (points of profit maximization consistent with perfect competition).
10. A mortality rate for capital that is constant, in percentage terms, and the same for all vintages and all regions.
11. The productivity of capital increasing from vintage to vintage at a constant percentage rate, the same for all regions.
12. Arguments of the production function restricted to privately owned capital stocks, of various vintages, and labor.

Not all of these assumptions are crucial, in the sense that their relaxation would complicate the analysis but not necessarily make it impossible. In a number of cases the fact that the empirical investigation has been conducted as if assumptions were true, while in fact they are not, will not seriously bias the estimates that Solow obtains. But in a number of cases they may introduce serious bias and it would be useful, in a more searching critique, to examine them one by one, to note first the effect that various degrees of inaccuracy of the assumptions would imply for estimates of critical parameters and second the extent to which such inaccuracies exist.

One should, in any event, distinguish carefully between assumption and empirical finding. For example, constant elasticity of substitution, as long as such elasticity is of the usual sign, implies that the marginal product of capital will never be negative (in fact, it will be positive), regardless of the capital-labor ratio. This may not be unreasonable in regard to the *gross* magnitude, value added, which is the dependent variable in much of Solow's current analysis. But it would be pure assumption to argue, as Solow has done elsewhere,[1] that variable factor proportions will then imply that any saving ratio is consistent with any rate of growth *and* positive net returns to capital. Estimating an elasticity assumed to be constant tells us little about whether the elasticity is in fact constant, particularly for ranges of factor proportions not included in the estimation.

Similarly, an estimate of the rate of productivity increase associated with technological advance assumed to be dependent only upon the application of new private capital to a homogeneous labor supply tells us nothing about the productivity that may be accruing or might accrue from education, training and redistribution of a heterogeneous and changing labor supply.

However, let us focus on just a few of the assumptions that may prove relevant to the completed estimates of this admittedly unfinished inquiry. For I shall now concentrate on the estimates of the elasticity of substitution between capital and labor which Solow offers on the basis of cross-sections of regional census data with regard to value added, payrolls, and labor force for each of the manufacturing industries which he considers. He notes that these estimates prove larger than estimates secured on the basis of international, "three-digit" cross sections reported upon in the paper by Arrow, Chenery, Minhas and Solow. I shall argue that the current estimates are in fact biased upward because of basic misspecifications and lack of identification of the underlying relations being measured. I shall argue in particular, that the inaccuracy of the assumptions of perfect competition and of equilibrium, the abstraction from the problems of risk and the insufficiency of arguments in the production function, all contribute to

[1] "A Contribution to the Theory of Economic Growth," *Quarterly Journal of Economics,* February 1956, pp. 65–94.

overestimates of the constant elasticity of substitution which Solow assumes.

The basis for the empirical analysis which Solow has completed, and to which much of the rest of this comment will be addressed, is the relation

$$\log \frac{Q}{L} = a \log W + b \tag{7'}$$

where, dealing with 1956 data for each of nineteen "two-digit" manufacturing industries, Q/L is the ratio of value added to the number of employees, and W is the ratio of payrolls to the number of employees for each of the nine census regions in the United States. Solow points out that, as demonstrated in the Arrow-Chenery-Minhas-Solow paper, on the basis of the assumptions of profit maximization in competitive labor and product markets, which implies that the product wage is equal to the marginal product of labor, the estimate of a is an estimate of the elasticity of substitution, σ. Solow's procedure then implies further that the various values of the wage in the various regions, more exactly, the ratios of payrolls to the number of employees, generate various factor ratios which in turn imply various ratios of value added to the number of employees, Q/L. This means that for each industry, the payroll-to-employee ratio determines the capital-employee ratio and consequently Q/L.

First, let us accept Solow's assumption that value added is related to the wage rate on the basis of a production function involving "capital" owned within the industry and "labor." But let us now add as arguments of this function a number of other capital and labor "factors," F_i, which might include capital *external* to the industry (railroads, highways, schools and general public services) and specially skilled workers (including managers and entrepreneurs). In a Solow-type CES equation, this would imply

$$Q = \gamma \left(\sum_{i=1}^{n} \delta_i F_i^{-\rho} \right)^{-\frac{1}{\rho}} \tag{E.1}$$

where $i = 1$ and $i = 2$ would relate to Solow's "capital" and "labor" respectively and $\Sigma \delta_i = 1$ (as in Solow's two-argument function). It will be noted that in Solow's CES function, as well as in many other "reasonable" production functions, this will mean that the more of any factor the higher will be the marginal product of other factors. (In mathematical terms, the cross partial derivatives will be positive.) But then regions with high endowments of factors not specified by Solow (F_i, for $i > 2$), would tend to have high marginal products of both labor and capital within the industry and hence high values of both wage and nonwage income.

If the cross partial derivatives of the function in logarithmic form were equal, that is, if increased endowments of these other factors increased the marginal products of Solow's "labor" and "capital" in proportion, the estimate of a, which Solow takes to be the elasticity of substitution, would be biased toward unity. (The estimate of a would tend to be greater or less than unity to the extent that the cross partials of other factors with "capital" were greater or less than the cross partials of other factors with labor.) This would occur even if, as seems more likely to me, the true elasticity of substitution between capital and labor is much closer to zero than Solow likes to think.

But now let us introduce profit maximization to a world with changing demand and entrepreneurs acting on the basis of probability distributions of expected returns. In such a world, with neither factor markets nor product markets perfectly competitive, decision makers adjust their payrolls partly to current demand and partly to the expectation of permanent demand. Salaried employees are not fired and do not even suffer reductions in pay when demand and output fall. Borrowing obviously from another field of economic inquiry, we may suggest that output and payrolls may both be viewed usefully as related separately to permanent and transitory components of a fluctuating demand. However, payrolls will be relatively more sluggish than output in reacting to changes in demand. Thus, letting w = the logarithm of the ratio of payrolls to the number of employees, and letting v = the logarithm of the ratio of value added to the number of employees, we conjecture that the true relations underlying Solow's observations may better be written:

$$w_P = k_P v_P + c_P, \qquad (7.1)$$

$$w_T = k_T v_T + c_T, \text{ where } 0 < k_T < k_P \leq 1 \qquad (7.2)$$

and, with $w = w_P + w_T$ and $v = v_P + v_T$, the "reduced form,"

$$w = kv + c. \qquad (7.3)$$

This is to say that long run changes in output per man, whether based on productivity or increases in the value of output related to changing demand (or changing degrees of monopoly), may (if $k_P = 1$) reflect themselves in proportionate changes in wage and salary payments per employee but short-run fluctuations in output result clearly in less than proportionate changes in payrolls. Thus, if one were to ignore the distinction between v_P and v_T but instead estimate k in (7.3), the estimate obtained would be less than unity. The greater the discrepancy between k_P and k_T and the greater the value of the ratio

$$T = \frac{\text{variance of } v_T}{\text{variance of } v},$$

the smaller the estimate would be.

Now it may be noted that the k we would be estimating would be the reciprocal of Solow's a, which is his estimate of the elasticity of substitution. Hence the lower the value of k the greater the value of Solow's estimate of the elasticity of substitution.

To the extent that the regional observations used by Solow in making his estimates include a transitory variance of demand and hence of output, he will overestimate—even if other necessary assumptions are met—the elasticity of substitution. This leads us immediately to two conclusions: 1. Since in all cases some of the variance of output must be transitory in nature, there will be a general overestimate by Solow of elasticities of substitution. 2. The extent of this overestimate can be predicted on the basis of estimates of the proportion of variance of output which is accounted for by its transitory component. In fact, the relation between the "true" elasticity of substitution, which Solow would obtain if there were no transitory variance, and the estimate which he actually obtains as a result of transitory variance and other disturbances (as we shall see), may be written as

$$\frac{\sigma}{\sigma_b} = 1 - T\left(1 - \frac{k_T}{k_P}\right), \tag{E.2}$$

where σ = the "true" elasticity of substitution

σ_b = Solow's biased estimate of the elasticity of substitution

T = the proportion of the variance of the logarithm of output accounted for by its transitory component

and k_T and k_P = the coefficients of transitory and permanent output as indicated in (7.2) and (7.1).

The underlying reasoning is that in response to temporary declines in demand there are substantial declines in v and lesser drops in w. Thus one will find both transitory components, of v and w, negative. The observed or measured w below the mean of w will tend to be observations with w_T negative but relatively close to zero, and v_T also negative but of relatively great absolute value. One can hence infer that on the average, for every observation (v_i, w_i), there is a vector (v_{P_i}, w_{P_i}) such that, since the means of v_T and w_T can be assumed to be zero, for v_i and w_i less than their means, $v_{P_i} > v_i$ and $w_{P_i} > w_i$. The reverse would be true for v_i and w_i greater than their means but what is crucial is that the regression coefficient of v_T on w_T would be greater than the regression coefficient of v_P on w_P. Perhaps all this can be seen best by writing the regression equations in the direction in which Solow estimated them. He in fact estimated a in

$$v = aw + b. \tag{7}$$

I say that underlying this relation is the equilibrium or "permanent" relation in which Solow is really interested,

$$v_P = a_P w_P + b_P, \tag{E.3}$$

and the transitory relation (or rather, relation involving the transitory components),

$$v_T = a_T w_T + b_T, \tag{E.4}$$

where $a_T > a_P$. This last inequality, for which one can offer good justification both in terms of theory and data, will imply that $a > a_P$, with the ratio of a to a_P also depending, of course, on the ratios of variances of transitory and permanent components.[2]

[2] A rigorous treatment of the relation between coefficients of measured variables and coefficients involving their permanent components may be found in the writer's "The Permanent Income Hypothesis: Comment," *The American Economic Review,* December, 1958, especially, pp. 985–990. It is to be noted, however, that the argument there is focussed on the special case highlighted by Milton Friedman in which the transitory and permanent components are uncorrelated for each variable and the regression coefficient involving the transitory components is equal to zero. It should be noted that in the present case transitory and permanent components of each variable are judged to be positively correlated (both being influenced in the same direction, but in different magnitudes, by changes in demand) and the regression coefficient of the transitory components, taking the relation in the same direction as did Solow, is considered not only nonzero but larger in magnitude than the regression coefficient for the permanent components. Our argument may be put diagrammatically, to illustrate

Solow observes that the elasticities he estimates in the current investigation are higher than those obtained in earlier empirical work with the same model but with three-digit industries. This he explains by the greater scope for indirect substitution in two-digit industries. Our current argument, however, suggests a quite different explanation. Demand conditions are likely to vary less between regions, at a given time, than between products. If the demand for radios is down in one region it is likely to be down in all. But the demand for radios may be down while the demand for turbine-generators, also in the two-digit category (Number 36), may be up. Turbine-generators may be made largely in Schenectady and radios elsewhere so that the interproduct difference will show up as a regional variation as the product classes become larger.

While we have focussed on a "permanent output" hypothesis as an explanation of the discrepancy between Solow's current and other estimates of the elasticity of substitution, our argument can be generalized to include all factors that result in interregional differences in value added which are less than proportionately related to payrolls. We should single out, in particular, differences in degrees of monopoly in product markets. We may concede that there is some tendency for monopoly profits to be passed on to employees but casual empiricism would suggest that the pass-on is less than proportionate. Again it may be argued that product markets in manufactured goods are likely to be national in character and that differences in degrees of monopoly would not show up in a cross section of analyses of identical products, but will

---

the shift from the "permanent" relation Solow requires to the relation, including transitory and permanent components, which he actually measures in the following figure:

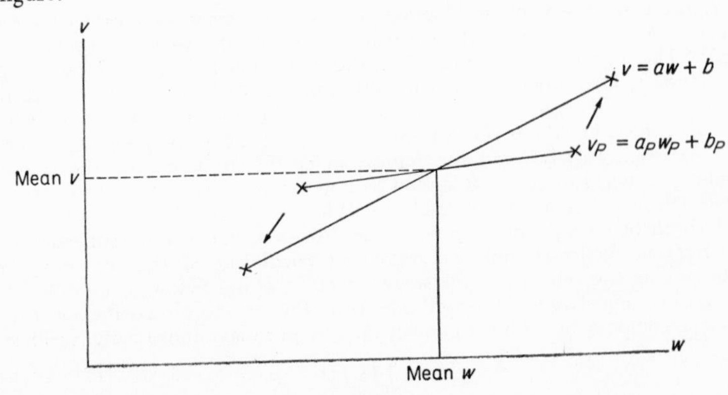

show up as a result of interregional differences in product mix in broader product classes. It may be added that product markets are not, of course, fully national in character, so that differences in degrees of monopoly may manifest themselves even in cross sections of more narrowly defined product groups, thus contributing to overestimates of elasticity of substitution by Solow in such cases as well. However, the overestimate is likely to be larger the larger the product classes, and hence the larger the interregional variation in degrees of monopoly related to interregional differences in product mix.

The general point of this critique should by now be clear. As in virtually all serious econometric inquiry, the crucial problems are those of specification and identification. One may concede that there is an underlying relation tying the share of capital to a production function and capital-labor ratios as posited by Solow. But there is clearly also a set of underlying relations involving the value of current product and current payrolls which reflect degrees of monopoly, distinctions between transitory and permanent elements, exposure to risk, and other factors. My own hypothesis is that Solow has measured an unspecified linear combination of these various relations. He has no more right to say that his estimates apply to the elasticity of substitution than his less sophisticated precursors, observing prices and quantities of commodities sold or rates of interest and saving, could properly use them to estimate elasticities of demand or interest elasticities of consumption or saving. I personally would surmise that the elasticity of substitution between capital and labor is both very low (nearer to zero than one) and variable, getting lower as the capital-labor ratio is pushed to the point where the marginal *net* product of capital would become zero and then negative. I base this hypothesis on the fact that a production function with these characteristics would be consistent with the chronic and related problems involving growth and stability which we observe and I consider it important to explain. But this leads back to an older controversy that I have enjoyed with Solow. I am happy to confine the present argument to issues closer at hand.

NESTOR E. TERLECKYJ, Office of Management and Organization, Bureau of the Budget

Professor Solow suggests a very interesting new analysis ingeniously and impressively formulated, and demonstrates its application to a body of data. The empirical results are tentative, as the data apparently are not sufficient to bear the full burden of analysis.

Solow proposes a new way to estimate the production functions of industries and their shifts through time. The procedure is designed to yield estimates of elasticities of substitution of technological progress and of the rates of return. These results are obtained through a combination of cross-section and time series analyses.

The production function used by Solow is homogeneous of degree one in labor and capital, and the time shift representing technical progress appears in the present exposition exclusively as the trend in productivity of new capital goods produced in successive periods. Aside from its conceptual restrictiveness, this assumption seems to place a very heavy burden on the capital investment data in empirical application.

The elasticity of substitution for any given industry is assumed to be constant over the whole function and through time, but can have any value. This appears preferable to fixing its value in advance, particularly since, as Solow suggests, the actual estimate may in a large measure depend on the level of industry definitions used. Estimation of the elasticity of substitution rests on the assumption of competitive equilibrium.

In Solow's model, productivity of capital produced in any given year remains constant throughout the life of the asset. As time goes on, individual items of old capital are retired from use. Thus, Solow's concept of capital consumption involves scrapping of assets operating at their original efficiency, rather than deterioration of capital goods through use and the passage of time. I have no quarrel with this formulation on pragmatic grounds, particularly as I think it permits us to account for obsolescence where it is important. Nevertheless, it abstracts from quality deterioration on the one hand, and on the other, from improvements involving relatively minor investment, as well as from "external economies" generated by growth of experience over time. These abstractions, to be sure, may be more of a limitation on applications at the microeconomic level than for analyses cast within a broader framework.

Capital stock, then, at any point in time consists of items of different vintages and each vintage has its own constant productivity. Solow assumes a homogeneous labor force which is assigned to capital of different vintages so as to equalize the marginal productivity of labor. Since the model requires that the unit productivity of capital of any given vintage remain constant at all times, it implies flexibility in the capital-labor ratios for all the various vintages of capital.

Through a series of substitutions in the formulas, Solow expresses output as a function of the wage rate and the labor input alone, netting out capital. This allows him later on to estimate the elasticity of substitution from regional cross-section data when the regional age composition of capital is unknown. The estimate of the elasticity of substitution, after a simple transformation, later serves in the time series analysis to estimate the remaining parameters of the production function. In the present paper Solow assumes elasticities of substitution to be constant through time. It may be pointed out, however, that the technique proposed by Solow may be used to generate a whole time series of the estimates of the elasticities of substitution. Such estimates would provide a test for the important assumption of no time trends in elasticities of substitution. Estimates of other constants in the production function, notably the rate of technical change, depend on the value of elasticity of substitution.

In the present application of his analysis, Solow makes what appears to be a very strong assumption that the average life of capital is constant across industries and over time. This assumption, however, is not inherent in his approach. The interindustry variation in the life of capital may be taken into account with the help of outside data, and the time variation may be allowed for by building a time trend in the life of capital into the model (or by limiting the time period of analysis to subperiods of relatively constant average lives of durable assets).

The Solow model includes an exponential growth of productivity, which here is the same as the rate of growth in productivity of new capital. This, I believe, defines the length of the period over which Solow's approach may be expected to give most useful results. Obviously, the period cannot be too short, otherwise the cycle and other short-run changes would introduce too many disturbances into estimates of productivity trends. On the other hand, the period of analysis cannot be too long, because then the long waves and secular accelerations in productivity growth which came to light in John Kendrick's work might be expected to vitiate the exponential fit.

The empirical results, on the whole, are tentative, and they are offered in the spirit of a tentative report on a pilot project.[1] The obvious problem seems to be the narrowness of the information base. At most only nine observations are available for the cross-section analysis, and again the period employed in the time series estimates covers only a decade. Until the analysis is tested on a stronger body of data, it seems impossible to evaluate the firmness of the results it yields. Further testing would also indicate whether any assumptions need to be modified and how.

The analysis formulated by Professor Solow certainly deserves careful study. Although it has many facets, each interesting in its own right, I find its greatest appeal in the promise it holds—in conjunction with complementary research—to indicate answers to some very important questions about productivity growth.

As the next step, it appears to be worthwhile to test Solow's model on a large body of data, together with other models, such as production functions which allow imputation of productivity gains to labor input and functions containing a "disembodied" productivity trend. The various estimates of productivity change would then be usefully compared with each other and with independent estimates, such as those yielded by Kendrick's study. Such an exercise obviously would involve a major research project but the mechanics of computation can probably be handled easily by electronic computers.

JOHN W. KENDRICK, George Washington University

My admiration was aroused by Professor Solow's ingenious attempt to estimate elasticities of substitution indirectly from regional data. Since I happen to have made estimates of both real inputs and prices of the two major factor groupings, labor and property, I thought it would be interesting directly to compute elasticities of substitution for the same manufacturing industry

[1] I would like to raise one point concerning the interpretation of time series results. It is suggested in the paper that the very sharp and sudden drop in productivity from 1956 to 1957 which appears on the scatter diagrams is to be attributed to the 1957–58 recession. One would expect the 1953–54 recession to produce a similar result since it was not too different from the 1957–58 decline either in depth or seasonal timing, and investment held up quite well. The scatter diagrams, however, do not indicate any effect of the earlier recession. This seems to argue strongly against a purely cyclical explanation of the break in productivity trends. Also, seemingly inconsistent with the cyclical explanation is the fact that in all cases productivity in the trough year 1958 appears higher than in 1957, while one would be inclined to expect the opposite on the basis of an idle-capacity explanation.

TABLE 1
MANUFACTURING GROUPS: FACTOR INPUTS AND PRICES, 1957 AND ELASTICITY OF SUBSTITUTION, 1953–57

	INDEX NUMBERS, 1957 (1953 = 100)				
	Factor Input		*Factor Price*		Elasticity of
	Labor	Capital	Labor	Capital	Substitution[a]
Total Manufacturing	95.1	112.2	123.5	94.6	.62
Beverages	78.0	83.9	121.7	103.5	.45
Food	100.4	105.0	121.0	101.1	.25
Tobacco	86.4	104.2	134.8	109.1	.88
Textile mill products	83.7	93.3	114.0	94.8	.59
Apparel	95.0	98.8	117.4	75.4	.09
Lumber and wood products	85.0	113.2	120.9	57.6	.40
Furniture and fixtures	99.6	116.1	118.2	108.9	1.86
Paper, pulp, and products	103.0	133.0	124.4	77.9	.55
Printing and publishing	106.2	108.0	121.1	110.6	.18
Chemicals	104.9	116.0	125.5	107.5	.65
Petroleum and coal products	94.5	125.6	129.0	72.6	.51
Rubber products	98.9	113.7	119.5	79.8	.35
Leather and products	95.3	104.0	116.8	96.9	.47
Stone, clay, and glass	100.5	132.9	124.0	90.4	.89
Primary metals	93.9	117.0	129.8	98.9	.81
Fabricated metal products	88.5	117.1	123.7	86.1	.78
Machinery (exc. electrical)	96.5	113.3	121.9	88.5	.50
Electrical machinery	100.1	94.8	119.2	127.6	.80
Transportation equipment	96.6	116.0	120.6	90.9	.65
Miscellaneous, incl. instruments	97.6	95.9	124.8	110.3	−.14

SOURCE: Estimates by John W. Kendrick, assisted by Maude R. Pech, based on concepts, sources, and methods described in *Productivity Trends in the United States*, Princeton University Press for NBER, 1961.
[a] Ratio computed by arc formula.

groups used by Solow (see Table 1). These estimates are based on relative prices and quantities for the years 1953 and 1957, which span the year to which Solow's estimates relate.

The elasticities shown in my table must, therefore, be interpreted in a dynamic context. To be taken as indicative of elasticities under static, equilibrium conditions, not only must all the assumptions underlying Solow's model be made, but also the assumption that the shapes of the relevant production functions did not change between the two periods. From the dynamic viewpoint, the "historical" elasticities of substitution are useful summary descriptions of what happened over a given period to the interrelation of changes in relative prices and in relative input quantities. This interrelationship is, of course, the chief element in explaining changes in income shares.

Now for a word about the concepts underlying the several variables used in the elasticity calculations. Labor input is man-hours worked in each of the twenty major groups, but in the manufacturing segment as a whole it is man-hours worked in each group weighted by base-period average hourly labor compensation in each. Property input is assumed to move proportionately to real capital stocks (plant, equipment, and working capital) in each group, and in the manufacturing segment the real stock in each group is weighted by base-period rates of return. This is the reason that cycle-peak years were chosen for the comparisons.

The price of each factor class is calculated as the factor cost of each (compensation of labor and of capital) divided by the input of each. Thus, the "price" of labor is its average hourly compensation in each industry group—an average influenced by inter-industry shifts within each group, but not among groups as far as the segment is concerned. The average hourly earnings of employees is imputed to the relatively small number of proprietors and unpaid family workers in the various groups. The price of capital in each group is, in effect, the product of the average price of the underlying capital goods and the average rate of return (capital compensation—interest, rent, and profit before tax—divided by the value of the capital assets in current replacement values). The rates of return are affected by interindustry shifts within each of the manufacturing groups, but not among the groups in the segment as a whole. These concepts are discussed in more detail in my National Bureau study, *Productivity Trends in the United States* (1961).

The elasticities of substitution computed from my estimates differ widely from those obtained in Solow's regression equations, and the former appear to be more plausible. All but one are less than unity, and all but one indicate a negative relation between the rates of change in relative prices and in relative quantities. I believe that further progress in the estimation of elasticities of substitution and analysis of changing factor shares lies along the road of refining concepts and measures of capital inputs and their prices.

Short-Run Movements of Income Shares

CHARLES L. SCHULTZE

UNIVERSITY OF MARYLAND

Introduction

Recent neo-Keynesian literature on the business cycle assigns a major role to shifts in the functional distribution of income. Kaldor,[1] Duesenberry,[2] Hickman,[3] and others have pointed out that the systematic shift between profits and other forms of income during cyclical swings in income, implies a systematic variation in the over-all saving rate. The propensity to save out of profits—particularly corporate profits—is substantially higher than the propensity to save out of other forms of income. As a consequence, the over-all marginal propensity to save out of total gross national income is much higher during cyclical fluctuations than the average long-run saving rate. Viewed another way, the cyclical change in disposable personal income is less than proportional to the cyclical change in total gross income, not only because of the behavior of transfer payments and government tax receipts, but also because of the shift in income distribution between retained profits and earned personal income. In addition, therefore, to the automatic stabilizing effect of fluctuations in the personal saving rate, which characterizes the "ratchet" or "permanent income" hypotheses, there exists the very significant stabilizing impact of systematic cyclical shifts in income distribution.

Because of the differential savings rates out of profits and other forms of income, the endogenous mechanism by which initial shocks are propagated throughout the economy cannot be articulated without specifying the functional relationship between changes in income and the distribution of those changes among the

NOTE: The preparation of this paper was aided by a grant from the Graduate School, Indiana University. The author's research assistant, Robert Schock, contributed importantly to all stages of the project. Stuart Erholm assisted in the statistical compilation.

[1] Nicholas Kaldor, "Economic Growth and the Problem of Inflation," *Economica*, August 1959, see especially pp. 214–220.

[2] James Duesenberry, *Business Cycles and Economic Growth*, New York, 1958, Chapter 3. See also James Duesenberry, Otto Eckstein, and Gary Gromm, "A Simulation of the United States Economy in Recession," *Econometrica*, October 1960, pp. 781–786.

[3] Bert Hickman, *Growth and Stability of the Postwar Economy*, Washington, D.C., 1960, pp. 221–232.

various factors of production. This paper attempts to provide a set of functional relationships which illuminate the factors affecting cyclical shifts in income distribution. Its orientation, however, is not mainly towards an explanation of short-run shifts in the distribution of income for its own sake. Rather it concentrates on those aspects of the income distribution process which themselves affect the level and rate of change in income and output. As a consequence major attention is devoted to an explanation of the cyclical behavior of corporate profits, although some analysis has also been made of changes in other income shares.

In Table 1, changes in nonfarm private gross national income, gross corporate profits, gross retained profits, and disposable income from cyclical peaks to cyclical troughs have been tabulated for the downturns of the past forty years. In every case, the ratio of the decline in gross corporate profits[4] to the decline in gross national income is substantially greater than the average long-run ratio of profits to income. And in turn, since dividend payments are a lagged function of past profits and dividends, the ratio of the decline in gross retained profits to the decline in total gross profits tends to be very high. Reflecting these relationships, the ratio of the decline in disposable income to the decline in gross national income is significantly smaller, during all but the major depressions, than the long-run average ratio of disposable to total income. It may be noted that disposable income tended to rise, relative to total income, during the downturns of 1924 and 1927, and in these instances the relation of disposable income to GNP could not be explained by automatic changes in taxes and transfer payments.

There is one further feature of Table 1 which warrants comment. The fall in gross profits relative to the fall in GNP in 1929–33 was much smaller than the relative decline in profits during milder recessions. In particular, the proportion of income declines absorbed by gross corporate profits, and more noticeably by retained profits, in the postwar recessions was a good bit larger than in 1929–33 and, in the case of retained profits, somewhat larger than in 1937–38. (Without quarterly data for the 1920's it is difficult to make relevant comparisons for the 1924 and 1927

[4] We use gross profits (i.e., profits before taxes *plus* depreciation) as the relevant variable, not only because it is gross margins which are relevant for a determination of disposable income, but also because, at least in the short run, changes in depreciation and taxes are assumed to be borne by the corporations and not shifted; i.e., the behavior of *gross* profit margins is determined by economic factors, while net profits may be viewed as an accounting residual.

TABLE 1
CHANGE IN NONFARM PRIVATE GNP AND SELECTED COMPONENTS, RECESSION PERIODS
(billions of 1954 dollars)

Period	GNP	Gross Corporate Profits[a]	Gross Retained Corporate Profits[a]	Disposable Personal Income	Consumption Expenditures
1923–24	−.2	−1.3	−1.2	+1.7	+4.8
1926–27	−.3	−2.5	−3.2	+2.5	+3.1
1929–33	−55.2	−20.4	−14.2	−41.4	−24.6
1937–38	−8.4	−4.0	−.7	−8.5	−2.2
4Q 1948-2Q 1949	−7.0	−4.3	−4.0	−1.4	+3.0
2Q 1953-1Q 1954	−12.8	−6.7	−6.4	−1.0	−2.8
3Q 1957-1Q 1958	−19.4	−8.7	−8.5	−4.3	−4.0

NOTE: Except for consumption outlays, the data are deflated by the GNP implicit deflator. Consumption outlays for 1922–28 are the constant dollar consumption figures given in Simon Kuznets, *Capital in the American Economy: its Formation and Financing*, Princeton for NBER, 1961, Appendix Table R-2, cols. 1, 4, and 7. The 1929–59 consumption data are Department of Commerce estimates. Other data are described in Appendix 3 to this paper.

[a] Profits are before taxes and are adjusted for inventory valuation.

recessions.)[5] Does this reflect a structural change in the cyclical shift in income distribution, or does it reflect the fact that the absorption of income declines by gross profits tends to become smaller the further income declines? If the former is true, then the structural change has strengthened the automatic stabilizers in the economy; but if the latter is the case, then we may conclude that the stabilizing influence of cyclical shifts in income distribution tends to weaken as the economy moves further into recession. More precisely, insofar as there is a shift away from profits towards personal income during recessions, the value of the multiplier is reduced and the secondary effects of an initial shock to the economy are damped. But insofar as the rate of shift away from profits becomes smaller the further income declines, the "damping factor" begins to lose its strength, and the secondary consumption effects of further declines in income become larger. The importance of this question for cyclical analysis is obvious. Hence, a large part of the analysis in this paper has been devoted to determining whether the marginal ratio of profit change to GNP change is itself a function of the rate or extent of the GNP change.

One word of caution. The analysis is confined to cyclical shifts in income distribution. We have left to Messrs. Solow and

[5] Harold Barger's quarterly income data, which are available for the 1920's and 1930's, do not include the corporate product data required for the regression equations of this paper.

Lebergott the task of disentangling the factors affecting secular shifts in factor shares. The problem they deal with, we have hidden away in a drawer labeled "time trend," in the belief that the cyclical variance in factor shares can be legitimately analyzed without a full-blown treatment of the secular variance.

All of the analysis is carried out in terms of private nonfarm income and product. In minor recessions the behavior of farm income and output is largely autonomous with respect to the behavior of total GNP. In part, this stems from the fact that "autonomous" variations in supply, due to weather, combined with the inelasticity of demand for most farm products, tend to produce changes in farm income which have little relation to the over-all behavior of the economy. The exclusion of the farm sector from the analysis makes the results less general. Its inclusion, however, would have required a fairly elaborate agricultural model, the construction of which is beyond the competence and outside the inclinations of the author.

The Share of Gross Corporate Profits

The share of gross corporate retained profits (corporate profits before taxes + IVA + depreciation − dividends) in gross national income, is, as we have noted, a major determinant of the ratio of disposable income to gross national income. If, when income declines cyclically, the share of gross retained profits falls, this implies that the marginal ratio of gross retained profits to GNP is larger than the average ratio, and conversely that the marginal ratio of the change in disposable income, other things being equal, is smaller than its average ratio; hence, disposable income fluctuates less than proportionately with changes in total income.

The share of retained profits in GNP is the product of three independent ratios:

$$\frac{\pi_r}{Y} = \frac{\pi_r}{\pi} \cdot \frac{\pi}{Y_c} \cdot \frac{Y_c}{Y} \tag{1}$$

where

π_r = gross retained profits
π = gross profits
Y_c = gross product originating in corporations
Y = nonfarm private gross national product (= gross national income).

Similarly:

$$\frac{\Delta\pi_r}{\Delta Y} = \frac{\Delta\pi_r}{\Delta\pi} \cdot \frac{\Delta\pi}{\Delta Y_c} \cdot \frac{\Delta Y_c}{\Delta Y} \tag{2}$$

The first basic relationship—retained profits relative to total profits—has been carefully investigated by Lintner,[6] and no attempt is made in this paper to extend his findings (although we do comment on their significance). Our major concern is with the other two relationships.

Insofar as the share of corporate product in total product is systematically related to the cyclical behavior of the economy, the share of gross profits in GNP cannot be explained without explaining the relations between corporate product and total product. We turn first, however, to gross profits as a share of corporate gross product.

GROSS PROFITS AS A SHARE OF CORPORATE GROSS PRODUCT

The initial hypothesis we have tested is that the share of gross profits in corporate gross product is composed of two elements:

1. A secular component, which may change slowly over time in response to such factors as changes in factor scarcities, changing degree of monopoly, non-neutral innovations, etc.
2. A cyclical component, which responds to deviations in corporate product from its full capacity "norm." This component has zero value when corporate product is at its normal full capacity level.

Apart from long-run secular changes, the gross profit share will thus vary about a normal ratio as gross corporate product varies about its "normal" full capacity level. This is a "ratchet" theory of profits, with the modification that the prior peak ratchet element tends to move up over time.[7] Thus the share of gross profits will decline, even if corporate product is stable, so long as capacity is growing.

[6] John Lintner, "Distribution of Incomes of Corporations Among Dividends, Retained Earnings, and Taxes," *American Economic Review*, May 1956.

[7] Edwin Kuh, on whose imaginative study ("Profits, Profit Markups, and Productivity; an Examination of Corporate Behavior Since 1947," in U.S. Congress, Joint Economic Committee, *Employment, Growth and Price Levels*, Part 15, 1960) this paper heavily leans, uses a similar approach to explain the behavior of prices and productivity in the corporate sector.

Other authors have used a straight ratchet theory to explain corporate profit behavior.[8] Theoretically this is less satisfying than the excess capacity theory which we advance here. Theory would lead one to choose an excess capacity hypothesis on two grounds. First, as output falls relative to capacity, unit overhead costs rise, with resulting lower profit margin. Since we have included depreciation in the gross margin figure, the relevant overhead costs here exclude depreciation. This rise in overhead costs per unit, especially salaries and interest, and the consequent downward pressure on the profit share, should occur even if output does not decline absolutely, so long as capacity rises relative to output. Secondly, a rise in excess capacity should put pressure on profit margins via its influence on *ex ante* markups. Under orthodox price theory this is quite obvious. But even if one believes that some sort of full cost pricing practice characterizes American industry, it is clear that the markups are not completely immune to the pressure of excess supply. Finally, the excess capacity hypothesis can help explain the phenomenon which often occurs during the later stages of a boom, i.e., profit margins decline during a period in which the absolute level of income is still rising. A pure ratchet theory could not account for this fact.

The term "excess capacity" has so far been used in a very loose sense. Theoretical considerations would indicate that what we need is not the deviation of output from full capacity, where full capacity is defined in terms of the maximum output capable of being produced by existing facilities. Rather we should define capacity in terms of some "optimum" operating rate—presumably the point of minimum average unit costs.

When fitting a regression equation of gross profits against deviations in output from capacity, the actual point of utilization which we choose as "normal" does not matter in terms of goodness of fit. But, it does affect the constant in the equation, i.e., if we measure deviations of actual output from a physical maximum capacity, all deviations will be negative; if we choose some "optimum" level of utilization as our base line, both positive and negative deviations will occur. The correlation coefficient and the *b* coefficients will not be affected, but the constant in the equation will; i.e., the con-

[8] Franco Modigliani, "Fluctuations in the Saving-Income Ratio; a Problem in Economic Forecasting," *Studies in Income and Wealth 11*, New York, NBER, 1949, pp. 403–407.

stant a in

$$\frac{\pi}{Y_c} = a + b\frac{\Delta Y_{ck}}{Y_c}; \ \Delta Y_{ck} = \text{deviation (in dollars) of corporate product from capacity} \quad (3)$$

will be higher, the higher the level of utilization from which we choose to measure our deviations.[9] If we are to interpret a as the normal share of profits around which cyclical fluctuations take place, it is desirable to allow, in the estimating procedure, for positive as well as negative deviations.

The actual estimation of a capacity series for corporate gross product involves, of course, much cruder statistical techniques than is implied in the foregoing discussion. One possible method is to use a corporate capital stock figure as a measure of changes in capacity. During the past four decades, however, capital-output ratios have been declining. A capital stock figure would, therefore, underestimate the growth in capacity. What we have done, in lieu of actual capacity figures, is to define "normal capacity output" in terms of a trend of actual output fitted to relatively full employment years only. This allows for positive as well as negative deviations between actual output and normal capacity output. Deviations of actual from capacity output were computed annually for the years 1922–41 and quarterly for the postwar years, 1948–59. Gross corporate product was estimated by adding corporate depreciation to national income originating in corporations. The rate of growth in normal full capacity output was determined in two parts for 1922–41. One trend was fitted to 1922–29. Somewhere in the early thirties, however, there was clearly a decline in the rate of growth in capacity. Hence, a separate capacity growth line for the thirties was estimated simply by taking the growth rate in real corporate product between 1929 and the average of 1940–41. For any single year normal capacity output was defined to be the prior peak output plus the normal capacity growth rate. Similar techniques were employed in the postwar period. As in the case of the prewar period, two trend rates of growth were used; one from 1948 to 1953, and a second, lower rate, from 1953 to 1959.[10] For prewar and postwar periods,

[9] In his comment, which follows, Bert Hickman correctly points out that the regression coefficients *are* affected by the choice of the "optimum" of capacity utilization. However, as Hickman demonstrates, the slope and elasticity values are not affected by this choice.

[10] Actually, the latter period was one of both lower capacity growth rates and

separately, the following equation was fitted:

$$\frac{\pi}{Y_c} = a + b\frac{\Delta Y_{ck}}{Y_c} + c(t) \tag{3a}$$

In the postwar period the equation was fitted for the following subperiods:

1. 1948–1959.
2. 1948–1950 cycle (3Q 1948 to 3Q 1950).
3. 1953–1955 cycle (1Q 1953 to 4Q 1955).
4. 1957–1959 cycle (1Q 1957 to 2Q 1959).
5. all cycles taken together (i.e., "plateau" periods were omitted).

The time variable in 1922–41 was set to zero in 1929. In the postwar subperiods the time variable was set to zero at the beginning of each subperiod. This time variable, of course, has to carry all of the intricate factors which determine changes in the normal (i.e., full capacity) profit share.

The results are given in Table 2. The most striking feature of the regressions is the narrow range of the coefficients for the output deviation variable. Given the volatility of profits, it is quite striking that the percentage change in the profit share per 1 per cent deviation of output from normal was almost the same in 1922–41 as in 1948–59. Considering the fact that we are fitting ratios, and that the postwar data are quarterly, the correlation coefficients are quite high. (We could, of course, have obtained much better fits by using absolute data.)

As one would expect, the postwar fit is noticeably improved when the various recessions are taken separately. The better fit of 1922–41 is also to be expected. Because of the great depression, the variance in actual relative to capacity output was so large as to swamp those factors affecting the behavior of profits which are not themselves systematically related to the business cycle. In the postwar period the smaller variance of output deviations tends to increase the importance of such factors, leading to a poorer fit. As we shall note below, the postwar fit is improved when we introduce some of these factors explicitly into the equations. The coefficient of $\Delta Y_{ck}/Y_c$ estimated for the whole period is lower than the coefficient estimated for recessions and recoveries alone. In

lower capacity utilization. Hence a straight line was extended from 1953 to the second quarter of 1959, and the figure for the latter was raised by one per cent to allow for the less than full employment conditions which prevailed.

general this reflects the fact that during plateau periods the influence of output deviations is smaller than during periods in which output is changing sharply.

The equations in Table 2 can be transformed into the elasticity and the slope of changes in profits relative to deviations from normal in corporate product; i.e., the proportion of changes in

TABLE 2
REGRESSION EQUATIONS OF GROSS PROFIT AGAINST DEVIATIONS OF OUTPUT FROM CAPACITY[a]

Period	a	b	c	R
1922–1941	27.9	.195 (.001)	.151 (.052)	.979
1948–59	28.9	.187 (.039)	−.030 (.013)	.735
1948–50 cycle	28.9	.203 (.037)	.191 (.059)	.944
1953–55 cycle	26.9	.237 (.044)	.213 (.058)	.910
1957–59 cycle	27.2	.212 (.033)	.286 (.057)	.938
cycles only	28.7	.200 (.042)	−.021 (.015)	.759

[a] The equation fitted was $\frac{\pi}{Y_c} = a + b\frac{\Delta Y_{ck}}{Y_c} + c(t)$.

$\frac{\pi}{Y_c}$ and $\frac{\Delta Y_{ck}}{Y_c}$ are expressed in percentage terms.

gross corporate income from normal that are absorbed by changes in gross corporate profits. From equation (3), we derive:

$$\frac{\Delta\pi}{\Delta Y_{ck}} = a + b \tag{4}$$

and

$$\mu_\pi = \frac{\Delta\pi}{\Delta Y_{ck}} \cdot \frac{Y_{ck}}{\pi} = 1 + \frac{b}{a} \tag{5}$$

where

ΔY_{ck} = the absolute deviation in corporate gross product from normal

μ_π = the elasticity of the change in profits with respect to corporate output deviations.

Table 3 gives the values of the slopes and elasticities for the various periods. The ratio of the change in gross profits to the change in corporate gross product from normal is remarkably constant in all the periods under consideration. A drop in corporate product

TABLE 3
PROFIT-DEVIATION SLOPES AND ELASTICITIES

Period	Slope: $\frac{\Delta\pi}{\Delta Y_{ck}}$	Elasticity: μ_π	"Normal" Ratio: $\frac{\pi}{Y_{ck}}$
1922–41	.474	1.70	.279
1948–59			
whole period	.476	1.65	.289
1948–50 cycle	.492	1.70	.289
1953–55 cycle	.506	1.88	.269
1957–59 cycle	.484	1.78	.272
cycles only	.487	1.70	.287

below normal of, say $10 billion, leads to a decline in gross profits of $4.7 to $5.0 billion, assuming that we start from a situation in which actual and normal product are equal. Given the normal profits/income ratios which have existed during the period, the implied elasticity ranges between 1.7 and 1.9.

Note that the marginal ratio of changes in profits to deviations in corporate product from normal is substantially larger than the secular, full capacity ratio of profits to gross product. Measured from normal capacity, declines in income lead to more than proportional declines in profits by a factor of almost two.

The slopes and elasticities calculated in Table 3 refer to the relationship between profit changes and deviations in corporate product from its normal full capacity level. But we are interested in the change in profits relative to the actual change in output; i.e., to determine the change in disposable income per unit change in GNP, we need the change in profits per unit change in GNP, *not* the change in profits per unit deviation of GNP from the normal. In other words, as one stage in this process, we must convert $\Delta\pi/\Delta Y_{ck}$ into $\Delta\pi/\Delta Y_c$. This conversion can be made, once we specify the rate at which normal gross product is growing relative to the actual gross product. Equation (4) gives us

$$\frac{\Delta\pi}{\Delta Y_{ck}} = a + b.$$

From this we can deduce that,

$$\frac{\Delta\pi}{\Delta Y_c} = a + b\left(1 - \frac{q(1+q)^{j-1} \cdot Y_{ck}(t-j)}{r(1+r)^{j-1} \cdot Y_c(t-j)}\right) \tag{6}$$

where the term $Y_{ck}(t-j)/Y_c(t-j)$ represents the initial ratio between normal and actual gross product, and

q = the rate of change in "normal" gross product
r = the rate of change in actual corporate gross product
j = the number of periods over which the change in product extends.

Given the values of a and b from the regression equations, we can calculate the marginal rate of change in profits relative to the change in corporate product. The results for $a = .29$, $b = .20$, and $q = .01$ per quarter (roughly the postwar values), are given in Table 4. Note that the slopes change slightly as the period is lengthened. This results from the compounding effects of $(1+q)^{j-1}/(1+r)^{j-1}$ as j is extended. Unless r is a very large figure, however, this effect will be relatively insignificant.

Strikingly, the constant ratio between changes in gross profits and changes in corporate gross product from normal is converted into a nonlinear relationship when we measure the ratio between changes in gross profits and changes in actual corporate gross product. The verbal explanation for this is quite simple, and, when once elaborated, intuitively obvious. Granted that the ratio of profits to corporate gross product depends on the degree of excess capacity, the profit ratio will decline if capacity rises while output remains unchanged. (The function which determines $\Delta\pi/\Delta Y_c$ is obviously undefined when $\Delta Y_c/Y_c = r = 0$.) Now imagine that output falls very gradually, and capacity is still rising. The decline in profits relative to the decline in output will be very large; profits would be declining even if output remained unchanged. The faster the fall in output, the closer ΔY_{ck} is to ΔY_c, and the closer $\Delta\pi/\Delta Y_c$ approaches $\Delta\pi/\Delta Y_{ck}$.

As may be seen in Table 4, when the rate of growth in actual income equals the rate of growth in capacity, the average and marginal profit ratios are the same—the share of profits is constant, except for the time trend, which we are ignoring here. Also, when output rises by less than the growth in capacity, the profit share falls, and the marginal profit ratio is less than the average. Indeed, if output rises very slowly, the absolute level of profits may decline, i.e., $\Delta\pi/\Delta Y < 0$.

The share of declines in total income absorbed by corporate profits tends to be quite large, *but* this absorption rate decreases the faster the rate of decline in income. Insofar as the ratio of

TABLE 4
THE RATE OF CHANGE IN PROFITS RELATIVE TO CHANGES IN CORPORATE PRODUCT

	$\Delta\pi/\Delta Y$			
	Length of period over which slope is calculated			
r (per quarter)	1Q	2Q	3Q	4Q
.03	.42	.43	.43	.43
.01	.29	.29	.29	.29
.005	.09	.09	.09	.08
.0025	−.31	−.32	−.32	−.33
−.005	.89	.90	.90	.91
−.01	.69	.69	.70	.70
−.03	.56	.56	.56	.57

NOTE: Calculations assume $Y_{ck} = Y_c$ in initial period, and that $a = .29$, $b = .20$, $q = .01$ per quarter.

changes in disposable income to changes in GNP is affected by the behavior of corporate profits, the marginal ratio of disposable income to GNP will be quite small for moderate rates of decrease in GNP. The greater the rate of decline in GNP, however, the less will be the absorption of that decline by corporate profits, and the greater the absorption by disposable income. While this point has important implications for multiplier theory, it should not be overrated. The rate of decline in output during moderate recessions is not so very different from the rate of decline during larger recessions. It is the duration of contraction, not so much the rate of decline, which differentiates recessions of varying severity.

Our conclusions so far relate only to the behavior of gross profits relative to gross corporate product; to relate profits to total gross national product we must examine the share of corporate product in total product.

The Share of Gross Corporate Product

The corporate form of organization is much more prevalent in some industries than in others. In manufacturing, for example, corporate product accounts for an overwhelming proportion of total product. In services and trade, on the other hand, the proportion is much smaller. Hence, apart from long-run trends in the share of corporate product in individual sectors, the share of corporate product in total gross national product will depend on the industrial composition of output. As that composition shifts toward those sectors in which corporations account for the bulk of activity, the corporate share in total GNP will rise; and vice versa.

If the industrial distribution of GNP were random with respect to cyclical variation, the corporate share of GNP could only be determined by a specific examination of the nature of each cycle. However, there is good a priori reason—and as we shall see abundant empirical evidence—to support the hypothesis that there are systematic cyclical changes in industrial composition, which, in turn, have a systematic effect on the share of corporate product. More specifically, value added in commodity-producing industries fluctuates much more sharply than value added in service or distribution industries. The former are mainly organized in the corporate form; the latter much less so. Consequently, as output falls below capacity, the proportion of output originating in the corporate sector tends to decline; the opposite occurs as output rises relative to capacity.

To test this hypothesis we write:

$$\frac{Y_c}{Y} = a + b\frac{\Delta Y_k}{Y} + c(t) \tag{7}$$

where $\Delta Y_k = (Y - Y_k)$, the deviation in real private nonfarm product from "normal." We have estimated normal gross product by the same techniques as those used to estimate normal corporate product. The results of fitting equation (7) to the data are summarized in Table 5.

Table 6 shows the results of converting the coefficients of the regression equation into the slope and elasticity coefficients, $\Delta Y_c/Y_k$ and μ_{Yc}. Using exactly the same procedure as outlined earlier for finding $\Delta\pi/\Delta Y_c$, we can calculate $\Delta Y_c/\Delta Y$, given the *a* and *b* values of the regression equations and the rate of growth in capacity GNP. As in the case of the profit-corporate product relationship, the marginal ratio of the change in corporate product to the change in total product tends to become smaller as the rate of decline in GNP becomes larger. Since $\Delta\pi/\Delta Y = (\Delta\pi/\Delta Y_c)\cdot(\Delta Y_c/\Delta Y)$, the marginal ratio of the change in profits to the change in GNP declines very rapidly with an increase in the rate of decline of GNP (or with an increase in the excess of the rate of growth in GNP over its normal capacity growth rate).

There is a crucial difference, however, between the results of the corporate *product* share regression (Table 5) and the corporate *profits* share regression (Table 2). In the case of profits, we found that the regression coefficients (and consequently the slope and elasticity coefficients) were fairly uniform over a number of cycles widely varying in duration and amplitude. In the case of the corporate product share, however, the coefficient relating that share to deviations in GNP from normal differs from cycle to cycle. More importantly, the coefficient seems to be smaller, the larger the amplitude of cyclical fluctuation. The values of b in the various cycles covered were:

1922–41	.128
1948–50	.397
1953–55	.184
1957–59	.164

The reason for this is quite probably that we have attempted to capture a nonlinear phenomenon with a linear function.[11] In other words the relative magnitude of the decline in the corporate product share when GNP declines below normal is itself a decreas-

TABLE 5
REGRESSION EQUATIONS: SHARE OF CORPORATE PRODUCT RELATED TO CHANGES IN GNP

Period	a	b	c	R
1922–41	55.1	.128 (.028)	.143 (.116)	.959
1948–59				
whole period	57.1	.240 (.030)	.069 (.027)	.775
1948–50 cycle	58.1	.397 (.059)	−.101 (.062)	.941
1953–55 cycle	58.0	.184 (.030)	.057 (.032)	.892
1957–59 cycle	58.5	.164 (.015)	.006 (.012)	.984
cycles only	57.2	.221 (.027)	.045 (.007)	.860

NOTE: $\frac{Y_c}{Y}$ and $\frac{\Delta Y_k}{Y}$ are expressed in percentages. The regression equation fitted was: $\frac{Y_c}{Y} = a + b\frac{\Delta Y_k}{Y} + c(t)$.

[11] It should be stressed that the corporate product share is now being related to deviations of actual from normal GNP. The nonlinearity involved enters at this stage. It is clear, from the earlier discussion that the linear relationship $Y_c/Y = f(\Delta Y_k/Y)$ converts to a nonlinear relationship when we measure Y_c/Y as a function of $\Delta Y/Y$.

TABLE 6
CORPORATE PRODUCT-DEVIATION SLOPES AND ELASTICITIES

Period	Slope: $\frac{\Delta Y_c}{\Delta Y_k}$	Elasticity: μ_{Y_c}	"Normal" ratio: $\frac{Y_c}{Y_k}$
1922–41	.679	1.23	.551
1948–50			
whole period	.811	1.42	.571
1948–50 cycle	.978	1.68	.581
1953–55 cycle	.764	1.32	.580
1957–59 cycle	.749	1.28	.585
cycles only	.793	1.39	.572

ing function of the magnitude of the GNP deviation. As a consequence, the 1922–41 period, which is dominated by the huge fluctuations in output during the 1930's, exhibits a lower b coefficient than any of the postwar cycles. On the other hand, the 1948–50 fluctuation in nonfarm product was much smaller than the other cycles; hence the b coefficient is quite large.

If the relationship $Y_c/Y = f(\Delta Y_k/Y)$ is really nonlinear, then $\Delta Y_c/\Delta Y_k$ will decrease as ΔY_k increases. In that case the calculations of $\Delta Y_c/\Delta Y$ in Table 7 *understate* the degree to which $\Delta Y_c/\Delta Y$ decreases as the (absolute) rate of change in ΔY increases. Table 7 shows that $\Delta Y_c/\Delta Y$ falls with r', assuming a *constant* $\Delta Y_c/\Delta Y_k$ for declines of all magnitudes. However, if $\Delta Y_c/\Delta Y_k$ itself decreases with an increase in ΔY_k, clearly $\Delta Y_c/\Delta Y$ will fall even more than shown in Table 7, as the size of ΔY increases.

If we go back to the basic hypothesis upon which the relationship of the corporate product share to deviations in GNP was founded, it is not hard to discover the reason for the nonlinear shape of the relationship. As total output falls below normal capacity levels, output and income in those industries in which the corporate form of organization is most important tends to decline more than proportionately. In a mild recession almost all of the decline in activity is centered in the commodity-producing sectors of the economy. Indeed, declines in inventory investment alone account for a major part of the total fall-off in activity. As the recession deepens, however, the downturn begins to extend into other areas, particularly trade and services. As a consequence, the *marginal* ratio of the decline in corporate product to the deviation

TABLE 7

VALUES OF $\frac{\Delta Y_e}{\Delta Y}$ FOR VARIOUS VALUES OF r'[a]

r' (per quarter)	$\Delta Y_e/\Delta Y$ (for first quarter of change)
.03	.69
.01	.58
.005	.41
.0025	.07
−.005	1.09
−.01	.92
−.03	.81

NOTE: Calculations assume $Y_k = Y$ in initial period.
[a] Given $a = .580$, $b = .17$, $q' = .01$ per quarter.

in GNP from normal becomes smaller the further the downturn proceeds.

A direct comparison of deviations in GNP with changes in the share of output represented by services and by (nonfarm) commodity production strengthens the preceding hypothesis. Table 8 summarizes the results of regressions relating the share of commodities and of services in GNP to the deviation in GNP from normal. The table shows the slope and elasticity coefficients, derived from the regressions:

$$\frac{C_o}{Y} = a_1 + b_1 \frac{\Delta Y_k}{Y} + c_1(t)$$

$$\frac{S_e}{Y} = a_2 + b_2 \frac{\Delta Y_k}{Y} + c_2(t)$$

(where $\frac{C_o}{Y}$ and $\frac{S_e}{Y}$ are the shares of commodity and service production in total nonfarm private GNP).

The last column in the table gives the multiple regression coefficients of the original regressions upon which the slope and elasticity coefficients were based.

In the 1922–41 period, the elasticity of commodity production relative to GNP deviations was much smaller than in the postwar cycles. The converse holds true for the elasticity of service production. It is possible, of course, that the difference in elasticity between prewar and postwar is due to a change in economic structure, making the commodity production share more sensitive and the service production share less sensitive to GNP deviations, relative to their prewar sensitivities. Since there have been no postwar cyclical declines approaching the magnitude of the 1937–

38 downturn, much less the 1929–33 debacle, there is no way of testing this. On balance, I do not believe we can attribute the changed elasticities to structural differences. The logic of the case for a nonlinear relationship, however, is quite strong. In moderate recessions service production does not fall significantly, if at all. The same is true of activity in the distributive sector. On the other hand, when the decline in economic activity begins to reach depression proportions, output and income in these sectors do begin to fall significantly, with a corresponding reduction in the proportion of the output decline absorbed by commodity production.

TABLE 8
REGRESSION RELATING SHARE OF COMMODITIES AND SERVICES IN GNP TO DEVIATION IN GNP: SLOPE AND ELASTICITY COEFFICIENTS

	Commodity Production			*Service Production*		
Period	Slope	Elasticity	*R*	Slope	Elasticity	*R*
1922–41	.585	1.13	.917	.114	.38	.960
1948–59						
whole period	.889	1.45	.963	−.029	−.11	.959
1948–50 cycle	.874	1.46	.439	.055	.19	.883
1953–55 cycle	.871	1.48	.774	.088	.30	.919
1957–59 cycle	.829	1.45	.800	.079	.24	.898

NOTE: The regressions for each *individual* postwar cycle were run without the time variable.

If we combine the behavioral relationships described in the last few pages we reach the following conclusions:

1. When total nonfarm private GNP (= GNI) declines, the proportion of the declines absorbed by gross corporate profits is much larger than the average long-run ratio of profits to income.
2. In mild recessions, this marginal ratio of profit change to GNP change is very large relative to the average ratio. The ratio tends to decline as the *rate* of decline in GNP increases: it remains, however, above the average long-run ratio of profits to income.[12]

[12] From equation (6), it is clear that $\Delta\pi/\Delta Y_c$ approaches the value $(a + b)$ asymptotically as the rate of decline in Y_c approaches infinity. In other words, the slope $\Delta\pi/\Delta Y_c$ becomes a closer and closer approximation to the slope $\Delta\pi/\Delta Y_{ck}$ $[= (a + b)]$ as the rate of change in Y_c increases. Since a is the average ratio of gross profits to gross income, the marginal ratio always remains above the average ratio, whenever Y_c is absolutely declining.

3. The ratio of corporate profit change to income change tends to become smaller as the *magnitude* of the decline in GNP increases. This phenomenon is due to the fact that initial declines in GNP are borne almost exclusively by sectors in which the corporate form is dominant, in particular the commodity producing sectors; as the economic decline continues, however, it tends to extend beyond these sectors into those where the corporate form is less important.[13] The marginal ratio of the change in corporate product to the change in GNP, however, still remains larger than the average ratio between the two magnitudes.

Even under the assumption that corporate dividends fell proportionately with corporate gross profits (which they do not), the recession shift from profits to other forms of income would be stabilizing in terms of consumption outlays. The marginal ratio of corporate taxes plus corporate saving to gross corporate profits (even granted the dividend-proportionality assumption) is much higher than the marginal ratio of personal taxes plus personal saving to personal income. In other words, a very large proportion of the decline in gross corporate profits is absorbed by decreases in government revenues and saving; a much smaller proportion of declines in personal income is absorbed by savings and government revenues. The fact that the marginal ratio of gross corporate profits to gross national product is much higher than the average ratio between these two variables, implies that the marginal ratio of disposable income, and hence of consumption, to gross national income is much smaller than the average ratio. Indeed, since it is the deviation in GNP from normal capacity levels which controls this relationship, a very small decline in GNP may be fully absorbed in profits, with no aggregate decline in other forms of income. However, this stabilizing influence tends to become weaker—though it does not disappear—as the rate and magnitude of the downturn become larger. In other words, quite

[13] In fitting a corporate profit function for postwar cycles, Duesenberry, Eckstein, and Fromm ("Simulation of the United States Economy") find that splitting GNP into final sales and inventory investment substantially improves the results. The reason for this is probably that the proportion of GNP accounted for by corporate gross product is significantly related to the level of inventory investment. The tendency of the commodity output share of GNP to vary inversely and the service output share to vary directly with cyclical changes in output, is partly accounted for by the very large values for changes in inventory investment which characterize cyclical movements in GNP.

apart from the stabilizing features of our tax and transfer payment system, and of Duesenberry and Friedman consumption functions, consumption outlays are well insulated against moderate shocks to the economy. Larger initial shocks, however, carry with them not only larger, but proportionately larger, impacts. Quite crudely expressed, the multiplier has a very low value for small changes in nonconsumption spending; its value tends to increase, however, as the recession worsens. The multiplier is, in a word, nonlinear, depending directly on the magnitude of the change in GNP.

The hypothesis that the share of corporate profits in corporate income originating and the share of the latter in nonfarm private GNP depend on deviations in GNP from a normal capacity level, can explain a number of additional aspects of the cyclical behavior of corporate profits.

Both Lintner[14] and Hickman[15] have noted that the change in profits, relative to the change in income, is larger during the downswing of the cycle than during the upswing. This asymetrical behavior is predicted by our hypothesis. If π/Y_c and Y_c/Y both deviate from normal as GNP deviates from normal, then the marginal ratio, $\Delta\pi/\Delta Y$, will be larger during a downturn than during an upturn which exhibits the same rate of change. If, for example, GNP declines at a rate of 2 per cent per quarter, the rate at which it is deviating from a growing capacity will be larger than 2 per cent. On the other hand, a recovery of 2 per cent per quarter will imply that the reduction in the deviation from normal is proceeding at less than 2 per cent per quarter. As a consequence, the decline in the profit share is more rapid during a downturn than the increase in the profit share during a recovery of corresponding speed. In terms of marginal ratios, $\Delta\pi/\Delta Y$ will be larger during the downturn than during the recovery. Suppose GNP falls 10 per cent in four quarters. If capacity is growing at 1 per cent per quarter, the deviation of GNP from normal would be 14 per cent at the end of the year, and the profit share would fall by an amount governed by this deviation. A 10 per cent rate of increase in GNP from the trough (with the increase measured as a percentage of the same base on which the decrease was measured) would still leave GNP approximately 8 per cent

[14] Lintner, "Distribution of Incomes."
[15] Hickman, *Growth and Stability*.

below normal at the end of the year. Even though GNP had attained its prior peak level, profits would be lower than at prior peak, because of the growth in capacity. Hence $\Delta\pi/\Delta Y$ during the recovery would have been less than the $\Delta\pi/\Delta Y$ during the preceding downturn, even though the magnitude and rate of GNP change were the same in both phases.

There is another reason why the change in profits relative to the change in GNP is cyclically asymmetrical. A typical upturn, measured from trough to peak, normally encompasses two subphases: first a recovery of GNP to normal, and then a period of slower growth after normal capacity utilization is approached or surpassed. In the early, pure recovery, phase of the upturn the ratio $\Delta\pi/\pi Y$ will be larger than the normal secular ratio of profits to income, although less than the $\Delta\pi/\Delta Y$ which characterized the downturn. During the next phase of the cycle, since GNP usually rises no faster (and often slower) than capacity, $\Delta\pi/\Delta Y$ will be much lower, somewhere in the neighborhood of (and often below) the normal secular π/Y ratio. A calculation of $\Delta\pi/\Delta Y$ from trough to peak will yield a weighted average of the separate ratios for the two phases, and should be significantly lower than the marginal ratio which characterized the downturn.

In many cycles the growth in GNP during the latter stages of the upturn is slower than the growth in capacity. As a consequence, the share of profits in GNP will tend to decline moderately before the cycle peak is reached. Osborne and Epstein[16] in an analysis of the corporate profit share since World War I, found that this was a typical pattern; the peak ratio of profits to GNP was attained before the cycle peak was reached. Our hypothesis tends to predict such behavior.

Hickman[17] has observed that, on an annual basis, consumption outlays continued to rise during the mild recessions of 1924 and 1927. Part of this may indeed be due to a Friedman type distributed lag in the consumption function. However, the hypothesis that the profit share falls when GNP declines below capacity, would also help to explain this phenomenon. Granted a Lintner-type function for dividends,[18] a decline in the profit share implies

[16] Harlowe Osborne and Joseph Epstein, "Corporate Profits Since World War II," *Survey of Current Business*, January 1956.

[17] Hickman, *Growth and Stability*.

[18] Even with a constant ratio of dividends to payout, a shift in the profit share would raise the disposable income share, unless the combined share of retained profits and corporate taxes in total profits were no higher than the effective rate of taxation on personal income.

a rise in the disposable income share. In the annual data, 1924 and 1927 show up as little more than a cessation of growth. But this was enough to create a rise in excess capacity and a fall in the profit share. Disposable income continued to rise, and so did consumption.

RETAINED CORPORATE PROFITS

The impact on disposable income of a change in the profit share will depend, of course, on the dividend policy of corporate management. Even if dividend payment ratios remain unchanged—i.e., dividends change proportionately with after-tax profits—a decline in the corporate profit share would raise the share of disposable income. At the present time dividends account for about 20 per cent, on the average, of total gross corporate profits. (They represent, of course, a much higher proportion—about 55 per cent—of net profits after tax.) If this proportion were maintained, each $1 billion shift in income away from gross profits would result in an increase of $0.8 billion in personal income, and a somewhat smaller increase in disposable income, depending on the marginal effective tax rate on dividend recipients and on other income recipients. A simple algebraic model will illustrate these relations. (It should be remembered that we are making the drastic assumption that dividends change proportionately with gross profits.) Assume a decline in corporate gross profits, $\Delta\pi$, within a fixed total GNP.

$$\Delta Y_d = \Delta\pi - .2\Delta\pi - t\Delta\pi + .2t'\Delta\pi$$

where

ΔY_d = change in disposable income
$.2\Delta\pi$ = decline in dividends
t = marginal effective personal tax rate on incomes other than dividends
t' = marginal effective tax rate on dividend income.

Then

$$\Delta Y_d = \Delta\pi(.8 - t + .2t')$$

In order that ΔY_d be zero, when there is a shift in income between gross profits and other types of income, we must have,

$$t = .8 + .2t'$$

Even if the marginal effective tax rate on dividends were as low as 20 per cent, the marginal effective rate on other forms of income would have to be 85 per cent in order to cancel out the effect of a shift in income distribution. As a matter of fact, the value of t is probably between 15 and 20 per cent. With a marginal effective tax rate on dividends of, say 40 per cent, a shift of \$1 billion of income away from gross profits to order forms of income would raise disposable income by about \$0.7 billion. In other words, the "sticky" behavior of dividends is not a necessary condition in order for a shift away from corporate profits to raise disposable income. The very high average proportion of gross corporate profits accounted for by depreciation, taxes, and retained earnings is sufficient to explain the phenomenon. It is gross corporate profits which are relevant, in the short run at least. Changes in depreciation simply reallocate a gross flow between two accounting categories, net profits and depreciation. Further, whatever one believes about the incidence of a change in corporate tax rates, surely a short-run change in corporate tax liabilities, brought about by a change in profits, does not affect the gross margin. The relatively high tax rates simply mean that government revenues absorb a large part of any change in gross profits.

Once we take into account the fact that dividends are "sticky," the impact on disposable income of a change in gross corporate profits is increased. Lintner's work in this area is too well known to require detailed repetition. Using annual data for 1918–41, Lintner[19] found dividends (D_t) to be a function of current profits before IVA and after taxes (P_t), and a lagged dividend variable (D_{t-1});

$$D_t = .352 + .150P_t + .700D_{t-1} \qquad R = .967$$

Duesenberry, Eckstein, and Fromm[20] fitted the same equation to quarterly data for 1947–57 and found,

$$D_t = -.53 + .079P_t + .91D_{t-1} \qquad R = .962$$

As they point out, the increased size of the lagged dividend coefficient and the reduced size of the current profits coefficient are to be expected when shifting from an annual to a quarterly basis. In both cases, however, the coefficient of current profits is very low compared to the coefficient of lagged dividends. A decline in profits has a very damped impact on dividends, and a very disproportionate effect on retained earnings.

[19] Lintner, "Distribution of Incomes," in *AER*, May 1956.

[20] In "Simulation of the United States Economy," *Econometrica*, October 1960.

The Lintner dividend equation is approximately equivalent to making dividends a function of a weighted moving average of past profits, with the current term of the moving average receiving rather small weight (particularly in the quarterly series). Consider a situation in which profits have been rising before a turning point. During the early stages of the downturn dividends may not decline at all, indeed they may rise slightly, if the decline is shallow.[21] The further profits decline, however, the larger will be the effect of further declines on dividends. If profits stabilize at a lower level, dividends, and hence disposable income, will continue to decline for a while.

We pointed out earlier, that the nature of our gross profits hypothesis implied that gross profits absorbed a very large part of declines in income. The hypothesis also implies, however, that the proportion absorbed by profits tends to fall as the rate and magnitude of the economic decline become larger. Corporate dividend policy, as described by Lintner's equations, magnifies the impact of this pattern of profit behavior on disposable income. In mild and short-lived recessions, not only do gross profits absorb a very sizeable proportion of the decline in disposable income, but in turn, most if not all of the gross profit decline is absorbed by corporate taxes and retained earnings; the reduction in dividends will be very small, or nonexistent. The faster and the further the decline in income, however, the smaller the marginal ratio, $\Delta\pi/\Delta Y$. Similarly, the steeper and longer the decline in profits, the greater the impact on dividends, as the moving average of profits (on which dividends depend) begins to fall rapidly.

Thus, the stabilizing effect of changes in income distribution away from profits and toward other forms of income is very powerful. Small shocks to the economy encounter a powerful built-in stabilizer—quite apart from Federal budget stabilizers.[22] The marginal rate of change of disposable income relative to GNP changes is quite small. But an increase in the size of the initial shock has a more than proportional effect on the economy. The

[21] That is, the new terms in the moving average, while below their immediate predecessors, may still exceed the terms in the distant past which are being dropped.

[22] The fact that corporate taxes take such a large part of corporate profits does affect the average and marginal behavior of dividends. Hence, indirectly, part of the stabilizing effectiveness of shifts in the corporate profits share can be traced to the structure of tax rates. See below, p. 167.

ratio of changes in disposable income relative to changes in GNP becomes larger, as the rate, magnitude, and duration of the downturn increase. Hence, the larger the shock to the economy, the proportionally greater the cumulative secondary effects are likely to be, at least insofar as the stabilizing role of profits is concerned.

TABLE 9
GROSS PROFIT, RETAINED PROFIT, AND OTHER RATIOS, IN VARIOUS RECESSIONS

Period	*Marginal Ratios*					*Average Ratios*			
	$\frac{\Delta\pi}{\Delta Y_c}$ (1)	$\frac{\Delta Y_c}{\Delta Y}$ (2)	$\frac{\Delta\pi}{\Delta Y}$ (col. 1 × col. 2) (3)	$\frac{\Delta\pi_r}{\Delta\pi}$ (4)	$\frac{\Delta\pi_r}{\Delta Y}$ (col. 3 × col. 4) (5)	$\frac{\pi}{Y_c}$ (6)	$\frac{Y_c}{Y}$ (7)	$\frac{\pi_r}{\pi}$ (8)	$\frac{\pi_r}{Y}$ (9)
1929–33	.50	.69	.35	.74	.26	.29	.55	.60	.09
4Q 1948-2Q 1949	.56	1.44	.82	.92	.76	.29	.58	.81	.14
2Q 1953-1Q 1954	.58	.86	.50	.96	.48	.28	.58	.82	.13
3Q 1957-1Q 1958	.56	.84	.47	.97	.46	.27	.58	.81	.12

NOTE: Data were deflated by the private nonfarm GNP deflator before the changes were calculated (see below, pp. 36–37). Average ratios were calculated for the peak year or quarter. Private nonfarm product was measured on the income side of the accounts, i.e., GNP minus statistical discrepancy, since we wish to measure changes in profits against changes in total gross income. (See Appendix 2.)

Table 9 gives some of the more important average and marginal ratios for the 1929–33 depression and for each of the postwar recessions. The ratios behave more or less as our hypotheses would indicate. The marginal ratios between changes in profits and changes in corporate product, between the latter and changes in GNP, and between changes in retained gross profits and changes in GNP were substantially larger than the average ratios. In the 1929–33 downturn, gross retained profits, which in 1929 accounted for only 9 per cent of GNP, absorbed 26 per cent of the decline in GNP. In the 1957–58 recession, gross retained profits absorbed 47 per cent of the fall in GNP, although they were only 12 per cent of GNP in 1957.

The ratio of the change in gross profits to the change in corporate product was slightly higher in the postwar cycles than in 1929–33. In the formulation presented earlier, this marginal ratio should be larger, the smaller the rate of decline in GNP. In the postwar cycles, the rate of decline in GNP was smaller, but not much smaller, than in 1929–33; the major difference was in the magnitude, not in the speed of the decline.

The second ratio, the change in corporate product relative to the change in GNP, depends both on the rate and the magnitude of the decline in GNP. This shows up particularly in the figure for 1949. The percentage decline in private nonfarm GNP during that downturn was only 2.5 per cent, compared to 4.5 per cent in 1954 and 5.5 per cent in 1958.[23] On the other hand, the much greater magnitude of the 1929–33 downturn was associated with a $\Delta Y_c/\Delta Y$ ratio only moderately smaller than in 1953–54 and 1957–58. Insofar as these few recessions can be taken as evidence, it may be that the marginal ratio between corporate product and GNP falls most rapidly for small increases in the magnitude of the GNP decline and then falls at a reduced rate as the magnitude of the downturn is further increased.[24]

As the Lintner equations imply, the marginal ratio between retained earnings and profits was much lower in the deep depression of 1929–33 than in the shallower and shorter recessions of the postwar period. Only a small part of the dividend decline took place in the first year of the 1929 downturn; most of it occurred in subsequent years, as the moving average of profits began to decline sharply. An additional reason for the larger relative decline in dividends in the 1929–33 period lies in the fact that at that time they comprised a larger fraction of gross profits. The substantial increase in corporate profits taxes since the 1920's did not result in a significant rise in gross before-tax profit margins. Not only were after-tax margins reduced, but most of the reduction took place at the expense of dividends; retained earnings as a percentage of before-tax profits did not decline very much. Hence, our concept of gross retained earnings (corporate profits before taxes plus depreciation minus dividends) is currently a much larger proportion of total gross profits than in 1929.[25]

The final marginal ratio in Table 9, $\Delta\pi_r/\Delta Y$, was significantly

[23] The relative magnitude of the 1949 decline is much larger than 2.5 per cent when *total* GNP is used as a measure; the magnitude of the 1949 decline in private nonfarm GNP is significantly smaller than the decline in total GNP.

[24] For a further discussion of the factors affecting the corporate product share in GNP, see below, pp. 171 ff.

[25] The ratio was .60 in 1929 and .80 in 1957.

higher in each downturn than its average value at the peak. However, gross retained corporate earnings accounted for about one-half of the decline in total nonfarm income in the last two recessions, compared to about one-quarter in 1929–33. In both the 1929–33 and the postwar downturns corporate profits acted as a stabilizing influence, but much more so in the postwar cycles. While some of this difference is due to a change in economic structure (particularly to the smaller *average* ratio of dividends to gross retained earnings which characterized the postwar period), our basic hypothesis implies that a good part of the difference is simply due to the greater magnitude and duration of the decline in income in 1929–33.

RATIOS OF DEFLATED VERSUS CURRENT DOLLAR FIGURES

All of our marginal ratios have been based on the assumption that deviations in the share of profits in corporate product (and of corporate product in GNP) are a function of deviations in *real* output from normal capacity levels. The theoretical basis for this relationship is the hypothesis that the two major factors affecting the profit share—changes in unit costs and the markup on costs—are themselves systematically related to the degree of excess capacity. Thus, two recessions with the same deviation of real product from normal capacity output would, in our formulation, be characterized by the same decline in the profit share, even though the absolute level of prices fell more in one recession than the other. The excess capacity variable is supposed to "carry" any shift in the price-cost margin. Hence, if the deviation in GNP from normal, and therefore the deviation of profits from normal, were the same in two recessions, the ratio $\Delta\pi/\Delta Y_c$ would be the same, but only if $\Delta\pi$ and ΔY_c were measured in constant dollars, with both terms deflated by the same deflator. When the marginal ratio of profits to corporate product is measured in *current* dollars, a given decline in the share of profits will require a larger $\Delta\pi/\Delta Y_c$ the smaller the price decrease. A simple example may help make this clear:

Let Y_c = corporate product in constant dollars
y_c = corporate product in current dollars
π = corporate profits in constant dollars
z = corporate profits in current dollars

Assume an initial situation as follows:

$$Y_c = y_c = 100$$
$$\pi = z = 10$$
$$\frac{\pi}{Y_c} = \frac{z}{y_c} = .10$$

When real income declines by 20 per cent, the profit share $z/y_c(= \pi/Y_c)$ declines to .08. If the level of prices remains unchanged, the situation is as follows:

A.
$$Y_c = 80$$
$$y_c = 80$$
$$\pi = 6.4$$
$$z = 6.4$$
$$\frac{\Delta\pi}{\Delta Y_c} = \frac{\Delta z}{\Delta y_c} = \frac{3.6}{20} = .180$$
$$\frac{\pi}{Y_c} = \frac{z}{y_c} = .08$$

In exactly the same situation, except that prices decline by 10 per cent, we have:

B.
$$Y_c = 80$$
$$y_c = 72$$
$$\pi = 6.4$$
$$z = 5.8$$
$$\frac{\Delta\pi}{\Delta Y_c} = .180$$
$$\frac{\Delta z}{\Delta y_c} = \frac{4.2}{28} = .150$$
$$\frac{\pi}{Y_c} = \frac{z}{y_c} = .08$$

In our formulation the deviation in real output from normal carries with it the impact on profits of any change in relative prices (i.e., prices relative to wages). The degree of absolute price flexibility plays no independent role, except that of *numeraire*. The profit share is determined without reference to the absolute price level. But for the profit share to fall to a lower level, the marginal ratio of the profit decline to the product decline must be higher than the average profit share. In order to reach any given level, the marginal must exceed the average by an amount which depends on the size of the decline in product. If real product falls, say, 20 per cent below capacity, the share of profits in product will fall by a certain amount. But if prices decline, the magnitude of the current dollar decline in product will, of course, be larger than the magnitude of the constant dollar decline. Hence, the marginal ratio of profit change to product change will be smaller when both changes are measured in current dollars than when they are both measured in constant dollars.

There is a determinate relation between the ratios $\Delta\pi/\Delta Y_c$ and $\Delta z/\Delta y_c$. Given the equation determining the profit share, $\pi/Y_c = a + b\Delta Y_{ck}/Y_c$, we can obtain the marginal ratio $\Delta\pi/\Delta Y_c$. Assume, also, for the sake of simplicity that there is no growth in capacity, and that $Y_{ck} = Y_c$ in the initial period.

Let $\dfrac{\Delta\pi}{\Delta Y_c} = b$

$\dfrac{\Delta z}{\Delta y_c} = q$

p = the per cent change in prices during the interval $t = 1$ to $t = 2$

$Y_{c1} = y_{c1};\ \pi_1 = z_1$

$Y_{c2} = \dfrac{y_{c1}}{(1+p)};\ \pi_2 = \dfrac{z_2}{(1+p)}$

For any particular $\Delta Y_c/Y_c$, there will result a particular profit share in period 2.

Since
$$\frac{\pi_2}{Y_{c2}} = \frac{z_2}{y_{c2}}$$

Then
$$\frac{ay_{c1} + b\left(\dfrac{y_{c2}}{(1+p)} - y_{c1}\right)}{\dfrac{y_{c2}}{(1+p)}} = \frac{ay_{c1} + q(y_{c2} - y_{c1})}{y_{c2}} \tag{8}$$

$$q = \frac{y_{c1}(ap - b - bp) + by_2}{\Delta y_c} \tag{9}$$

Letting
$$\frac{\Delta y_c}{y_{c1}} = r',$$

$$q = \frac{p(a-b)}{r'} + b \tag{10}$$

And since $r' = r + p + pr$, where $r = \Delta Y_c/Y_{c1}$,

$$q = \frac{p(a-b)}{r + p + pr} + b \tag{11}$$

When $p = 0$, $q = b$. When r is negative, $b > a$; hence, during a recession, $q < b$ when prices decline and $q > b$ should prices increase.

The same formulation can be made for the relation between $\Delta Y_c/Y$ and $\Delta y_c/y$. If one computes the marginal ratios with *undeflated* data, the 1929–33 ratios are very much smaller than the postwar ratios. But this is a spurious result. Prices fell substantially in 1929–33, but, aside from 1949, they did not decline in the postwar recessions. The further prices fall, the smaller the marginal ratios must be in order to reduce the average ratio by a given amount. Conversely, the marginal ratio of undeflated disposable income to GNP and the marginal ratio of consumption to GNP fell far more in 1929–33 than in postwar cycles, if we base the ratios on undeflated data.

The marginal profit ratios in Table 9 were calculated from deflated data, in order to avoid the purely formal, arithmetical effect of changes in prices on the ratios. Even after correction the 1929–33 ratios were smaller than the postwar ones. These differences are "legitimate" and reflect a real difference in behavior; the much wider divergence in undeflated ratios does not.

To use the marginal ratios developed in the earlier part of this paper for prediction, where prediction in current dollar terms is desired, it would be necessary to convert the ratios to current dollar terms by use of equation 11.

OTHER FACTORS INFLUENCING THE BEHAVIOR OF THE CORPORATE PRODUCT SHARE

So far we have concentrated on the behavior of corporate product and corporate profits as determined by deviations in output from normal. Insofar as the structural relationships which determine the profit share are themselves imperfectly correlated with the deviation of output from normal, we should expect to get a better fit by directly relating the profit share and the corporate product share to these structural factors.

The basic rationale for expecting a systematic deviation in the corporate product share as total private nonfarm output deviates from normal lies in the fact that there are systematic cyclical shifts in the industrial composition of output. However, the change in industrial output mix is not perfectly correlated with output deviations. While the general direction and magnitude of shifts in industrial composition will be the same in most cycles, each cycle will have its own distinctive characteristics. As a consequence, if we add to our earlier equation, $Y_c/Y = a + b(\Delta Y_k/Y) + c(t)$, a specific allowance for mix changes, we should expect to find a significant improvement in the fit if the change in mix varies substantially from cycle to cycle. To examine the possibility we fit:

$$\frac{Y_c}{Y} = a + b\left(\frac{\Delta Y_k}{Y}\right) + c(t) + d\left(\frac{Com}{Y}\right) + e\left(\frac{Ser}{Y}\right) + f\left(\frac{Const}{Y}\right)$$

(where $\frac{Com}{Y}$, $\frac{Ser}{Y}$, and $\frac{Const}{Y}$ equal, respectively, the shares of commodity, service, and construction output in total private nonfarm product).

The results are shown in Table 10. In 1922–41 and in each of the separate postwar cycles the mix added significant additional information to that given by the time trend and the output deviation. There is already a high intercorrelation between the mix and the output deviation. This is the reason we get generally good results from fitting the corporate share to output deviations. However, in each single postwar cycle, and in the 1922–41 period the variation in mix, over and above the systematic cyclical variation, is sufficient to yield significant partial correlations for the mix.

TABLE 10
CORPORATE PRODUCT SHARE RELATED TO OUTPUT DEVIATION AND OUTPUT COMPOSITION

Period	$R_{1.23}$[a]	$R_{1.23456}$[a]	$R_{1456.23}$[a]	$R_{1.3456}$[a]
1922–41	.959	.989	.869	.958
1948–59	.775	.833	.290	.806
1948–50	.941	.992	.935	—
1953–55	.892	.957	.785	—
1957–59	.984	.989	.620	—
All cycles	.860	.886	.435	.859
Plateaus	.160	.650	.637	.452

[a] $R_{1.23}$ = multiple correlation coefficient of $\frac{Y_c}{Y}$ on $\frac{\Delta Y_k}{Y}$ and (t).

$R_{1.23456}$ = multiple correlation coefficient of $\frac{Y_c}{Y}$ on $\frac{\Delta Y_k}{Y}$, (t) and mix.

$R_{1456.23}$ = partial correlation coefficient of $\frac{Y_c}{Y}$ on mix, holding $\frac{\Delta Y_k}{Y}$ and (t) constant.

$R_{1.3456}$ = multiple correlation coefficient of $\frac{Y_c}{Y}$ on (t) and mix.

For the postwar period as a whole, and for the postwar cycles combined, however, the addition of mix variables adds little to the correlation. This is probably due to excessive aggregation in our mix variables. When mix changes are very large, as in 1922–41, or are measured over one cycle only, the intragroup mix is small compared to the intergroup mix. Had we fitted a more detailed mix pattern we probably would have achieved better results. On the other hand, the mix categories we chose—commodities, construction, and services—are particularly well suited for use in an aggregative forecasting model.

As might be expected, the correlation between Y_c/Y and $\Delta Y_k/Y$ was very poor during plateau periods (the periods between the end of recovery and the next cycle peak). During such periods the relationship between $\Delta Y_k/Y$ and mix is likely to be minimal, with the mix governed by other than cyclical factors. Even adding mix as a separate variable does not give us a very good fit, again because during such periods changes in intergroup mix are likely to be small compared to intragroup mix.

Insofar as the mix of nonfarm private GNP is not systematically cyclical in nature—and there is no reason to expect each cycle to be exactly alike with respect to mix—then the change in Y_c/Y can vary from cycle to cycle. If we wish to be perfectionists in forecasting $\Delta\pi/\Delta Y$ (which depends on $\Delta Y_c/\Delta Y$), then we must specify the particular shifts in the composition of output. Since the multiplier is affected by variations in $\Delta\pi/\Delta Y$, it is in part dependent on the composition of output. To take account of such variations in aggregate models is, however, a counsel of perfection, particularly since so much of the variance in Y_c/Y can be satisfactorily explained by deviations in output from normal. In other words, there is enough constancy in the cyclical variation in output composition to permit the use of $\Delta Y_k/Y$ as a proxy variable for variations in mix.

From the regression weights yielded by fitting Y_c/Y to the composition of output we can derive a set of coefficients which give the change in the corporate product for any given change in mix. These are shown in Table 11. For a 1 per cent shift in the composition of private nonfarm output from commodities to services, for example, a decrease of .8 per cent in the share of corporate product was to be expected in both periods. These percentages, reflecting the relative weight of the corporate form of organization

TABLE 11

CHANGE IN THE CORPORATE PRODUCT SHARE FOR SPECIFIED CHANGES IN OUTPUT COMPOSITION

Period	1 per cent change from:	Percentage point change in corporate product share
1922–41	Commodities to Services	−.80
	Commodities to Construction	−.26
	Construction to Services	−.54
1948–59	Commodities to Services	−.77
	Commodities to Construction	−.27
	Construction to Services	−.50

SOURCE: Derived from the coefficients of the multiple regression equation:

$$\frac{Y_c}{Y} = a + b\left(\frac{Com}{Y}\right) + c\left(\frac{Ser}{Y}\right) + d\left(\frac{Constr}{Y}\right) + e(t)$$

in the various sectors, were (as would be expected) about the same in both periods. Despite the fact that the coefficients were so similar in both the prewar and postwar periods, however, their standard errors were larger than the coefficients themselves in all cases. The large standard errors stem from the fact that the three composition variables, expressed as a share of private nonfarm product, add to unity in each observation time period. Thus each composition variable has a perfect negative correlation with the sum of the other two.

Other Income Shares

Table 12 gives the results of estimating other major income shares with the same type of regression as utilized in explaining the corporate profit share.

There are two features of Table 12 which deserve particular comment. During the 1922–41 period a negative output deviation was accompanied by a negative change in the share of unincorporated business income. The opposite, however, held true in the postwar period. The reason for this probably lies in the lack of proper specification of the model. As we stressed earlier, the incidence of moderate declines in output is almost wholly in the corporate sector. Consequently, the absolute level of unincorporated output originating falls little, if at all. Even if there is some squeeze in the margins of unincorporated business, so that its share of income originating in its own sector decreases, the rise in the share of the unincorporated sector more than offsets the

TABLE 12
RESULTS OF REGRESSION EQUATIONS ON OTHER MAJOR INCOME SHARES[a]

Period	a_i	b_i	c_i	R
1922–41				
Unincorporated business and professional income	10.2	.042 (.005)	.023 (.020)	.903
Property income[b]	12.6	−.046 (.008)	−.551[c] (.046)	.946
Compensation of employees	51.4	−.026 (.027)	−.044 (.041)	.640
1948–59				
Unincorporated business and professional income	10.4	−.052 (.003)	−.053 (.010)	.954
Property income	5.2	−.063 (.025)	.018 (.002)	.954
Compensation of employees	54.4	−.040 (.036)	.004 (.015)	.490

[a] All data refer to the private nonfarm sector. Shares and output deviations are expressed in percentage terms. $\text{Share}_i = a_i + b_i \frac{\Delta Y_k}{Y} + c_i(t)$.

[b] Rent and interest.

[c] The time variable has a value of 0 for all years prior to 1930.

fall in the internal profit share. Further, a large part of the "unincorporated business and professional income" is really wages, and hence the pure profit element is much smaller than the statistical share would indicate. For these reasons, a moderate decline in output will raise the statistically reported unincorporated business income share. Declines in total output of depression magnitude, however, will be accompanied by a decline in the absolute level of output in the noncorporate sector. After a point, the fall in the internal share of unincorporated business profits more than offsets the rise in the share of unincorporated business output. Further, the marginal ratio of the change in unincorporated output to the change in total output tends to rise as the output decline becomes larger. (This is the converse of the nonlinearity in the corporate product share, which we observed earlier.) As a consequence, in the 1922–41 regression, which is dominated by the great depression, the share of business income varies directly with the deviation in total output; in the postwar regression on the other hand, it varies inversely with output deviations.

In theory, this problem could have been partly solved by the same technique as we used to explain deviations in the corporate product share. The share of unincorporated profits in total income equals the share of profits in unincorporated product times the share of the latter in total product. Each ratio should be fitted separately. This would have been an extremely difficult task, however, in view of the nature of the statistics. The profit element of the unincorporated business sector is so mingled with wages (and other) elements, that we did not attempt a further breakdown of the data.

The fact that the share of unincorporated business income tends to increase in mild recessions, is a partial offset to the stabilizing influence of a declining corporate share. The saving rate out of unincorporated entrepreneurial income is much higher than the saving rate out of other forms of personal income.[26] Insofar as the shift in income distribution is from corporate profits to unincorporated business profits, the net reduction in the saving rate is less than if the shift were to other forms of income. On balance, of course, the shift away from corporate profits during a recession is still stabilizing with respect to consumption outlays. First, by no means all of the shift is towards unincorporated income; note the signs on the coefficients of the other income shares. Second, the marginal saving rate out of unincorporated business income, while higher than saving rates out of other forms of income, is less than that of corporate profits. Third, as our 1922–41 regression indicates, a large enough decline in income will lead to a *decline*, rather than an increase in the share of unincorporated business income. Finally, the unincorporated business income share is only in part entrepreneurial income. If we had data on the pure entrepreneurial part of the total, we should undoubtedly find that the shift toward such income, during mild recessions, was much smaller than that shown in the postwar regression reported in Table 12.

In both periods, the correlation coefficient for the employee compensation share was disappointingly low. The regression coefficients, however, did have the "right" signs. We tried adding a variable representing the difference between the wage change of the period and the "normal" increase in productivity, on the assumption that such changes would have a lagged response in

[26] See, for example, Irwin Friend and I. B. Kravis, "Entrepreneurial Income, Saving, and Investment," *American Economic Review*, June 1957; and L. R. Klein and A. S. Goldberger, *An Econometric Model of the United States: 1929–1952*, Amsterdam, North Holland Publishing Co., 1957.

prices, and hence, depending on the sign, would tend to raise or lower the wage share. However, the addition of this variable improved the fit very little; moreover, its coefficient was exceedingly small (although significant).

In part, the poor fit of the wage share results from a combination of factors. The wage share in the corporate sector is somewhat larger than the statistically reported wage share in the noncorporate sector. Hence, the tendency of the wage share to rise as output declines is partially offset by the greater than proportional decline in the corporate sector. The over-all wage share, as a function of deviations in output, thus depends not only on the relation between wage shares and output deviations in each sector, but also on the composition of output. Unlike the corporate profit share, these two factors work in opposite directions as output deviates from normal, so that the resultant fit between the over-all wage share and the over-all output deviation tends to be loose.

Appendix 1

THE 1937–38 RECESSION

In one major respect changes in factor shares during the 1937–38 recession do not fit the pattern described in this paper. The decline in gross corporate product relative to the decline in private nonfarm product was *larger* than in the 1953–54 or 1957–58 recessions. Our hypothesis would have predicted the opposite result, since the magnitude of the decline in output was greater in 1937–38 than in these later recessions.

The basic ratios are as follows:

$$\frac{\Delta\pi}{\Delta Y_c}\,(.380) \times \frac{\Delta Y_c}{\Delta Y}\,(.920) = \frac{\Delta\pi}{\Delta Y}\,(.350)$$

$$\frac{\Delta\pi}{\Delta Y}\,(.350) \times \frac{\Delta\pi_r}{\Delta\pi}\,(.195) = \frac{\Delta\pi_r}{\Delta Y}\,(.074)$$

The marginal ratio of the decline in gross profits to the decline in corporate product, $\Delta\pi/\Delta Y_c$, behaves as our hypothesis would indicate. It is much lower than in the postwar recessions; we would expect this, because the rate of decline in corporate product was very large. Indeed between the third quarter of 1937 and the second quarter of 1938, industrial production declined by 36 per cent—a rate of decline much larger than in 1953–54 or 1957–58.

The decline in corporate product relative to the fall in GNP, on the other hand, was larger than in the last two postwar recessions. This is possibly due to the fact that an unusually large part of this recession was concentrated in the commodity producing sector of the economy. It is possible, of course, that the statistics on gross corporate product are not sufficiently accurate during these earlier years to stand the weight of marginal calculations, particularly in a short-lived, though very deep, recession. Although the marginal ratio $\Delta Y_c/\Delta Y$ was unusually large from the point of view of our hypothesis, the marginal ratio $\Delta\pi/\Delta Y$ ($= \Delta\pi/\Delta Y_c \cdot \Delta Y_c/\Delta Y$) was more or less in line with its expected value, in the sense that it was noticeably lower than the ratios for the postwar cycles.

The ratio of the decline in gross retained profits to total profits is very much smaller than in any other recession with which we have dealt. The reason, of course, is that the tax on undistributed profits, which had been in force during 1936 and 1937, was removed in 1938. As a result, retained earnings, as a proportion of total profits, were sharply increased in that year. The marginal ratio has no meaning in terms of structural relationships.

Appendix 2

THE STATISTICAL DISCREPANCY

During recessions the decline in GNP when measured from the income side of the accounts frequently tends to be smaller than when measured from the product side, i.e., the statistical discrepancy decreases. We have chosen to measure our marginal ratios in terms of changes in GNP measured from the income side. All of our data, including the corporate product data, were derived from income statistics. Even the measures of farm and government product, subtracted from GNP to arrive at private nonfarm product, were estimated from income data. The table below gives the marginal $\Delta\pi_r/\Delta Y$ ratios for each recession in terms of a product measurement of GNP, for comparison purposes. The regression equations for 1922–41 were all based on GNP data measured on the income side of the account. Due to an oversight, not caught until all of the computations were complete, the postwar regressions were based on GNP measured from the product side. Since the recession declines in GNP are slightly larger, measured by product data, our b coefficients in the various regressions where $\Delta Y_k/Y$ is a variable are biased slightly downward, compared to the 1929–41 values. Raising the b coefficients would strengthen rather than weaken all of the major observations made earlier with respect to the relationship between the 1922–41 and the 1948–59 regressions.

	1929–33	*1948–49*	*1953–54*	*1957–58*
$\Delta\pi_r/\Delta Y$	.27	.74	.46	.42

Appendix 3

DATA SOURCES

1922–29: The factor income shares, aside from corporate profits, were based on Simon Kuznets, *National Income and its Composition, 1919–38*, New York, NBER, 1941. The Kuznets data were used to extrapolate the relevant Department of Commerce 1929 data back through the 1920's. In the case of *interest*, Kuznets' figure was adjusted (with other Kuznets data) to exclude net interest paid by government. *Corporate profits* before tax + IVA were taken from Raymond W. Goldsmith's GNP tables in Part V, Vol. III of *A Study of Savings in the United States* (Princeton N.J., 1956). The other items of reconciliation between GNP and national income were taken from the same source. Gross national product was thus built upon the income side. From 1922 to 1929 this estimate was quite close to the GNP estimate of Kendrick (given in Goldsmith, *Study of Savings*), the Department of Commerce (*U.S. Income and Output*, Table I-16) and Kuznets (two Kuznets estimates were available; the first from his *Capital in the American Economy: Its Formation and Financing* (Princeton for NBER, 1961), and a second, based on the national income data in his *National Income* and adjusted by the present author to the Department of Commerce concept wherever possible, and raised to a GNP level with the reconciliation items given by Goldsmith).

The various GNP estimates differed among themselves to some extent, but not seriously, between 1922 and 1928. However, an attempt to extend the data back to 1919, in order to cover the 1920–21 recession, ran into serious difficulty. First the Kendrick,

Department of Commerce, and Kuznets estimates differed widely in all three years, 1919, 1920, and 1921. Second—and even more frustrating—the Kuznets factor income data, plus the Goldsmith profit and reconciliation items, added up to a figure far below any of the GNP estimates. Some items of income or other charges are clearly underestimated, if any of the various GNP estimates are to be believed. In Variant I of Appendix Table R-2 in *Capital in the American Economy*, Kuznets adds a capital consumption allowance estimate to his earlier national income estimates and comes up with a GNP figure which is not too far from the Commerce estimate for 1919, 1920, and 1921 (after allowing for the more important conceptual differences such as indirect taxes, corporate taxes, etc.). However, the figures used in Kuznets' Appendix Table R-2 for reproduction cost depreciation seemed to be noticeably higher than the Fabricant estimates of capital consumption allowances, which had been the main basis for deriving the net profit figures in the original national income estimates. Moreover, one of the major items of the Fabricant capital consumption allowance was the figure for the reproduction cost depreciation on residental housing. Yet the Kuznets description of the technique used to derive net rent, in *National Income*, seems to imply an original book value depreciation figure. Adding back a reproduction cost estimate of capital consumption allowances would thus seem to overstate gross product since there was a sizeable excess of reproduction cost over original cost during the years in question. Therefore, even though Kuznets was able to reach a total GNP not too far below the Commerce estimates for 1919 through 1921, the resulting distribution of gross income, for the reasons described above, gave what seemed to be a distorted picture. There appeared to be no major problems in other years.

All of the gross income shares were adjusted to exclude income originating in the farm sector. Before using the Kuznets data on unincorporated business income and net interest to extrapolate the Department of Commerce data back through 1922, income of farm proprietors and farm net interest were excluded. Farm capital consumption allowances, as estimated by the Department of Commerce (in the August 1954 *Survey of Current Business*) were subtracted from total capital consumption allowances.

Corporate gross product was defined to equal corporate income originating plus corporate depreciation. No attempt was made to allocate indirect taxes to the corporate sector. The corporate income originating for 1922–28 was taken from the appendix table in Osborne and Epstein (*Survey of Current Business*, January 1956). Corporate depreciation was taken from Fabricant, through 1937, and extrapolated through 1941 with data generously furnished the author by Osborne.

For the 1922–41 period the wage and price data used in the estimate of actual and normal costs are only rough approximations to the corporate wage and price data theoretically required. The private nonfarm GNP deflator was used to represent the price of corporate product. Average hourly earnings, again for the private nonfarm sector, were taken from the Joint Economic Committee publication, *Productivity Prices and Incomes* (Materials prepared by the Committee Staff), 1957, Table 48, p. 141. The productivity figures used were those appearing in BLS Bulletin 1249, *Trends in Output per Man-Hour in the Private Economy*, December 1959, Table 5, based on Kendrick's private nonfarm man-hours and the Department of Commerce private nonfarm GNP. Since the data were all in index number form, they were first converted to absolute values (except the price index, and here the "quantity" figure, of course, is set in terms of units to yield a price of $1.00 in 1954, the base year).

The figures on the output of commodities, services, and construction, were taken from Kuznets, *National Product since 1869* (New York, NBER, 1946), and linked to Department of Commerce data in 1929, the latter contrlling as to level. For the 1929–41 period, services include only consumer services. Construction includes both public and private construction. The data for 1948–59 are based on the more exhaustive detail given in the new Department of Commerce quarterly estimates on gross national product by type of product (*Survey of Current Business*, November 1960).

1929–41: Except as indicated above, the data are all taken from Department of Commerce estimates.

1948–59: The basic GNP and income share data are from Department of Commerce sources. However, Commerce does not publish a quarterly series on private nonfarm product. To arrive at this figure a quarterly estimate of government and farm product was made, based on partial data. Government wages and salaries are published quarterly, and the adjustment to compensation of government employees requires only the interpolation of minor adjustment items, available annually. Farm gross product was estimated by interpolating the annual adjustment items between income of farm operators and farm gross product, and adding this to the available quarterly figures on income of farm operators.

Corporate gross product, the corporate wage and price indexes, and the corporate productivity figure were taken from Kuh ("Profits, Profit Markups, and Productivity"). His estimates of corporate gross product from 1956 through 1959 were revised in line with the latest Commerce estimates. All of the data were extended, using the techniques described by Kuh, through the last two quarters of 1959. (Kuh's estimates end in the second quarter of 1959.)

The estimations of "normal" private nonfarm GNP, normal gross corporate product, and normal productivity gains are described in the text.

COMMENT

BERT G. HICKMAN, The Brookings Institution

Professor Schultze introduces his stimulating paper with the observation that other writers have recently emphasized the role of cyclical shifts in the profit share as a short-term consumption stabilizer. He has pushed well beyond other studies, however, in his attempt to quantify some of the principal influences governing fluctuations in the profit share and to assess how those influences may themselves vary with the phase of the cycle and, as among cycles, which differ in amplitude, duration, or both.

Schultze's basic hypothesis is that the share of profits in produced income is positively related to the level of capacity utilization, for two main reasons. "First, as output falls relative to capacity, unit overhead costs rise, with resulting lower profit margin . . . . Secondly, a rise in excess capacity should put pressure on profit margins via its influence on *ex-ante* markups." He postulates a "normal" profit share associated with "normal capacity output" and relates short-term variations in the profit share to positive and negative deviations of output from normal capacity. He employs the conventional definition of normal capacity as that output at which average unit costs are minimized.

More discussion of these postulates would have been welcome, since they form the theoretical rationale for the causal interpretations which are offered of the regression results, and yet there are conceptual barriers to accepting the interpretations without reservation. On Schultze's definitions, for example, the profit share should fall below normal for output deviations to *either* side of normal capacity, provided product price remains constant either absolutely or as a proportion of factor prices. If normal capacity is the output for which average unit cost is a minimum, it is irrelevant that unit overhead cost will decrease when output exceeds normal, since the resulting rise of variable cost per unit must by definition exceed the fall of overhead cost per unit.[1]

How then, may one account for the fact that Schultze's regressions do indeed show that the profit share is above or below its "normal" according to whether output is above or below "normal capacity"? One possibility is that the empirical estimate of capacity corresponds to the theoretical norm of minimum average cost, but that the rise of average cost, which occurs when output exceeds capacity, is more than compensated for by a concomitant price increase. In that case Schultze's second postulate—that *ex-ante* markups will vary directly with the level of capacity utilization—would be operative even though the first were not.

There is good reason to be suspicious of the foregoing rationalization, of course, since there is nothing in the author's estimation procedure to make it likely that the capacity index is an accurate measure of theoretical normal capacity. He has estimated capacity in such a way as to permit positive as well as negative output deviations, but that in itself tells us nothing about the behavior of unit costs on either side of estimated capacity.

Another, more plausible rationalization would run as follows. Assume that average variable costs typically are either falling or constant through a large range of observed output, as has often been claimed in empirical cost studies, and that the range of rising marginal and average costs is reached only rarely and sustained only briefly during business upswings. Then Schultze's empirical estimate of capacity may lie far to the left of the point of minimum

[1] One could not escape the difficulty by measuring output deviations from maximum attainable capacity (the output at which average total cost approaches a vertical asymptote) since the profit share would then increase through an initial range of negative output deviations and decrease thereafter. Similarly, if normal capacity were defined as the output at which average variable cost were minimized, the only result would be to introduce an initial range in which positive output deviations would increase the profit share—the latter would still fall for larger positive deviations.

average cost, allowing plenty of scope for the margin-increasing effect of falling unit overhead cost as output rises above estimated capacity. Thus, it is unnecessary to rest all the weight of explanation on variations in *ex-ante* markups.

Schultze also argues that "the excess-capacity hypothesis can explain the phenomenon which often occurs during the later stages of a boom, i.e., profit margins decline during a period in which the absolute level of income is still rising." This argument rests on the assumption that an increase of capacity in the face of an unchanged output, will have the same kind of depressing effect on profit margins as would a decline of output relative to an unchanged capacity. The assumption is certainly open to question. Insofar as costs are concerned, an increase of capacity—that is, a rightward shift of the short-term cost curve—could easily reduce unit costs at the old level of output if there were economies of scale, and could do so even in the face of constant returns to scale if the firm had previously been operating on the rising portion of its cost curve. In addition, a firm would not necessarily reduce its *ex-ante* markup while demand remains high and merely because it has increased its capacity; quite possibly it deliberately attempts to maintain a normal margin of overcapacity at the existing level of output.

An alternative hypothesis may be offered to explain the lead of profit margins over the downturn of aggregate income. It is indeed a fact that when aggregate production rises more slowly in the later stages of a boom there is both an increase of aggregate capacity, relative to aggregate output, and a decline in the aggregate profit margin. This empirical correlation does not in itself establish a causal relationship, however. As numerous National Bureau studies have demonstrated, another development which regularly accompanies a deceleration in the rate of increase of aggregate output, is an increase in the proportion of firms experiencing absolute declines of output. Thus, in a substantial number of firms—a number approaching 50 per cent as the rate of increase of aggregate output approaches zero—profit margins will be falling because of output declines, despite the fact that aggregate output is still rising.

It remains true, nonetheless, that the data show that in a majority of firms, profit margins decline before output starts to fall—that is, profit margins must be falling in some firms despite stable or rising outputs. It may be that the explanation of depressed margins in these cases is the one offered by Schultze (that capacity increases faster than output), but this cannot be established by appeal to aggregative data since it would be necessary to show that capacity was increasing relative to output in those particular firms. Moreover, there is another route by which margins could be depressed in those firms whether or not capacity rose relative to output.

There will be a general pressure on profit margins during normal business expansions because of increases in money wages. (By normal expansion I mean one not characterized by extreme inflationary pressure owing to widespread excess demands, as in 1947–48 or 1950.) It is irrelevant in this context whether the wage increases are autonomous or induced in the particular sectors in which they originate. It need only be noted that wage increases tend to become generalized throughout the economy, whereas the ability to offset wage increases by price increases will vary according to the demand prospects of individual firms and the market structures of the industries in which they are located. Hence, it is quite possible for profit margins to fall for firms whose outputs are stable or rising, not because cost curves have shifted to the right owing to increases of capacity, but because they have shifted upward owing to increases in wage rates which cannot be fully compensated for by price increases under existing demand conditions. Indeed, an expansion of capacity in such cases might reduce unit costs and prevent margins from falling as much as otherwise. It should be unnecessary to add that this entire argument presumes a general constraint on aggregate money demand, or to note that this is an eminently realistic assumption.

My next comments are directed to the empirical measurement of capacity and its effect on the numerical estimates of the marginal response of profits to output. Schultze states that the specification of a higher or lower level of capacity against which to measure output deviations would affect the *a* coefficient of his basic regression, which measures the "normal" profit share, but not the *b* coefficient, which measures the deviation of the profit share from normal for a given deviation of output from normal. Evidently he is assuming that a proportional change in the level of capacity against which each output deviation is measured would change all output deviations by the same absolute amount and merely shift the vertical axis. This is not correct. Each deviation is computed as actual output minus capacity output divided by actual output. A given proportional change in the level of capacity will alter a large deviation relatively less than a small one, affecting the values of both a and b.[2]

Apart from the mathematical point involved, the effects of capacity measurement on the regression parameters is important because Schultze's estimates of the response of corporate profits to output change depend on them. Thus, the ratio of the change of corporate profits to a given deviation of corporate income from normal is equal to $(a + b)$, and the corresponding elasticity is given by $(1 + b/a)$. If it were indeed true that only the value of a were affected by the specification of capacity level, this would mean that the derived profit-deviation slope would be dependent on that choice. It is therefore of considerable interest to note that not only do both coefficients depend on the specification of capacity, but that their sum, and hence the derived slope, is invariant to that specification.

Thus, let each period's estimated capacity be raised or lowered in the same proportion, so that the new capacity level for each period is k times the old one. Then, if a and b were the coefficients of the original linear relationship between profit share and output deviations, it can be shown from the formulas for the slope and intercept of a straight line that the corresponding new values will be as follows:

$$a' = a + b(1 - 1/k) \tag{1}$$

$$b' = b/k \tag{2}$$

$$a' + b' = a + b \tag{3}$$

These relationships hold whether the transformation is for an exact equation or a least squares regression. Hence, a change in the specification of capacity by a constant proportion will not affect the marginal relationship between profits and output deviations $(a + b)$, although it will alter the corresponding elasticity $(1 + b/a)$.

Thus far I have discussed the marginal relationship between corporate profits and output *deviations*. It can also be shown that the corresponding relationship between profits and output *changes* is invariant to the specification of capacity. A casual glance at the formula for the marginal relationship between corporate profits

[2] A given absolute change of capacity would also affect the relative deviations unevenly.

and corporate output would seem to contradict this statement, since a is a free constant in the formula whereas b is multiplied by another factor. The multiplicative factor itself depends on the specification of capacity, however, and in such a way that a change in the specification alters the values of a, b, and the multiplicative factor, in a manner which leaves the marginal profits-output relationship unaffected.

It may be concluded, then, that a proportional change in the specification of capacity in the profit share regression, or of "normal GNP" in the corporate product share regression, would not alter the derived marginal relationships and hence would not affect the implicit multiplier values. Thus Schultze's major quantitative results are not biased by the arbitrary nature of his capacity estimates.

The remainder of my remarks will be directed to the implications of Schultze's findings for cyclical stability. First, it is clear that gross corporate saving is a powerful automatic stabilizer insofar as consumption demand is concerned. Moreover, this was true even in prewar years, so that the multiplier was already comparatively small before the government fiscal stabilizers became important. The fiscal stabilizers have indeed diminished the value of the multiplier, since, as Schultze observed in connection with corporate taxes (and as is also true of personal taxes), the increased tax rates have not depressed corporate or personal saving propensities. As I have reported elsewhere, however, the resulting decrease in the value of the multiplier is quite modest, especially for mild contractions.[3]

Secondly, the marginal response of corporate saving to national product is larger for contractions than expansions. For this reason, and because of ratchet or permanent income effects on personal saving propensities, the multiplier is cyclically variable. The cyclical asymmetry of corporate saving is partly due to the dividend lag analyzed by Lintner. Also important, however, is the fact that gross profits absorb more of a decrease than they do of an increase of national product. Schultze explains this tendency by three factors: (1) the continued growth of capacity during the downturn and recovery; (2) the fact that commodity production, and hence corporate output, absorbs more of a fall of national product than it does of the subsequent rise; (3) the fact that profit

[3] See footnote 22 of Schultze's paper.

margins must rise more slowly once the excess capacity inherited from the contraction has been eliminated during the recovery phase of the upswing. I have already expressed doubts about the importance of the first of these three factors. A decrease of utilization brought about by an increase of capacity need not necessarily depress profit margins.

Finally, we come to Schultze's penetrating observations about the extent to which induced changes in corporate saving will be stabilizing during contractions which differ in amplitude and duration. Here as elsewhere he makes effective use of his resolution of the marginal corporate saving ratio into three components: the marginal response of corporate profits to corporate income, the marginal response of corporate income to total income, and the marginal response of corporate saving to corporate profits. The second and third of these relationships are strongly affected by the magnitude and duration of the decline, and hence account for most of the difference in corporate saving behavior as between mild and severe contractions.

I have nothing to add to the Lintner-Schultze analysis of the tendency for the marginal ratio of corporate saving to corporate profits to diminish as the contraction deepens and lengthens in duration. With regard to the remaining relationship, however—that between corporate product and national product—it should be noted that Schultze has abstracted from the relationship of investment to income change.

I do not have in mind the possible connection between corporate saving as a source of funds and corporate investment, since external funds are plentiful during contractions. Rather, my concern is with the fact that inventories are held primarily in connection with the production and distribution of commodities. Thus, the fact that most of the initial decline of final expenditure is at the expense of commodities instead of services may stabilize consumption through its effect on corporate saving, but it causes inventory investment to decline more than it otherwise would. Conversely, when at a later stage services begin to absorb more of the fall in final demand, the favorable effect on inventory demand will tend to offset the unfavorable effect on corporate saving. Thus, variations in the value of the multiplier associated with shifts in the composition of output are nullified at least partly by offsetting variations in the value of the acceleration coefficient.

Long-Run Changes in the Distribution of Income by Factor Shares in Canada

S. A. GOLDBERG
DOMINION BUREAU OF STATISTICS

Introduction

In economic literature, there has always been a lively interest in the relative amounts of the national product (or income) accruing to the factors of production. Theoretical discussions usually distinguished three factors: land, labor and capital, with a fourth—enterprise—first hovering uneasily on the horizon and later descending to claim a coordinate and, at times, somewhat commanding position. Empirical studies, while paying appropriate respects to the theoretical distinctions, tended to become soiled quickly with the stark realities of statistical exigency, leading to the adoption of either a simplified functional classification of income into (a) labor and (b) property, occasionally separated into land and capital; or a rather institutional classification which reflected legal property relationships—most frequently, wages and salaries, net income of unincorporated business and investment income, with the latter subdivided at times into corporation profits, net rents and interest. In either case the relationship between the statistical categories and their theoretical counterparts has been rather uneasy.

In general, the main conclusion of earlier empirical work was that the shares of labor and property fluctuated around a line that tended to be horizontal. In more recent years, less of a consensus has prevailed, some studies emerging with a constant long-run ratio and others with a decided upward trend in favor of labor. More recently, too, short-term fluctuations have been receiving increasing attention. Various explanations have been brought forward for the changes, or lack of them, in the observed data but it is generally acknowledged that a completely satisfying theoretical framework for studying and explaining the observed distributions of factor incomes and changes in them is still lacking. It is, presumably, one of the objectives of further

NOTE: S. A. Goldberg and F. H. Leacy are responsible for all aspects of the paper and supplement, respectively: none of the statements made or unpublished statistics shown may be attributed to the Dominion Bureau of Statistics. The authors wish to acknowledge a deep debt of gratitude to their colleagues who have collaborated with them in the statistical work: in particular, Jenny R. Podoluk, D. H. Jones, P. S. Sunga, and E. C. West.

empirical work in this field to provide raw material for formulating eventually more effective theoretical tools in the field of income distribution. Another objective, of very recent origin, is to add ultimately to the evolving arsenal of anticipatory indicators for the purpose of detecting emerging cyclical developments in the economy.

To our knowledge no comprehensive study of the factor shares has been carried out with Canadian data and the purpose of this paper is to provide a beginning in the filling of this gap. We wish to stress the word "beginning." The central task to which we have addressed ourselves is merely to make a (reasonably comprehensive) statistical exploration of the behavior of the factor shares in Canada over a relatively long period; in the attached supplement, F. H. Leacy covers similar ground for shorter time segments. Only marginal attention could be devoted to related developments and no effort has been made to explain the observed relationships in terms of cause and effect. These narrow terms of reference, while they are in line with our interpretation of our assignment, have been imposed on us also by a growing realization that our subject matter is highly complex and somewhat amorphous, and that a realistic explanation of the observed changes would require more detailed study of related developments than it would be possible for us to make within the time at our disposal, and more penetrating insights into economic processes than we can claim.

The paper is divided into two parts, preceded by a summary statement of procedures and results. Most of the statistical material is shown in the appendix. Part I is devoted to a discussion of concepts and definitions and provides some comparisons of ratios, using a variety of definitions of income. Part II deals with long-run developments in the shares of net domestic income and its subdivisions. Main attention is devoted to the period from 1926 to date but some comparisons are made with years prior to 1926. While general reference is made to all factor incomes, detailed attention is devoted to the labor share. An institutional approach has been adopted but the two-way functional classification of income into labor and property income is briefly discussed.

Before turning to the summary, a word may be said here about terminology in order to avoid confusion: (a) the words "wages,"

"wages, salaries and supplementary labor income," and "labor income" are used to mean the same thing. Unless otherwise stated supplementary labor income is always included with the total. (b) The word "share" is used always in the sense of a percentage of a total; it is used interchangeably with the word "ratio." Thus the wage share and the wage ratio represent the same thing in our terminology. Dollar amounts accruing to individual factors are referred to as "returns" to that factor. (c) The words "domestic income" always refer to the net domestic income at factor cost. Income originating in any subdivision of domestic income (such as in a particular industry or sector) is referred to as the "product" of that industry or sector. Thus, income originating in the private business sector is called the private business product.

Summary of Procedures, Main Results and Conclusions

It was necessary at the outset to decide which definition of income and factor returns to use in the statistical compilations. Domestic income was selected as the main variant but alternative definitions are discussed and ratios based on them compared, in part because the ensuing similarities and differences in the changes of the factor shares are of some consequence, and in part as a means of emphasizing the uncertainties inherent in our subject matter.

A decision had to be made, also, regarding the procedures to employ for the purpose of summarizing the statistical results. The simple technique of comparing five-year arithmetic averages of annual ratios, of more or less comparable years, at the beginning and end of the period under consideration, is used. However, heavy reliance has been placed on charted year-to-year movements to provide a background against which to view the changes in the five-year averages.

By coincidence, the first five years (1926–30) of the official time series on the national accounts are broadly comparable with the last five years (1954–58) for which data were available in more or less final form when the work on this paper began. These periods are, therefore, used in the main comparisons.

The periods are comparable in the sense that economic activity and employment were, on the whole, at a high pitch, although there was some variation among individual years: 1926 to 1928 were years of sharp upswing, 1929 a year of high activity but little growth and 1930 a year of decided downswing; a relatively mild pause in 1954 was followed by two years of intense growth, and two years of little (or no) growth but, on the whole, high activity. Persons without jobs and seeking work averaged 3.7 per cent of the labor force in 1926–30 and 4.5 per cent in 1954–58.

The terminal periods are, however, characterized by different price movements. The earlier period, 1926–30, is notable for the great stability that prevailed in the price level. In more recent years, by contrast, two years of price stability (1954 and 1955) were followed by pronounced upward movements in prices. These periods differ also in other respects, particularly in industrial structure and legal form of business organization; indeed, a substantial portion of Part II of the paper is devoted precisely to a discussion of these differences and to an attempt to evaluate statistically the impact of some of them on the observed changes in the factor shares. The most important of these differences are mentioned in the brief summary of the statistical results that follows.

There was a considerable rise in the wage share (some 17 per cent)[1] from 1926–30 to 1954–58, accompanied by a substantial decline in the share of net unincorporated income, both farm (—50 per cent) and nonfarm (—30 per cent). The relative importance of investment income remained fairly constant in the two periods, reflecting the net outcome of a percentage rise in the share of corporation profits, that almost matched that of salaries and wages, offset by a decline in the share of interest, rents, and other investment income.

Different definitions of income affect mainly the changes in the share of investment income and only moderately those of the other components. The four sectors contributing to domestic income—persons, general government, government business, and private business—are heterogeneous, and their contribution to production is valued differently in the national accounts. When the changes in the factor shares of the private business portion are examined separately, they appear to have been broadly similar to those of domestic income described above, although the rise in the wage ratio is moderately higher (20 per cent).

[1] The percentage figures shown in this summary refer to percentage changes in the *shares*, on the base of 1926–30. To illustrate, the wage share increased from 56.7 in 1926–30 to 66.2 in 1954–58, or by 9.5 points, amounting to nearly 17 per cent.

The percentage of wages and salaries paid out to total income originating differs among the various industries comprising the private business product. Accordingly, varying rates of growth of the constituent industries may be reflected in changes in the over-all wage ratio of the private business product. When allowance is made for this factor the remaining change in the wage ratio may be attributed to developments within industries. It appears that a large portion (roughly 60 per cent) of the observed increase in the over-all wage share of the private business product is due to interindustry shifts of the type mentioned, reflecting mainly the declining importance of the contribution of the agriculture industry to the total product.

The increase in the wage ratio that remains after the adjustments mentioned in the preceding paragraph have been made, is appreciable (roughly 7 to 8 per cent), but its meaning is hard to appraise:

a. One of the differences between the terminal periods is that the relative importance of nonfarm unincorporated business has declined, and the question naturally arises as to the extent to which the remaining increase in the wage share reflects a change in institutional practice *within* industries—a shift from unincorporated to the incorporated form of business organization. Such a shift can give rise to a lifting of the wage ratio because wages paid out are a larger fraction of income originating in incorporated business than in unincorporated business. It has not been possible to handle this problem satisfactorily in the absence of the appropriate statistics, but some rough calculations suggest that a portion of the remaining increase reflects a shift to the incorporated form of business organization.

b. The remaining rise in the wage ratio may reflect the changing composition of the labor force (within industries). This point is of added relevance in view of the fact that the increase in the wage share occurred mainly after 1946, coincident with an apparent upward drift in the relative importance of occupations involving a greater amount of training and skill.

c. The percentage of wages and salaries to sales or total income for incorporated establishments seems to decline as the size of establishment increases, so that different size distributions of establishments (within industries) in the periods being compared may "produce" a change in the over-all wage ratio of the private business product.

Although the periods 1926–30 and 1954–58 appear to be reasonably appropriate for comparisons such as are made in this paper the question does arise whether undetected cyclical and other factors of a passing nature, peculiar to the one or the other period, may have contributed to the observed changes in the factor shares. To throw some light on this question special estimates of domestic income and wages and salaries were prepared for the years 1919 to 1925. Preliminary results of this work indicate that (a) before removal of interindustry shifts, the ratios for the domestic income of the earlier years are, on the whole, in the neighborhood of the average for 1926–30; and (b) after removal of interindustry shifts the ratios of the earlier years are, on the whole, of the same order of magnitude as the average for 1954–58. These findings make it even more doubtful that trend significance can be attached to the increase, from 1926–30 to 1954–58, in the wage ratio of the private business product (and *a fortiori* domestic income), after removal of the effect of the changing relative importance of constituent industries.

The changes in the over-all wage share after removal of the influence of interindustry shifts appear moderate in comparison with the wide variation in the changes of the ratios of the constituent industries. This relative inertness in the longer-run movements of the over-all ratios compared with the pronounced variation among those of constituent components is apparent in the industrial classes of domestic income and private business product, as well as in manufacturing. It is, of course, reasonable to expect substantial differences in the changes of the ratios among individual industries as the cyclical and other circumstances peculiar to each industry differ; and a certain amount of cancellation when the detailed parts are combined into larger aggregates. Be that as it may, the diverse behavior of the constituent parts throws considerable doubt on the adequacy of global explanations of the movements in the aggregate shares (of the economy as a whole or of the total private business product) that appeal to over-all variables, for example, of capital, labor inputs and prices.

While study of developments in individual industries and groups of industries will throw much needed light on the meaning of the movements of the aggregate ratios, and the forces underlying them, the process of aggregation from detailed industries into larger segments should not, in our view, stop short of the economy as a whole since "everything depends on everything else." For example, the labor employed by government, even though it is not matched in the conventional national income statistics with corresponding estimates of capital service, surely competes with labor employed in the private sector. Similarly, residential capital should not be left out in a general theory. Furthermore, in view of the difficulties inherent in separating net income of unincorporated business into its components (of labor income and investment income) a general theory of the distribution of income by factor shares should attempt to handle this income component as a single entity.

I: Changes in Factor Shares on the Basis of Different Concepts and Definitions

Section 1 of this first part of our paper is devoted to a discussion of definitional and conceptual problems. The main purpose of this discussion is to indicate that, while we prefer the domestic income concept, there are some uncertainties regarding the precise delineation of aggregate income that cannot be resolved unequivocally; and further, that the composition of the constituent factor returns is rather heterogeneous, with ensuing implications as to the meaning of the observed changes in the ratios. Section 2 is designed to display the quantitative impact of various definitions on the changes in factor shares, thus providing perspective within which to view the changes described in the second part of the paper.

1. DEFINITIONS OF FACTOR SHARES: TOTAL AND COMPONENTS[2]

Just as market values can be separated into prices and quantities so can factor returns be thought of as quantities of factors (e.g. number of man-hours) multiplied by their unit prices (e.g. wage rates).[3] The total national income may be regarded simply as

[2] In writing this section we have benefited from Simon Kuznets, "Quantitative Aspects of Economic Growth of Nations: IV. Distribution of National Income by Factor Shares," *Economic Development and Cultural Change*, April 1959, Pt. II, esp. pp. 1–7.

[3] This way of looking at the matter is, of course, more difficult for investment income, and more difficult still for net unincorporated income. The phrase

the sum of factor returns arrived at in this way, and changes in the shares of factors may be thought of as reflecting changes in relative unit prices and relative amounts of factors employed in production. Complications arising from market imperfections and institutional arrangements aside, the ultimate causes of changes in the total income and the relative size of its constituent parts must be sought, of course, in changes in demand and prices for commodities and services, changes in technology, and changes in the supply and quality of the several factors of production, and in the interactions of these changes. We mention here this rather oversimplified generalization merely to provide some sort of a setting within which to view the considerations that follow.

Of more immediate concern is that the calculated size and changes of total income and its parts depend not only on the fundamental forces just mentioned but also upon the definitions employed. Naturally the definitions selected should reflect as closely as possible the fundamental forces at play, but which definitions actually come closest to achieving this is to some extent a matter of judgment, although statistical convenience necessarily plays a part in the choice.

The two most widely used definitions of the total product in studies such as this are the net national income at factor cost (to be referred to henceforth as national income), and the net domestic income at factor cost (to be referred to henceforth as domestic income). The difference between these two aggregates, it will be recalled, is that the former excludes and the latter includes payments abroad of factor income, while the former includes and the latter excludes receipts from abroad of factor incomes.[4] We have decided to use domestic income and its subdivisions as the main denominator in the calculations of part II, but in section 2, below, comparisons are made among ratios using a variety of definitions of income.

Our preference for domestic income is to some extent dictated by statistical convenience, as it is easier to handle industry and sector distributions of income on this basis. More fundamentally,

---

"wage rates" is used here to include not only wages and salaries but all other labor costs that are included in "wages, salaries and supplementary labor income."

[4] In the Canadian National Accounts only interest and dividends are involved. Payments to and receipts from abroad of wages and salaries, which are believed to be quite small, are not taken into account in the compilation of national income.

we prefer the domestic concept because it comes closer to a conception of income as it emanates from the point of production before the intervention of quasi-administrative decisions such as are involved in the distribution of dividends.

Likewise, our preference for the net concept, as opposed to the gross, is based on the simple view that allowances for capital consumption represent not a return *to* capital but a return *of* capital. It is, of course, true that the available (book value) depreciation figures leave a lot to be desired: a significant and varying proportion of profits may be impounded in them, depending on the extent to which the taxation incentive to shorten the lives of assets through write-offs is balanced by the tendency to undervalue capital consumption in relation to rising cost of replacement. It should be added, however, that there is some doubt as to the extent to which higher cost of replacement reflects higher prices rather than more efficient plant and equipment. If estimates of capital consumption valued at replacement cost and based on "realistic" assumptions of asset life were available, we would probably use them, and adjust profits and net unincorporated income accordingly, just as we have used the inventory valuation adjustment. In the absence of such estimates the available net figures have been used, with the proviso, however, that the significance of the changes in the resulting ratios must be appraised in the light of the uncertain composition of the depreciation data.

We must admit, however, that our preference for aggregates (and components) containing implied replacement cost depreciation (and inventories calculated on the basis of the value of physical change rather than the change of book values) results in considerable discomfort because (questions of reliability of the adjusted statistics aside) we are not sure which figures—the book values or the adjusted magnitudes—have a greater influence on the actions of entrepreneurs.

The use of net concepts is in close harmony with general practice and the requirements of theory.[5] More controversial is the treatment of interest on the public (and to a lesser extent, the consumer) debt. It would seem that this controversy stems basically

[5] The gross concept is implicitly preferred in the Canadian National Accounts; this is reflected in the fact that the tables on the industrial distribution of domestic income show only the gross figures. See *National Accounts, Income and Expenditure 1926–1956* (Dominion Bureau of Statistics, Ottawa).

from the unresolved problems of measuring adequately the output of noncommercial institutions; these problems, referred to again later, have had to be skirted in the construction of national accounts, in the absence of statistical solutions that are not at variance with common sense. The Canadian practice[6] of excluding all interest on the public debt and replacing it with an admittedly rough and incomplete estimate of imputed rents on government buildings, represents something of an act of desperation; and we have used it here in the absence of practical alternatives with greater appeal.

We have taken it for granted, so far, that incomes before taxes are the relevant magnitudes for our purposes. Yet the question may well be asked whether the typical businessman is guided by anticipated incomes before taxes or after taxes; for example, in making decisions regarding relative amounts of capital and labor to combine in production. In general, does labor respond to wages before taxes or net of taxes and other deductions in making decisions regarding alternative job opportunities or amounts of labor service to sell?

It would not be proper to take a strong position on matters about which so little is known. We are disposed to favor the before-tax figures because they appear to be more relevant in a substantially competitive economy—an economy in which all comers face the same structure of tax rates, where the quest for larger shares of markets (or the maintenance of existing ones) is an overriding consideration in making decisions, and where sheer bulk of personal and business income is a mighty prestige factor, even though the incomes may be reduced substantially by the state.

Income after taxes is really the more suitable concept in an analysis centered around the command over resources arising from the income stream, including capital transactions, in contrast with a study of income shares as they emerge from the productive process directly—the so-called "primary distribution of income."[7] A familiar variant of the former concept is disposable income, per-

[6] For a description of the Canadian practice and the reasons underlying it, see R. B. Crozier "The Treatment of Interest on the Public Debt in the National Accounts," *The Canadian Journal of Economics and Political Science*, November 1959.

[7] See, for example, Jesse Burkhead, "Changes in the Functional Distribution of Income," *Journal of the American Statistical Association*, June 1953.

sonal or business. This, however, would exclude capital gains and losses, in the absence of the appropriate information in Canada. Disposable income is more comprehensive than domestic income to the extent that it includes transfer incomes as well as those paid out in production; it is less comprehensive in that it excludes income arising in production that has not been paid out, although this exclusion is more applicable to personal disposable income than business disposable income. At any rate, the personal disposable concept, including its before-tax variant, lends itself readily to analysis of distributions of incomes by size of incomes and other characteristics of households and individuals. It should be emphasized that, despite the fact that the distribution of income by factor shares is in many ways related to the distribution of income by size of income, one cannot reach conclusions about changes in the latter from observed changes in the former without courting misleading inferences.

Various definitions of total income affect the constituent shares differently and we now turn to a more detailed consideration of the nature of the components. Each of the main headings of domestic income—salaries and wages, investment income, and net unincorporated income—is composed of heterogeneous items which, while possessing a common, unifying thread, are substantially unlike. Moreover, characteristics attributed to one class are also found, in some instances to a significant degree, in the others. Such heterogeneity is inherent in all classifications of complex phenomena and would not be serious in a study of changes in relative shares if it could be assumed that the relative importance of the characteristics remains substantially constant. Such an assumption would almost certainly be wrong, probably in proportion to the length of the time interval being considered, but to determine quantitatively the size and direction of such changes is a formidable task beyond our reach. However, the significance one attaches to the data described later is surely influenced, or should be, by the image one forms of the composition of the constituent parts and the possible changes in them, and we therefore summarize briefly several characteristics of the factor shares, purely as a reminder.

Turning first to the labor share, equated in the official statistics (and in this paper) with "wages, salaries and supplementary labor income," it should be noted that it is at once incomplete and too comprehensive. It is incomplete in that it excludes the contribution to production of certain classes of individuals, namely unpaid family workers and working owners of unincorporated business; and, of lesser importance, certain emoluments taking the form of investment income, for example interest on pension funds. It is too comprehensive, in that it includes the return from working of all classes of paid employees, whatever their function in the organization—top executives, managers, and superintendents, as well as the whole range of skilled and unskilled clerical and manual workers. Many executive functions involve a degree of inventiveness and risk (both to the person concerned and the business) very much like the "enterprise" for which part, at least, of profits is considered the theoretical reward; and the psychological identification with the concern of the individuals fulfilling these functions resembles more that of owners than of employees.[8] Furthermore, a substantial amount of prior investment in time and money on training and education, which resembles physical capital accumulation, is clearly involved in the execution of many jobs. Although the return to this "human capital" appears in practice as an indistinguishable component of salaries and wages, it may be more properly regarded, from some points of view, as a form of investment income.

Casual observation suggests that significant changes may indeed have taken place in the occupational composition of the labor force since the end of World War I and particularly since World War II, even if the so-called "managerial revolution" is not taken into consideration.[9]

[8] In the case of closely held owner-managed corporations the distinction between salaries and investment income is even more arbitrary as it may reflect primarily the influence of tax considerations.

[9] Census information on occupational changes is difficult to interpret. However, an examination of the data between 1931 and 1951 suggests that there has been some upgrading, which may have continued at an accelerated pace since 1951. In a recent unpublished study, W. R. Dymond, Director, Economics and Research Branch, Department of Labour (Canada), comes to the following conclusion: "It is abundantly clear that the fastest growing occupations are the ones requiring relatively high levels of training and education. The professional group has been increasing most rapidly . . . . An outstanding development in the last 10 to 15 years has been the creation of a whole range of new jobs at the level between skilled trades and the professions, which may loosely be classified as technician occupations." Statistics of the annual census of manufacturing show that the ratio of "production and related workers" to total employees has been declining since the twenties and particularly since the second world war for manufacturing as a whole. The "non-production workers" include supervisors, engineers, technicians, office personnel and others but even among the "production workers" a

To the extent that market transactions are accepted as the relevant guides in the classification and valuation of factor services, it can be argued that, when labor services with more, or more up-to-date, training and education are offered on the market these are nonetheless pure and simple labor services, albeit of higher quality,[10] in the sense of being more suitable and effective to emerging technological requirements. The fact that the labor is of higher quality will be reflected in the price which market demand and supply fixes. More often than not the "upgrading" of the quality of labor will be preceded by the appearance on the scene of higher quality capital—in the same sense of being more up-to-date and effective—and the market forces will also fix the price of its services, in which the new characteristics will be reflected. It is the ratio of this new price for the services of capital to that of labor (as well as the relative quantities of each being combined in the

---

greater number of trained people may be included. An examination of labor force data indicates that the percentage of nonfarm female workers in total nonfarm paid workers has risen since the end of the war. In 1947 the percentage was 25.9 and in 1958, 28.8. This rise since the war has taken place outside of manufacturing. Women command lower wage rates than men and it may therefore be thought that a rise in the proportion of women in the labor force would pull down the share of wages. This is not necessarily so, as the comparison must take into account, also, the extent to which wage rates of female workers have risen compared with those of men; it is possible that the present differential in the wage rates between men and women is smaller, on average, than it was in the late twenties or right after the war.

Census information and data on school enrollment from the Education Division (D.B.S.) indicate that there has been an increase in the number of years of schooling of the Canadian population. In 1921 the average (mean) number of years of schooling of Canadians was 9.1 years and in 1951, 10.5 years; the median years of schooling for Canadians ten years and over, not in school, is estimated at 6.9 years in 1921 compared with the Census figure of 8.25 years in 1951; the per cent of the school population, ages 5–19, in school, was 61.5 per cent in 1921 and 66.7 per cent in 1951. The 1961 Census may show an acceleration of these trends. More revealing than these global averages, perhaps, is the following table showing the percentage of the population attending school by age groups:

Age Group	*1921*	*1951*
Total 5–24	49.3	52.2
5–9	65.5	65.2
10–14	88.7	93.0
15–19	24.8	40.5
20–24	2.3	4.9

NOTE: Not including Newfoundland, Yukon, and Northwest Territories.

SOURCE: *Ninth Census of Canada, 1951,* Ottawa, 1956, Vol. X, *General Review,* Chapter XI, Table II, p. 214.

[10] R. M. Solow, "A Skeptical Note on the Constancy of Relative Shares," *The American Economic Review,* September 1958, p. 630.

new situation) that will be reflected in the relative factor shares.

While the employer may find it more relevant to regard all hired help simply as labor, though of varying quality (and no portion as capital), this is not necessarily so from the point of view of the individual concerned or that of society; and, as Kuznets pointed out,[11] it may not be the most useful way of looking at the problem for studies of economic growth. We cannot pursue this matter further here and it may suffice merely to point out that considerations such as those mentioned above add elements of vagueness to the significance of changes in the observed ratios of factor shares which are described later. We skip over other impurities in the definition of labor income[12] to a brief consideration of the other factor shares.

Investment income[13]—the return to owners of capital used in production—is also incomplete to the extent that it excludes returns to owners of property of unincorporated business concerns. Furthermore, the size and fluctuations of this return obviously depend on how capital is defined—whether consumer durables and outlays on long-run research and development, for example, are included or excluded; as well as whether or not interest on the public and consumer debt and depreciation allowances are included, as already intimated. If one is prepared to overlook the implications of the issues just raised and adopt the conventional definitions of the national accounts, the resulting *aggregate* of investment income is reasonably clear-cut; but once one starts examining its constituent parts strong ambiguities emerge: corporation profits include transfer incomes to the extent that they contain interest on the public and consumer debt; net rents appear as corporation profits when accruing to corporations but as a separate income component when accruing to individuals, and this is also true of interest; government investment income is a composite of miscellaneous receipts reduced by interest on government debt; net rents and net interest[14] contain elements of labor income (which, however, are likely to be quantitatively unimportant).

[11] Kuznets, in *Economic Development and Cultural Change*, April 1959, p. 5.

[12] To illustrate, labor income is defined in gross terms—to the extent, for example, that expenses on transportation to and from work and other expenses arising from the job are not deducted; on the other hand, certain benefits in the form of subsidized cafeterias, for example, are not added. Some part, at least, of expense accounts may also add to the real income of the recipient.

[13] This paragraph benefited from comments by T. K. Rymes.

[14] For example, when an individual manages his own estate.

To simplify our task we deal below mainly with the aggregate of investment income.

Perhaps the most difficult income component to handle satisfactorily is net income of unincorporated business. For some purposes (such as the determination of the value of parameters used in simplified production functions) this "factor share" is most conveniently regarded as a composite of two distinct shares—labor income and investment income—which ought to be separated into its parts. For other purposes, such as studying separately the behavior and development of segments of business with distinct sociological and economic characteristics, the net income should be kept intact.

There is, of course, no reason why both these purposes could not be served by appropriate arrangement of the statistical material; and the case against splitting the composite of net income of unincorporated business has to be made on other grounds. We touch on the statistical aspects of this problem later; it may suffice to indicate here that we would be as hard put to separate net unincorporated income into its theoretical components as we would be to break down, for example, corporation profits into interest, rents, "pure" profits, and so on. The entity "net unincorporated income" should perhaps be likened, not to a *mixture* of elements, but to a chemical compound in which the constituent elements have become transformed into something which is neither labor nor capital but a synthesis of both. Thus it happens, as Kuznets points out,[15] that when the return to capital of unincorporated business is estimated residually, what appears to be an unreasonably low figure is obtained; and similarly, when the return to labor is calculated in this manner. The point is that the unincorporated owner's *own* labor and the capital employed in the business may not be two independent factors whose services can be priced independently of each other or priced on the basis of market criteria relevant to other sectors of the economy.[16]

[15] See Kuznets, in *Economic Development and Cultural Change,* April 1959, pp. 26–27. It should be noted, however, that high postwar tax rates may have had some depressing influence on the size of the net income estimates, as the incentives and ability to understate taxable incomes are probably greater for this factor share than for the others. Furthermore, the estimates of a number of components of net income of incorporated business are based on poor data.

[16] The concept of substitution of capital for labor when their relative prices change is difficult to apply to the labor that the working-owner contributes to the enterprise. It is interesting to note in this connection that, despite the rapid

2. COMPARISONS OF CHANGES IN FACTOR SHARES USING VARIOUS DEFINITIONS

We now turn to a comparison of factor shares using the various definitions of income discussed above. In each case the components have been recalculated to conform to the contents of the aggregate. The ratios are shown in Table 1 for the years 1926–30 and 1954–58. In addition, accompanying charts show comparisons, for the whole period from 1926 to 1958, for selected components that were thought to be of special interest.

Turning first to a comparison of the ratios of domestic income and national income, it will be seen that the increase in the relative wage share is appreciably greater, and the decline in the share of net unincorporated income somewhat smaller, in domestic income than in national income, but the most notable difference is in regard to investment income. Whereas investment income, as a percentage of domestic income, was practically the same in the five-year periods 1926–30 and 1954–58, it shows a rather pronounced rise when adjusted to a national income concept and expressed as a percentage of national income; reflecting, of course, the influence of changes in net factor payments to foreigners.[17] In the earlier period these payments represented 5.1 per cent of domestic income but in the more recent years the percentage had fallen to 1.6 per cent. Examination of Chart 1 indicates, further, that the differences in the ratio of investment income widened during the depression of the thirties, reflecting the fact that payments of dividends and interest abroad were sustained at high levels even in the face of rapidly falling profits. In the depth of the depression net interest and dividends paid to foreigners amounted to fully 9 per cent of domestic income. During the war and postwar years, however, payments abroad became relatively less important in relation to domestic income and, as a consequence,

mechanization on Canadian farms and the ensuing displacement of man by machines, this has not led to a displacement of the farmers' own labor—the number of hours worked on the farm by farm operators not having changed, apparently, in the postwar years. General observation suggests that, in the case of many professional people, mechanization in their offices is not accompanied by a reduction in their own labor; and that small business proprietors tend to work as hard in bad times as in good times though for different reasons.

[17] It should be noted that these figures are purely formal to the extent that the national income figures include undistributed income accruing to foreigners.

TABLE 1

COMPARISON OF CHANGES IN FACTOR SHARES USING DIFFERENT DEFINITIONS

	1926–30 (1)	1954–58 (2)	Point Change (col. 2 minus col. 1) (3)	Percentage Change (col. 3 ÷ col. 1) (4)
1. *Domestic Income*				
Wages and salaries	56.7	66.2	9.5	16.8
Investment income	20.3	20.2	− 0.1	− 0.5
Net unincorporated income	23.0	13.6	− 9.4	−40.9
Corporation profits[a]	10.6	12.2	1.6	15.1
2. *National Income*				
Wages and salaries	59.8	67.3	7.5	12.5
Investment income	16.0	18.9	2.9	18.1
Net unincorporated income	24.2	13.8	−10.4	−43.0
3. *Gross Domestic Income*				
Wages and salaries	49.8	57.3	7.5	15.1
Investment income	26.9	28.4	1.5	5.6
Net unincorporated income	23.4	14.4	− 9.0	−38.5
4. *Domestic Income plus Interest on Public and Consumer Debt*				
Wages and salaries	53.9	63.9	10.0	18.5
Investment income	24.2	22.9	− 1.3	− 5.4
Net unincorporated income	21.9	13.2	− 8.7	−39.7
5. *Domestic Income after Tax*				
Wages and salaries after tax	57.2	69.0	11.8	20.6
Corporation profits after tax[a]	10.0	7.7	− 2.3	−23.0
6. *Personal Income before Tax*				
Wages and salaries	61.3	69.9	8.6	14.0
Investment income received by persons	12.8	8.9	− 3.9	−30.5
Net unincorporated income	24.5	14.4	−10.1	−41.2

SOURCES: Personal income data (item 6) are taken from the Canadian National Accounts publications without adjustment. All other data are from Tables A-1 through A-5.

[a] These figures of corporation profits are not entirely on a domestic basis; while they exclude interest and dividends received from abroad, they include only dividends, but not interest, paid abroad by corporations.

the ratios of investment income in the two aggregates have tended to converge.

When comparisons are made between the relative factor shares of net domestic income and gross domestic income (that is, before deduction of depreciation allowances in the total and components) rather less striking differences emerge for the two terminal periods:

CHART 1
Factor Shares in Relation to National and Domestic Income

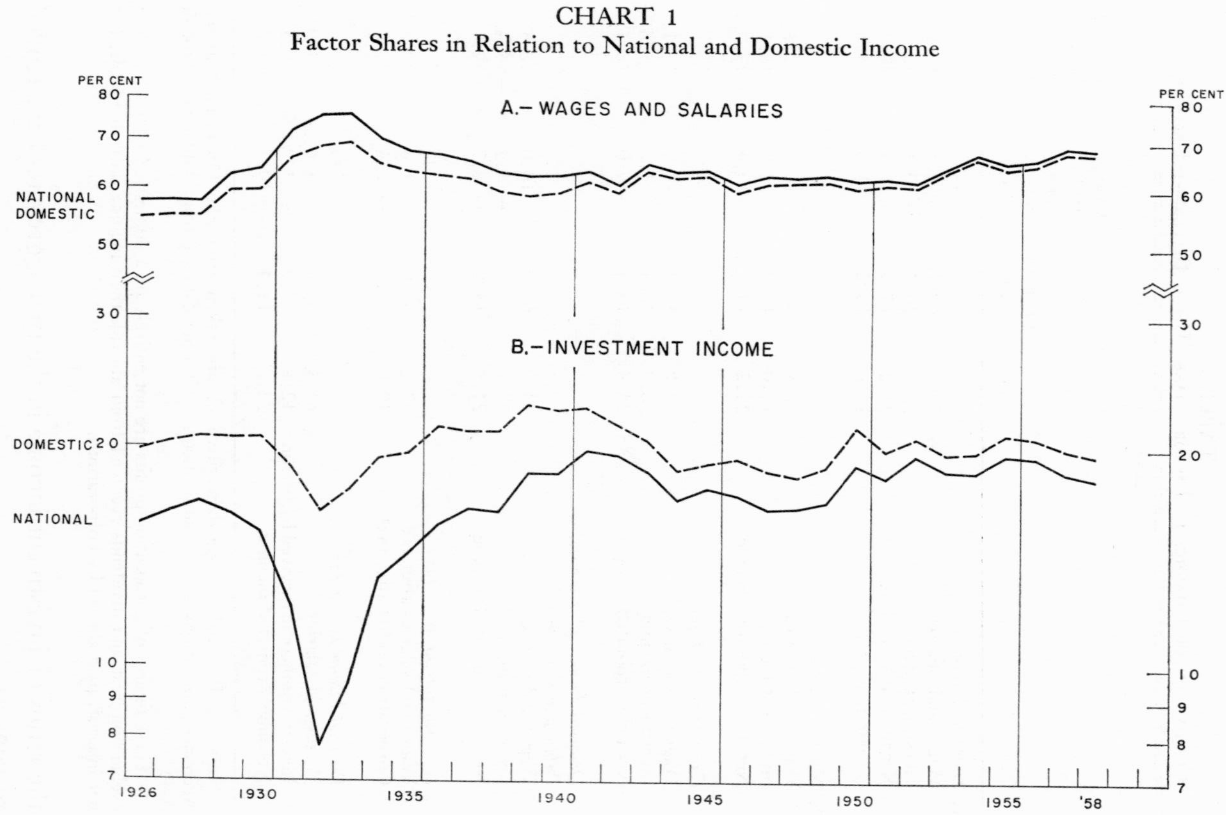

the rise in the ratio of wages and salaries and the decline in that of unincorporated business were somewhat smaller in the gross figures, while the ratio of gross investment income rose moderately. However, Chart 2 (lines 3 and 5) and Chart 3 (lines 1 and 3) indicate that the differences in the amplitude of the movements of the wage and investment income ratios were considerable. The ratio of gross investment income shows a much shallower trough in the thirties, reflecting the fact that, with only a fraction of capacity being utilized, depreciation allowances represented a larger proportion of gross profits. The curve of the gross ratio also remained flatter in the postwar years until 1950 and from 1955 on. In the latter case, this probably reflected changes in the income tax laws that encouraged companies to charge higher capital cost allowances.

Although interest on the public debt was much higher in more recent years than in the twenties it did not rise as fast as the domestic income. Accordingly, when interest on the public debt is added to investment income and aggregate income, the resulting ratio shows a moderate decline, compared with no change in the ratio of domestic income. This decline is dampened somewhat by the inclusion, in the figures of Table 1, of interest on consumer debt which had risen more sharply than domestic income in the postwar years. However, the weight of interest on consumer debt was not great enough to alter appreciably the general picture.[18] Chart 3 (lines 2 and 3) shows, further, that the amplitude of the movements of the two income variants has been appreciably different. In particular, in the early thirties, the cyclical trough of the investment income ratio disappears with interest on the public debt included, reflecting a moderate depression-induced swelling of the public debt during these years, in contrast with rapidly shrinking profits.

Turning to the before-tax and after-tax comparisons, it will be seen that from 1926–30 to 1954–58, the wage ratio rose considerably more after exclusion of taxes than in the before-tax calculations. As might be expected, the opposite is true for corporation profits: while corporation profits before tax, as a percentage of domestic income, rose from 10.6 to 12.2, or by some 15 per cent, the after-tax ratios declined from 10.0 to 7.7, or

[18] Similarly net imputed rent on government buildings has *not* been deducted but exclusion of rents would not alter the ratios perceptibly.

CHART 2
Wages and Salaries in Aggregate Income, Various Concepts

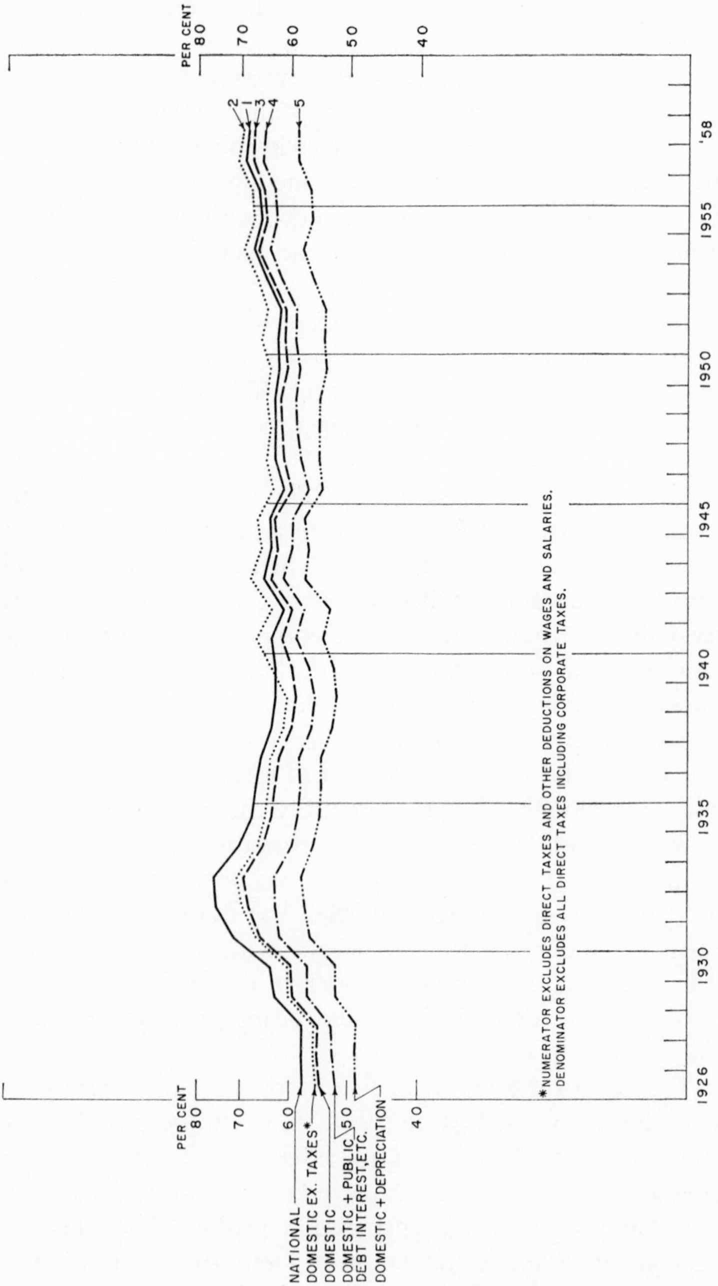

PER CENT 80 70 60 50 40

2 1 3 4 5

1926 1930 1935 1940 1945 1950 1955 '58

NATIONAL
DOMESTIC EX. TAXES*
DOMESTIC
DOMESTIC + PUBLIC DEBT INTEREST, ETC.
DOMESTIC + DEPRECIATION

*NUMERATOR EXCLUDES DIRECT TAXES AND OTHER DEDUCTIONS ON WAGES AND SALARIES. DENOMINATOR EXCLUDES ALL DIRECT TAXES INCLUDING CORPORATE TAXES.

CHART 3

Investment Income in Aggregate Income, Various Concepts

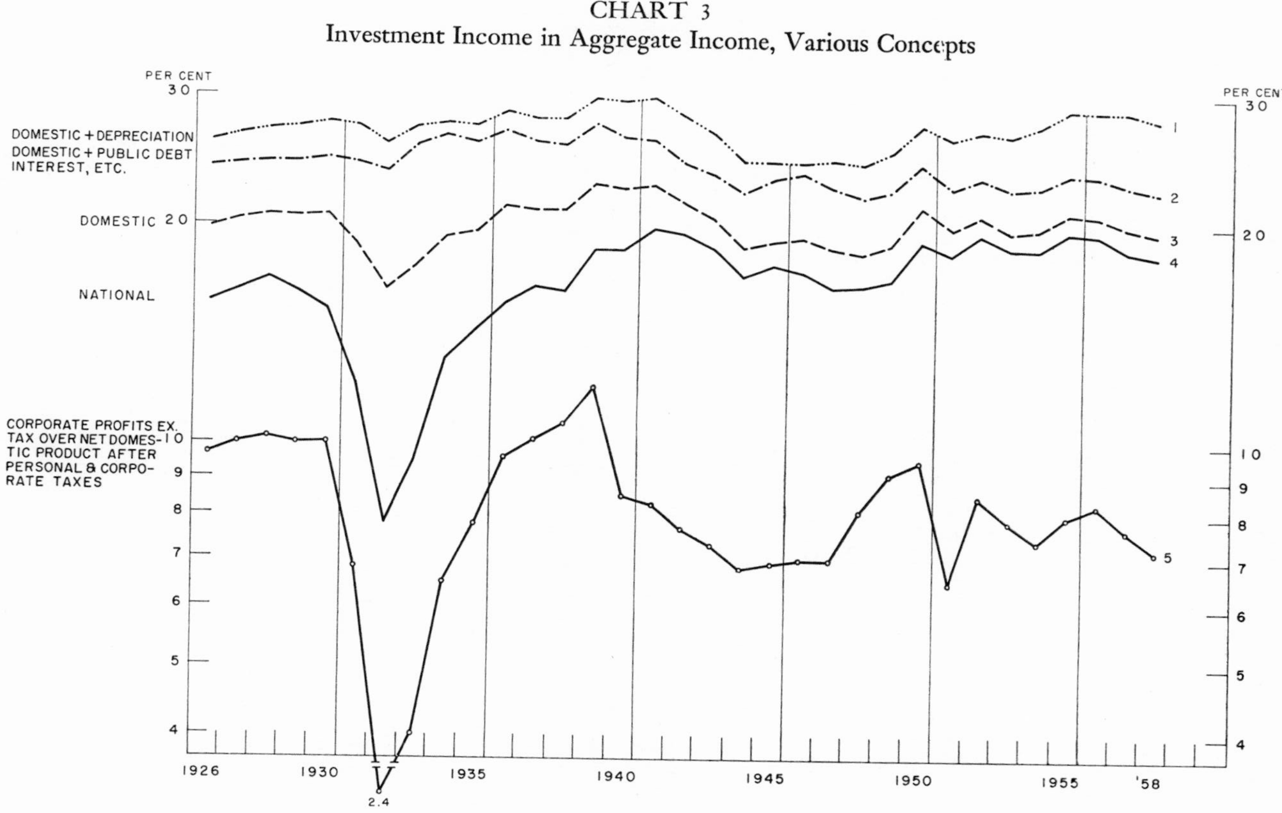

by 23 per cent.[19] Chart 2 (lines 2 and 3) shows that the spread in the wage ratios before and after taxes fluctuated within a narrow band until 1939; between 1939 and 1940 the band widened abruptly and remained wider, with some variations, until 1952, at which time, it tended to narrow. The widening between 1939 and 1940 was caused by a jump in corporate tax rates which resulted in an increase in corporation income tax from 18.4 per cent of profits in 1939 to 44.4 per cent in 1940. Taxes and other deductions accounted for 2.9 per cent of wages in 1940, practically unchanged from the previous year, and although this percentage rose to nearly 9 per cent in 1942, taxes on profits and other incomes also rose.

In summary, Table 1 and the charts suggest that while the relative factor shares calculated on the basis of different definitions exhibit striking similarities in general behavior, they also show some notable differences. In the longer-term comparison from 1926–30 to 1954–58, a considerable increase is shown for the wage ratio and a substantial decline for the ratio of net unincorporated income, no matter what definition is used. On the other hand, the situation is rather more indeterminate in regard to the longer-run changes and fluctuations of the ratio of investment income.

II: Longer-Run Changes in Factor Shares of Domestic Income and Its Subdivisons

In what follows we concentrate attention on domestic income and its subdivisions but, as we shall see, it is difficult to arrive at unequivocal conclusions even within the restricted framework of a single definition of total output.

We begin (Section 1) with an examination of the changes in the factor shares in the two terminal periods 1926–30 and 1954–58, leading up to the question of the extent to which certain structural and institutional changes in the economy may be reflected in the observed rise of the wage ratio. Section 2 is devoted to a discussion of the influence on factor shares of changes in the relative importance of the four sectors of the economy—persons, general

[19] Only wages and salaries and corporation profits are included in these comparisons because it has not been possible to separate other direct taxes between those falling on net unincorporated income, on the one hand, and on investment income received by persons on the other. Employer and employee contributions to social insurance and government pension plans have been included with taxes on wages.

government, government business and private business. This analysis leads to the somewhat surprising conclusion (Section 3) that, on balance, the influence of these changes has been rather small, so that the behaviour of the private business product is shown to be substantially similar to that of the total domestic income.

Changes in the relative importance of the various industries comprising the private business product are next considered (Section 4). The impact of these changes on the longer-run movements of the wage ratio has been substantial, reflecting mainly the decline of the relative importance of agriculture which, being almost wholly unincorporated, is characterized by a very small wage ratio. The point emerges, incidentally, that the movements of the wage ratios in the various industrial groups have been very different.

A more detailed examination of the factor shares of the nonfarm private business product is made in Section 5. The discussion focuses attention on the extent to which the observed increases in the standardized wage ratios may reflect the declining importance of net income of unincorporated business within industries. The reasons for the decision not to split net unincorporated income between wages and investment income are specified.

Attention is then turned (Section 6) to the question of whether a more detailed standardization for changing industry weights than was made in Section 4 would affect the changes in the wage ratios significantly. To answer this question detailed data on the census of manufacturing are used; the general conclusion is that more detailed standardization would not affect the over-all results significantly, in manufacturing at least. The manufacturing data emphasize again that the relatively moderate increase in the wage ratios of the total represents compensating results of rather substantial diverse movements in the parts.

A brief discussion then follows (Section 7) on the possible influence of changes in size of establishment on the wage ratio. Section 8 displays some tabular material for the years prior to 1926 that throws further doubt on the trend significance of the increases in the wage ratios for the period from 1926 to 1958.

1. CHANGES IN FACTOR SHARES OF DOMESTIC INCOME

It has been shown above that the wage ratio in total domestic income rose from an average of 56. 7 for the five-year period 1926–30 to an average of 66.2 for the years 1954–58, or by 9.5 points representing 16.8 per cent. Accompanying this pronounced rise was a drastic reduction in the relative position of net farm unincorporated income to approximately one-half of the 11 points which it had represented in the earlier period; and a lesser, but nevertheless substantial, reduction of net income of nonfarm unincorporated business from 12 to 8.3 points. As already noted, the ratio of investment income remained substantially at the same level in the two periods.[20]

Reference to the preceding charts and Chart 4, below, indicates that the changes summarized in Table 2 have been accompanied

TABLE 2

CHANGES IN FACTOR SHARES OF DOMESTIC INCOME, 1926–30 TO 1954–58

	1926–30 (1)	1954–58 (2)	Point Change (col. 2 minus col. 1) (3)	Percentage Change (col. 3 ÷ col. 1) (4)
Wages and salaries	56.7	66.2	9.5	16.8
Investment income	20.3	20.2	−0.1	− 0.5
Net nonfarm unincorporated income	12.0	8.3	−3.7	−30.8
Net farm unincorporated income	11.0	5.3	−5.7	−51.8
Corporation profits[a]	10.6	12.2	1.6	15.1

SOURCE: Table A-1.

[a] See note a, Table 1.

[20] As before, these figures *include* the inventory valuation adjustment. Ratios *excluding* this adjustment are shown in Appendix Table A-1. For individual years of the two terminal periods, 1926–30 and 1954–58, the ratios in Appendix Table A-1 are similar whether or not the IVA is included, with the exception of 1930. The (positive) IVA for 1930 is very high relative to profits and net income and, in the face of the rather moderate price declines of that year, may be overstated. In a comparison of changes between the two terminal periods the effect of such overstatement would, of course, be to overstate somewhat the rise of the wage ratio (and understate that of investment income) when the IVA is included; and to understate somewhat the rise in the wage ratio (and overstate that of investment income) when the IVA is excluded. Changes in the factor shares between the two terminal periods with the IVA excluded were as follows:

	1926–30 (1)	*1954–58* (2)	*Point Changes* (col. 2 − 1) (3)	*Percentages Changes* (col. 3 ÷ col. 1) (4)
Wages and salaries	57.5	66.0	8.5	14.8
Investment income	19.5	20.4	0.9	4.6
Net nonfarm unincorporated income	11.9	8.4	−3.5	−29.4
Net farm unincorporated income	11.1	5.2	−5.9	−53.2

CHART 4
Domestic Income by Factor Shares

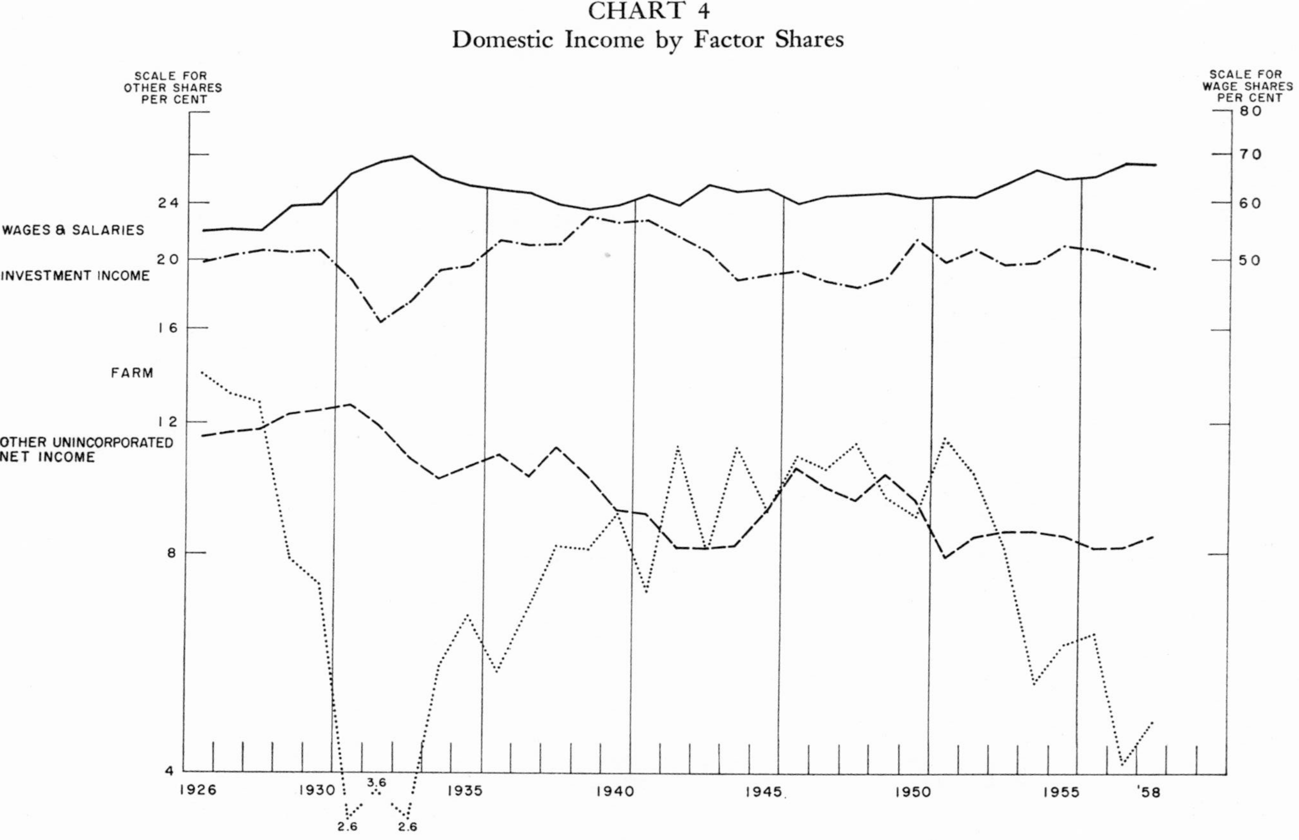

by considerable fluctuations, the amplitudes as well as the phasing of which differed as between the various factor shares. This is elaborated in the Supplement. A number of other noteworthy characteristics are evident from an examination of Chart 4, which are briefly summarized here.

First, the rise of the relative position of the wage share, while considerable, is of rather recent origin. Comparisons between the ratios in the late twenties and those of postwar years prior to 1953 show smaller gains.

Secondly, the rise in the wage ratio since 1952 is almost matched by a corresponding and coincident decline in the relative position of net farm income. Thus the wage ratio increased from 60.7 in 1952 to 67.4 in 1958, or by 6.7 points; net farm income during the same years dropped from 10.3 to 4.7, or by 5.6 points. It is interesting to note, further, that the decline in the relative position of net farm income has not been part of a gradual downward drift but, rather, has taken place in sudden drops. As late as 1951 the ratio of net farm income was 11.4 compared with 12.8 in 1928 and 7.9 in 1929; in 1950 it was 10.3.[21]

Thirdly, the apparent stability of total investment income is the net result of some contrary movements within the parts; in particular, corporation profits have risen considerably as shown in Table 2, with a corresponding decline in the remainder of investment income.

Fourthly, in contrast with the stability of aggregate investment income, the decline in the relative importance of net nonfarm unincorporated income reflects a persistent downward drift.

The last observation, together with the movements of the ratio of net farm income and corporation profits, raises the question whether the observed increases in the wage ratio in the postwar years, compared with the late twenties, reflect mainly a secular de-

[21] It should be noted, incidentally, that the substantial drop in the relative position of net farm income cannot be attributed to the exodus from the farms which commenced after 1946, accompanied as this exodus was by intense mechanization and ensuing increase in productivity. Whereas "persons with jobs" in agriculture (excluding paid workers) declined from 1,039,000 in 1946 to 780,000 in 1952, the ratio of net farm income hovered within a range of 11.2 and 10.3 during this period. The decline in "persons with jobs" in agriculture (excluding paid workers) continued at a somewhat lower rate between 1952 and 1958 when it reached 615,000, but this time it was accompanied by the very substantial drop in the ratio of domestic income, from 10.3 to 4.7. This drop, it would appear, reflects, in part at least, adverse developments in the prices of farm products compared with nonfarm products.

cline in the unincorporated business portion of the economy (farm and nonfarm). Agriculture is almost entirely unincorporated in Canada and is characterized by a very low wage ratio compared with the average of nonagricultural industries; the wage ratio of nonfarm unincorporated business is lower than for incorporated business.[22] In both cases the wage ratios are lower, in part at least, because the implied wages of unpaid family workers and of working owners are included in net income. At any rate, when parts of the economy exhibiting low wage ratios become relatively less important, and those with higher wage ratios more important, the over-all ratio for the economy will rise even if there is no change in the wage ratio within each part.

The impact on the wage ratio of the declining importance of unincorporated business is part of a more general influence arising from changes in the structure of the economy, namely, the changing relative importance of the various sectors and industries comprising the domestic income. Since the wage ratios in these various sectors and industries differ considerably, changes in their relative importance will be reflected in the factor shares. We discuss later (Section 5) the possible impact on the wage ratio of the secular decline of unincorporated income.[23]

2. THE TRANSITION FROM DOMESTIC INCOME TO PRIVATE BUSINESS PRODUCT

As is well known, the conventional national accounts divide the economy into the two main parts: that which produces goods or services for a price designed to cover cost of production at the

[22] In the absence of comprehensive Canadian statistics, this statement is based on United States data. There is no reason why Canadian experience should differ in this regard. The following ratios of salaries and wages to income originating are taken from Edward F. Denison, "Income Types and the Size Distribution" *American Economic Review*, May 1954, Table 1:

	1929	*1941*	*1951*
Nonfarm corporations	74.1	72.6	72.9
Nonfarm proprietorships and partnerships	48.4	47.1	50.3

[23] The analysis that follows is an adaptation of the one used by a number of other people, particularly Edward F. Denison in the *American Economic Review*, May 1954, and in "Distribution of National Income: Pattern of Income Shares since 1929," *Survey of Current Business*, June 1952. See also, Odd Aukrust "Trends and Cycles in Norwegian Income Shares," *Income and Wealth*, Series VI, London, 1957; M. Kalecki, *Theory of Economic Dynamics*, London, 1954; and John T. Dunlop, *Wage Determination Under Trade Unions*, New York, 1944.

very least—the so-called business (commercial) sector; and that which does not, or the so-called noncommercial sector. Each of these sectors is subdivided further into (a) private or personal and (b) government.

The treatment accorded the two main sectors is unequal. Whereas the valuation of the product of business is complete, in the sense that all elements entering into market prices are accounted for, that of the noncommercial sector is not, as only wages and salaries are counted.[24] The partial coverage of the contribution of the noncommercial sector to the domestic income has been accompanied by a considerable increase in its relative importance, though not as large as might be supposed (Table 3).[25]

TABLE 3
PERCENTAGE DISTRIBUTION OF DOMESTIC INCOME BY SECTORS

Year	Persons[a]	General Government	Government Business	Private Business
1926	3.2	5.7	6.8	84.3
1929	3.4	5.9	6.9	83.8
1930	3.6	6.8	6.6	83.0
1933	4.3	10.2	7.8	77.7
1939	3.0	8.0	6.5	82.5
1945	1.5	16.8	7.0	74.7
1946	1.7	9.7	7.1	81.5
1947	1.8	7.0	6.5	84.7
1950	1.9	7.3	6.4	84.4
1954	2.3	9.9	6.7	81.1
1958	2.4	11.2	6.8	79.6

SOURCE: Table A-6.
[a] Includes private noncommercial institutions.

The main distinction between government business and private business is that the latter may be assumed to aim to maximize profits and is not likely to withstand prolonged losses; the former, by contrast, does not necessarily aim to maximize profits and its losses

[24] The salary and wage figures may, however, "undervalue" the services in question compared with the business sector. This is illustrated by the fact that, in the United States for example, several individuals have recently accepted top government jobs at a fraction only of their pay in private industry but their new jobs are certainly no less "important."

[25] It is interesting to note that the private business sector emerged from the war relatively more important, in terms of its contribution to the domestic income, than it entered; the sustained decline in its relative importance started after the Korean War.

are likely to be subsidized out of general government revenues. Indeed, a private concern may be converted into a public body after a prolonged period of sustained losses, as happened, for example, in the case of concerns that now comprise the Canadian National Railways. At the other extreme, there is the case of the Provincial Liquor Control Boards, included with government business in the Canadian accounts, which have a legal monopoly and whose profits are not unlike indirect taxes in many respects. At any rate, the institutions classified in the government business sector, as a group, while similar in many respects to their private business counterparts, are sufficiently unlike to warrant isolating them in order to permit separate analysis of private business. In this way, a more homogeneous group whose operations are more directly determined by competitive market forces is obtained.[26]

Table 3 indicates that the relative importance of the government business sector has remained remarkably constant over the period. This constancy has, however, been accompanied by an appreciable decline in the wage ratio of the government business product from 68.4 in 1926–30 to 62.1 in 1954–58, reflecting, mainly, developments in government business enterprises classified as public utilities, communications and retail trade.

3. CHANGES IN FACTOR SHARES OF THE PRIVATE BUSINESS PRODUCT

By eliminating from domestic income the noncommercial sectors (whose total income originating is wages and salaries) and the government business sector, we are left with private business product. When the changes of the factor shares of private business product are calculated and compared with those of domestic income we find a rather similar picture. Although the increase in the wage ratio of the private business product was moderately higher than that of domestic income.[27] The fluctuations in the fac-

[26] A considerable amount of rearrangement of the basic information was necessary in order to separate the private business sector, as the published estimates include totals only for the business sector as a whole. This work and the calculations of the various ratios were done in the National Accounts Division and Labor Division under the supervision of P. S. Sunga.

[27] The rise in the wage ratio of domestic income from 1926–30 to 1954–58 is practically the same as that of the *total* (private and government) business product (Table A-11). It may occasion surprise that addition of the (100 per cent wage income) noncommercial sector, which was relatively more important in the later period, does not lift the wage ratio. Consider, however, the dual in-

tor shares over the period were also similar to those of domestic income, on the whole, although there were some differences in detail.[28]

The similarities in the general movements of the relative factor shares of domestic income and the private business product are clearly apparent when Charts 4 and 5 are compared. However, the contours of the movements in Chart 5 are somewhat sharper; in particular, the inverse correlation between the wage ratio and the investment income ratio stands out more prominently. For

TABLE 4
CHANGES IN FACTOR SHARES OF THE PRIVATE BUSINESS PRODUCT

	1926–30 (1)	1954–58 (2)	Point Change (col. 2 minus col. 1) (3)	Percentage Change (col. 3 ÷ col. 1) (4)
Wages and salaries	51.0	61.4	10.4	20.4
Investment income	21.7	21.8	0.1	0.5
Net nonfarm unincorporated income	14.2	10.3	−3.9	−27.5
Net farm unincorporated income	13.1	6.5	−6.6	−50.4
Corporation profits[a]	12.7	15.2	2.5	19.6

SOURCE: Table A-7.
[a] See note a, Table 1.

this reason, and also because the cyclical analysis of the supplement to this paper is carried out more suitably on the basis of the private business product, we shall continue the discussion on this basis but broadly similar results would have been obtained had we continued on the basis of domestic income.

---

fluence of the noncommercial sector:

1. If the wage ratio in the business sector remains constant in two periods and the relative importance of the noncommercial sector increases from period 1 to period 2, then addition of the noncommercial sector will result in a rise of the wage ratio; the wage ratio of domestic income will show an increase even though that of the business sector remains constant.

2. If the wage ratio in the business sector rises from period 1 to period 2 and the relative importance of the noncommercial sector remains constant, then addition of the latter to the former results in a *smaller* increase of the wage ratio. The actual wage ratio is the net result of these two influences and in the comparison between 1926–30 and 1954–58 they have almost cancelled each other out.

[28] From 1929 to 1930 the wage share goes down slightly in the private business sector and rises somewhat in domestic income, reflecting an (absolute) increase in government payrolls.

CHART 5
Private Business Product by Factor Shares

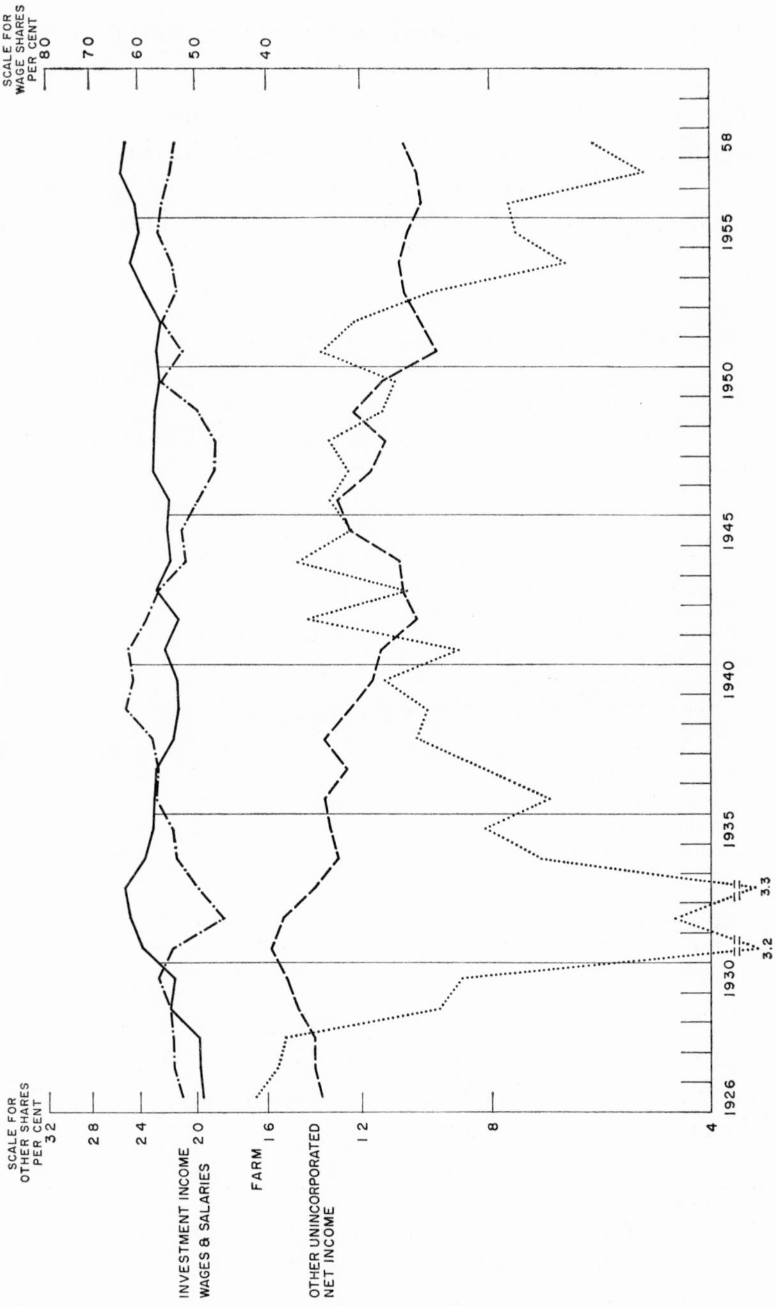
SCALE FOR WAGE SHARES PER CENT
80
70
60
50
40
SCALE FOR OTHER SHARES PER CENT
32
28
24
20
16
12
8
4
INVESTMENT INCOME
WAGES & SALARIES
FARM
OTHER UNINCORPORATED NET INCOME
1926
1930
1935
1940
1945
1950
1955
58
3.2
3.3

4. THE INDUSTRIAL COMPOSITION OF THE CHANGE IN THE WAGE RATIO OF THE PRIVATE BUSINESS PRODUCT—STANDARDIZATION

The industrial groups comprising the private business product sector have contributed rather differently to the rise in the over-all wage ratio of 10.4 points (or 20.4 per cent), some industries showing declines and others substantial increases, as indicated in Table 5. The wage ratios of the service-producing industries have

TABLE 5
PERCENTAGE CHANGE IN THE WAGE SHARE OF THE INDUSTRIES OF THE PRIVATE BUSINESS PRODUCT: 1926–30 TO 1954–58

Industry	1926–30	1954–58	Points Change	Percentage Change	Weights in 1949
Commodity-producing industries					
Agriculture	16.1	11.9	−4.2	−26.1	12.7
Forestry	91.3	86.0	−5.3	− 5.8	2.2
Fishing[a]	23.1	33.5	10.4	45.0	.6
Mining	58.9	61.1	2.2	3.7	4.2
Manufacturing	68.4	73.8	5.4	7.9	34.6
Construction	77.9	74.1	−3.8	− 4.9	6.7
Service-producing industries					
Transportation, communication and public utilities	68.3	70.7	2.4	3.5	6.8
Wholesale trade	68.8	73.4	4.6	6.7	6.0
Retail trade	53.8	64.3	10.5	19.5	10.8
Finance, insurance and real estate	31.0	32.9	1.9	6.1	7.1
Service (proper)	37.9	52.7	14.8	39.1	8.4
Total private business product	51.0	61.4	10.4	20.4	100.0

SOURCE: Table A-9.
[a] Part of the increase in the wage ratio in fishing reflects a discontinuity that occurred in the estimates beginning with the year 1952.

all shown gains, though of varying size; those of service (proper) and retail trade have risen most. The ratios of agriculture, forestry and construction have declined but those of the remainder of the commodity-producing industries have risen.

It is apparent from Table 5 that the wage ratios of only two industries, service (proper) and fishing with a combined weight in 1949 of only 9.0 per cent, have risen more than the over-all ratio. Retail trade, with a 1949 weight of 10.8 per cent, has risen almost as much as the over-all ratio. The remaining industries have shown much smaller increases or actual declines. This suggests that simultaneously with the movements of the shares *within* industrial groups, there have been shifts as *between* industries resulting in some additional lifting in the over-all wage ratio of the private business product.

In order to isolate the impact of interindustry shifts we have recalculated the wage ratios on the assumption that the relative importance of the constituent industries (as measured by the relative contribution of each industry to the private business product) that prevailed in the year 1949 remained fixed throughout the period 1926–58. We shall refer henceforth to these fixed weighted ratios as the standardized series, in contrast with the implied currently (changing) weighted series which we shall call the unadjusted ratios. The year 1949 has been chosen because it is generally considered the first "normal" postwar year and is used in many Canadian index numbers, but calculations with 1928 and 1956 industry weights were also made.

Turning first to the total private business product we find that the rise in the wage ratio from 1926–30 to 1954–58 was only 4.1 points or 7.4 per cent, using 1949 industry weights. Thus, of the increase of 10.4, or 20.4 per cent, in the unadjusted series, the larger portion reflects a change in the relative importance of the various industries during the periods being compared.[29] Substantially similar results have been obtained with 1956 and 1928 industry weights.

Secondly, it will be seen that much of the change in the ratio, when standardized figures are used, reflects the influence of agriculture, a result that could be surmised from Chart 5. The unadjusted wage ratio, calculated with agricultural income excluded from the numerator and denominator, has risen only 6.9 points, or 11.8 per cent (compared with 20.4 per cent when agriculture is included). When the wage ratio of the nonagricultural private business product is standardized for changes in the relative importance of industries, the rise in the wage ratio declines further to 5.3 points or 8.7 per cent. Evidently the sharp reduction in the relative importance of income originating in agriculture during the two periods being compared has contributed more to the apparent rise in the unadjusted wage ratio of the total private business product than the combined changes of all the other industries.

[29] It should be noted that we have ignored the effect of the interaction of weight changes and ratio changes which cannot be assigned to either.

TABLE 6
CHANGES IN UNADJUSTED AND STANDARDIZED WAGE RATIOS: 1926–30 TO 1954–58

	1926–30	1954–58	Point Change	Percentage Change
Total private business product				
Unadjusted	51.0	61.4	10.4	20.4
Standardized	55.5	59.6	4.1	7.4
Nonfarm private business product[a]				
Unadjusted	58.6	65.5	6.9	11.8
Standardized	61.2	66.5	5.3	8.7
Total domestic income				
Unadjusted	56.7	66.2	9.5	16.8
Standardized	60.7	63.7	3.0	4.9
Nonfarm domestic income[a]				
Unadjusted	63.9	69.8	5.9	9.2
Standardized	66.0	70.0	4.0	6.1

SOURCE: Tables A-1, A-8, A-10, A-12, and A-13.
[a] Includes farm rents, paid and imputed.

As a matter of interest, we made similar calculations for the wage ratio of domestic income. As might be surmised from the comparisons already shown in preceding sections comparable results are obtained, although the rise in the wage ratio from 1926–30 to 1954–58 was more moderate (see Table 6).

5. THE SHARES OF THE NONFARM PRIVATE BUSINESS PRODUCT

We turn now to a somewhat closer examination of the movements of the standardized factor shares of the nonfarm portion of private business product,[30] focusing attention on the possible influence on the wage ratio of changes in the form of business organization. Chart 6 summarizes the movements in the standardized shares. It will be seen that the upward drift of the wage ratio is visible from 1946 on, earlier than in the preceding charts. The pronounced, though irregular, downward drift of the ratio of net unincorporated income is seen to be steeper in the postwar period as a whole than for the years 1926 to 1945; the downward drift was

[30] As will be observed from Chart 6, the trend of the wage ratio tends to be flat because of the effect of the great depression in the earlier years of the time series. A least square line has been fitted to the nonfarm standardized wage ratio from 1926 to 1958, deleting the complete cycle from 1929 to 1937 (and tested for significance). As might be expected this gives a linear fit with a strongly significant, upward trend of practically the same slope as a line joining the average ratio for the two terminal periods 1926–30 and 1954–58.

CHART 6
Nonfarm Private Business Product, Standardized Factor Shares

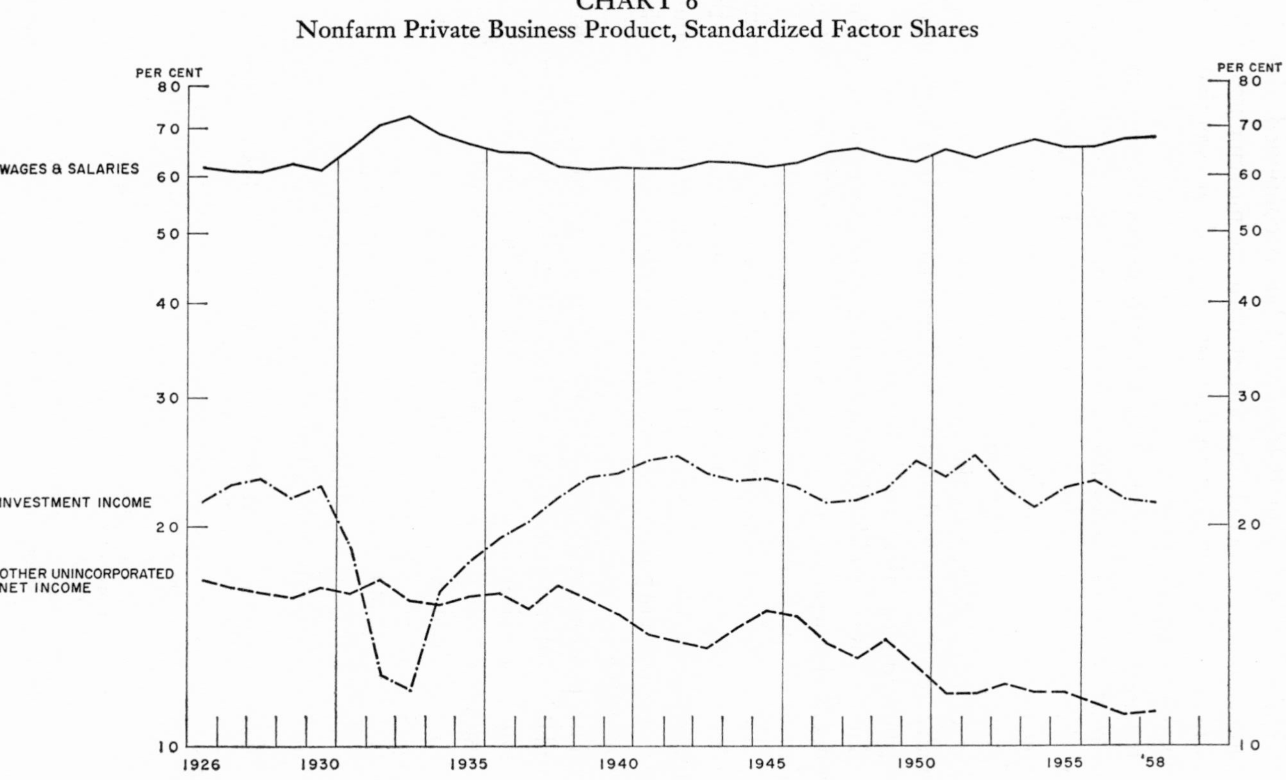

particularly sharp from 1946 to 1951 but it continued, though at a slower rate, after 1951, in contrast with the movements in Chart 5 where the ratio is seen to fluctuate around an essentially horizontal line after 1951.[31]

It should be emphasized that Chart 6 shows the movements of the relative factor shares after elimination of the effects of changes in the relative importance of industries. The standardization procedure also abstracts from the effect of the changing importance of various forms of business organization—but only to the extent that this is reflected in the changing industrial pattern; it leaves unaffected changes in the ratios resulting from shifts in the form of business organization *within* industries.

Such a shift could take the form, for example, of established concerns incorporating themselves in order to gain a tax advantage. The wages and salaries paid by these firms have already been included with labor income before the incorporation and continue to be so included; what happens after the incorporation is that the sum of wages and profits (and interest) is higher by the amount that net unincorporated income has been reduced.[32] But in what proportions?

The proportion could, of course, be estimated roughly using available information as a guide. Then, by adding the split amounts to labor income and investment income respectively, a consolidated dual classification of income would be produced with the disturbing effects of shifts between forms of business organization removed from the data.[33]

We have decided not to split unincorporated income, not only for reasons already mentioned above (see Part I) but also because, while the desirable procedure for carrying out the segregation is

[31] Tax incentives to convert to the incorporated form of business organization were considerable after the war, especially after 1949 when tax regulations were introduced lowering tax rates on the first $10,000 (subsequently raised to $35,000) of profits. Beginning with 1946 the Census of Manufacturing began collecting data by form of organization: these show a decided drift toward the incorporated form. The relative movements of net income of unincorporated business described in the text are, of course, the net result of a number of interacting factors and not just the drift toward incorporation.

[32] Similar reasoning can, of course, be applied where net unincorporated income drops in relative position because larger proportions of new firms assume the incorporated form when they get established.

[33] See, for example, I. B. Kravis, "Relative Income Shares in Fact and Theory," *The American Economic Review*, December 1959; and Edward C. Budd, "Factor Shares, 1850–1910," *Trends in the American Economy in the Nineteenth Century*, Studies in Income and Wealth 24, Princeton University Press for NBER, 1960.

complex, the necessary statistical data for carrying it out are not readily available.

The proportions of labor input and capital input in net unincorporated income undoubtedly vary substantially as between industries,[34] from instances where almost the entire net income could properly be allocated to wages (e.g., such self-employed professionals as accountants, lawyers, doctors,[35] private detectives, entertainers) to cases where substantial proportions may be attributed to capital (restaurants, funeral parlors and certain manufacturing). The proportions will also vary with the prevalence of owner-occupied unincorporated business establishments, the capital component being lower in rented premises. Further, the proportions will vary with size of concerns, the portion properly attributed to capital probably being greater as the size of establishment increases. Finally, the apportionment will vary with the extent of mechanization over time (such as, for example, has taken place in agriculture), and the degree of utilization of unpaid labor.

Thus it would appear that a realistic apportionment of net unincorporated income between capital and labor should be calculated separately for each industry, by size groups, by form of ownership of premises and on the basis of changing, not constant, ratios. Furthermore, in order to make the calculation on any basis, appeal would have to be made to statistical data reflecting, in many ways, substantially different market situations (as already suggested), such as those pertaining to the corporate sector and the regular labor market.

Since we are unable to split net income, it would be desirable at the very least to make separate calculations of the factor shares by legal form of business organization. In this respect we have been handicapped in the handling of our subject in this paper because of the absence in Canada of such estimates for the nonagricultural portion of the economy. However, we have carried out some calculations which are aimed to approximate, albeit incompletely, the incorporated part of the nonfarm private business product.

[34] In unpublished comments on Kravis' paper George Jaszi emphasized this point.

[35] The expenditures involved in the training of professionals, such as doctors, could, of course, be regarded as a capital outlay, the return to which should be included with investment income as already indicated. Further, the capital they employ is mainly social capital, such as hospitals and other expenditures by government on health.

As a first step to an approximation of changes in the wage ratio of incorporated business we have recalculated the ratios of each industrial group for the years 1926–30 and 1954–58 excluding net income of unincorporated business and net rents received by persons. These exclusions bring the data closer to the factor shares of the corporate sector. The revised wage ratios were then standardized, using 1949 industry weights. The results are summarized in Table 7.

TABLE 7
PERCENTAGE CHANGES OF WAGE SHARE IN NONFARM PRIVATE BUSINESS PRODUCT, EXCLUDING NET INCOME OF UNINCORPORATED BUSINESS AND NET RENTS

	1926–30 (1)	1954–58 (2)	Point Change (col. 2 minus col. 1) (3)	Percentage Change (col. 3 ÷ col. 1) (4)
Unadjusted	75.2	76.9	1.7	2.3
Standardized	75.9	77.2	1.3	1.7

As might be expected Table 7 shows a substantial reduction in the rise of the wage ratio (compared with the corresponding ratio in Table 6). However, since salaries and wages paid out by unincorporated business have been included and since, in line with the reduction in the unincorporated portion of the economy the weight of these wages has undoubtedly declined, the actual increase of the wage ratio in the corporate portion is undoubtedly higher than that shown in Table 7. The most reasonable conclusion perhaps is that the rise of the standardized wage ratio in the corporate portion of the economy from 1926–30 to 1954–58 was positive but considerably smaller than the 8.7 per cent of the total nonfarm private business product. In other words, it seems likely that a portion of the 8.7 per cent reflects a shift from the unincorporated to the incorporated form of business organization.

6. CHANGES IN THE WAGE RATIO IN MANUFACTURING

Standardization in Greater Industrial Detail

We have seen above that the differences between the standardized and unadjusted wage ratios in the nonfarm private business product were small. However, since the standardization was carried out at a rather aggregative level, which permits considerable shifts to take place within groups,[36] the question arises whether significantly different results would be obtained if it had been carried out at a finer level of detail.

We were able to carry out more detailed standardization for the industries classified in manufacturing in the standard industrial classification, but before examining the results, the characteristics of the data are summarized here so that their limitations may be kept in mind.

First, the denominator used here is the larger aggregate of census value added (which differs from income originating in manufacturing, used above, in that it includes, in addition to income originating, depreciation allowances, cost of repairs, office supplies and purchased services such as advertising and insurance). The ratio of income originating to census value added in manufacturing, while not exhibiting any pronounced trend, is appreciably lower in the period 1954–58 than in 1926–30, apparently reflecting, mainly, a greater importance of purchased services in the later period (although the possibility of unknown differences in valuations affecting the figures of census value added in the two periods cannot be excluded). On this account, we would expect the ratio of wages and salaries to census value added to have risen correspondingly less than that of wages and salaries to income originating.

Secondly, the coverage of the wages and salaries data is somewhat different from that used earlier. In the first place, supplementary labor income is excluded because the information is not available for individual manufacturing industries. Since supplementary labor income has become an increasingly important component of total payrolls in manufacturing, having risen from an average of 2 per cent of the total in 1926–30 to 3.8 per cent in

[36] Separate income figures for only eleven industrial groups are available in the Canadian National Accounts for the whole period back to 1926, reflecting data deficiencies and unresolved difficulties in classification. Whereas wage income and, to a considerable extent, net unincorporated business income are classified on an establishment basis, corporation profits and depreciation are available only on a company basis. Accordingly, the finer the industrial classification the less comparable are the factor shares within industries. Even in the more aggregative published figures difficulties in the comparisons are present because manufacturing overlaps to some extent with mining, on the one hand, and forestry on the other. It is felt that in these cases the overlap is not sufficiently large to invalidate the comparisons made. It should be mentioned, though, that we have encountered some disconcerting anomalies that we were unable to remove between the movements of the ratios of payrolls to census value added in mining, on the one hand, and those of payrolls to income originating in mining, on the other. In an unpublished memorandum, H. J. Adler of the National Accounts Division lists at least a dozen factors that might be responsible for such differences.

1954–58, the ratio of wages and salaries to census value added will again show a correspondingly smaller rise than that of wages and salaries to income originating.

There are several other differences which, however, may be expected to cancel out more or less completely: the most important of these is that the census figures include, in addition to payrolls, the withdrawals of working proprietors; but they excluded, until the year 1949, a portion at least of salaries paid in head offices which were situated in a separate physical location, unattached to any other manufacturing establishment of the firm. The inclusion of working proprietors' withdrawals understates the rise in the wage ratio because the relative importance of withdrawals to the total wage bill has been declining; the exclusion of a portion of unattached head offices in the earlier period overstates the rise in the wage ratio. Since, roughly, similar order of magnitudes are involved in the understatement and overstatement (between 2 and 3 per cent of payrolls) the over-all wage ratio may be assumed to be unaffected.

Revisions for the factors just described have been made in the National Accounts, but only for manufacturing as a whole. Since in the present section attention is directed to individual industries within manufacturing, as well as the total, the unrevised data will be used.

Turning now to the data as they emanate from the census of industry,[37] we compare first the movement in the ratios of wages and salaries (exclusive of supplementary labor income), standardized for eighteen industrial groups (using the percentage of census value added of each industry to the total of all industries in 1949 as the fixed weights), with the unadjusted ratios, that is, with the implied changing current weights. This comparison is made in Table 8 (columns 1 and 2).

It will be seen, first, that in neither case does the ratio exhibit any pronounced trend, although the average in 1954–58 is somewhat higher than that of 1926–30. Secondly, the standardization does not give rise to any appreciable differences in the movements of the ratios, except for the depression years of the thirties. Thirdly, in contrast with the ratios of the private business product standardization in manufacturing does not give rise to a lower wage ratio in the longer-run comparison; in fact the standardized wage

[37] In a number of cases the census of industry data had to be adjusted to render them more comparable over time.

TABLE 8

WAGES AND SALARIES (EXCLUDING SUPPLEMENTARY LABOR INCOME) AS A PERCENTAGE OF CENSUS VALUE ADDED—MANUFACTURING

	Total Manufacturing		*Durable Goods*		*Nondurable Goods*	
	Un-adjusted	Standard-ized	Un-adjusted	Standard-ized	Un-adjusted	Standard-ized
1926	48.8	48.9	55.7	55.1	44.5	44.0
1927	47.5	47.8	53.6	53.4	43.7	43.5
1928	46.2	46.7	52.3	52.7	42.2	42.2
1929	45.3	45.5	50.6	50.5	41.6	41.6
1930	47.1	48.1	54.2	54.6	42.6	43.1
1931	48.4	50.1	55.7	57.2	44.5	44.7
1932	49.6	53.1	60.2	62.7	45.4	45.7
1933	47.4	51.1	52.2	57.9	45.5	45.9
1934	46.3	49.2	50.1	54.8	44.6	44.9
1935	48.5	50.5	54.3	56.5	45.7	46.0
1936	47.5	49.3	51.1	53.6	45.5	46.0
1937	47.8	49.4	49.0	51.9	47.0	47.4
1938	49.4	51.0	51.7	54.0	48.0	48.6
1939	48.2	49.7	51.6	53.6	46.2	46.8
1940	47.4	48.0	50.2	51.1	45.4	45.7
1941	48.6	48.5	50.5	50.7	46.8	46.9
1942	50.9	49.9	54.0	53.4	47.5	47.2
1943	52.1	51.1	57.1	55.9	46.3	47.4
1944	50.5	49.7	55.5	54.4	45.2	46.1
1945	51.8	51.3	57.5	56.5	46.7	47.2
1946	50.2	50.8	59.3	59.2	44.3	44.3
1947	48.6	48.8	54.5	54.5	44.2	44.4
1948	48.8	48.8	53.9	53.8	44.8	44.9
1949	48.6	48.6	52.7	52.7	45.4	45.4
1950	46.6	46.8	50.3	50.3	43.7	44.2
1951	47.2	47.8	52.0	52.1	43.2	44.5
1952	48.5	48.9	53.4	53.2	44.2	45.5
1953	48.7	48.9	52.6	52.5	45.1	46.1
1954	50.2	51.0	55.3	55.8	45.9	47.3
1955	47.8	48.5	51.9	52.5	44.1	45.5
1956	48.5	49.4	52.1	52.8	45.2	46.7
1957	50.1	51.0	54.4	55.0	46.3	47.9
1958	50.1	51.1	55.7	56.1	45.5	47.2
Averages						
1926–30	47.0	47.4	53.3	53.3	42.9	42.9
1954–58	49.3	50.2	53.9	54.4	45.4	46.9
Points change	2.3	2.8	.6	1.1	2.5	4.0
Percentage change	5.0	5.9	1.1	2.1	5.8	9.3

ratio is somewhat higher. However, the difference is really too small to be significant, particularly in view of the imperfections in the data described above. At any rate, these comparisons suggest that the increases of the wage ratios of the nonfarm private business product, shown in the preceding sections, would not be materially altered by a more detailed standardization, although this inference must be qualified by the possibility that different results might be obtained in a more detailed standardization of the other industrial groups.[38] Even within manufacturing, it can, of course, be argued that standardization on a more detailed basis than the eighteen industries we have used might produce significantly different results.

Industrial Composition of Changes in the Over-All Manufacturing Wage Ratio

The rather inert behavior of the over-all wage ratio in manufacturing (with supplementary labor income excluded) is in sharp

TABLE 9
PERCENTAGE CHANGES OF WAGE RATIO IN VARIOUS MANUFACTURING INDUSTRIES
(census value added)

Industry	Percentage Change in Wage Ratio: 1926–30 to 1954–58
Electrical apparatus	27.1
Textile products	20.0
Chemical and allied	18.9
Foods and beverages	18.6
Miscellaneous industries	18.0
Rubber products	14.1
Knitting mills	10.0
Leather products	6.6
Printing, etc.	5.9
Clothing	5.8
Paper products	3.2
Iron and steel	3.1
Nonmetallic minerals	2.8
Wood products	0.9
Nonferrous metals	0.2
Transportation equipment	− 6.2
Tobacco products	−25.7
Petroleum and coal	−29.5
Totals	
Unadjusted	5.0
Standardized	5.9

[38] Some experimental calculations with mining data, carried out by E. C. West of the National Accounts Division, suggest that more detailed standardization in mining would not give rise to significantly different changes in the wage ratio.

contrast with the substantially diverse movements of the wage ratios of the constituent industries. The diverse behavior of the wage ratios is illustrated in Table 9 which ranks the individual manufacturing industries by size of percentage change in the wage ratio from 1926–30 to 1954–58.[39]

Changes in the Wage Ratio Using Different Aggregate Classifications

Closer examination of Table 9 suggests that there is a measure of underlying regularity, within the cross-currents of large variability, not only when the constituent industries are combined into a total for all manufacturing, but also for major subgroupings of the total on the basis of broad technological and market criteria. With the exception of electrical apparatus, all the industries in Table 9 that have exhibited small changes in the wage ratio are classified in durable manufacturing. On the other hand, most of the industries showing large increases are the ones classified in nondurable manufacturing; the outstanding exceptions being tobacco products and petroleum and coal. The combined wage ratio for the durable manufacturing group as a whole shows no perceptible trend. Although that of the nondurable group exhibits a discernible upward drift, especially in the standardized form, it is small compared to the variations in the constituent industries. The amplitude of the fluctuations of the durable group is larger than that of the nondurable group (see Table 8).

The individual manufacturing industries can, of course, be combined on the basis of a number of criteria other than durability of product. One such classification is the so-called "primary" and "secondary" manufacturing grouping.[40] While a large portion of

[39] An examination of the industrial distribution of detached head office salaries and withdrawals of working proprietors for recent years suggests that allowances for these factors would not affect the over-all picture conveyed by Table 9.

[40] The classification is that developed in D. H. Fullerton and H. A. Hampson, *Canadian Secondary Manufacturing Industry*, Royal Commission on Canada's Economic Prospects, Ottawa, 1957. Primary manufacturing industries are those which involve "either relatively minor processing of domestic resources (i.e., in which the value added by manufacture is relatively low), or those high intensive and often extremely complex industries which produce industrial materials from (Canadian) basic natural resources for sale mainly in export markets. Flour milling, cheese factories and saw and planing mills are examples of the first type, while pulp and paper production (excluding finished paper goods) and smelting and refining are examples of the second." In contrast, the secondary manufacturing industries "are characterized by a rather higher degree of processing and much greater dependence on the domestic market. They tend to be located close to the centre of the market, while primary industries are usually found at or near the resource on which they are based." These industries draw on foreign

the primary industry group is export oriented it includes several industries that export very little of their produce. On the other hand, two industries classified as secondary[41] have a considerable export content. By adding the latter to the primary group, and subtracting the nonexport industries a somewhat amended classification is obtained of "export" and "domestic" industries. The unadjusted wage ratios for these four major groupings have been calculated and plotted. The results are shown in Chart 7.

While these groupings represent different classification criteria, the long-run drifts of the (unadjusted) wage ratios fall within very narrow limits, despite the wide variation of the ratios of the individual industries of which they are composed.

Thus it appears that there are compensating forces present which produce relatively small changes in the longer-run comparisons of the wage ratios of the broader industrial groupings. However, in view of the strong element of dispersion underlying these movements one may well ask whether the search for the "invisible hand" causing regularities would not benefit greatly from prior study of the changes in the ratios of the more detailed industries or small groups of industries and the factors responsible for them.

7. NOTE ON POSSIBLE INFLUENCE ON THE FACTOR SHARES OF CHANGES IN SIZE OF BUSINESS UNIT

In appraising the significance of changes in the relative factor shares between two periods, account has to be taken not only of changes in industrial structure of the type already discussed but also those which take the form of changes in the relative size of business units within industries (changes between industries having been eliminated by the standardization).

Information on the changes in relative size of business units in Canada is scanty.[42] Some sketchy data we have examined suggest

---

as well as domestic suppliers for raw materials and tend to be more labor intensive than the basic resource industries. Examples are textiles, clothing, transportation equipment and electrical apparatus and supplies (see *ibid.*, pp. 3 and 4). An average of about one-quarter of census value added in manufacturing is accounted for by the primary group and three-quarters by the secondary groups. For a listing of industries included with each of these groupings see Appendix A of the report.

[41] The two industries are agricultural implements and distilled liquors.

[42] See, however, the authoritative study by Gideon Rosenbluth, *Concentration in Canadian Manufacturing Industries*, Princeton, 1957. This study (p. 21), which

CHART 7

Wage and Salary Share in Manufacturing by Manufacturing Divisions

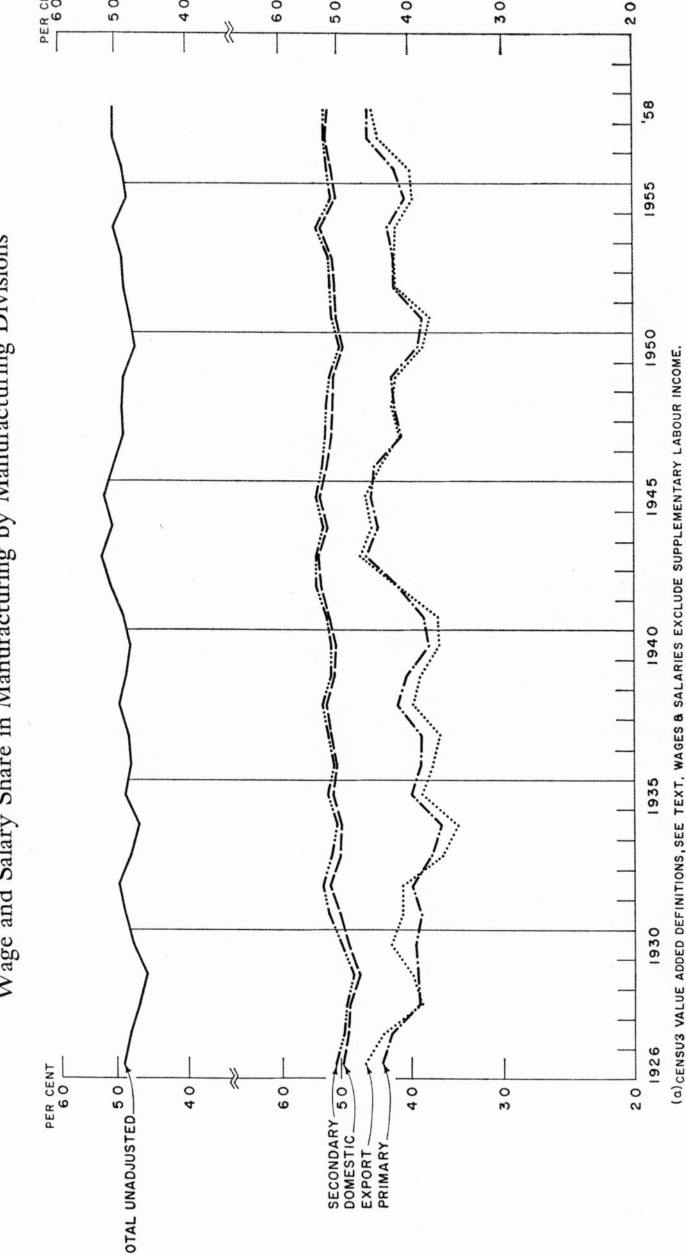

that there is an inverse relationship between the wage ratio and the size of establishment of incorporated firms. In incorporated manufacturing establishments, for example, the ratio of salaries and wages to census value added goes down as the size of establishment increases, when the value of shipments is used as the criterion of size. In 1958 this ratio was as follows:[43]

Value of Shipments	*Ratio*
Under $25,000	86.5
$25,000 to 100,000	68.1
$100,000 to 500,000	59.4
$500,000 to 1,000,000	56.4
$1,000,000 to 5,000,000	51.5
$5,000,000 and over	43.4

The ratio of wages and salaries to profits before tax for independent incorporated retail stores also declines, in general, as the size of establishment increases, when sales are used as the criterion of size.[44] Time did not permit us to study these data adequately, nor to disentangle the size effect from the industry and other effects. The data are mentioned here merely for the purpose of reaffirming the conclusion to which we are tending: that the significance of the observed changes in the wage ratio cannot be determined from aggregative data alone; rather it would require much more detailed information and analysis than we were able to muster for this paper.

8. COMPARISONS WITH YEARS PRIOR TO 1926

The comparisons of the wage ratio have been made for the periods 1926–30 and 1954–58 and the question arises whether comparisons with earlier years would give rise to significantly different results. In order to throw some light on this question the official figures of labor income and domestic income were extended back to 1919, using published and unpublished information and estimates of income originating by industry prepared some years ago by the

---

is confined to manufacturing, shows that there has been a decline in plant concentration in manufacturing from 1922 to 1948.

[43] The ratios for unincorporated establishments are complicated by the inclusion of withdrawals of working owners in the wage figures. The source of the data on which the calculations are based is *General Review of Manufacturing Industries of Canada*, Dominion Bureau of Statistics, Ottawa, 1957 and 1958.

[44] See, for example, *Operating Results, Retail Trade, 1956,* Dominion Bureau of Statistics, Ottawa.

Dominion Bureau of Statistics in connection with its work on national income.[45]

The nature and reliability of these estimates are described in a memorandum that will be made available on request. It will suffice to note here that, while they agree reasonably well in total with estimates for the same years made by others, we do not attribute to them the same degree of reliability as those of the official series. Moreover, further checking than we have been able to do until now may give rise to some revisions.

The figures were prepared on a *domestic* income basis only. The ratios are shown in the following table:

TABLE 10
RATIO OF WAGES AND SALARIES TO DOMESTIC INCOME 1919–25

	Unadjusted		*Standardized (1949 industry weights)*[a]	
Year	Total	Nonfarm	Total	Nonfarm
1919	55.1	65.2	60.0	65.5
1920	57.3	68.3	63.2	69.1
1921	60.5	68.6	65.1	70.7
1922	56.5	65.6	62.1	67.8
1923	57.2	66.7	63.2	69.0
1924	60.3	68.1	65.3	70.9
1925	54.0	65.6	62.2	68.2
1926–30	56.7	63.9	60.7	66.0
1954–58	66.2	69.8	63.7	70.0

[a] Substantially the same results are obtained with 1928 industry weights.

In interpreting these ratios it has to be kept in mind that the figures for the year 1919 may reflect the aftermath of World War I; 1920 was a year of high inflation and 1921 a year of sharp, though short-lived, recession; there was also, apparently, some recession in 1924. The unadjusted total domestic income is, in addition, strongly influenced by (the characteristically erratic) developments in agriculture.

Be that as it may, the average ratio of total domestic income, including agriculture, for the period from 1919 to 1925 is of the same order of magnitude as the average for 1926–30. On the other hand, with agriculture excluded, the average ratio for the

[45] The estimates were made by D. H. Jones of the Central Research and Development Staff, Dominion Bureau of Statistics.

period 1919 to 1925 is half way between those of the late twenties and the late fifties; the standardized ratios are closer to those of the more recent years than for 1926–30. On the whole we must conclude that, after allowance for interindustry shifts, the ratios of the earlier years cast further doubt on the trend significance of the increases between 1926–30 and 1954–58 of the private business product and, *a fortiori*, the domestic income described in the preceding sections. While further work on the estimates for the years from 1919 to 1925 may give rise to revisions, it is unlikely that these will be of sufficient magnitude to alter this conclusion.[46]

Wage ratios have also been calculated for manufacturing industries, using comparable definitions and classifications, back to 1917, and are shown in Table 11:[47]

TABLE 11
WAGES AND SALARIES AS A PERCENTAGE OF CENSUS VALUE ADDED IN MANUFACTURING 1917–25

Year	Unadjusted	Standardized (1949 industry weights)
1917	41.0	40.9
1918	43.2	43.4
1919	44.3	44.6
1920	45.8	46.2
1921	47.9	48.7
1922	47.9	48.8
1923	49.1	50.1
1924	50.6	51.4
1925	49.7	50.2
1926–30	47.0	47.4
1954–58	49.3	50.2

An examination of these figures indicates, again, that the wage ratio for manufacturing as a whole was higher from 1921 to 1925 than the average for 1926–30; from 1917 to 1920 the ratios were

[46] This paragraph benefited from comment by David C. Smith, who in addition pointed out that it is possible that an actual decline may be shown in the standardized wage ratio from 1919–25 to 1954–58 if other factors, particularly the shift from unincorporated to incorporated business within industries, are taken into account. This result may be accentuated somewhat if the calculations are made on a gross basis, that is, before deduction of depreciation allowances.

[47] This work, which required considerable reclassification of individual industries and estimation of several components, was carried out by Miss J. R. Podoluk, who also prepared ratios for later years. The preparation of the manufacturing data was carried out in connection with a major project on historical statistics comprising a large number of statistical areas in addition to manufacturing, which is being completed under the direction of Professors M. C. Urquhart and K. Buckley.

lower. However, the ratios for 1917 to 1919 undoubtedly reflect developments peculiar to World War I and its aftermath and one cannot impute longer-run significance to them.

We have examined also the wage ratios in manufacturing calculated on the basis of information gathered primarily from decennial censuses for the following years: 1915, 1910, 1900, 1890, 1880 and 1870. The denominator used for calculating these ratios was census value added less materials purchased only. There are some anomalies present in these ratios that it was not possible to remove despite a very careful sifting of the data.[48] The ratios for 1915 and 1900 appear to be of the same high level as those for 1923–1925. Although these high ratios could be explained on the basis of assumptions about related developments, we are disposed rather to suspect that hitherto uncovered differences in definitions and classifications are responsible for the high level of the ratios in these two years. If these years are disregarded, the standardized ratios in particular are significantly lower than for the years 1920–25. However, manufacturing becomes an increasingly smaller proportion of the economy as we go back in time and it would not, of course, be appropriate to generalize from manufacturing to the economy as a whole. Since the relative importance of net unincorporated income looms larger in the earlier periods, one could surmise that the ratio of wages paid out probably declines as we go back in time. This, however, raises the question of whether comparisons of the wage ratios for periods which are substantially unlike do not inevitably mirror the basic differences that existed in the industrial structure and institutional arrangements, despite adjustments that may be made to the (generally poorer) data to eliminate these factors.

Supplement

Short-Term Fluctuations of Wage Shares

F. H. Leacy

DOMINION BUREAU OF STATISTICS

It is a commonplace that because wages and salaries are a large component of nonfarm private business product, they are highly

[48] T. K. Rymes prepared and analyzed the figures prior to 1917 for the historical study referred to above. The ratios are not reproduced here.

correlated with that total, and that the total as well as the components display cyclical variability. But the ratios between them are much more subtle, *since they reflect differential rates of change during business cycles.* For example, if wages and salaries are less flexible to cyclical forces, or display less amplitude of variation during expansions and contractions than private business product, then the wage share itself will behave in an inverted fashion. We start out by examining the extent to which this hypothesis is borne out by the data; it will be seen that there are many exceptions to the general rule.

Section 1 describes very briefly the general behavior of factor returns. We then proceed to a description of the cyclical movements of factor returns and shares in the total nonfarm private business product and its major industry divisions, followed by a brief glance into manufacturing by eighteen groups and by selected export, primary, and other major groupings. The cyclical behavior of the industry wage shares is examined first in terms of the fixed set of turning points known as "reference dates"; and second in terms of the varying "specific dates" which each individual industry displays. Since annual data leave much to be desired in this kind of analysis, a special compilation was made of postwar quarterly data, seasonally adjusted, for the four industry groups of mining, manufacturing, transportation and utilities, and trade. These postwar data are also used to examine the timing of turning points in the wage share. The share may turn down later than the peaks of each individual industry's product, or turn up later at troughs. To what extent these timing lags supplement the earlier findings regarding inverted behavior of the wage share, is also considered.[1]

1. Income Components and Their Cyclical Variability

It will be recalled that the investment income share appeared to have greater cyclical volatility than the wage and salary share.

[1] The wage share can be regarded as labor costs per dollar of output; if the latter is deflated, we have labor cost per unit of output, or simply unit labor costs. Moore and Hultgren have shown that unit labor costs lag behind the turns in general business activity. See *Current Economic Situation and Short-Run Outlook,* Hearings, Joint Economic Committee, 86th Congress, December 7th and 8th, 1960, p. 94. See also, *Business Cycle Indicators* (Geoffrey H. Moore, ed.), Princeton for NBER, 1961 and Thor Hultgren, *Changes in Labor Costs During Cycles in Production and Business,* New York, NBER, Occasional Paper 74, 1960, p. 73.

The charts shown in the paper on long-term changes were designed for use in cyclical analysis as well as long-run changes. They show percentage variation and provide a visual measure of what might be called "coefficients of variation." An examination of Charts 4, 5 and 6 indicates that the investment income share displays more percentage variation than the wage share. In addition, the investment income share is almost perfectly inverse to the wage and salary share, suggesting that these two items interact with one another[2] despite the complications introduced by net unincorporated income.

But these share charts, of course, do not show which factors contribute the most variation to their sum (in dollar terms). We therefore examined the factor returns of the nonfarm private business product, with investment income divided into corporation profits, net rents, and interest and have concluded that there is less percentage variation in wage and salary returns than in either profits or net unincorporated income (both adjusted for inventory valuation). However, rents and interest follow relatively smooth paths. The main body of the industrial analysis which follows was carried out with charts showing dollar figures of the factor returns as well as their shares, but they are not reproduced here.

2. *Reference Cycle of Behavior of Wage Shares*

In order to describe the behavior of the wage share during recurrent expansions and contractions of general business activity (the so-called reference cycles), we have charted the main industrial divisions of nonfarm private business product, and have indicated the alternate periods of expansion and contraction by plain and shaded areas (see Chart 8). In delineating these periods, the reference dates developed by E. C. Chambers for Canadian business cycles have been utilized.[3] The dates of these reference cycles, incidentally, resemble very closely (frequently within one or two months), those used for the United States economy by the National Bureau.

[2] If we add $10 to wages which hitherto were $50 and do this at the expense of another factor, say profits, which hitherto were $20, we have added 20 per cent to wages and deducted 50 per cent from profits. Thus, if one factor were gaining or losing absolute amounts at the expense of another, we would expect to see quite diverse movements cyclically, on semilog share charts.

[3] E. C. Chambers, "Canadian Business Cycles Since 1919: A Progress Report," *Canadian Journal of Economics and Political Science*, May 1958, p. 181. We have added turning points in January 1944, April 1957, and April 1958.

CHART 8

Wage and Salary Share of Nonfarm Private Business Product

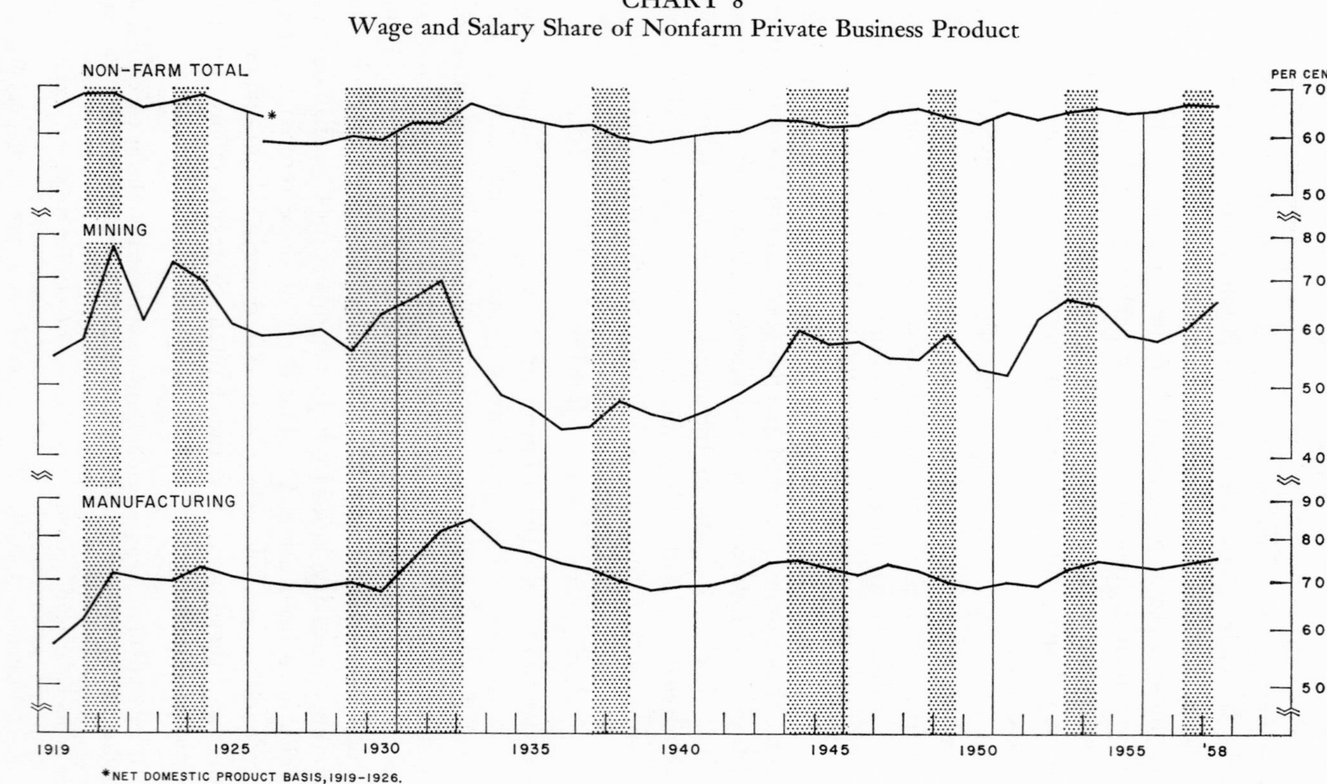

CHART 8 (continued)

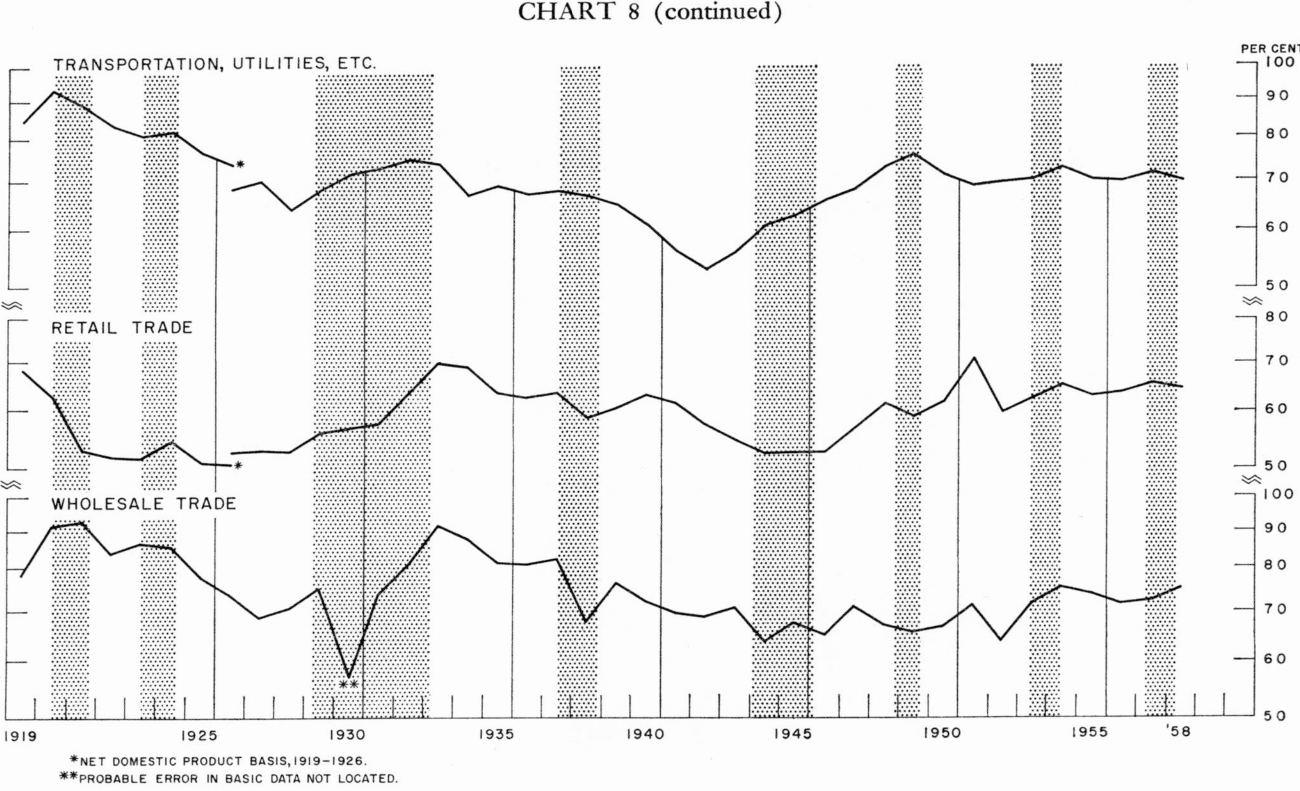
TRANSPORTATION, UTILITIES, ETC.
RETAIL TRADE
WHOLESALE TRADE
PER CENT
100
90
80
70
60
50
80
70
60
50
100
90
80
70
60
50
1919
1925
1930
1935
1940
1945
1950
1955
'58
*NET DOMESTIC PRODUCT BASIS, 1919-1926.
**PROBABLE ERROR IN BASIC DATA NOT LOCATED.

CHART 8. (concluded)

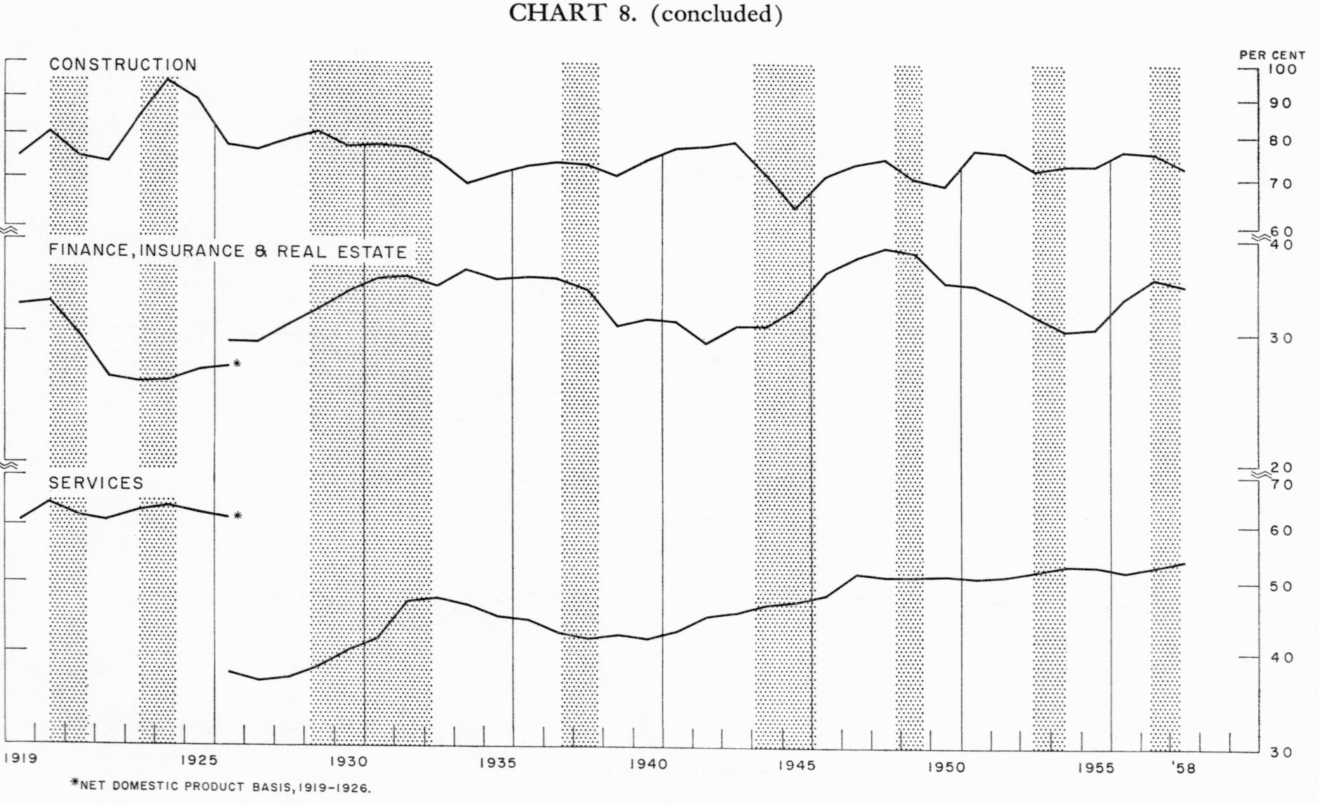

*NET DOMESTIC PRODUCT BASIS, 1919-1926.

Despite the shortcomings of annual data for cyclical analysis, the chart and the following tables provide the initial suggestion that there is some degree of inverse behavior of wage shares during reference cycles. This is illustrated by the predominance of minus signs in Table 1 (part A) and plus signs in Table 2 (part A). This inverse behavior does not hold in the period 1938–48, nor does it hold strongly in the mild cycles of the postwar period.

TABLE 1
WAGE SHARES OF PRIVATE BUSINESS PRODUCT DURING EIGHT REFERENCE EXPANSIONS[a]

	May 1919 to June 1920	Sept. 1921 to June 1923	Aug. 1924 to Apr. 1929	May 1933 to July 1937	Oct. 1938 to Jan. 1944	Feb. 1946 to Oct. 1948	Sept. 1949 to May 1953	June 1954 to Apr. 1957
A Industries in which countercyclical behavior predominates								
Mining, quarrying, and oil wells	+	−	+	−	+	−	+	−
Manufacturing	+	−	−	−	+	0	+	0
Transportation, public utilities, etc.	+	−	−	−	−	+	−	−
Wholesale trade	+	−	−	−	−	0	+	−
Retail trade	−	−	−	−	−	+	0	0
B Industries in which cyclical conformity predominates								
Forestry	+	+	0	+	+	+	+	+
Construction	+	+	−	−	0	+	+	+
C Industries not displaying either behavior								
Finance, insurance and real estate	+	−	+	0	−	+	−	+
Service	+	0	−	−	+	+	+	0
D Total nonfarm private business product wage share								
Total nonfarm	+	−	−	−	+	+	+	+

[a] Change between beginning and ending level of annual average, plotted at mid-year.

Moreover, while it is evident in mining, manufacturing, transportation, communication and public utilities, and wholesale and retail trade, it is not evident in forestry, construction, finance, and services. Forestry and construction with very high wage shares appear to move in the same direction as reference cycle phases.[4] Finance and services, with relatively low wage shares, have very little cyclical volatility of either wages and salaries or private business product, and no particular correlation with reference phases can be seen. Manufacturing itself is a heterogeneous aggregate behaving very much like the nonfarm private business product, as far as reference cycle responses of wage shares are concerned. But there is sufficient hint of negative correlation here

[4] Our data are less adequate for these industries than for most others.

TABLE 2
WAGE SHARES OF PRIVATE BUSINESS PRODUCT DURING EIGHT REFERENCE CONTRACTIONS

	June 1920 to Sept. 1921	June 1923 to Aug. 1924	April 1929 to May 1933	July 1937 to Oct. 1938	June 1944 to Feb. 1946	Oct. 1948 to Sept. 1949	May 1953 to June 1954	April 1957 to April 1958
A Industries in which countercyclical behavior predominates								
Mining, quarrying, and oil wells	+	−	+	+	+	+	−	+
Manufacturing	+	+	+	−	−	−	+	+
Transportation, public utilities, etc.	−	+	+	−	+	+	+	−
Wholesale trade	+	−	+	−	+	−	+	+
Retail trade	−	+	+	−	+	−	+	−
B Industries in which cyclical conformity predominates								
Forestry	−	−	−	−	−	−	−	−
Construction	−	+	−	0	−	−	+	−
C Industries not displaying either behavior								
Finance, insurance, and real estate	−	+	+	−	+	−	−	−
Service	−	+	+	−	+	0	+	+
D Total nonfarm private business product wage share								
Total nonfarm	+	+	+	−	−	−	+	0

to make it seem worthwhile to go further. We next examine these data in specific cycles.

3. Specific Cycles in Wage and Salary Shares

NONFARM PRIVATE BUSINESS PRODUCT BY MAIN INDUSTRY DIVISIONS

The industrial parts of nonfarm private business product display some variety of timing behavior. The term "specific" implies that we are not now concerned with business cycle reference dates, but rather with the turning points of the total product of each individual series.

In percentage terms, wages and salaries vary less than the total product, and corporate profits after I.V.A. vary more than the total. The effect on the wage shares is that they vary inversely with the total during a majority of specific cycles. This behavior is most apparent in mining, less apparent in manufacturing (which contains some diverse elements), clear in the transportation, communication, storage and public utility group, and also quite clear in wholesale and retail trade. Additional confirmation of the above is apparent from the study of postwar seasonally adjusted data below.

In order to condense these notes, the above findings will not be repeated for each individual industry. Rather we note exceptions and add comments on special factors.

Forestry, as noted above, has a very high wage content (90 per cent). Wages and salaries in this industry appear to vary in specific cycles just as the total industry product varies, with the result that the wage share appears to be positively correlated with output values. Despite the high level of wages and general agreement among short swings in wages and the total product, four lags of the shares behind the total are noted in the four most recent postwar turning points.

The *mining* industry, more than any other, displays a strong inverse correlation between the wage share and the total industry product. This appears to be associated with large variations in corporate profits after I.V.A., which on average are as large as wages and salaries.[5] The specific cycle turning points in the industry product (and profits) frequently lead the turning points in general business activity by a year or more.

The timing pattern of *manufacturing* wage shares is almost identical to that of the all-industry total. The wage share is inverse in the twenties, thirties, and fifties, but it moves in the same direction as total product in the forties. The group is large and heterogeneous, so that its total wage share reflects a great deal of cancellation of widely varying individual components.

Construction, like forestry, has a large (75 per cent) wage share which is quite flat and to a considerable extent positively correlated.

The *transportation*, *communication*, *storage and public utilities* group has been adjusted to exclude government-owned business enterprises, which represent an important proportion of the total in this group. Its private business content behaves quite like the general rule for the all-industry total, as well as manufacturing and mining, displaying negatively correlated wage shares and fairly large positively correlated profit variations.

Wholesale and retail trade wage shares vary countercyclically. In addition, both profits and net unincorporated income exhibit greater short-term variability than wages or industry product, accounting in the statistical sense for wage share inversion.

[5] Classification problems may affect this statement.

In *finance, insurance and real estate*, the wage and salary share is small, varying between 30 and 40 per cent of total product. The largest component of the product of this industry is net paid and imputed rents, and short cycles are not shown by either the total or its main components. Therefore, inverse behavior is not visible, except for the period 1928–34, when the total and main components declined and the wage share increased.

The combined *service industries* have approximately equal amounts of wages and salaries and net unincorporated incomes, which follow a similar and smooth path, increasing to 1928, decreasing to 1933, and rising thereafter. The wage share has no noticeable cyclical events except a rise from 1926 to 1933, a decline from 1933 to 1939 and a general rise thereafter.

The following table summarizes the above and in addition provides some indication of leads and lags of wage shares and profits, as shown by annual data.

TABLE 3

Summary of Specific Cyclical Behavior of Wages and Salaries and Corporate Profits after I.V.A.

	Do Wages Vary Less Than Total?	Does Wage Share Lag Total?	Is Wage Share Inversely Correlated with Total?	Does Profit Variation Exceed Wage Variation?	Do Profits Lead at Specific Peaks and Troughs?
Nonfarm private business product	yes	yes	yes	yes	occasionally
Mining	yes	yes	yes	yes	coincident
Manufacturing	yes	yes	yes	yes	occasionally
Construction	not clear	no	yes, in post-war period	not clear	no
Transportation	yes	ccasionally	yes	yes	no
Wholesale trade	yes	no	yes	yes	no
Retail trade	yes	no	yes	yes	no
Finance, insurance and real estate	yes	no	yes	yes	no
Service	no	no	no	no	no

SPECIFIC CYCLES IN WAGE AND SALARY SHARES IN CENSUS VALUE ADDED—EIGHTEEN MAJOR GROUPS

We now turn to a brief description of the movements of the wage share in specific cycles of the eighteen major manufacturing groups. The definitional aspects of census value added statistics were discussed in the preceding paper. At first sight it seems that the finer the industrial detail the more extreme the cyclical variability of wage shares—at least the cyclical cross-currents are so numerous that one is bewildered by their variety. However, closer examination indicates that it is possible to group the industries into several classes as far as the cyclical behavior of their wage shares is concerned.

It is suggested that the wage share patterns may be classified into four groups:

1. Foods and beverages, textiles, knitting mills and clothing, leather products, and printing are consumer nondurables with only a moderate amount of cyclical variation in wage shares, but all higher at the end than at the beginning of the series. Rubber products and miscellaneous manufacturing belong here, as far as demand factors are concerned, but their patterns are not alike and other reasons would have to be sought for their behavior, e.g., in terms of technology, markets and organizational structure in these industries. Tobacco has a downward share drift and unusual behavior throughout.

2. Electrical apparatus, chemicals, iron and steel, and transportation equipment, which are, of course, mainly producers' durable goods industries, all exhibit fairly strong amplitudes and considerable similarity of timing of wage shares at peaks and troughs.

3. Wood and paper products and nonmetallic minerals have only a moderate amount of wage share variation, despite the fact that they are related to the highly variable demand sectors of exports and construction.

4. Extreme variations are shown by petroleum, coal, and nonferrous metals; and, as was discovered earlier for mining, there must be large variation in some other factor such as corporation profits in these industries. They are also, except coal, related to exports.

A complete durable and nondurable classification was carried out, which showed greater cyclical variation in durable goods industries than in nondurables. The latter had a flat pattern reflecting cancellation of its parts. Much finer detail, together with an end-use classification, would be required to do the above analysis properly.

SELECTED PRIMARY AND EXPORT INDUSTRIES IN MANUFACTURING

As described in the preceding paper, it was possible to arrange the finest available industrial detail at the three-digit level according to (a) primary and secondary and (b) export and domestic groups. This rearrangement appears in Chart 7 where it will be noted that cyclical patterns of wage shares in primary and export industries display considerable amplitude by comparison with those of domestic and secondary industries. Since primary and export industries are largely overlapping in content and are dominated by sawmills, pulp and paper products and nonferrous smelting and refining, the cyclical patterns of their wage shares are very similar in amplitudes and turning points. On the other hand, the domestic and secondary industries display a remarkably unchanging pattern through time, the result of a substantial amount of cancellation of wide individual differences among their component groups.

4. Postwar Quarterly Data, for Net Domestic Product Originating in Major Industry Groups

In preceding sections we concentrated on the main hypothesis that wage shares display countercyclical behavior, as a concomitant of the lesser volatility of wages and salaries, by comparison with other factors that enter the total product. Not only were there numerous exceptions to the general rule in the form of increasing diversity as we looked into the various industrial groupings, but there were noted in passing a number of instances where even the annual data showed timing discrepancies at peaks and troughs. In particular, Table 10 showed several industry groups wherein wage shares turned up or down at a later date than the total product. Thus, it was suspected that the earlier hypothesis was oversimplified and should be supplemented by a more careful examination of leads and lags of factor returns and share ratios in specific cycles. Since annual data are not adequate for this sort of work, we were fortunate in obtaining preliminary and unpublished postwar quarterly data, seasonally adjusted, for four major industry groups (mining, manufacturing, transportation and public utilities, and trade). These data are on a domestic income basis and have not been adjusted to remove government-owned business enterprises. They have been adjusted for inventory valuation, which alters turning points considerably.

SPECIFIC CYCLES IN WAGE SHARES AND RELATED ITEMS

Chart 9 for the mining, quarrying, and oil industry indicates that profits are quite volatile, that they are highly correlated with domestic income and have the same turning points. By contrast, wages and salaries lag at the three peaks and at one of the two troughs and are relatively stable. Although the wage share undoubtedly behaves countercyclically, it is not perfectly so; it is therefore suggested that the lag of wages is an extra complicating factor over and above relative wage stability in determining the countercyclical movement of the wage share.

Chart 10 for manufacturing indicates that there are four turning points in which profits turn ahead of wages. But the turning points in the industry product do not appear to be as strongly correlated with profits as was the case in mining. However, the conclusion is still possible that the wage share is inverted in such a manner that it goes up during contractions and goes down during the initial half of expansions, at least.

Chart 11 for the group of transportation, public utilities, etc. indicates that profits after inventory valuation adjustment are rather stable by comparison with the other charts. Also, other investment income (not charted) is large and quite stable. Wages and salaries move parallel to the industry product and although they are not much more stable than total product, some wage share inversion is noticeable. Again we see that the wage share goes up during all of the contraction in total product and declines mainly in the early half of expansion.

In Chart 12 for wholesale and retail trade combined, there is a considerable amount of wage share inversion accompanied by profit variability. The wage share increases right through the contraction phase of total output, and may then decline during the first half of expansion.

A reference cycle analysis was also carried out with the same four charts, leading to the general conclusion that wage shares decline during a considerable part of reference expansions and increase in reference contractions. However, the mining industry leads the 1953 reference peak by a year and one-half and recovers early as well. Another exception is for wholesale and retail trade,

CHART 9
Net Domestic Product and Selected Components: Mining

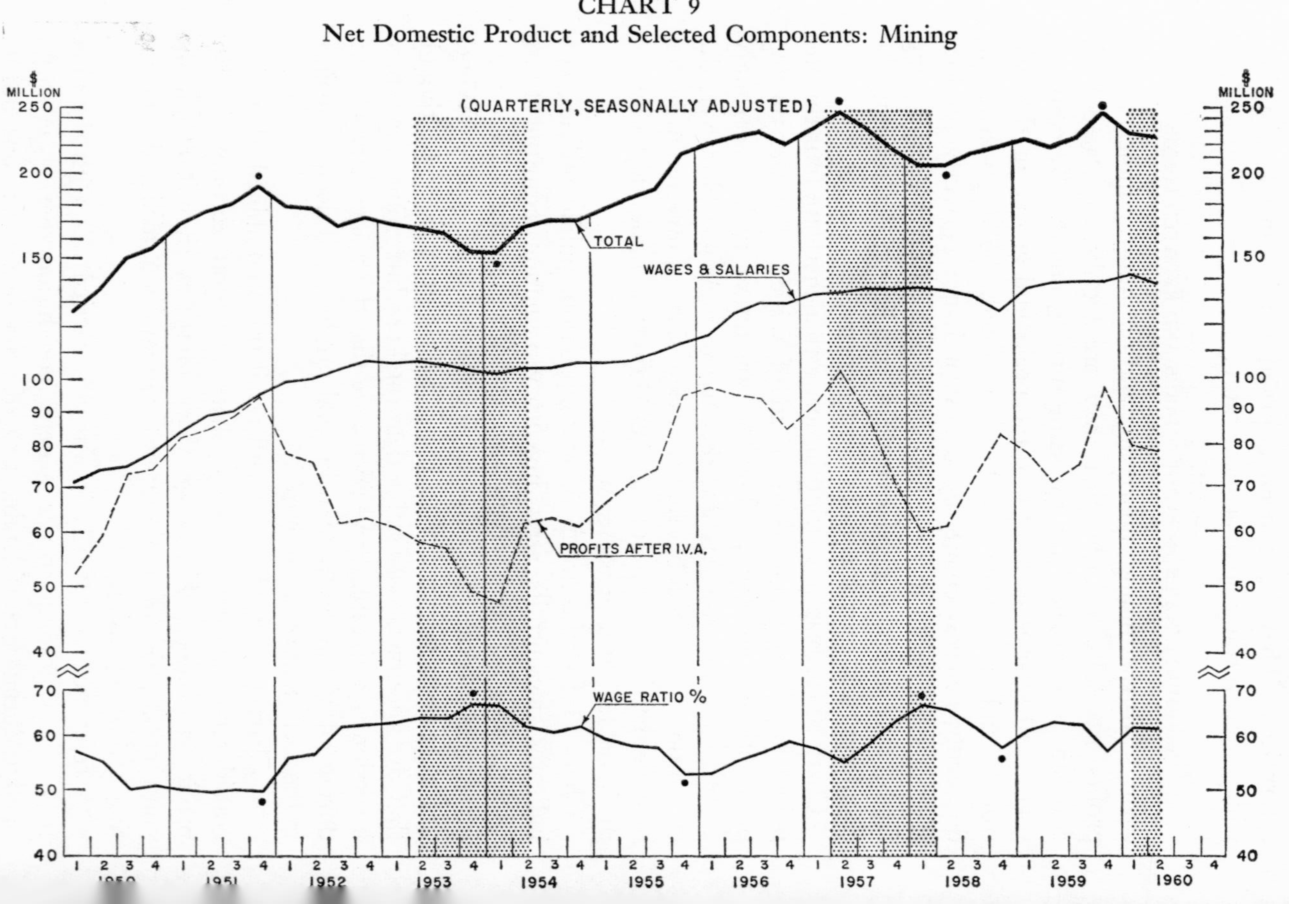

CHART 10
Net Domestic Product and Selected Components: Manufacturing

(QUARTERLY, SEASONALLY ADJUSTED)

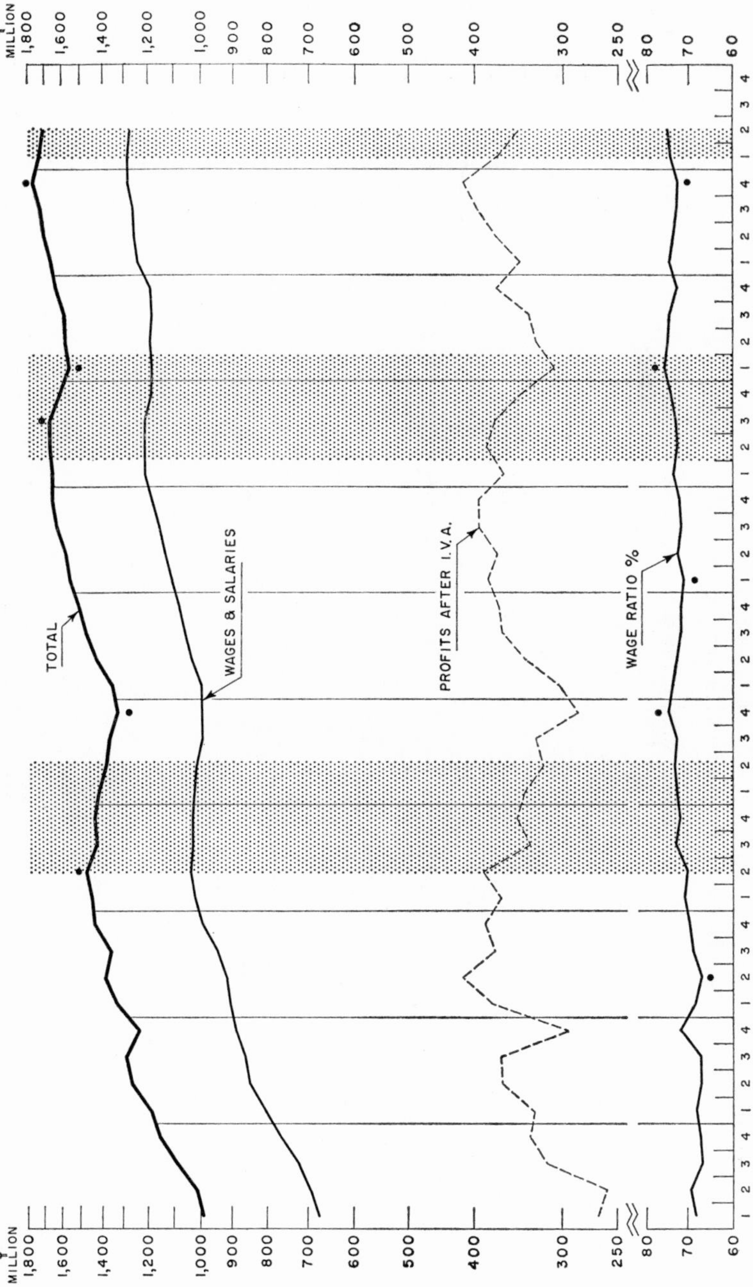

CHART 11
Net Domestic Product and Selected Components: Transport, Etc.
(QUARTERLY, SEASONALLY ADJUSTED)

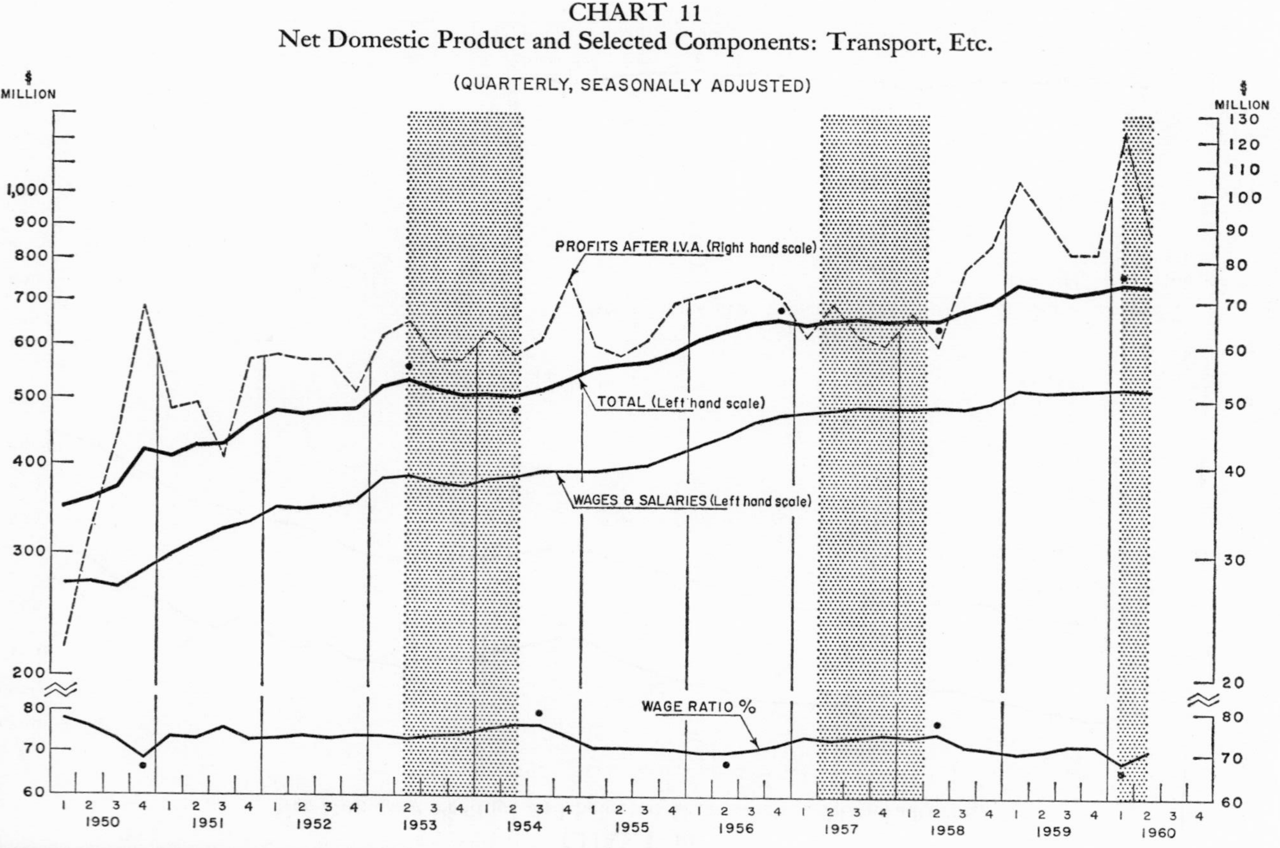

CHART 12
Net Domestic Product and Selected Components: Total Trade
(QUARTERLY, SEASONALLY ADJUSTED)

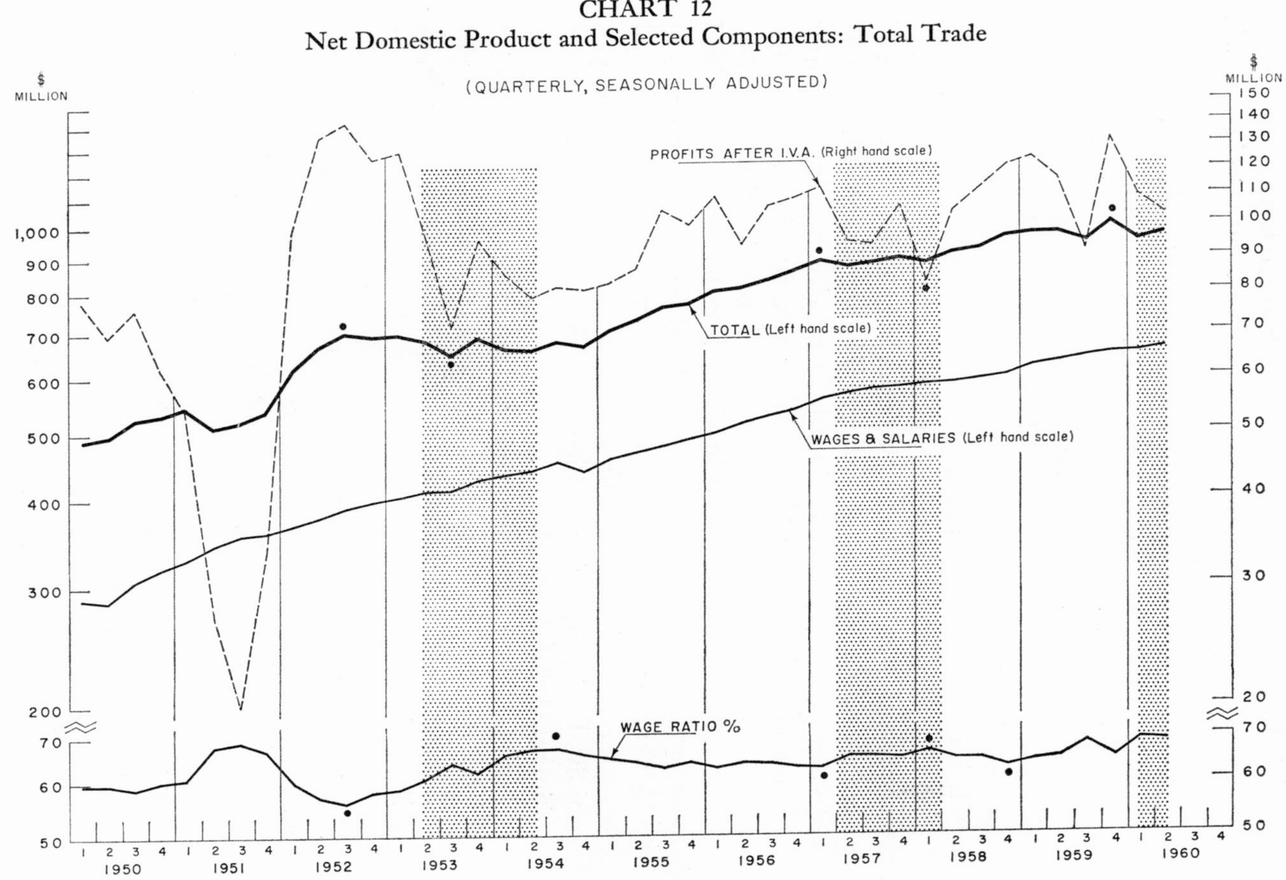

which leads the 1953–54 downturn. Since reference cycles are not as clear cut as specific cycles, the following conclusions will refer to specific cycles only.

In most of the above specific cycles, the reciprocal of the wage share is a leader of total product peaks. This is the result of the finding that wage shares generally declined only during the first half of these postwar expansions. The same claim cannot be made for the troughs in these data. Here the wage shares are usually at a maximum and are coincident.

It is very difficult to translate the above straightforward description of events, as portrayed by statistical charts, into some kind of generalization or hypothesis which might be easier to comprehend or to remember for future testing. The simple initial hypothesis of wage share inversion as a result of relative stability of returns to this factor, by comparison with profits, is not too far off the mark. But it must be qualified by the observation that, according to our data, there are frequent very short lags of wages behind total product, accompanied, usually, by short leads of profits. In addition to these short leads and lags of factor returns at peaks and troughs, there is also a differential rate of response of wages, mainly during expansions, which gives rise to a quarter-cycle lead of inverted shares at peaks.

Business cycle literature contains references to items closely related to wage shares, such as labor costs per unit of real output and net product price indexes (referring to the output minus input prices which are a by-product of the double deflation process sometimes used in arriving at real output). The closeness of this relationship is demonstrated by the fact that if weighting systems and procedures are properly chosen, the wage share is equal to a cost-price ratio.[6] It has long been known that unit labor costs "tend to rise in contraction and to fall at least during the earlier stages of expansion."[7] More recently there have been several additions to the list of leading indicators. Corporate profits before taxes and a price-unit labor cost ratio in manufacturing which

[6] $$\text{Wage share} = \frac{\text{wages and salaries}}{\text{total product}} = \frac{\text{wages and salaries} \div \text{real output index}}{\text{total product} \div \text{real output index}} = \frac{\text{unit wage costs, index}}{\text{net product price index}}$$

[7] Wesley C. Mitchell, *What Happens during Business Cycles,* N.Y., NBER, 1951, p. 133. Hultgren's *Changes in Labor Cost* contains a great deal of additional information on this point.

is the reciprocal of the wage share, are included as leaders, while unit labor costs are included as laggers.[8] Although we have not worked with product prices or deflated total product in this paper, it is suggested that this might be a suitable topic for future research.

Summary and Conclusions

Annual data from 1926 to 1958 for nonfarm private business product indicate that the cyclical variability of wages and salaries is frequently smaller than that of other factor returns, in terms of percentage variation. This is mainly true of the total and the groups of mining, manufacturing, transportation and public utilities, and wholesale and retail trade. It does not hold in the 1938–48 period, nor in the industries of forestry, construction, finance, insurance and real estate, and services. Wherever the above finding is true, the wage share displays inverted behavior and it is easier to see this in the specific cycles of each industry's total product than in reference cycles in business at large.

The eighteen major groups within manufacturing were grouped experimentally according to their common patterns of wage share behavior. No important findings can be claimed from this experiment, except that finer detailing and more examination of related factors is called for. At the finest level of detail available to us, we were able to separate (a) export versus domestic industries and (b) primary versus secondary industries. The export and primary groups displayed the most variation in wage shares.

Postwar quarterly data, seasonally adjusted, for four industry groups indicated that the initial hypothesis of inverted cyclical behavior of wage shares required further qualification. The wage share patterns were never the exact opposite of the total product patterns and at certain stages of cyclical phases the wage shares moved in the same direction as the total. No simple sine-curve or straight-line model containing various leads and lags, will serve to summarize the complicated behavior of wage shares. Nevertheless, it is suggested that an important thing about cycles in wage shares is that they continue on down for some time after the total product has begun to expand. Later in expansion, the wage shares turn up. According to our data, the wage shares continue in an upward direction right through the succeeding contraction. They

[8] Moore and Hultgren in *Current Economic Situation* (see note 1).

turn down only when total product turns up and therefore do not lead the trough as they had previously turned in advance of the peak. Taking the cycle as a whole, and subject to the above qualifications, wage shares may be regarded as an inverted series.

APPENDIX

Note on Tabular Material

Only a brief note on sources is provided here. The data for 1926–58 are based on official published sources and worksheets of the National Accounts and Labor Divisions of the Dominion Bureau of Statistics. For a detailed description of sources and methods reference should be made to *National Accounts, Income and Expenditure, 1926–56* and *National Accounts, Income and Expenditure, 1959.* In several cases adjustments were made to published information, the most important of which is the inclusion of imputed rent on government-owned buildings with the finance, insurance, and real estate industry, rather than services as in the published figures. Substantial rearrangement of worksheet data was involved in segregating the private business sector, as the worksheets had been set up to produce totals only for the private and government business sector as a whole. Some rearrangement of the information was also involved in securing data for domestic income, by industry, as the worksheets had been designed to produce industry distributions on a gross domestic basis only. The published figures of the inventory valuation adjustment were separated into incorporated and unincorporated, for each individual industry, on the basis of admittedly arbitrary judgments and scattered statistics on legal form of business organization. The taxation data used to calculate factor shares after taxes were based on various editions of *Taxation Statistics* published by the Canadian Department of National Revenue. Since 1946 the personal income tax payable for each income size class was split pro rata according to the ratio of wages and salary income to total taxable income assessed. For the earlier years, income tax paid by "employees" was taken as synonymous with income tax paid out of salary-wage income. The estimates of 1919–26 were carried out by D. H. Jones of the Central Research and Development Staff, Dominion Bureau of Statistics, and a memorandum on sources and methods prepared by him will be made available on request.

TABLE A-1
PERCENTAGE DISTRIBUTION OF DOMESTIC INCOME BY FACTOR SHARES

Year	Wages and Salaries	Investment Income	Net Nonfarm Unincorporated Income	Net Farm Unincorporated Income[a]	Total
		INCLUDING INVENTORY VALUATION ADJUSTMENT			
1926	54.7	19.8	11.5	14.0	100.0
1927	55.0	20.2	11.7	13.1	100.0
1928	54.8	20.6	11.8	12.8	100.0
1929	59.3	20.5	12.3	7.9	100.0
1930	59.6	20.6	12.5	7.3	100.0
1931	65.9	18.8	12.7	2.6	100.0
1932	68.2	16.3	11.9	3.6	100.0
1933	69.2	17.4	10.8	2.6	100.0
1934	65.0	19.2	10.2	5.6	100.0
1935	63.2	19.6	10.6	6.6	100.0
1936	62.4	21.2	10.9	5.5	100.0
1937	61.9	21.0	10.3	6.8	100.0
1938	59.5	21.0	11.2	8.3	100.0
1939	58.7	22.9	10.3	8.1	100.0
1940	59.2	22.4	9.3	9.1	100.0
1941	61.2	22.7	9.0	7.1	100.0
1942	59.3	21.4	8.1	11.2	100.0
1943	63.5	20.4	8.1	8.0	100.0
1944	62.0	18.7	8.2	11.1	100.0
1945	62.6	19.0	9.2	9.2	100.0
1946	59.5	19.2	10.5	10.8	100.0
1947	61.0	18.6	9.9	10.5	100.0
1948	61.2	18.2	9.4	11.2	100.0
1949	61.4	18.8	10.3	9.5	100.0
1950	60.3	21.2	9.5	9.0	100.0
1951	60.9	19.8	7.9	11.4	100.0
1952	60.7	20.6	8.4	10.3	100.0
1953	63.6	19.7	8.7	8.0	100.0
1954	66.3	19.8	8.6	5.3	100.0
1955	64.7	20.9	8.4	6.0	100.0
1956	65.0	20.7	8.1	6.2	100.0
1957	67.8	20.0	8.1	4.1	100.0
1958	67.4	19.5	8.4	4.7	100.0

(continued)

TABLE A-1 (concluded)

Year	Wages and Salaries	Investment Income	Net Nonfarm Unincorporated Income	Net Farm Unincorporated Income[a]	Total
		EXCLUDING INVENTORY VALUATION ADJUSTMENT			
1926	55.3	19.1	11.4	14.2	100.0
1927	55.3	19.8	11.7	13.2	100.0
1928	54.8	20.6	11.8	12.8	100.0
1929	59.1	20.6	12.4	7.9	100.0
1930	62.8	17.4	12.1	7.7	100.0
1931	69.2	16.2	12.0	2.6	100.0
1932	70.9	14.0	11.4	3.7	100.0
1933	68.7	18.0	10.8	2.5	100.0
1934	64.2	19.9	10.4	5.5	100.0
1935	62.8	19.9	10.7	6.6	100.0
1936	61.8	21.8	10.9	5.5	100.0
1937	60.6	22.1	10.6	6.7	100.0
1938	60.5	20.0	11.0	8.5	100.0
1939	58.0	23.6	10.4	8.0	100.0
1940	57.8	23.5	9.8	8.9	100.0
1941	59.7	23.8	9.6	6.9	100.0
1942	58.5	22.2	8.3	11.0	100.0
1943	63.0	20.9	8.2	7.9	100.0
1944	61.7	19.0	8.3	11.0	100.0
1945	62.3	19.2	9.3	9.2	100.0
1946	58.0	20.8	10.7	10.5	100.0
1947	57.8	21.7	10.5	10.0	100.0
1948	58.7	20.6	9.9	10.8	100.0
1949	60.9	19.3	10.4	9.4	100.0
1950	58.8	22.7	9.6	8.9	100.0
1951	58.7	21.7	8.6	11.0	100.0
1952	61.0	20.2	8.4	10.4	100.0
1953	63.5	19.8	8.6	8.1	100.0
1954	66.6	19.5	8.6	5.3	100.0
1955	64.1	21.6	8.4	5.9	100.0
1956	64.4	21.2	8.3	6.1	100.0
1957	67.6	20.1	8.2	4.1	100.0
1958	67.3	19.6	8.4	4.7	100.0

[a] Undistributed Wheat Board profits included.

TABLE A-2
PERCENTAGE DISTRIBUTION OF NATIONAL INCOME BY FACTOR SHARES[a]

Year	Wages and Salaries	Investment Income	Net Unincorporated Income (Farm and Nonfarm)	Total
1926	57.5	15.7	26.8	100.0
1927	57.7	16.2	26.1	100.0
1928	57.5	16.8	25.7	100.0
1929	62.6	16.1	21.3	100.0
1930	63.5	15.3	21.2	100.0
1931	71.4	12.1	16.5	100.0
1932	75.1	7.8	17.1	100.0
1933	75.8	9.5	14.7	100.0
1934	70.0	13.1	16.9	100.0
1935	67.4	14.3	18.3	100.0
1936	66.8	15.7	17.5	100.0
1937	65.5	16.4	18.1	100.0
1938	63.1	16.2	20.7	100.0
1939	62.2	18.4	19.4	100.0
1940	62.3	18.4	19.3	100.0
1941	63.3	19.9	16.8	100.0
1942	60.8	19.5	19.7	100.0
1943	65.0	18.6	16.4	100.0
1944	63.3	17.0	19.7	100.0
1945	63.7	17.6	18.7	100.0
1946	61.0	17.2	21.8	100.0
1947	62.6	16.4	21.0	100.0
1948	62.5	16.5	21.0	100.0
1949	62.9	16.9	20.2	100.0
1950	61.9	19.0	19.1	100.0
1951	62.1	18.2	19.7	100.0
1952	61.5	19.5	19.0	100.0
1953	64.4	18.7	16.9	100.0
1954	67.3	18.6	14.1	100.0
1955	65.7	19.7	14.6	100.0
1956	66.1	19.4	14.5	100.0
1957	69.0	18.5	12.5	100.0
1958	68.5	18.1	13.4	100.0

[a] I.V.A. included.

TABLE A-3

PERCENTAGE DISTRIBUTION GROSS DOMESTIC INCOME BY (GROSS) FACTOR SHARES[a]

Year	Wages and Salaries	Gross Investment Income	Gross Unincorporated Income (Farm and Nonfarm)	Total
1926	48.4	26.0	25.6	100.0
1927	48.5	26.5	25.0	100.0
1928	48.3	27.0	24.8	100.0
1929	51.9	27.2	21.0	100.0
1930	51.8	27.7	20.6	100.0
1931	56.1	27.3	16.7	100.0
1932	56.9	25.8	17.2	100.0
1933	57.5	27.1	15.4	100.0
1934	55.4	27.5	17.1	100.0
1935	54.4	27.3	18.3	100.0
1936	54.1	28.6	17.3	100.0
1937	54.1	28.0	17.9	100.0
1938	52.1	28.0	19.9	100.0
1939	51.4	29.8	18.8	100.0
1940	51.9	29.6	18.6	100.0
1941	53.8	29.8	16.4	100.0
1942	52.7	28.3	19.0	100.0
1943	57.0	26.7	16.3	100.0
1944	56.3	24.4	19.3	100.0
1945	57.0	24.4	18.7	100.0
1946	54.0	24.3	21.7	100.0
1947	54.7	24.5	20.9	100.0
1948	54.7	24.3	21.0	100.0
1949	54.5	25.2	20.3	100.0
1950	53.3	27.4	19.3	100.0
1951	53.9	26.2	20.0	100.0
1952	53.8	26.9	19.3	100.0
1953	55.9	26.5	17.5	100.0
1954	57.6	27.3	15.1	100.0
1955	56.0	28.9	15.2	100.0
1956	56.3	28.8	14.9	100.0
1957	58.2	28.8	13.0	100.0
1958	58.3	28.0	13.7	100.0

[a] I.V.A. included.

TABLE A-4

PERCENTAGE DISTRIBUTION OF DOMESTIC INCOME PLUS INTEREST ON PUBLIC AND CONSUMER DEBT BY FACTOR SHARES[a]

Year	Wages and Salaries	Investment Income Plus Interest[b]	Net Unincorporated Income (Farm and Nonfarm)	Total
1926	51.9	23.9	24.2	100.0
1927	52.2	24.1	23.6	100.0
1928	52.3	24.2	23.5	100.0
1929	56.6	24.2	19.3	100.0
1930	56.6	24.6	18.8	100.0
1931	61.6	24.2	14.2	100.0
1932	62.2	23.6	14.2	100.0
1933	62.3	25.7	12.0	100.0
1934	59.3	26.4	14.3	100.0
1935	58.2	26.0	15.8	100.0
1936	57.9	26.9	15.2	100.0
1937	58.0	26.0	16.0	100.0
1938	56.0	25.8	18.3	100.0
1939	55.2	27.5	17.3	100.0
1940	56.2	26.2	17.5	100.0
1941	58.5	26.1	15.4	100.0
1942	57.1	24.3	18.6	100.0
1943	61.0	23.6	15.4	100.0
1944	59.5	22.1	18.5	100.0
1945	59.4	23.0	17.5	100.0
1946	56.3	23.6	20.1	100.0
1947	57.9	22.7	19.4	100.0
1948	58.4	21.9	19.7	100.0
1949	58.8	22.3	18.9	100.0
1950	58.0	24.2	17.9	100.0
1951	58.8	22.5	18.7	100.0
1952	58.7	23.2	18.1	100.0
1953	61.5	22.4	16.2	100.0
1954	63.8	22.7	13.4	100.0
1955	62.4	23.6	14.0	100.0
1956	62.8	23.3	13.8	100.0
1957	65.5	22.7	11.8	100.0
1958	65.0	22.3	12.7	100.0

[a] Includes I.V.A.

[b] Interest on public and consumer debt.

TABLE A-5

PERCENTAGE DISTRIBUTION OF DOMESTIC INCOME BY FACTOR SHARES[a]
(after taxes)

Year	Wages and Salaries After Taxes[b]	Corporation Profits After Direct Taxes	Other Income After Direct Taxes[c]	Total
1926	55.0	9.7	35.3	100.0
1927	55.4	10.0	34.6	100.0
1928	55.3	10.2	34.5	100.0
1929	60.0	10.0	30.0	100.0
1930	60.1	10.0	29.9	100.0
1931	66.7	6.8	26.5	100.0
1932	69.2	2.5	28.3	100.0
1933	70.6	4.0	25.4	100.0
1934	66.2	6.5	27.3	100.0
1935	64.6	7.8	27.6	100.0
1936	64.0	9.6	26.4	100.0
1937	63.6	10.1	26.3	100.0
1938	61.0	10.7	28.3	100.0
1939	60.2	12.0	27.8	100.0
1940	63.2	8.5	28.3	100.0
1941	66.3	8.3	25.4	100.0
1942	63.4	7.7	28.9	100.0
1943	67.8	7.3	24.9	100.0
1944	65.4	6.8	27.8	100.0
1945	66.3	6.9	26.8	100.0
1946	63.0	7.0	30.0	100.0
1947	64.7	7.0	28.3	100.0
1948	63.9	8.1	28.0	100.0
1949	64.4	9.1	26.5	100.0
1950	63.9	9.5	26.6	100.0
1951	65.6	6.5	27.9	100.0
1952	64.3	8.5	27.2	100.0
1953	66.6	7.9	25.5	100.0
1954	69.2	7.4	23.4	100.0
1955	67.6	8.0	24.4	100.0
1956	67.9	8.4	23.7	100.0
1957	70.5	7.7	21.8	100.0
1958	69.8	7.2	23.0	100.0

[a] Includes I.V.A.

[b] In addition to taxes on wages and salaries, employer and employee contributions to social insurance and government pension plans have been deducted.

[c] Succession duties have not been deducted.

TABLE A-6
PERCENTAGE DISTRIBUTION OF DOMESTIC INCOME BY SECTORS

Year	Persons[a]	General Government	Government Business	Private Business	Total
1926	3.2	5.7	6.8	84.3	100.0
1927	3.2	5.7	6.7	84.4	100.0
1928	3.1	5.5	6.9	84.5	100.0
1929	3.4	5.9	6.9	83.8	100.0
1930	3.6	6.8	6.6	83.0	100.0
1931	4.1	8.6	7.3	80.0	100.0
1932	4.3	10.1	7.7	77.9	100.0
1933	4.3	10.2	7.8	77.7	100.0
1934	3.9	9.4	7.4	79.3	100.0
1935	3.7	8.7	7.1	80.5	100.0
1936	3.4	8.2	7.3	81.1	100.0
1937	3.2	7.6	6.6	82.6	100.0
1938	3.2	7.9	6.2	82.7	100.0
1939	3.0	8.0	6.5	82.5	100.0
1940	2.6	10.2	6.5	80.7	100.0
1941	2.2	11.4	6.4	80.0	100.0
1942	1.7	12.8	5.9	79.6	100.0
1943	1.4	15.4	6.6	76.6	100.0
1944	1.4	16.0	6.5	76.1	100.0
1945	1.5	16.8	7.0	74.7	100.0
1946	1.7	9.7	7.1	81.5	100.0
1947	1.8	7.0	6.5	84.7	100.0
1948	1.9	7.0	6.3	84.8	100.0
1949	2.0	7.5	6.3	84.2	100.0
1950	1.9	7.3	6.4	84.4	100.0
1951	1.9	7.6	6.4	84.1	100.0
1952	1.9	8.1	6.2	83.8	100.0
1953	2.0	8.7	6.6	82.7	100.0
1954	2.3	9.9	6.7	81.1	100.0
1955	2.2	9.9	6.8	81.1	100.0
1956	2.2	9.7	6.8	81.3	100.0
1957	2.3	10.5	6.9	80.3	100.0
1958	2.4	11.2	6.8	79.6	100.0

[a] Includes private noncommercial institutions.

TABLE A-7

Percentage Distribution of Private Business Product by Factor Shares[a]

Year	Wages and Salaries	Investment Income	Nonfarm Net Unincorporated Income	Farm Net Unincorporated Income[b]	Total
1926	48.9	20.9	13.6	16.6	100.0
1927	49.2	21.4	13.9	15.5	100.0
1928	49.3	21.6	13.9	15.2	100.0
1929	54.1	21.8	14.7	9.4	100.0
1930	53.5	22.6	15.1	8.8	100.0
1931	59.6	21.4	15.8	3.2	100.0
1932	61.8	18.3	15.3	4.6	100.0
1933	62.9	19.9	13.9	3.3	100.0
1934	58.8	21.3	12.9	7.0	100.0
1935	57.1	21.5	13.2	8.2	100.0
1936	57.0	22.8	13.4	6.8	100.0
1937	56.7	22.6	12.5	8.2	100.0
1938	53.4	23.0	13.5	10.1	100.0
1939	52.8	25.0	12.4	9.8	100.0
1940	52.9	24.3	11.6	11.2	100.0
1941	55.0	24.8	11.3	8.9	100.0
1942	52.4	23.4	10.1	14.1	100.0
1943	56.6	22.4	10.6	10.4	100.0
1944	54.0	20.6	10.7	14.7	100.0
1945	54.4	20.9	12.4	12.3	100.0
1946	54.1	19.8	12.9	13.2	100.0
1947	57.0	18.9	11.7	12.4	100.0
1948	56.9	18.8	11.1	13.2	100.0
1949	56.8	19.8	12.2	11.2	100.0
1950	55.8	22.2	11.2	10.8	100.0
1951	56.2	20.8	9.4	13.6	100.0
1952	55.6	22.1	10.0	12.3	100.0
1953	58.7	21.1	10.5	9.7	100.0
1954	61.3	21.5	10.7	6.5	100.0
1955	59.8	22.4	10.4	7.4	100.0
1956	60.3	22.1	10.0	7.6	100.0
1957	63.1	21.7	10.1	5.1	100.0
1958	62.3	21.2	10.5	6.0	100.0

[a] Includes I.V.A.

[b] Includes undistributed Wheat Board profits.

TABLE A-8
PERCENTAGE DISTRIBUTION OF NONFARM PRIVATE BUSINESS PRODUCT BY FACTOR SHARES[a]

Year	Wages and Salaries	Investment Income	Nonfarm Net Unincorporated Income	Total
1926	58.5	24.1	17.4	100.0
1927	58.1	24.5	17.4	100.0
1928	58.0	24.7	17.3	100.0
1929	59.7	23.2	17.1	100.0
1930	58.8	23.7	17.5	100.0
1931	62.2	20.5	17.3	100.0
1932	66.2	16.7	17.1	100.0
1933	66.5	18.1	15.4	100.0
1934	64.2	21.2	14.6	100.0
1935	62.8	22.0	15.2	100.0
1936	61.5	23.4	15.1	100.0
1937	62.0	23.8	14.2	100.0
1938	59.4	24.9	15.7	100.0
1939	58.4	27.2	14.4	100.0
1940	59.5	27.0	13.5	100.0
1941	60.3	26.9	12.8	100.0
1942	60.8	27.1	12.1	100.0
1943	63.0	24.9	12.1	100.0
1944	63.0	24.1	12.9	100.0
1945	61.8	23.8	14.4	100.0
1946	62.0	22.8	15.2	100.0
1947	64.8	21.5	13.7	100.0
1948	65.3	21.7	13.0	100.0
1949	63.6	22.3	14.1	100.0
1950	62.2	25.0	12.8	100.0
1951	64.8	24.2	11.0	100.0
1952	63.1	25.3	11.6	100.0
1953	64.8	23.4	11.8	100.0
1954	65.5	23.0	11.5	100.0
1955	64.4	24.2	11.4	100.0
1956	65.0	24.0	11.0	100.0
1957	66.4	22.8	10.8	100.0
1958	66.1	22.6	11.3	100.0

[a] Includes I.V.A. and farm rents paid and imputed.

TABLE A-9
Ratio of Salaries, Wages and Supplementary Labor Income to Income Originating in the Private Business Sector, by Industry[a]

Year	Agri-culture	Forestry	Fishing	Mining	Manu-facturing	Construc-tion	Transpor-tation, Com-munications, Utilities	Trade	Finance, Insurance, and Real Estate	Service	Total
1926	14.1	92.2	21.2	58.3	69.2	77.1	68.0	59.0	29.1	37.5	48.9
1927	14.3	91.0	22.6	58.7	68.4	76.3	69.9	57.8	29.0	36.7	49.2
1928	13.7	92.9	21.2	59.5	68.2	78.6	64.0	58.0	30.6	37.0	49.3
1929	19.4	90.8	23.3	55.4	69.1	80.6	68.1	61.3	32.2	38.2	54.1
1930	19.2	89.8	27.3	62.6	67.3	77.0	71.4	56.2	34.0	40.1	53.5
1931	31.2	81.6	30.8	65.3	74.0	77.5	72.4	62.7	35.3	41.6	59.6
1932	25.2	88.5	33.3	69.2	81.5	76.9	74.9	69.6	35.7	46.9	61.8
1933	30.0	89.3	30.0	54.8	84.5	73.9	73.9	77.0	34.6	47.1	62.9
1934	20.9	91.9	28.6	48.2	77.5	68.8	69.8	75.0	36.6	46.3	58.8
1935	19.2	93.0	25.0	46.2	76.0	70.8	68.8	68.9	35.1	44.8	57.1
1936	21.5	92.6	22.2	43.2	73.3	72.3	67.2	68.2	35.5	44.2	57.0
1937	18.5	91.3	22.2	43.7	72.1	73.0	67.6	70.0	35.4	42.4	56.7
1938	15.9	84.9	25.0	47.3	69.7	73.0	66.7	61.6	34.2	41.9	53.4
1939	15.9	82.7	22.2	45.4	67.8	70.3	64.9	65.7	30.6	42.1	52.8
1940	13.5	86.7	22.7	44.7	68.5	73.6	60.5	66.2	31.3	42.0	52.9
1941	14.4	87.5	20.0	46.2	68.9	76.8	55.7	64.3	32.0	42.9	55.0
1942	8.9	87.5	20.5	48.3	70.6	77.0	52.8	61.1	29.2	44.9	52.4
1943	11.9	88.2	21.6	51.7	73.8	78.1	55.5	59.8	30.7	45.2	56.6
1944	8.7	93.0	21.8	59.7	74.3	70.5	60.6	56.0	30.6	46.3	54.0
1945	10.4	87.3	20.6	57.0	72.4	63.8	62.1	57.3	32.3	46.9	54.4

(continued)

TABLE A-9 (concluded)

Year	Agri-culture	Forestry	Fishing	Mining	Manu-facturing	Construc-tion	Transpor-tation, Com-munications, Utilities	Trade	Finance, Insurance, and Real Estate	Service	Total
1946	9.9	89.0	21.4	57.3	71.2	70.2	65.8	56.7	36.1	47.9	54.1
1947	10.1	90.8	28.0	54.6	73.1	72.8	68.0	61.3	38.0	51.1	57.0
1948	8.5	91.2	27.7	54.0	72.0	74.2	72.5	63.3	39.1	50.7	56.9
1949	9.5	81.6	27.0	59.0	69.7	69.8	75.6	61.1	38.7	50.7	56.8
1950	9.6	78.1	25.6	52.4	68.3	68.5	70.9	63.4	35.0	50.8	55.8
1951	7.4	90.5	25.9	51.7	69.6	76.5	68.4	71.0	34.9	50.4	56.2
1952	7.5	90.7	32.8	61.8	68.8	75.8	69.1	61.2	33.3	50.8	55.6
1953	8.9	86.0	35.7	65.8	72.3	71.9	69.9	65.4	31.7	51.8	58.7
1954	11.6	81.8	34.4	64.3	74.1	72.9	72.6	68.5	30.2	52.7	61.3
1955	11.0	80.6	33.9	58.5	73.3	73.0	69.9	66.6	30.3	52.7	59.8
1956	10.3	86.7	31.9	57.4	72.7	76.2	69.5	66.4	33.4	51.5	60.3
1957	14.2	90.9	34.4	59.9	73.9	75.9	71.5	68.0	35.7	52.7	63.1
1958	12.4	90.2	32.9	65.2	75.0	72.5	69.8	68.3	34.9	53.9	62.3

[a] Includes I.V.A.

TABLE A-10
WAGES, SALARIES AND SUPPLEMENTARY LABOR INCOME AS A PERCENTAGE OF INCOME ORIGINATING IN THE PRIVATE BUSINESS SECTOR—STANDARDIZED (1928, 1949, and 1956 weights)[a]

Year	Total: 1928 Weights	Total: 1949 Weights	Total: 1956 Weights	Nonfarm[b]: 1928 Weights	Nonfarm[b]: 1949 Weights	Nonfarm[b]: 1956 Weights
1926	49.8	55.3	57.0	58.6	61.4	61.0
1927	49.5	54.9	56.4	58.1	60.8	60.4
1928	49.3	54.8	56.4	58.0	60.7	60.5
1929	51.7	56.8	58.3	59.6	62.2	62.0
1930	51.1	55.7	57.2	59.0	61.0	60.8
1931	56.5	60.9	62.0	62.7	65.3	64.9
1932	59.2	64.8	66.1	67.6	70.6	70.0
1933	61.1	66.8	67.7	68.7	72.2	71.3
1934	56.5	62.2	63.4	65.2	68.2	67.4
1935	54.5	60.2	61.4	63.2	66.1	65.5
1936	54.0	59.2	60.5	62.0	64.7	64.2
1937	53.2	58.6	60.0	61.7	64.5	64.0
1938	50.7	55.8	57.3	59.2	61.6	61.2
1939	50.0	55.2	56.5	58.3	61.0	60.4
1940	49.7	55.2	56.7	58.6	61.3	60.8
1941	49.7	55.2	56.7	58.3	61.1	60.7
1942	48.3	54.4	56.1	58.0	61.1	60.6
1943	50.2	56.3	58.0	59.6	62.8	62.3
1944	49.7	55.8	57.4	59.7	62.6	62.1
1945	49.4	55.1	56.7	59.0	61.7	61.1
1946	50.1	55.6	57.4	60.0	62.3	61.9
1947	52.1	57.8	59.6	62.4	64.7	64.3
1948	52.4	57.9	59.9	63.1	65.1	64.7
1949	51.6	56.8	58.6	62.0	63.7	63.3
1950	50.4	55.6	57.3	60.4	62.4	61.8
1951	51.9	57.7	59.6	62.8	65.0	64.5
1952	50.6	56.2	58.0	61.2	63.2	62.8
1953	52.2	58.1	59.8	62.8	65.3	64.6
1954	54.2	60.0	61.5	64.6	67.0	66.3
1955	52.7	58.6	60.1	63.0	65.5	64.8
1956	52.8	58.6	60.3	63.2	65.6	65.1
1957	54.8	60.3	62.0	64.7	67.1	66.5
1958	54.6	60.4	62.1	65.0	67.4	66.8

[a] Includes I.V.A.
[b] Includes farm rents paid and imputed.

TABLE A-11
PERCENTAGE DISTRIBUTION OF NET DOMESTIC INCOME BY FACTOR SHARES—TOTAL BUSINESS SECTOR, PRIVATE AND GOVERNMENT[a]

Year	Wages and Salaries	Investment Income	Nonfarm Net Unincorporated Income	Net Farm Unincorporated Income[b]	Total
1926	50.3	21.7	12.6	15.4	100.0
1927	50.6	22.1	12.9	14.4	100.0
1928	50.5	22.6	12.9	14.0	100.0
1929	55.1	22.6	13.6	8.7	100.0
1930	54.9	22.9	14.0	8.2	100.0
1931	61.0	21.6	14.5	2.9	100.0
1932	62.9	19.0	13.9	4.2	100.0
1933	64.0	20.4	12.6	3.0	100.0
1934	59.7	22.2	11.7	6.4	100.0
1935	58.0	22.4	12.1	7.5	100.0
1936	57.6	23.9	12.3	6.2	100.0
1937	57.3	23.5	11.6	7.6	100.0
1938	54.4	23.6	12.6	9.4	100.0
1939	53.6	25.8	11.5	9.1	100.0
1940	53.2	25.7	10.7	10.4	100.0
1941	55.0	26.3	10.5	8.2	100.0
1942	52.4	25.1	9.4	13.1	100.0
1943	56.2	24.5	9.7	9.6	100.0
1944	54.0	22.6	9.9	13.5	100.0
1945	54.2	23.2	11.3	11.3	100.0
1946	54.2	21.7	11.9	12.2	100.0
1947	57.2	20.4	10.9	11.5	100.0
1948	57.4	20.0	10.3	12.3	100.0
1949	57.4	20.8	11.4	10.4	100.0
1950	56.3	23.3	10.4	10.0	100.0
1951	56.8	21.9	8.7	12.6	100.0
1952	56.3	22.9	9.3	11.5	100.0
1953	59.2	22.1	9.7	9.0	100.0
1954	61.6	22.5	9.9	6.0	100.0
1955	59.8	23.7	9.6	6.9	100.0
1956	60.3	23.5	9.2	7.0	100.0
1957	63.0	23.0	9.3	4.7	100.0
1958	62.2	22.6	9.7	5.5	100.0

[a] Includes I.V.A.
[b] Includes undistributed Wheat Board profits.

TABLE A-12
WAGES, SALARIES AND SUPPLEMENTARY LABOR INCOME AS A PERCENTAGE OF DOMESTIC INCOME—STANDARDIZED
(1928 and 1949 industry weights)[a]

Year	*Total Domestic Income* 1928 Weights	1949 Weights	*Nonfarm Domestic Income* 1928 Weights	1949 Weights
1919	56.0	60.0	64.4	65.5
1920	59.0	63.2	68.0	69.1
1921	60.4	65.1	68.7	70.7
1922	57.1	62.1	65.6	67.8
1923	58.0	63.2	66.7	69.0
1924	60.1	65.3	68.4	70.9
1925	56.8	62.2	65.7	68.2
1926	55.5	60.5	63.7	66.1
1927	55.2	60.1	63.4	65.6
1928	54.8	59.8	63.0	65.3
1929	57.1	61.7	64.6	66.8
1930	57.1	61.2	64.7	66.3
1931	62.1	66.1	68.3	70.2
1932	64.6	69.5	72.5	74.8
1933	66.3	71.3	73.6	76.3
1934	61.6	66.7	69.7	72.2
1935	60.1	65.1	68.3	70.6
1936	59.3	64.0	66.8	69.1
1937	58.6	63.5	66.6	68.9
1938	56.7	61.3	64.9	66.8
1939	55.8	60.5	63.7	65.8
1940	54.9	60.0	63.2	65.6
1941	54.4	59.6	62.4	65.0
1942	52.9	58.5	61.6	64.5
1943	54.1	59.7	62.5	65.5
1944	53.8	59.5	62.7	65.6
1945	53.4	58.8	62.0	64.6
1946	54.6	59.6	63.5	65.6
1947	56.5	61.7	65.8	67.9
1948	57.2	62.2	66.9	68.7
1949	56.8	61.4	66.2	67.7
1950	55.5	60.2	64.6	66.3
1951	56.8	62.0	66.6	68.6
1952	55.9	60.9	65.6	67.3
1953	57.3	62.6	67.0	69.0
1954	58.7	64.0	68.2	70.3
1955	57.5	62.8	66.8	69.0
1956	57.6	62.8	67.0	69.1
1957	59.4	64.5	68.5	70.5
1958	59.4	64.6	68.8	70.9

[a] Includes I.V.A.

TABLE A-13
WAGES AND SALARIES AND DOMESTIC INCOME, TOTAL AND NONFARM
(million dollars)[a]

Year	*Domestic Income* Total	*Domestic Income* Wages and Salaries	*Nonfarm Domestic Income*[b] Total	*Nonfarm Domestic Income*[b] Wages and Salaries
1919	3,958	2,181	3,175	2,071
1920	4,541	2,602	3,617	2,470
1921	3,454	2,091	2,893	1,985
1922	3,589	2,028	2,946	1,934
1923	3,829	2,191	3,130	2,088
1924	3,641	2,194	3,067	2,090
1925	4,139	2,236	3,243	2,128
1926	4,337	2,373	3,542	2,261
1927	4,572	2,513	3,789	2,401
1928	4,966	2,722	4,141	2,609
1929	4,969	2,948	4,385	2,835
1930	4,688	2,794	4,166	2,694
1931	3,664	2,416	3,414	2,338
1932	2,906	1,983	2,664	1,922
1933	2,594	1,796	2,397	1,737
1934	2,994	1,947	2,697	1,885
1935	3,305	2,088	2,956	2,021
1936	3,603	2,250	3,273	2,179
1937	4,113	2,547	3,702	2,471
1938	4,242	2,524	3,758	2,447
1939	4,485	2,633	3,993	2,555
1940	5,324	3,152	4,707	3,069
1941	6,531	3,994	5,934	3,908
1942	8,301	4,923	7,231	4,828
1943	9,004	5,722	8,138	5,619
1944	9,776	6,066	8,544	5,959
1945	9,836	6,154	8,785	6,045
1946	9,793	5,827	8,582	5,707
1947	10,634	6,482	9,348	6,352
1948	12,258	7,496	10,712	7,365
1949	13,212	8,115	11,795	7,981
1950	14,545	8,766	13,044	8,622
1951	16,923	10,304	14,795	10,147
1952	18,922	11,478	16,763	11,316
1953	19,533	12,419	17,762	12,263
1954	19,308	12,799	18,109	12,660
1955	21,060	13,617	19,591	13,456
1956	23,547	15,314	21,877	15,142
1957	24,304	16,472	23,082	16,299
1958	25,122	16,925	23,697	16,749

[a] Includes I.V.A.
[b] Includes farm rents paid and imputed.

The manufacturing ratios are based on information shown in the various issues of *General Review of the Manufacturing Industries of Canada* published by the Dominion Bureau of Statistics and worksheets of the Industry and Merchandising Division. In a number of cases the published information was adjusted in order to render the data more comparable. For example, for the years 1952 to 1955, the published data on the value of shipments had to be adjusted for changing inventories. For years prior to 1926 substantial reallocation of individual industries was necessary in order to produce a comparable set of statistics.

COMMENT

M. C. Urquhart, Queen's University

I should like to begin my comments, as a user of Canadian data, by expressing my personal appreciation for the new data that are presented in this paper over and above those on factor shares. These data include new series on private product, which I am sure involved a great deal of work, and new estimates of national income extending backward from 1926 to 1919, an important period in Canadian economic history.

The following is an attempt to appraise the meaning of the results on factor shares that Goldberg has prepared. The comments should not be taken as being critical of the work itself.

My main contention, both for reasons given by Goldberg and for other reasons, is that if we include in labor share of income that part of the unincorporated enterprise income which should be attributed to it (in one way or another), while there is some presumption that the share of labor income in the economy as a whole may have risen very moderately in the last forty years, it is yet not clearly evident that this is so. Without applying high-powered statistical techniques, one might well maintain that the null hypothesis that factor shares have not changed has not been disproved. Goldberg's results show:

1. With the unincorporated income undistributed between labor and property shares but counted as a part of domestic income, in a comparison between 1926–30 and 1954–58: (a) the wage share rose considerably from 1926–30 to 1954–59; (b) the property share remained unchanged as a percentage of the total. This means that the property share as a proportion of that part which

had been separated into a return on labor and property had fallen.

2. When the data for private domestic product were standardized in the sense in which Goldberg uses the term, for shifts among industries, much of the increase in the wage share between 1926–30 and 1954–58 is removed (about 60 per cent of it). Most of this effect of standardization, though not all, is attributed to the decline in the importance of agriculture. Actually, insofar as agriculture is concerned, the standardization in large part adjusts for the fact that agriculture is predominantly unincorporated and that the actual wage share reported is accordingly very low. Had a wage been imputed to farmers and unpaid family workers it would, of course, have been greatly higher than shown though still, perhaps, somewhat less than in the rest of the economy.

3. When private domestic product is further corrected for the existence of unpaid labor in nonfarm unincorporated business only about a 2 point rise or a 4 per cent increase in the labor share remains.

4. Actually, Goldberg's tabulation of the unstandardized wage share for that part of production that corresponds fairly closely to the corporate sector of nonfarm private business shows a rise of only 1.7 points or 2.3 per cent. Standardization changes this very little.

5. The publicly-owned business sector actually showed a fall in the wage share (from 68.4 per cent to 62.1 per cent). The larger part of this sector, which is made up of the publicly owned railways and public utilities, is similar to private business in its operations. The operation of the liquor stores, on which a profit is recorded, really involves, however, a substantial element of taxation and is unlike operations in the private sector of the economy. If this sector were added to the private sector it would mean an even smaller increase in the wage share in the resulting total than that estimated for the private sector alone.

6. On the other hand, the direct government income created, of which a major share is for labor services, has increased considerably in relative importance; its growth in relative importance would tend to make the wage share rise.

7. The preliminary results for the data from 1919–25 (when standardized) cast further doubts on the firmness of an hypothesis that there has been a long trend towards a rise in the over-all share of labor income in the economy.

These results which Goldberg has pointed out, it seems to me, clearly cast doubt on there being a significant upward trend in the over-all labor income share (including imputed labor income) in the period under consideration. There are also other reasons that contribute to the uncertainty of inferring, from the data presented, a rise in the wage share.

The two periods which Goldberg has chosen for his main comparisons clearly and fortunately have many similarities, but considerable differences do remain. In pointing these out, I direct my remarks particularly to the property share of income, thereby, of course, making an inference about the labor share.

One point of difference between the periods is that prices were falling slightly in the 1926–30 period, particularly in the last year, and were rising in the 1954–58 period. Consequently, the inventory revaluation adjustment, which is included in investment income in these estimates, was positive (and in 1930 quite large) in the former period and negative in the 1954–58 period. The net inventory valuation adjustment amounted to about plus 9 per cent of investment income in the 1926–30 period, most of it coming in 1930, and about minus 2 per cent of investment income in 1954–58. Had the IVA been omitted the share of property income as well as the share of labor income would have risen between the two periods at the expense of unincorporated income. While I do not disagree with including the inventory valuation adjustment in making estimates of national income, two things should be kept in mind. The first is that the knowledge of accounting methods used in the evaluation of inventories, particularly in the first period, is limited, and the estimates of the inventory valuation adjustment are not as firm as other estimates. The second point is that the inventory valuation adjustments probably reflect windfall gains or losses on the part of business which may affect their behavior.

Another important point with regard to the firmness of the data used in calculating factor shares relates to the estimates of capital consumption allowances. The size of these allowances in all but the unincorporated sector bears entirely on the estimates of net property income. The estimates of capital consumption in the business sector rely heavily on data from income tax returns and are presumably based predominantly on historical cost. The amount of capital consumption allowances will, therefore, depend on the price history of the periods prior to the two periods for which comparisons are being made. The general wholesale price index in 1926–30 was 50 per cent above that for 1910–14; prices in the 1917–20 period had risen much higher than in the 1910–14 period and were considerably higher than in the 1926–30 period. They were relatively stable from 1921 on after the decline in prices in 1920. The general wholesale price index in 1954–58 was 130 per cent above that for 1935–39 and there had been no intervening period of price decline.

The implications of the effects of this different price history on the estimates of depreciation is not entirely clear. One would expect it to cause capital consumption allowances, as recorded, to be relatively smaller, compared with allowances calculated on a replacement cost basis, for 1954–58 than for 1926–30. If this presumption is correct, it would mean that there might have been a tendency for net profits, as recorded, to have an upward bias in 1954–58 as compared with 1926–30.

Another point affecting the capital consumption allowances is that there was a change in the tax laws in 1949 which permitted the substitution of depreciation at a constant percentage rate on a diminishing balance for the older straight-line methods. For example, motor trucks could be depreciated at a rate of 30 per cent of the diminishing balance. This method, if used, means that higher amounts of depreciation than under the straight-line method are charged in earlier years of an asset's life and, consequently, less in later years. We do not know enough about how widely this method was adopted to be able to say for sure what its effect would be in the 1954–58 period. My guess is that with the very high rates at which capital goods were being put in place from 1950 onward, and particularly in 1954–58, it meant a considerable increase in the capital consumption allowances and a consequent lowering of stated investment income.

While I have not a clear judgment whether capital consumption allowances were relatively overstated in 1954–58 compared with 1926–30, the main point I would make is that more precise estimates of capital consumption allowances on a consistent replacement cost basis (and I do not suggest that it would have been possible for Goldberg to get these) might have altered the estimates of depreciation substantially and hence the estimates of investment income. The magnitude of the possible adjustments on this score is emphasized by the fact that capital consumption allowances have recently run at between two-thirds and three-quarters of net investment income. It is interesting to note that gross investment income (Table 1 of Goldberg's paper) as a percentage of gross domestic income rose over the period under review.

A further point relates to how shares are affected by the fact that regulated companies' profit positions are affected by the prices they are permitted to charge. Regulated companies are apt to be more squeezed in periods when prices are rising than when prices are falling. This, of course, is evident from the time which it takes to have regulated rates changed. The rise in prices in the 1950's compared with quite stable prices from 1921 to 1930 would suggest that investment income in regulated companies, owing to the time that it takes to adjust rates, might have been relatively lower in the 1950's than in the 1920's.

My conclusion from Goldberg's paper is that, if there has been a change in factor shares in the last forty years in Canada, it has probably been toward an increase in labor's share in income. However, the evidence of an increase in labor's share is by no means conclusive. Goldberg's paper has provided much new and important information on this matter. There remains more work to be done, however, before a clear inference that there has been a change in factor shares can be drawn.

EDWARD C. BUDD, Pennsylvania State University

Simon Goldberg and Frank Leacy have produced a most interesting and worthwhile paper—one containing such a wealth of material that it would be impossible to comment on all aspects at length. I will therefore confine my attention to the longer-run changes in factor shares, by Mr. Goldberg.

The author has chosen to concentrate on those income concepts which are clearly most relevant for the analysis of distributive shares: domestic income (which excludes net income from abroad), private business product (which excludes income originating in households, nonprofit institutions, government and government enterprises), and nonfarm private business product. For these concepts, a comparison of the results in his paper with data for the United States shows that over the period as a whole (1926–58) the movement of Canadian income shares was quite similar to that for the United States. A comparison of the two countries for the terminal periods used in his paper is given in Table 1. While

TABLE 1
DISTRIBUTIVE SHARES IN ALTERNATIVE INCOME CONCEPTS, 1926–30 AND 1954–58, CANADA AND THE UNITED STATES[a]
(per cent of total)

	Canada			United States		
	1926–30	1954–58	Percentage Point Change	1926–30	1954–58	Percentage Point Change
1. *Domestic income*[b]						
Employee compensation	56.7	66.2	+ 9.5	60.3	70.4	+10.1
Net unincorporated income	23.0	13.6	− 9.4	17.4	12.9	− 4.5
Nonfarm	12.0	8.3	− 3.7	10.5	9.2	− 1.3
Farm	11.0	5.3	− 5.7	6.9	3.7	− 3.2
Corporation profits	10.6	12.2	+ 1.6	10.7	11.3	+ .6
Rent and interest[c]	9.7	8.0	− 1.7	11.6	5.4	− 6.2
2. *Private business product*						
Employee compensation	51.0	61.4	+10.4	56.2	65.2	+ 9.0
Net unincorporated income	27.3	16.8	−10.5	19.2	15.2	− 4.0
Nonfarm	14.2	10.3	− 3.9	11.6	10.8	− .8
Farm	13.1	6.5	− 6.6	7.6	4.4	− 3.2
Corporation profits	12.7	15.2	+ 2.5	11.8	13.2	+ 1.4
Rent and interest[c]	9.0	6.6	− 2.4	12.8	6.4	− 6.4
Business product originating in farms	17.8	7.7	−10.1	11.0	5.5	− 5.5
3. *Nonfarm private business product*						
Employee compensation	58.6	65.5	+ 6.9	61.4	68.3	+ 6.9
Net unincorporated income	17.3	11.2	− 6.1	13.0	11.5	− 1.5
Corporation profits	14.5	17.1	+ 2.6	13.3	14.1	+ .8
Rent and interest[c]	9.6	6.2	− 3.4	12.3	6.1	− 6.2

[a] Income and share concepts for the United States have been adjusted as closely as possible to the definitions used by Goldberg and Leacy. For 1929 and 1954–58, shares were computed from estimates of the National Income Division of the U.S. Department of Commerce. For 1926–28 (and earlier years) computations were made from estimates prepared by the author, based largely on Simon Kuznets, *National Income and Its Composition, 1919–1938*, New York, NBER, 1941.

[b] "Domestic Income" for the United States does not include imputed rent on government-owned buildings and the profits of government enterprises. U.S. estimates do not cover the former, and include subsidies with the latter. The profits of government enterprises rose from 1.2 per cent of Canadian domestic income in 1926–30 to 2.4 per cent in 1954–58; the wage and salary share in Canadian domestic income would have been .7 percentage points higher in 1926–30 and 1.5 points in 1954–58, were such profits eliminated from the income concept.

[c] Comprises net interest (exclusive of interest on consumer debt), net rental income of persons, and, for Canada, government investment income (for domestic income) and withholding taxes on interest, dividends, rents and royalties paid to nonresidents.

the wage share (that is, the share of employee compensation) is lower in Canada than in the United States, the percentage point change in this share for the period as a whole is virtually identical regardless of which of the three income concepts is used. There are, on the other hand, some interesting differences in the other shares. While in each country the share of corporate profits rose and the shares of unincorporated enterprises, rent, and interest fell, the relative fall in unincorporated enterprise income and the rise in corporate profits was much sharper in Canada, while the decline in rent and interest shares was more marked in the United States.

While the official Canadian statistics start with 1926, Goldberg has carried the estimates for domestic income, at least, back annually to 1919. These estimates indicate that the similarity in the behavior of the wage share for the two countries does not hold for the twenties as a whole. From the beginning to the end of this decade, the wage share in Canada fell slightly, whereas in the United States it rose. The data for this earlier period are summarized in Table 2.

TABLE 2
SHARE OF EMPLOYEE COMPENSATION IN DOMESTIC INCOME, SELECTED PERIODS, CANADA AND THE UNITED STATES
(per cent of total)

	Domestic Income		*Nonfarm Domestic Income*	
	Canada	U.S.	Canada	U.S.
1919	55.1	51.9	65.2	60.4
1920	57.3	55.6	68.3	62.4
1921–25	57.7	58.7	66.9	64.5
1926–30	56.7	60.3	63.9	65.4
1954–58	66.2	70.4	69.8	73.3

This paper, as well as the foregoing comparisons, is based essentially on an "institutional" classification of distributive shares. Wages (whether wages, salaries, or supplementary labor income) include only the compensation of hired workers, whether top management or unskilled labor. Property income is a residual—the difference between income and wages—and is itself classified primarily on a legal basis: income of unincorporated enterprises, corporate profits, and other investment income (rent and interest). While a further breakdown between rent and interest would be desirable, since the rental income of persons is more analogous to unincorporated enterprise income than it is to interest, no distinction is made in the published Canadian statistics.

The usefulness of any classification is of course dependent on the purposes to which it is put. If one is interested in incomes accruing to particular social or economic groups, e.g., farmers, professional persons, stockholders or employees, an institutional classification such as the preceding is of interest. If, however, one is interested in production and in the distribution of income as it is derived from production—and hence is interested in income accruing or imputable to the services of particular kinds of productive agents (human labor, reproducible physical assets, and non-reproducible natural resources) and to intangible assets arising from monopoly positions—something more is needed. About all that can be done with national income data is to ignore monopoly, lump together all income from physical assets, exclude transfer payments from the income concept, and find some basis for allocating the income of unincorporated enterprises. For this last share, the labor and property components are too important simply to be ignored by treating the share as either all labor or all property or as perhaps something imputable to neither.

Attacks in recent years on imputation of this share seem to me to have been overdone, and I do not share the view of those who argue that what the self-employed entrepreneur has joined in holy union, let no economist try to split apart. On the demand side it seems reasonable to suppose that the farmer, for example, *can* employ varying amounts of his or someone else's labor with his land or capital, or even vary the amount of land with his own given amount of labor, so that conceptually, at least, a marginal productivity approach is possible. But even if it were not, there *are* markets for the purchase, sale, and rental of physical assets and for the employment of labor, and these markets *do* produce prices, wage rates, and rental rates which can be used for imputing returns to agents whose services are not bought and sold on markets. If the person who is employing both his own labor and his own capital and land has no preference for either do-it-yourself or let someone-else-do-it-himself, then an imputation based on market prices will add up to the total income of the self-employed. The problem arises because the person has some kind of preference for self-use of his resources, and we do not know to which of the particular resources the preference is attached. Undoubtedly this is what Goldberg means when he states that "net unincorporated income should perhaps be likened . . . to a chemical compound in which the constituent elements have become transformed into something which is neither labor nor capital but a synthesis of both," or that "the unincorporated owner's *own* labor and the capital employed in the business may not be two independent factors whose services can be priced independently of each other, or on the basis of market criteria relevant to other sectors of the economy."

Nevertheless, it should be observed that the difference between a market price imputation and actual entrepreneurial income is considerably less than the error introduced by attributing all of it to one or the other of the agents. In fact, as Gale Johnson's article on the allocation of agricultural income showed some years back, whether we impute wages to farmers and treat rent as a residual, or impute rent and treat wages as a residual, over an average of years we get about the same result.[1] Kravis' results would also suggest that while the *levels* of shares would differ depending on the method of imputation used, the *trends* would not be much affected.[2] However, the data for making an adjustment by imputing either returns to labor or returns to the ownership of assets are apparently not available for Canada, and there is no point in continuing this particular quarrel.

While Goldberg confines his attention to an institutional classification, he properly stresses the importance of structural changes in the Canadian economy in interpreting the movement of shares. One of the most important of these is shifts in the composition of output. In both countries, for example, there has been a rise in the importance of general government, where, in common with households and nonprofit institutions, output is measured at labor input alone and hence the wage share is by definition unity. A glance at Table 1, however, shows that for both countries the percentage point rise in the wage share was about the same in private business product (where these sectors, together with government enterprises, are eliminated) as it was in domestic income. In fact, for Canada it was even greater in the former than in the

[1] D. Gale Johnson, "Allocation of Agricultural Income," *Journal of Farm Economics*, November 1948, pp. 724–749.

[2] Irving B. Kravis, "Relative Income Shares in Fact and Theory," *American Economic Review*, December 1959.

latter, arising in part from the inclusion in the Canadian estimates of the profits of government enterprises, which have risen as a per cent of domestic income over the period as a whole.

A far more important structural change was the drastic fall in the importance of agriculture's contribution to income, from 18 per cent to 8 per cent of private business product between the terminal periods in Canada, and from 11 per cent to 6 per cent in the United States. Eliminating agriculture from the income concept serves to reduce the rise in the wage share in both countries to the same 6.9 percentage points—in effect, the declining relative importance of agriculture accounted for about a third of the wage rise in Canada in private business product, compared with less than a quarter for the United States.

Another approach to isolating the effect of changing income composition is to determine what distributive shares would have been had the relative importance of various sectors or industries remained the same as in some given period. The author's "standardized series" is based on 1949 income weights. I have carried through the same computations for the United States data for three of the income concepts; the results are summarized in Table 3.[3]

The proportion of the wage share increase attributable to share increases within sectors (which can be measured by the ratio of the "standardized" share increase to the unadjusted share increase) differs noticeably for the two countries only for the nonfarm private business product. The greater proportion of the latter which appears to be due to weight shifts among sectors in the United States, however, can be accounted for by the much greater decline in rental income in the United States, the effect of which appears as a weight shift, since rental income is attributable en-

[3] For the analysis of sectoral changes in Tables 3 and 4, the first terminal period for the United States has been taken as 1929 rather than 1926–30, since data on industrial composition for 1926–28 comparable with subsequent years are not available. The year 1929 rather than the average of 1929 and 1930 has been used, since U.S. industrial composition in the latter year was affected much more by the depression than was Canada's. The wage shares unadjusted for changes in industrial composition of income for 1929, as compared with the Goldberg terminal period, are as follows:

	1929	*1926–30*
Domestic income	59.7	60.3
Private business product	55.6	56.2
Nonfarm private business product	60.9	61.4

Twelve sectors were used for the U.S. computations for private business product, compared with ten for Canada. This difference does not affect the results.

TABLE 3
STANDARDIZED WAGE SHARE, CANADA AND THE UNITED STATES
(per cent of total)

	CANADA				UNITED STATES			
	1926–30	1954–58	Point Change Stand.	Point Change Unadj.	1929	1954–58	Point Change Stand.	Point Change Unadj.
Domestic income	55.9	59.1	+3.2	+ 9.5	64.6	68.1	+3.5	+10.7
Private business product	55.5	59.6	+4.2	+10.4	59.6	63.4	+4.0	+ 9.6
Nonfarm private business prod.	61.2	66.5	+5.3	+ 6.9	64.0	68.3	+4.3	+ 7.4

tirely to the "real estate" industry. A rough calculation suggests that were rental income eliminated from the income concept, the proportion of the private nonfarm share increase attributable to share increases within industries would be the same for both countries—about four-fifths of the total. The hypothesis of share constancy cannot be rescued entirely by eliminating the effects of shifts in the industrial composition of income.

Another structural change considered by the author is the shift from unincorporated to corporate enterprise. After eliminating the shift implicit in the decline of the farm sector, which is, of course, dominated by the unincorporated form of enterprise, the shift for the United States has been minor. In 1929 nonfarm unincorporated enterprises accounted for 26 per cent of income originating in corporations and unincorporated enterprises combined; in 1954–58, their share averaged 25 per cent. The proportion of self-employed proprietors to total engaged in production in the private sector has shown only a minor decline, from 14 per cent in 1929 to 13 per cent in 1954–58. The change in the wage share within the two sectors was also quite similar: it rose in noncorporate enterprises from 46.1 per cent in 1929 to 50.4 per cent in 1954–58. The corresponding figures for the corporate sector are 74.6 per cent and 79.6 per cent.

Unfortunately, estimates of income originating by legal form of organization and of employees and proprietors are not available for Canada. As a substitute for the breakdown by corporate and unincorporated income originating, Goldberg has recomputed the wage share in nonfarm private business product after deducting income of unincorporated enterprises, and finds very little, if any, change in the share for the period as a whole. As the author recognizes, it would be dangerous to assume from this fact that the increase in the wage share in "standardized income" can be explained almost entirely by the shift to the corporate form, for the share increase is biased downward by the inability to exclude wages paid by unincorporated enterprises from total wages and income.

A more revealing procedure would be to determine the change in shares for those sectors dominated by the corporate form: mining, manufacturing, transportation, communication, public utilities, and finance. Only 10 per cent of unincorporated income in Canada, and 12 per cent in the United States, originates in these sectors, whereas they account for well over a half of private business product in both countries. The comparative data, standardized to eliminate any effect of intersectoral income shifts, are summarized in Table 4. Data are also given for manufacturing, which

TABLE 4
SHARE OF EMPLOYEE COMPENSATION AND OF UNINCORPORATED INCOME IN STANDARDIZED INCOME ORIGINATING IN PREDOMINANTLY CORPORATE SECTORS, CANADA AND THE UNITED STATES
(per cent)

	Canada			*United States*		
	1926–30	1954–58	Point Change	1929	1954–58	Point Change
Predominantly corporate[a]						
Share of:						
Employee compensation	62.6	67.0	+4.4	64.8	69.7	+4.9
Unincorporated income	4.3	2.2	−2.1	3.2	3.0	− .2
Per cent of self-employed to total engaged	n.a.	n.a.	n.a.	2.4	2.9	+ .5
Manufacturing						
Share of:						
Employee compensation	68.4	73.8	+5.4	74.2	77.6	+4.6
Unincorporated income	4.9	2.2	−2.7	2.6	1.5	−1.1
Per cent of self-employed to total engaged	n.a.	n.a.	n.a.	1.2	1.1	− .1

[a] Predominantly corporate includes mining, manufacturing, transportation, communications and public utilities, and finance, insurance, and real estate. The shares of employee compensation and of unincorporated income are "standardized," being based on the weight of each of the preceding sectors in 1949 income originating in the predominantly corporate sector. The per cent of self-employed to total engaged is based on 1949 employment weights.

n.a. = not available.

comprises over 60 per cent of income originating in this "predominantly corporate" sector.

The share increase in Canada for this predominantly corporate sector (4.4 percentage points) is only a little less than that in the standardized private business product. The unincorporated income share has, it is true, fallen by 2.1 percentage points. Before one concludes, however, that a shift to the corporate form is implied, he should note that in the U.S. data a *fall* in the share of unincorporated income has been accompanied by a slight *rise* in the proportion of self-employed to total engaged. Even the author's extreme assumption, that no wages are paid by unincorporated businesses, yields a share increase for this sector equal to 3.1 percentage points; more reasonable assumptions (e.g., the unincorporated wage share is two-thirds of the corporate wage share) yield an increase close to 4 points.[4]

It may be concluded, by way of summary, that a substantial part of the rise in the wage share was due to the relative decline of agriculture, a development that was common to both countries, although somewhat more important in Canada. Other shifts in output composition, as well as any shifts from the noncorporate to the corporate form of business organization, appear to have been relatively minor in their effect on the wage share.

A final word of caution should be inserted on attempts, such as the above, to account for share changes by analyzing the behavior of the aggregate in terms of the behavior of its components. Random forces are bound to produce dispersion in the behavior of the

[4] Let W_c and W_e be employee compensation originating in corporations and unincorporated enterprises respectively ($W_c + W_e = W$); Y_c and Y_e, income originating in the two respective sectors ($Y_c + Y_e = Y$); U, net income of unincorporated enterprises ($W_e + U = Y_e$). Further, let small letters denote the respective shares of each in $Y (y = 1)$. Then, by definition, the share of corporate employee compensation in income originating in corporations (the "corporate wage share") is

$$\frac{W_c}{Y_c} = \frac{W - W_e}{Y - (U + W_e)} = \frac{w - w_e}{1 - (u + w_e)}. \tag{1}$$

Since estimates of W_e are lacking for Canada, w_e cannot be computed. If we make the "extreme" assumption that $W_e = 0$, the corporate wage share is given by

$$\frac{W_c}{Y_c} = \frac{w}{1 - e}. \tag{2}$$

If $W_e > 0$, the corporate wage share can be computed from (1) by assuming a specific value for W_e/Y_e [$= w_e/(u + w_e)$], which should typically be less than w, e.g., two-thirds of w, as in the text above.

components and, unless we want to attribute the change to such random elements, we are likely to lose sight of the more basic forces which may show up only at a more aggregative level. Furthermore, the greater the extent of disaggregation, the less reliable the estimates become, and the variability of the components may be due simply to errors of measurement.

These comments are designed simply to extend the coverage of the author's paper and his work, which have gone a long way in eliminating a gap in our knowledge of Canadian income shares.

The Analysis of Factor Shares by Industry

MICHAEL GORT
STATE UNIVERSITY OF NEW YORK AT BUFFALO

A 13th century theologian who succeeded in measuring the head of a pin would not have found the information helpful without knowledge of the area of an angel's foot. And an economist who measures income shares by industry is not much better off until he resolves an almost equally metaphysical question—namely, what it is he has measured. The problem arises from the fact that, unlike information on the aggregate shares of capital and labor in the economy as a whole, data on factor shares for individual industries are of little intrinsic interest.

From the standpoint of income distribution, it matters little whether property holders or wage recipients derive their income from one industrial activity or another. Estimates of factor shares by industry are useful only indirectly. More specifically, the significance of measures of property income by industry lies primarily in their role either as indicators of capital inputs or as measures of the rewards to capital, expressed as rates of return. The use of estimates of property income to measure profitability is too familiar to warrant discussion at this point, but the implications of using these estimates to measure interindustry differences in capital inputs have not been adequately explored. Consequently, while this paper is mainly concerned with measurement problems, it first focuses on the above question.

Differences Among Industries in the Relation of Property Income to Output

Differences among industries in the ratio of earnings to output stem from two sources: variations in the production function and variations in rates of return. To what extent, then, can property income be taken as a measure of capital inputs? While the income that accrues to capital is, by definition, the value of the services of capital at market prices, for most analytical problems the desired measure of capital inputs is an estimate of the services of capital valued at their replacement cost. The extent, therefore, to which property income can be used for interindustry comparisons of capital-labor or capital-output ratios depends on the degree to which rates of return on replacement cost vary among industries. Assuming that the rewards for superior entrepreneurship are included in the compensation for managerial services, economic theory offers three possible reasons for differences in these rates of return. First, they may result from the presence of monopoly; second, from risk aversion (or risk preference) in conjunction with differences in risk between industries; and third, from temporary disequilibriums.

To date, attempts to establish a clear empirical relation between profit rates and monopoly have not met with much success,[1] so that one must at least tentatively conclude that in the American economy monopoly has not generated large and persistent differences among industries in rates of return. The role of the second factor, risk aversion, is still obscure and there is currently no evidence to support or confute a hypothesis about its influence. The third factor, that of temporary disequilibrium, is likely to be important. However, this source of variation in rates of return is, presumably, largely eliminated if returns are averaged over a period long enough to smooth out the effects of short-run fluctuations in output and of the lag in adjustment of supply to long-run shifts in demand. Our assumption is that when income is averaged over a period sufficiently long to smooth out the effects of temporary disequilibriums, there is a strong tendency to equality in rates of return to capital, when capital is valued at the replacement cost of its services. Thus, variations among industries in the ratio of average income to average output become useful measures of differences in the capital intensiveness of production. The critical question from the standpoint of measurement is the minimum duration of the period over which income must be averaged, for the choice of too long an interval may conceal significant changes in the production function.

A comparison of ratios of income to output with ratios of balance sheet values of capital to output appears in Table 1. For this table, gross income (without subtracting depreciation charges

[1] See, for example, Joe S. Bain, "Relation of Profit Rate to Industry Concentration: American Manufacturing, 1936–1940," *Quarterly Journal of Economics*, August 1951. Bain found no steady relation between the degree of concentration of production in a few producers and profit rates, though for one sample of forty-two industries he observed a higher profit rate for industries in which 70 per cent or more of the value of product was contributed by eight producers. In my own study, "The Analysis of Stability and Change in Market Shares" (*Journal of Political Economy*, February 1963), it was found that stability in market shares (another and perhaps more direct test of monopoly power than the concentration ratio) showed no clear relation to industry profit rates.

but after income taxes),[2] was averaged for the eight-year period, 1947–54 (and adjusted for changes in the price level). The relevant output was measured by the average of output for 1948 and 1953. When the income-to-output ratios using these measures are compared with ratios of capital assets to output for 1948 and 1953, there is obviously a strong relation between the two types of ratios. However, important differences in the ranking of industries on the basis of the two types of ratios arise, and the Spearman coefficient of rank correlation for the income-to-output and the 1948 asset-to-output ratios was only .702. Using the 1953 asset-to-output ratios, the Spearman coefficient was .695. Thus, despite the positive effect on the correlation coefficient resulting from the presence of common components in the denominators of the two sets of ratios, one set of ranks explained not quite one-half the variance in the ranks of the other set.[3]

The most important reason for differences in ranks based on income-to-output and asset-to-output ratios is that balance sheet values vary in relation to the replacement cost of tangible assets. It is only relative to *replacement* cost that returns can be expected to move, in the long run, towards equality. Because of the way in which book values are arrived at, these values are higher compared to replacement cost in industries with more rapid technological change.

Balance sheet values are conglomerate in the sense that, even if deflated for changes in the price level, they are composed of heterogeneous valuations. This stems from the fact that assets are acquired at more than one point in time and, hence, their book values reflect prices set under differing technologies. Since there is no evidence of a secular rise in rates of return, gains in technology appear to be translated into increases in real wages, leaving rates of return on new investment unchanged over time.[4] In con-

[2] It is the after-tax rates of return that, in the long-run, can be expected to move towards equality.

[3] When only the numerators of the ratios are correlated, a very high rank correlation coefficient results, but this is merely a consequence of the fact that both income and assets are a function of industry size. The Spearman coefficient for asset-to-output ratios in 1948 and 1953 was .833. This reflects a fair amount of instability considering that there were only five intervening years and that both 1948 and 1953 were generally years of peak output—a fact which greatly reduces the possibility that distortions in asset to output ratios will arise from the presence of excess capacity.

[4] For the period 1889–1957 real wages in manufacturing show an average annual percentage rise of 2.3. Assuming that labor inputs account for 70 per cent

TABLE 1
Ratios of Gross Income to Output and Capital Assets to Output, Twenty-two Manufacturing Industries, 1948–53

Industry	*Ratio of Gross Income to Output* 1948–53	*Ratio of Capital Assets to Output* 1948	1953
Beverages	.0372	.571	.413
Food	.0290	.347	.328
Tobacco	.0396	.569	.658
Textile mill products	.0527	.555	.631
Apparel	.0160	.338	.342
Lumber and wood products	.1219	1.112	1.135
Furniture	.0350	.376	.431
Paper, pulp, and products	.1054	.764	.753
Printing and publishing	.0695	.690	.669
Chemicals	.0858	.716	.840
Petroleum and coal products	.0567	.893	.763
Rubber	.0428	.518	.510
Leather	.0291	.407	.414
Stone, clay, and glass	.0845	.738	.686
Primary metals	.0727	.710	.764
Fabricated metal products	.0603	.575	.538
Machinery (except electrical)	.0745	.712	.657
Electrical machinery	.0552	.583	.527
Transportation equipment	.0377	.967	.666
Motor vehicles and parts	.0747	.493	.425
Instruments (professional, scientific, etc.)	.0702	.711	.655
Miscellaneous manufacturing	.0432	.669	.788

Source: Gross income taken from *Statistics of Income*. It is an average for the years 1947–54 of net income after taxes, plus depreciation and minus dividends received from other corporations. The values for each year were deflated by GNP price deflators (1929 = 100) to correspond to output, which was also expressed in 1929 prices. Data for output and for capital assets were taken from Daniel Creamer, Sergei P. Dobrovolsky and Israel Borenstein, *Capital in Manufacturing and Mining: Its Formation and Financing*, Princeton University Press for NBER, 1960, Table 26. The estimate of average output for the period 1948–53 is the average of output for the two individual years, 1948 and 1953.

sequence, as technology changes, the returns on old investment decline. In short, the market value of old "machines" declines not only because the remaining years of economic life are fewer, but also because old "machines" must compete with more efficient new ones which earn no more than the old ones did when they were new. While an adequate measure of capital consumption

of total inputs, the rise in total real costs from changes in wage rates is 1.6 per cent per year or almost equal to the average annual gain in total productivity (capital and labor) for the private domestic economy. Data on changes in wage rates and productivity taken from Solomon Fabricant, *Basic Facts on Productivity Change*, New York, NBER, Occasional Paper 63, 1959, Table 6.

could, in principle, allow for both sources of decline in the market value of old assets, none of the widely used methods of depreciation accounting achieve this objective. In particular, straight-line depreciation is designed primarily to measure declines arising from reductions in the period of remaining useful life. Thus depreciated book values generally tend to overstate the values of old relative to those of new assets, and the faster the rate of technological change the greater is this overstatement likely to be. Hence, when industries with differing rates of technological change are compared, those with more rapid technical gains will tend to have relatively lower income-to-asset ratios (assets measured by book values) and this is reflected in the previously noted differences in ranks based on income-to-output as compared with asset-to-output ratios.

While from the standpoint of value, balance sheet data tend to overestimate old capital as compared with new, depreciated book values as a gauge of current capacity to produce either output or income may err in the opposite direction. This is because depreciated book values take into account the period of remaining economic life. That is, assets represent a store of value rather than a flow of current services. In consequence, in industries with high rates of investment and, hence, a declining average age of assets, ratios of capital (as shown in balance sheets) to output will tend to rise even though the flow of the current services of capital is unchanged.[5]

Another problem is that idle assets do not contribute to income though they are included in measures of the stock of capital. The existence of idle assets stems partly from fluctuations in demand but partly also from the presence in most industries of obsolescent capacity held as a reserve for contingencies. Not all of this obsolete capacity will have been fully depreciated in balance sheet values of fixed assets.

The preceding discussion neither exhausts the possible distortions in capital-output ratios nor is it meant to establish an unqualified preference for a particular measure of capital inputs. The measure chosen must depend on the function it is intended to serve. The data presented, however, do show significantly different results when capital inputs are taken as the market price of the

[5] This point is developed in detail by Zvi Griliches in "Measuring Inputs in Agriculture: A Critical Survey," *Journal of Farm Economics*, December 1960.

current services of capital from those obtained when such inputs are measured on the basis of the book value of assets.

The Chief Problems of Measurement

Most of the difficulties in measuring factor shares by industry are the general obstacles to measuring property and labor income for the economy as a whole. However, they affect the various industries unequally and hence introduce questions of comparability for interindustry analysis of income shares. For measurement on an industry basis, the most serious of these general problems are (1) the difficulty of distinguishing property income from the compensation of property owners for labor services, and (2) that of separating current expenses from capital outlays. In addition, analysis on an industry basis is affected by a difficulty not present for analysis at the total economy level. Specifically, the activities of firms frequently are not restricted to a single industry, with the result that the allocation of income by industry of origin raises awkward estimating problems.

IDENTIFYING PROPERTY AND LABOR INCOME

The problem of distinguishing between the returns to capital and to labor arises mainly because in large sectors of the economy owners of property perform managerial and other services. This problem arises most frequently in the measurement of business income in industries where the noncorporate form of organization predominates (e.g., agriculture) but it is by no means restricted to these sectors. In owner-managed corporations the distinction between profit and officers' compensation is frequently quite arbitrary, being affected by such objectives as the minimization of tax liability. The distortion in the measure of business income is likely to be far greater in industries in which small firms account for a large proportion of output and income, partly because the salaries of the highest ranking officers are larger relative to reported profits for the smaller firms and partly, also, because a larger proportion of small firms are owner-managed. Because of wide differences among industries in size distributions of firms, the impact of distortions arising from arbitrary executive salaries is likely to be highly uneven among the various sectors of the economy.

Attempts to adjust profits for arbitrary officer compensation have shown that "excess compensation" may significantly affect rates of return for firms in the lower asset-size classes. For a sample of 500 small corporations, McConnell[6] compared officer salaries in owner-managed firms with those in which at least 15 per cent of the stock was held by nonofficers (the net excess of the former over the latter being a measure of "excess compensation"). He found that salaries for the former were substantially higher. Alexander[7] compared officer compensation per dollar of assets for deficit and income corporations, and classified the net excess of the latter over the former as profit. The rationale for this procedure was that owner-managers in deficit corporations have no incentive to withdraw more as compensation for services than their "true" salaries.

For the purpose of measuring the role of property as a source of income, both McConnell's and Alexander's adjustments depend on the assumption that the managerial services performed in the two classes of firms compared have approximately the same opportunity cost. Such services may differ markedly both in quality and quantity. If differences in executive salaries among owner- and nonowner-managed firms merely reflect differences in the market value of the services performed (as measured by the rates of compensation the executives would have secured in alternative employment), the net excess of one over the other cannot be classified as property income.

IDENTIFYING CURRENT COSTS AND CAPITAL OUTLAYS

As is well known, a substantial volume of outlays, though expected to yield income over more than one accounting period, is nonetheless reported as a current expense. This includes research and development outlays, expenditures on the promotion of new products, the cost of employee training programs, at least a part of advertising, and many others. Since these expenditures appear to be increasing more rapidly than total private investment, the relative understatement of returns to capital is likely to be rising. Of

[6] Joseph L. McConnell, "Corporate Earnings by Size of Firm," *Survey of Current Business*, May 1945.

[7] Sidney S. Alexander, "The Effect of Size of Manufacturing Corporations on the Distribution of the Rate of Return," *Review of Economics and Statistics*, August 1949. Alexander's adjustment shows a marked effect on rates of return in 1937 for firms with assets up to $100,000. At today's prices, the asset levels at which a significant effect would be present should, of course, be substantially higher.

special importance to the analysis of factor shares by industry is the fact that the distribution of investment outlays for intangibles is highly uneven over the industrial spectrum. For example, the 1959 research and development outlays as a percentage of total assets were more than sixteen times as large for the electrical machinery industry as for stone, clay, and glass products.[8] Generally, the relative volume of investment in intangibles is strongly correlated with firm size, with the result that distortions from this source in measures of returns to capital are concentrated in industries in which large firms account for a sizable proportion of industry output and income.[9]

The expensing of investment in intangibles is closely related to the general problem of arbitrary charges for capital consumption for fixed as well as for intangible assets. The magnitude of errors in charges for capital consumption for fixed assets is, once again, likely to be highly uneven among the industries. This stems not only from the fact that the economic life of assets is harder to forecast in some sectors than in others but also from sharp variations in the duration of their economic life. In industries in which assets are short-lived, capital consumption will generally be larger relative to gross income, with the result that potential errors in estimating net income are increased accordingly.

Factor Shares and the Heterogeneity of Output

There are three problems peculiar to measuring capital and labor income by individual industry. The first is more concerned with classification than with measurement and arises from the fact that some capital resources are leased rather than owned by the producer. The second stems from heterogeneity in the output of establishments, and the third, from the combination under common ownership of establishments in more than one industry.

The leasing of plant and equipment creates an arbitrary distinc-

[8] Research and development expenditures reported in U.S. National Science Foundation, *Review of Data on Research and Development*, Number 24, December 1960, and assets for 1956 as shown in U.S. Internal Revenue Service, *Statistics of Income*. Differences among industries in expenditure rates for research and development are materially reduced when outlays financed by the federal government are excluded, but they still remain large.

[9] For example, in 1958, of total company research and development outlays of roughly $8.2 billion, $6.9 billion was spent by firms with 5,000 or more employees. National Science Foundation, *Funds for Research and Development in Industry*, 1958 and 1961.

tion between returns to capital that are included in rent, on the one hand, and those shown as interest or earnings on equity, on the other. Clearly a building used by a petroleum refiner is a capital input in the petroleum industry regardless of the industry of the firm that is its legal owner. For most economic problems, the industry classification of returns on investment should be independent of the method of financing used (e.g., mortgage debt versus a rental contract). In short, for purposes of industry estimates of returns to capital, reported business income needs to be adjusted for the interest component of rental payments—that is, increased by this amount for rent payers and reduced for rent recipients.

For an allocation of income by industry, how serious is the problem raised by heterogeneity in the output of firms? The answer largely depends on the level of industry detail one chooses to use. At the two-digit level (as defined in the Standard Industrial Classification Code) nonhomogeneity in the output of *establishments* (as contrasted with firms) is negligible and the problem of income allocation is restricted to companies with establishments in more than one industry. At the higher levels of industry detail, plant heterogeneity increases[10] but the data which would permit an allocation of output or income by industry of the products produced (as contrasted with an allocation by the industry in which plants are classified) are not currently available.

It is much harder to measure by industry the returns to capital than wage and salary income. Leaving aside practical problems of data collection, the obstacles to measuring labor income by industry arise mainly in connection with administrative and supervisory employees and (to a lesser extent) sales personnel. On the basis of the 1954 Economic Census, employment in central administrative offices accounts for less than 3 per cent of the total employment of companies classified in manufacturing; and for central administrative and sales offices combined the percentage is less than 6.5. For the aggregate of companies in minerals extraction, wholesale and retail trade, and services, central and sales office

[10] At the four-digit level, almost 30 per cent of value added in manufacturing is contributed by plants whose secondary products account for more than 10 per cent of the plants' output. However, only 4 per cent of value added is contributed by plants whose secondary activities account for more than 20 per cent of plant output. Frank A. Hanna, *The Compilation of Manufacturing Statistics*, U.S. Department of Commerce, 1959, Table 4.

employment accounts for less than 2 per cent of total company employment. Moreover, the overwhelming majority of sales office employees, and probably most of those in central offices, serve production activities in a single rather than in several industries. To be sure, in multiindustry companies the higher salaried employees tend to direct activities in several industries, while the activities of employees receiving lower rates of compensation are restricted to individual industries. Thus, a larger share of labor income than of employees is subject to the allocation-by-industry problem. Furthermore, the earnings of administrative personnel in multiproduct plants are subject to the same allocation-by-industry problem as those of employees in central offices. Nonetheless, the proportion of total labor income not readily measurable by industry is substantially smaller than that of property income, and the discussion below will therefore focus on the latter problem.

Table 2, though based on employment data, gives a rough estimate of the distortions in industry distribution of business income that arise from classifying all the earnings of companies in their primary industries.[11] The table shows that, at the two-digit industry level, the aggregate employment of companies in six manufacturing industry classes differed from that of establishments in the same classes by more than 10 per cent of the former. At the one-digit level, establishment employment in mining and quarrying exceeded company employment by almost 30 per cent. Wholesale and retail trade and services also showed more employees on an establishment than on a company basis, but the discrepancies at this classification level were modest. Company employment in manufacturing moderately exceeded estabilshment employment. The problem increases as the level of industry detail used becomes greater, since a larger proportion of the activities of companies falls outside their primary industries when the latter are defined more narrowly. Table 3 shows that in 34 of 117 three-digit[12] industries, company employment differed from establishment employment by more than 10 per cent.

The extent of industrial heterogeneity in the employment of companies may differ from that for income for several reasons. The secondary activities of companies in some industries may be

[11] A firm's primary industry is one which, individually, contributes more to the firm's total employment (and, presumably, output) than any other activity.

[12] The industry classification used in U.S. Bureau of the Census, *Company Statistics*, 1958.

more (or less) capital intensive than the primary ones, with the result that a larger (or lesser) proportion of income than of employment emanates therefrom. Second, rates of return for some classes of companies may differ markedly between primary and secondary activities so that the industry composition of income differs from the composition of output. In addition, for many companies a sizable proportion of costs are common to plants in more than one industry. The more important of these costs are for general administration, engineering, research, and marketing (including advertising and the operation of sales outlets). The distribution of these costs by industry is not closely related to the distribution of employees and, in any event, the allocation of costs by industry raises conceptual as well as empirical problems.

Tables 2 and 3 are based on a definition of "company" which subsumes the establishments of all corporate subsidiaries under the latters' ultimate parent firms.[13] Users of information on the industry distribution of business income most often employ data contained in *Statistics of Income* and based on a definition of "company" that is substantially narrower than that used in Census data. Specifically, the degree to which parent-subsidiary relations are reflected in the identification of separate companies in *Statistics of Income* is based on the degree of consolidation of corporate tax returns. In 1957–58, for the aggregate of all industrial divisions, only about 13 per cent of the total assets of all corporations belonged to firms that submitted consolidated tax returns. Thus, for companies as defined in *Statistics of Income*, the discrepancy between company and establishment employment should be less for most industries than that shown in Table 2.[14]

Users of data from tax returns are confronted with still other sources of difficulty if they wish information over a period of time rather than for a single year. The degree of consolidation of tax

[13] All firms were asked in the 1954 Census to report the companies they controlled. This information constituted the basis for grouping subsidiaries with their parent companies.

[14] Virtually all tax returns were deconsolidated in 1934 and a measure of the effect of deconsolidation can be derived from data in the 1934 *Statistics of Income*. A relatively large interindustry shift in total receipts appears when the 1934 data are compared with what they would have been had the degree of consolidation and the industry classification of companies that submitted consolidated returns in 1933 remained unchanged. However, the degree of consolidation of returns was far greater in 1933 than currently. Moreover, the magnitude of the shift in some sectors raises some doubt about the consistency in the classification principles used in the two years.

TABLE 2
DISCREPANCIES BETWEEN INDUSTRY EMPLOYMENT ON A COMPANY AND ON AN ESTABLISHMENT BASIS, 1954[a]

Industry	Company Employment Minus Establishment Employment as Percentage of Company Employment
MINING AND QUARRYING	−29.2
Metal mining	−75.7
Anthracite mining	−3.5
Bituminous coal	−17.9
Crude petroleum and natural gas	−38.6
Nonmetallic minerals	−14.8
MANUFACTURING	1.7
Food	3.2
Tobacco	2.7
Textile mill products	1.4
Apparel	−2.4
Lumber and wood products	−1.2
Furniture	−4.0
Paper, pulp, and products	−2.9
Printing and publishing	0.0
Chemicals	6.0
Petroleum and coal products	−10.3
Rubber	17.9
Leather	2.0
Stone, clay, and glass	−1.5
Primary metals	13.2
Fabricated metal products	−9.4
Machinery (except electrical)	−5.3
Electrical machinery	10.3
Transportation equipment	−8.9
Motor vehicles and parts	25.3
Instruments (professional, scientific, etc.)	4.4
Miscellaneous manufacturing	−15.7
PUBLIC WAREHOUSES	−4.7
WHOLESALE TRADE	−5.3
Commission merchants	−1.9
Other wholesalers	−22.6
RETAIL TRADE	−1.1
Food stores	0.8
General merchandise	6.5
Apparel and accessories	−4.3
Furniture, home furnishings	−5.9
Automotive dealers, dealers in parts, etc.	−3.3
Drug stores	−1.2
Eating and drinking places	−0.2
Lumber, building materials, and hardware dealers	−4.5
Other retail trade	−11.0

(continued)

TABLE 2 (concluded)

Industry	Company Employment Minus Establishment Employment as Percentage of Company Employment
SELECTED SERVICE TRADES	−1.1
Personal services	−0.1
Business services	−4.0
Automobile repair services and garages	−0.4
Other repair services	−10.6
Motion picture theaters	1.4
Amusement and recreation services	−0.1
Other services	0.1

SOURCE: Based on data in U.S. Bureau of the Census, *Company Statistics*, 1958.

[a] "Company employment" consists of the employees of all companies classified in the industry regardless of the industries of establishments in which the employees work. "Establishment employment" consists of the employment of all establishments in the industry regardless of the industry in which the parent company is classified. For comparability, employment in central administrative offices was added to industry employment on an establishment basis inasmuch as it was automatically included in company employment.

TABLE 3

DISCREPANCIES BETWEEN EMPLOYMENT ON A COMPANY AND ON AN ESTABLISHMENT BASIS, 117 INDUSTRIES, 1958[a]

Net Difference Between Company and Establishment Employment as Percentage of Company Employment	Number of Industries
0– 2.5	31
2.6– 5	26
5.1–10	22
10.1–20	24
20 and over	14
Total	117

SOURCE: U.S. Bureau of the Census, *Company Statistics*, 1958.

[a] "Company employment" consists of the employees of all companies classified in the industry regardless of the industries of establishments in which the employees work. "Establishment employment" consists of the employment of all establishments in the industry regardless of the industry in which the parent company is classified.

returns has changed over time. For example, the proportion of total assets[15] contributed by consolidated returns (in all industries combined) rose from 8.7 per cent in 1948 to 12.3 per cent in 1954—a rise which, though not spectacular, may be sufficient to affect materially estimates of the magnitude of secondary activities for at least some industry classes of companies. Moreover, if a

[15] For corporations submitting balance sheets.

longer time span is taken, the change is more dramatic. For example, in 1933 consolidated returns accounted for 43.6 per cent of total assets in all industries combined.

Another problem, and one which for comparisons of income in successive years may be even more serious, is that of frequent changes in *Statistics of Income* data in the industry classification of some large companies. For example, from 1951 to 1954 at least one-fourth of the total assets reported for the highest asset-size class of companies (in *Statistics of Income*) disappeared in thirty-two three-digit manufacturing industries. Since these assets did not appear in the adjacent size class in the affected industries, one must presume that the disappearance was a result of reclassification. The gravity of this problem is considerably reduced if analysis is restricted to the two-digit industry level.

In summary, heterogeneity in the output of companies introduces an error in estimates of property income by industry source if all the income of companies is classified in their primary industries. This error is only moderate for most industry classes but fairly large for some, particularly at the higher levels of industry detail. The fact that most corporations currently submit unconsolidated federal tax returns reduces the error for measures of corporate income by industry based on data in *Statistics of Income*. However, this source often suffers from noncomparability of industry statistics over time resulting from changes in degree of consolidation of tax returns and from the frequent reclassification of companies for other reasons. The question to which we now turn concerns the ways in which estimates of business income may best be made for "pure" industries as contrasted with estimates of income from the conglomerate activities of companies.

Measuring Income for "Pure" Industries

Basically there are two approaches one can take. The first is to estimate profits directly from data for establishments. The second, and more promising, is to estimate the total earnings generated in a given industrial activity from the relation between profits and statistics available on an establishment basis (e.g., sales, value added, employment, etc.) for companies with homogeneous product structures. The latter approach should soon be rendered feasible by information currently being developed by the Bureau of the Census and Internal Revenue Service. This information will link Census establishment and *Statistics of Income* data for a sizable sample of medium-sized and large firms (including most large firms in sectors of the economy covered by the 1958 Economic Census).

A measure of operating income for an establishment can be derived from the difference between the value of sales (or shipments) and expenses of the establishment.[16] The estimate, however, would differ in several critical ways from a conceptually acceptable measure of profit. For shipments between plants of the same company, the prices at which such shipments are valued will frequently deviate from market prices. An arbitrary (nonmarket) price, either for the final product of a plant or for raw materials and other components incorporated in the final product, renders the measure of operating income also arbitrary. Second, for multiestablishment companies a sizable proportion of total expenses (e.g., those for sales, advertising, engineering and legal services, central administration, etc.) may be common to the activities of several plants. For many companies, these common costs are larger than reported net income. Consequently, measuring income on the basis of arbitrary allocations of these expenses—and only arbitrary methods are available with existing information—would be solving a problem by assuming it away. In short, this approach is not likely to prove fruitful.

The linking of Census statistics with data on earnings taken from tax returns makes it possible to compute for a given company ratios of earnings to sales, value added, or other establishment statistics. If these ratios are developed for companies with establishments in but a single industry, they can then be applied to total sales or value added in the industry to secure an estimate of industry income.[17] An assumption implicit in this procedure is that both the production function and the rate of return for a given

[16] Information on both expenses and the value of shipments is currently available in Census data for manufacturing and mining industries.

[17] Since firms within a given industry differ in degree of vertical integration, a ratio of earnings to value added should vary less among companies than that of earnings to sales, and is hence to be preferred. Unfortunately, however, information on value added is not currently available for all sectors of the economy. An alternative in these sectors is the use of ratios of earnings to employment. If separate estimates are made for each of several size classes of firms within an industry, ratios of earnings to employment may prove reasonably satisfactory. This is because within groupings of firms delimited by size as well as by industry, the variance in the relative magnitudes of capital and labor inputs is probably not large.

activity are generally the same whether or not the producing firm is engaged in activities in other industries as well. It is, of course, always possible to cite circumstances under which this would not be true, but the assumption is in general a plausible one if allowance is made for firm size. It will be noted that no assumption is made here that all firms in an industry are of equal efficiency. Rather what is assumed, first, is that diversified firms are *on the average* neither more nor less efficient than homogeneous ones, and second, that there are no important and persistent differences in *average* managerial efficiency between industries. The size of a firm affects ratios of earnings to sales or value added in two ways. First, it has been established that large firms use production methods that are more capital-intensive, as measured by capital-output ratios, than those of smaller firms.[18] Thus earnings relative to sales or value added should be positively correlated with firm size. Second, rates of return appear to vary with company size also, though in part, as previously noted, because of arbitrary executive salaries for the smaller owner-managed companies. It follows then that estimates of income made on the basis of the above ratios are best made separately for each size class of companies. Hence, among the data requirements for an effective use of this approach is an expansion of information on size distributions of firms by industry.[19]

If estimates of business income by industry are made on the basis of the aforementioned ratios, the choice of a sample of firms for these ratios should focus primarily on the selection in each industry of an adequate group of homogeneous firms over the entire size range of companies. Contrary to a common impression, relatively small multiestablishment firms frequently have a large volume of secondary production. Indeed, for multiestablishment firms diversification, as measured by the ratio of production in secondary to that in primary activities, is not strongly correlated with firm size.[20] Thus the selection of a sample of companies with homogeneous output is a problem not restricted to large

[18] Daniel Creamer, Sergei P. Dobrovolsky, and Israel Borenstein, *Capital in Manufacturing and Mining: Its Formation and Financing*, Princeton University Press for NBER, 1960, pp. 60–65.

[19] Size of firm can be envisaged in two ways: conglomerate size and size in individual industries. As a basis for grouping firms to reduce variability in capital-labor ratios, the latter is the more relevant.

[20] Michael Gort, *Diversification and Integration in American Industry*, Princeton University Press for NBER, 1962.

enterprises. However, at the upper tail of the size distribution, inclusion in the sample of an adequate group of firms is more difficult by virtue of the fact that in some industries all of the largest firms have a heterogeneous output.

A variety of checks are possible to assess the adequacy of estimated ratios of earnings to sales, value added, or employment. For example, for a given group of companies, the establishments and their output could be distributed by industry. By applying to the output in each industry class ratios of earnings to value added (derived from homogeneous firms), the total earnings of the group of companies can be estimated. This estimate can then be compared with aggregate reported income for the same companies.[21]

A discussion of methods of estimating income should not obscure the fact that for many industry classes (as may be judged from Table 2) the distortion arising from heterogeneity of company output is small and reported earnings on a company basis are acceptable unadjusted.

Rates of Return and the Heterogeneity of Output

For many problems, measures of property income by industry are useful only when expressed as rates of return on investment rather than as absolute amounts. The extent to which heterogeneity in output produces rates of return that differ between "pure" industries and those composed of conglomerate companies depends on two factors: the extent of secondary output for the latter and the magnitude of differences in rates of return between primary and secondary activities.

For most industry classes of firms, secondary activities are widely dispersed over the industrial spectrum with little concentration in individual narrowly defined sectors. This arises from two sources: first, companies classified in a given industry generally differ considerably in the nature of their secondary activities and, second, the nonprimary activities of individual large enterprises are themselves widely dispersed. The consequence of this is that the average rate of return for all the secondary activities in a given industry (the latter composed of conglomerate firms) is likely to approximate the average rate of return for all industries

[21] Information to permit tests of this type should be available from the linking of Census with Internal Revenue data.

in the economy as a whole. As a result, in a given industry class the rate of return for the primary activity and the average rate of return for the secondary ones are unlikely to be at opposite ends of the distribution of profit rates. This greatly reduces the importance of heterogeneity in company output as a problem in measuring profit rates for "pure" industries.

In the absence of income measures for firms with homogeneous product structures, estimates of rates of return for "pure" industries were made on the basis of a simplifying assumption. Specifically, the contribution of each activity to the total earnings of firms in a given industry was assumed to be proportional to that activity's share in the total employment of these firms. Since the purpose of such estimates was merely to provide a rough indication of the effect of heterogeneity on reported profit rates, the somewhat arbitrary nature of this assumption is not critical to the results. Accordingly, if R_j represents the reported profit rate for industry class j (composed of companies with conglomerate output), r_i represents the profit rate for "pure" industry i, and p_{ij} is the proportion of employment for companies in class j contributed by activities in industry i, we have the equation:

$$\sum_{i=1}^{n} p_{ij} r_i = R_j$$

Inasmuch as there is one equation for each industry class of companies, and since the number of such classes is equal to the number of unknowns (profit rates for "pure" industries), the values of the latter can be found by solving a set of simultaneous linear equations. In Table 4, rates of return for two-digit "pure" industries are obtained by a modified version of this method.[22]

Table 4 shows, as expected, that adjusted rates of return (those

[22] The modified method assumes that the rate of return for each industry class of manufacturing companies is derived from two sources: the profit rate in the primary activity and the average profit rate for all manufacturing activities exclusive of the primary one. In short, secondary activities are treated as a single industry. Thus, for example, the profit rate for food manufacturing is obtained by solving two simultaneous equations in which the profit rates for food companies and for all manufacturing companies are given (as well as the relative magnitude of secondary activities for food companies and the relative magnitude of food manufacturing for all manufacturing companies combined). The fact that secondary activities for most industry classes of companies are widely dispersed permits the use, for these activities, of an average profit rate in all industries.

TABLE 4

Rates of Return Reported and Adjusted for Nonhomogeneity of Output, 22 Manufacturing Industries, 1953 and 1954

(per cent)

Industry	*1953* Reported	*1953* Adjusted	*1954* Reported	*1954* Adjusted
Beverages	6.21	6.18	5.44	5.38
Food	6.05	5.99	5.93	5.90
Tobacco	5.78	5.75	6.49	6.50
Textile mill products	3.74	3.44	2.64	2.26
Apparel	3.09	2.85	3.10	2.88
Lumber and wood products	6.00	5.93	6.41	6.44
Furniture	5.15	4.94	4.81	4.60
Paper, pulp, and products	7.60	7.71	7.37	7.50
Printing and publishing	6.59	6.59	6.30	6.31
Chemicals	7.00	7.16	7.61	8.09
Petroleum and coal products	7.64	9.22	6.40	6.70
Rubber	6.07	5.86	5.73	5.52
Leather	4.43	4.15	4.75	4.56
Stone, clay, and glass	7.56	7.73	8.24	8.58
Primary metals	6.30	6.19	5.16	4.66
Fabricated metal products	6.51	6.50	6.01	5.95
Machinery (except electrical)	6.73	6.78	6.46	6.53
Electrical machinery	7.10	7.35	6.83	7.11
Transportation equipment	4.67	4.23	5.96	5.91
Motor vehicles and parts	8.09	9.03	8.37	9.69
Instruments (professional, scientific, etc.)	7.19	7.44	8.34	9.14
Miscellaneous manufacturing	4.99	4.57	4.97	4.64
All manufacturing	6.53		6.19	

Source: "Reported" rates of return were obtained from George J. Stigler, *Capital and Rates of Return in Manufacturing Industries*, Princeton for NBER, 1963. They are based on data, reported in *Statistics of Income*, for income (including interest payments) and total assets. The data for both income and assets were deflated by Stigler for price changes. "Adjusted" rates of return are developed from the "reported" ones. The adjustment, described in the text, is designed to show an estimated rate of return for the activities of companies restricted to their primary industries. That is, it attempts to exclude the effect on "reported" rates of return of the secondary activities of companies.

for "pure" industries) generally differed only modestly from those reported on a company basis—that is, generated by conglomerate activities. For 1953 and 1954, of all two-digit manufacturing industries, only petroleum refining in the former year and motor vehicles in both years showed sizable differences between adjusted and reported profit rates. Thus, in most industries heterogeneity in the product structures of companies is not a severe obstacle to measuring rates of return.

COMMENT

Robert M. Williams, University of California, Los Angeles

Professor Gort's paper discusses questions related to the measurement of returns to capital and labor in twenty-two manufacturing industries. The problems involved include the basic ones of identifying property and labor income plus problems peculiar to individual industries. These problems combine to make interindustry comparisons of factor income extremely difficult.

In identifying property and labor income, Gort discusses the problem raised by the arbitrary distinctions between profit and officers' compensation which owner-managers of small corporations make in the firm's accounts for income tax or other reasons. This well-known problem was discussed by several speakers at the conference. Similar problems of income definition and measurement occur in regard to expense accounts, stock options, and capital gains. These important sources of management compensation should be taken into account in any thorough analysis of factor incomes.

In addition, I suggest that the whole subject of executive salary determination be examined. Management groups of many large corporations whose stock is widely held are subject to little control by the stockholders. The latter legally own the business and, together with bondholders and other creditors, are entitled to receive all the property income generated by the firm. But, since the management group frequently determines its own compensation, this compensation might exceed or fall short of management's marginal revenue product which theoretically should determine its total income from the enterprise.

Executive compensation varies considerably between industries and companies, but executive performance appears to vary even more. In the automobile industry, for example, stockholders in General Motors Corporation consistently received a higher rate of return on their stock equity than was the case for other firms in the industry. Although the General Motors' management group was well paid as corporate compensation goes, it may have been grossly underpaid on the basis of its marginal revenue product. If so, the group was exploited in the interest of the stockholders. On the other hand, one can find examples of the reverse situation, where management performance is poor, its compensation probably exceeds marginal revenue product, and management is exploiting the stockholders. The proper definition and measurement of management's labor income is admittedly difficult, but this is a subject which deserves more consideration.

In discussing the problem of allocating factor income between industries for companies with heterogeneous outputs, Gort shows that the problem is less difficult for labor income than for property income because most employees can be identified with a particular product and industry. For the more difficult problem of allocating property income, Gort suggests two solutions which are useful but are not without serious limitations. The first method is to determine profit rates (as a percentage of some relevant base such as sales, value added, or employment) for companies with homogeneous product structures and then to use these rates in allocating profits of firms with heterogeneous product structures. This method requires the dubious assumption that all firms in an industry have the same profit rate. To cite one example, should we use the profit rate for the highly successful International Business Machines Corporation to determine the property income of computer divisions of less profitable firms which produce computers and also other items classified in other industry groups?

Gort's second suggested method for allocating property income by industry for firms with heterogeneous outputs requires the assumption that profit rates on sales in secondary industries will equal the average rate for the entire manufacturing sector. Application of this method of adjustment has the effect of raising the profit rate in the primary industry if the company's over-all profit rate exceeds the average for all manufacturing, and vice versa. This method of profit adjustment is illustrated in Gort's Table 4; in the motor vehicle and parts industry, for example, the reported profit rate for all firms classified in the industry in 1953 was 8.09 per cent, and Gort's adjusted profit rate for the industry is 9.03 per cent. This upward revision is based on the assumption that nonautomobile sales earned only the average for all manufactures, or 6.53 per cent. The effect of a similar adjustment for the apparel industry reduces its profit rate from 3.09 to 2.85 per cent.

The net effect of these profit rate adjustments is to increase the range of profit rates in 1953 for the twenty-two industries from 5.0 to 6.37 percentage points. Incidentally, this wide range of returns seems to contradict Gort's contention that rates of return tend to be the same in all industries. But returning to the point at issue here, I question whether returns from secondary industries tend to be nearer the average for all manufacturing than those for the primary activity engaged in by the firm. The firm's management ability is the controlling factor, and, in general, a firm may do everything it attempts well or badly rather than do some things well and others badly. General Motors Corporation, for example, seems to excel at most everything it attempts and has a policy of discontinuing activities which do not measure up to its profit standards.

Gort compares two ratios for twenty-two industries: property income to output and capital assets to output (see his Table 1). Essentially, he is correlating property income and capital assets by industry, and a high degree of correlation would be expected if industry rates of return on capital are anywhere near equal. The two pairs of ratios are fairly closely correlated, especially if two troublesome industries—transportation equipment and motor vehicles—are omitted from the calculation. To facilitate the reader's analysis of these interindustry differences, the data in Gort's Table 1 are restated in terms of industry ranks in my Table 1.

It is interesting to observe the degree of variation between the two sets of ratios of capital assets to output for 1948 and 1953. As my Table 1 shows, industry rankings change considerably over this five-year period. This change reflects a number of factors, including shifts in production functions, but perhaps most importantly, variations in the rate of capacity utilization.

I conclude with a word of caution; for an empirical study such as Gort's, which attempts to test hypotheses concerning industry differences in factor incomes, the concepts of factor income as well as the data available are imperfect. The concept of the industry itself is a source of difficulty. Even at the three- and four-digit level, "industries" include a wide variety of products with different production functions. Short-run comparisons are complicated by such problems as "sick industries," and the short run can last for decades, as in the case of the textile industry. Long-run comparisons are complicated by changing technologies. The aircraft industry, for example, is rapidly evolving into the missile industry, which in turn, soon may be transformed into the

TABLE 1

INDUSTRY RANKING BY RATIOS OF GROSS INCOME TO OUTPUT AND CAPITAL ASSETS TO OUTPUT, TWENTY-TWO MANUFACTURING INDUSTRIES, 1948–53

Industry	Ratio of Gross Income to Output 1948–53	*Ratio of Capital Assets to Output* 1948	*Ratio of Capital Assets to Output* 1953
Beverages	18	14	20
Food	21	21	22
Tobacco	16	15	10
Textiles	13	16	13
Apparel	22	22	21
Lumber and wood products	1	1	1
Furniture	19	20	17
Paper and products	2	4	6
Printing and publishing	9	10	8
Chemicals	3	6	2
Petroleum and coal products	11	3	5
Rubber	15	17	16
Leather	20	19	19
Stone, clay, and glass	4	5	7
Primary metals	7	9	4
Fabricated metal products	10	13	14
Machinery (except electrical)	6	7	11
Electrical machinery	12	12	15
Transportation equipment	17	2	9
Motor vehicles and parts	5	17	18
Instruments	8	8	12
Miscellaneous manufacturing	14	11	3

SOURCE: Gort's Table 1.

space industry. This change is accompanied by rapid and radical shifts in the proportions and composition of labor and capital inputs. Finally, problems arise from differences in accounting practices between industries and even between firms in the same industry. These differences further complicate interindustry comparisons and reduce the usefulness of analyses based on industry aggregates and averages.

HARLOW D. OSBORNE, Banco Central of Venezuela[1]

The Department of Commerce has been interested in this subject for many years. The cross-classification of factor earnings by industry and by form has been a central feature of the Department's national income reports ever since the first one was issued

[1] The author was formerly Chief, National Income Division, Department of Commerce.

in 1934. Economic analyses of cyclical and trend changes in the share distribution—as such, and as influenced by shifts in the industrial structure—have appeared at frequent intervals in the *Survey of Current Business* and its national income supplements.

Besides the particular application of these statistics which Gort has chosen for purpose of illustration, these data, of course, serve to illuminate many of the questions of long-term economic growth and social change, on the one hand, and the anatomy of business cycles, on the other, which have been discussed during this Conference.

The statistical problems of estimation noted by Gort are significant but are probably not serious enough to cast much doubt on conclusions of the sort that are commonly drawn from the data we have. The tables presented in the paper suggest that for most though not all major industries, these data distort the level of income and its distribution only to a relatively minor extent. With one or two important exceptions, moreover, movements through time are represented faithfully enough to meet the major analytical needs.

Exceptions occur, of course, and for some of these no cure is even in sight. The charging of research and development purchases to current expense, for example, affects both the numerator and the denominator of the capital-output ratio, and the tendency for the two effects to be offsetting will not prevent some distortion in the ratios for research-intensive industries relative to the all-industry average.

Though the problems are unimportant in some cases and seem insuperable in others, there are clearly substantial advantages to be gained by refining our statistical measures of the income shares originating in specific industries. Besides rendering the data more satisfactory in some of their present applications, such refinements should eventually make possible a whole series of new applications in studying cost structure, investment potential, and other aspects of individual industries. The careful job Gort has done in breaking down the statistical difficulties into bite-sized chunks for further quantitative study represents a stride in this direction.

I should like to emphasize what seem to me the salient features of his review by means of a graphic formulation of it. Besides providing a convenient framework to integrate one or two comments of my own with those he has made, this may perhaps prove useful as a mnemonic device.

Visualize then, if you will, a productive process. This process is absorbing labor and property services, along with raw or "intermediate" materials, supplies and services of many sorts; and each of these inputs is evaluated in terms of the cost payment made to obtain it.

At the other end of the process there emerges a product. The nature of this product is the main criterion for classifying the process in one or another of the many industries distinguished in the SIC.

This conceptual Garden of Eden is infested in practice by two sorts of reptiles which seem to me to be siblings if not twins. In real life, productive processes are so organized institutionally that too often we find a single economic entity turning out a heterogeneous set of products, and our ability to classify it by industry is of course impaired as a consequence. We find that many of the inputs consist of units which are likewise heterogeneous from the standpoint of our analytical needs—units, that is, which straddle our functional categories of labor services, property services, and intermediate products instead of fitting neatly into any one of these. We are troubled, I should say in summary, by the twin problems of heterogeneity in our units of input and heterogeneity in our bundles of output.

Inputs

Let us examine the problem by proceeding to fill in details on the input side of the production process.

One input factor or set of factors is delimited by the fact that payment for it takes the form of wages and salaries. A second set is defined in terms of its remuneration through interest or business net income; its gross value is sufficient to cover capital consumption charges also. A third group of inputs is distinguished by its involvement with purchases from other enterprises.

A problem emerges at once on the boundary line between the labor services which form set number one and the property services which form set number two. This is the problem posed by the heterogeneous input of the owner-manager. In the case of noncorporate business, there is commonly no institutional basis for splitting this. As Gort points out, moreover, even in the corporate sector the institutional basis available for a functional split of the owner-managers' contribution is rather artificial.

The line which separates the first two categories of inputs—and which must be drawn sharply if we are to have a precise statistical measure of either sort of input—is thus seen to be in fact a zone or band of indeterminate character.

Moving farther down the input line we come to a second major division, where the property services of set number two give way to the interbusiness cost purchases of set number three.

In this neighborhood, too, we find a number of outlays that might be included on either side of the line. Most of the research and development expenditures mentioned above, which contribute to the longer-term profitability of the process and are made to this end, are expensed in our present national income estimates. Being deducted in the calculation of business net income, in effect they enter our picture below the line in the value measure of intermediate product. For some purposes it might be more appropriate to capitalize them—i.e., treat them as a portion of business net income which has been realized as such and then reinvested. If this alternative is chosen, the immediate result is to raise the estimate of property income, but a more or less offsetting effect follows when capital consumption charges are deducted. The extent of the offset depends on the convention which is selected to govern the size and time-pattern of the charges.

Problems of this character are not unfamiliar in national income work. Some of them are recognized in the explicit allowance we make for capital outlays charged to current expense. This is restricted to outlays for tangible goods which for reasons of convenience or custom are not capitalized in ordinary business accounting but which will render significant productive services—thereby paying for themselves and returning a profit or loss—in a subsequent accounting period.

There are various other blurry spots along the line between property-service input and intermediate-product input. One of these has to do with productive services obtained by the payment of rent. Gort deals with this separately, but I think it can neatly be cited here.

Productive services remunerated by rent virtually always owe something to the managerial and other efforts of the lessor, as well as to the physical property concerned. Basically, the question here is whether the latter element is sufficiently predominant so that the former can be ignored without doing overmuch violence to reality. An alternative possibility, which would seem to me more realistic in most cases, is to view the rent payment as purchasing an intermediate product from the landlord-entrepreneur, who has produced it by combining the factor services of labor and property.

Nearly all intermediate products are produced with the aid of substantial capital nowadays—the carriage of freight and the supplying of electric power hardly less so than the services purchased by the payment of rent in an office building. The service bought in each case is clearly an input from the purchaser's standpoint. Whether it is an input sufficiently homogeneous at bottom to be attributed exclusively to one factor of production is not so clear.

In terms of the three-way division I am using, rent payments and capital outlays charged to current expense may be said to lie close to the border of property income. I would add that they have analogues along the region of labor income. Just as it is clear that producers' durables expensed on the books should be capitalized and the deduction added back to business net income, so pension and welfare fund payments by employers should be added to payrolls in measuring the market value of labor input. Employer outlays which go to provide fringe benefits in kind are not so clear a case. Multiuse facilities and other purchases which play a part in the productive process may also provide direct satisfaction to employees using them, and this makes it cheaper to recruit and retain workers. Besides the often-cited privileges of the expense account and the company cars and airplanes for executives, one might think of a wide range of conveniences which have become standard in modern factory practice after having been thought for many years to be unnecessary to the production process.

Let me summarize my review of the input heterogeneities in terms of the three zones of uncertainty noted above. First, there are units of input which straddle any simply drawn border between those intermediate products which go as fringe income to labor and those that do not. Passing across the zone of what are clearly labor earnings, we come to the earnings of owner-managers, which represent units of mingled labor and property services.

And still further on, beyond the area of what are unmistakably property services, we find rent, development, etc.—outlays which might or might not be regarded as intermediate-product purchases deductible in arriving at an income measure of property inputs.

In pursuing these interesting and fruitful lines of thought opened up by Gort, we should, of course, not lose sight of the fact that the bulk of all inputs is substantially free of such ambiguities and options. Payrolls make up two-thirds of the national income; and profits of million-dollar and larger corporations—calculated on principles widely understood and accepted (and not much affected by the owner-manager type of distortion, judging from McConnell's study)—represent as much as 90 per cent of all corporate profits and over 10 per cent of national income. Nevertheless enough inputs are of mixed character to create significant problems for the social accountant, and the specialized user should be aware of them.

Outputs

Turning now to the output side, we observe that the units of product are often entirely homogeneous within themselves and readily classifiable in terms of the SIC code. Unfortunately this is not enough. A statistical cross break of income by type and by industry requires that we classify not only the product but the whole process and the plant in which it is carried on, since most of the inputs (and other characteristics) of the process cannot be established for any unit narrower than the plant.

This situation gives rise to no problem when the output of the plant is homogeneous. It does make trouble whenever the output includes by-products or other secondary products. The industrial classification of the plant must then generally be made according to the *principal* product, as if this were the only product and, in many though not all compilations, as if the plant's total output, input and other dimensions were all aimed at providing this one product.

As Gort points out, the distortion that results in practice is not so very great when we are dealing with labor inputs, which for the most part can at least be identified with a particular plant as the unit to be classified. It frequently happens, though, that one plant is integrated with others, under the control of a multi-industry corporation or group of affiliated corporations. In this case, it has commonly not been feasible to tie down the measure of property services to any entity narrower than the corporation, the affiliated group as a whole (if a consolidated tax return is filed) or, at best, the corporate affiliates individually. The classification of property service inputs by industry becomes less accurate, of course, as the outputs of the legal entities employing these services become more heterogeneous: To the extent that this condition exists, services used in producing the secondary products are erroneously associated with the production of the primary product.

Such heterogeneity in the outputs of our institutional producing units makes trouble of three sorts for analysts using the data. The first comes in measuring an industry's magnitude, for comparisons over time or with other industries, when secondary production bulks large in the companies' outputs. The phenomenon Gort notes of multiindustry companies shifting back and forth across industry lines, which has occasionally plagued us in the preparation of our own tables, has its roots in such situations. Statistical measures of the comparative sizes of certain interrelated industries are seriously impaired for the same basic reason. The well-known difficulty of comparing petroleum extraction with petroleum refining as originators of profits and national income is a case in point.

Secondly, interindustry differences in the pattern of resource use, profitability, etc. tend to be watered down. This effect is illustrated neatly in Gort's assumption concerning the profitability of secondary operations in the industries covered by his Table 5. It is clear that the structural differences between auto and electrical machinery production, for example, will be understressed in data which reflect the extensive production of home appliances by companies in both these industry groups.

Finally, there is a tendency to distort the relative magnitudes of property and labor income within particular industries. The plant statistics basic to the industry measures of labor income covers some plants owned by corporations which are classified in the property-income statistics—in terms of their principal product —outside the industry being analyzed. This tends to make labor's percentage share appear higher than is really typical of the processes one commonly associates with the industry. On the other hand, the basic statistics of labor income for a given industry exclude plants whose processes belong outside this industry but which are owned by corporations classified inside. The income total reported for this industry will include the property income generated by these plants, but not the labor income; and the latter's share in the total will tend to be understated accordingly. There is a broad tendency for these two sources of noncomparability to offset one another. In certain cases, such as automobile manufacturing and petroleum and primary metals production, however, the offsets are very far from complete.

As I have already suggested, Gort's illustration of possible uses and interpretation of this sort of data is only one of a large number he might have selected from among the Conference papers and other relevant literature. The case he has chosen, however, is probably about as satisfactory for the purpose as any he could have found. The ratio of property income to total income is a statistic which is of wide interest, and significant in various analytical connections, and in a number of these it is readily replaceable by the profit-output ratio he has computed. The capital-output relationship is of similarly wide interest and multiple applicability.

Taking the profit-output and asset-output ratios as alternative measures of capital intensiveness, Gort notes that among manufacturing industries the rank-order correlation is not very high. It seems to me that the set of possible economic explanations he advances might go far to explain why the correlation is not higher, and that statistical problems cited earlier in the paper might also be found to play a recognizable part in the results.

I was interested enough to dig beneath the correlation coefficient a little, by means of a scatter diagram. From this it appeared that the income-output ratio for motor vehicles was out of line on the high side while the ratios for transportation equipment, petroleum products, tobacco and miscellaneous manufacturing were on the low side. If these deviations could be rationalized, the over-all relationship would look pretty good to me as these things go.

Gort might well have gone on to examine the "problem industries" individually in terms of the body of critical thought provided here and elsewhere in his paper. I believe that this addition would have increased the value of his contribution in several ways. It might have provided a focused summary, an indication of the relative magnitudes and bearings of the different sources of distortion he has noted, and a thumbnail guide to the dangers these may pose for long-term, short-term and static analyses of such data.

The Estimation of Produced Income by State and Region

GEORGE H. BORTS
BROWN UNIVERSITY

Produced and Received Income

Up to the present, our knowledge of the income generated in states and regions of the United States has been somewhat indirect. The major source of information is the annual series on personal income by states which is published by the National Income Division of the U.S. Department of Commerce. Personal income is composed for the most part of the factor payments received by the residents of a region;[1] it does not measure the factor payments attributable to the resources employed in a region, since the owner of a resource need not reside in the state or region where the resource is employed. Therefore an income concept based on residence may not be useful for the class of analytical problems dealing with the level and growth of income produced in different regions. There is, of course, no certainty of this; a statistical series derived from one income concept may be a useful proxy measure of an unknown series derived from a more appropriate concept. For example, personal income and produced income may in fact yield highly similar measures of the level and growth of economic activity in different states and regions. Richard Easterlin raised this question at the Regional Income Conference in 1955. He concluded that "the difference between the two concepts is significant, even for so comprehensive a measure as total income and for areas as large as census regions and states."[2]

NOTE: The author wishes to acknowledge with gratitude the extensive cooperation of Ernest J. Engquist, of the U.S. Internal Revenue Service, and Robert E. Graham, Jr., of the National Income Division, U.S. Department of Commerce. They provided unpublished source material which underlies many of the estimates.

Grateful acknowledgment is also due to Mary I. Pett and Morton Ehrlich for their help in the preparation of the estimates. The cost of carrying out this work was supported by a grant from the Ford Foundation.

[1] Strictly defined, personal income includes wages and salaries, dividends, interest, rents, proprietor's income, government interest, and government and business transfer payments. Personal income of course falls short of national income, which includes undistributed corporate profits, tax liability, and inventory valuation adjustment, as well as employer's contributions for social insurance; it excludes government interest and business and government transfers.

[2] See *Regional Income*, Studies in Income and Wealth 21, Princeton for NBER, 1957, p. 28. Easterlin estimated that in 1920 the quantitative difference between

His conclusions are based on computations made for the year 1920.

The object of this paper is to present and analyze estimates of produced income by state and region for 1929 and 1953. We shall determine whether produced income provides information which is not embodied in the personal income series that is currently published; whether this information is useful for the analysis of regional problems; and finally what changes in current methods of data collection would be needed to provide current estimates of produced income by state and region.

The analytical concept underlying this work might be called domestic produced income, which is the sum of the factor returns attributable to resources employed in a given region. This is to be distinguished from national income, which is the sum of the returns attributable to factors of production supplied by residents of the region. At the national level our concept differs from national income by the omission of a "rest-of-the-world account," which summarizes the net payments to domestically owned resources employed outside the region minus the payments to domestically employed resources owned by outsiders. The omission of this account means that our domestic income for each region will sum to domestic income for the United States, rather than to total national income. In 1953, the discrepancy between national income and domestic income came to $1.5 billion.[3]

The major problem in measuring domestic income for each state is to estimate the returns to resources over and above compensation of employees. Data on compensation of employees by state on a "where-worked" basis were provided by the National Income Division. Accordingly, the focus of this inquiry is the remaining portion which on the average comprises about 30 per cent of total national income. I refer to this remainder as net entrepreneurial income (or NEI) and we can see in what sense this title is appropriate.

---

income produced and income received was around ±5 per cent for the census regions.

[3] All national income data were derived from *National Income,* A Supplement to the *Survey of Current Business,* 1954 edition, Washington, 1954.

Personal income data were derived from *Personal Income by States since 1929,* Washington, 1956. While later editions of the *National Income* Supplement contain revisions of the 1953 data in the above volumes, these were retained as the basic sources, and revisions were not incorporated into our estimates.

National income may be written as the sum of the following components:

a. Compensation of employees	68.5
b. Income of unincorporated enterprises, etc.	12.6
c. Corporate income before income taxes } d. Inventory valuation adjustment	12.6
e. Net interest	2.8
f. Rental income of persons	3.5

The percentage following each category shows its portion of the total in 1953.

The 30 per cent remainder is a combination of returns to property and returns to entrepreneurs. The 12.6 per cent attributed to income of unincorporated enterprises is the only part which includes any income paid for personal services. However, even a good part of this category (comprising $38.6 billion in 1953) represents returns to property. This can be seen in the fact that, of the $38 billion, $12.5 billion was generated in agriculture, $3.0 billion in construction, and $12.4 billion in wholesale and retail trade. Each of these sectors, perhaps in descending order of importance, requires equity investment by the entrepreneur, and entrepreneurial income, as is well known, is only partly a return for personal services. In the material which follows, no estimate has been made of the portion of the $38 billion earned by unincorporated enterprises which is a return for personal services by the entrepreneur. The entire amount of income of unincorporated enterprises is included in the total of net entrepreneurial income.

Applications of Data on Produced Income

Data on produced income by state and region are highly useful for analysis of returns to productive factors. As a first approximation, we may regard the split between compensation of employees and net entrepreneurial income as representing the division between returns to labor and to capital in a two-factor analysis of production and distribution. This provides a view of the regional economy which appears useful to analyze regional differences in factor returns as well as the growth and decay of geographic areas. For we have at our disposal a means of interpreting capital accumulation, the growth of wages, and changes in the capital intensity of different sectors of the region's economy. The following applications come to mind:

1. Hanna has analyzed regional differences in wages and salaries per worker.[4] He finds that such differences may be explained partly by the regional composition of occupations and industries and partly by differences in earnings per worker in the same occupation and industry. Each of these influences is itself partly dependent upon the amount of capital employed and is explained by influences which also affect the return to capital. Perloff found that interindustry differentials in wages per worker are dependent upon the value added per worker which is in excess of the wages and salaries.[5]

Stein and Muth have analyzed regional differentials in wages per worker in specific industries in terms of differentials in the ratio of value added minus wages and salaries to the number of workers.[6] In these cases the explanatory variable (value added minus wages and salaries) is a gross measure of entrepreneurial income. It will play an important role in the estimation procedures discussed below.

2. Regional differences in the growth of wages and salaries per worker may be regarded as partly due to differences in the growth of the amount of capital employed per worker (thus affecting the marginal physical productivity of labor) and partly due to differences in the change of the prices of goods produced in each region.[7] Each of these characteristics is in turn an influence on the income produced by capital employed in the region, and may be inferred from a knowledge of the net entrepreneurial income in the region. Thus, knowledge of the income produced by capital and labor and of changes in these components is an important part of the analysis of regional differentials and regional growth.

[4] For an analysis of the influence of occupational and industrial composition on regional earnings differentials, see Frank A. Hanna, "Analysis of Income Differentials: Theory and Practice," in *Regional Income.*

[5] Harvey S. Perloff, "Interrelations of State Income and Industrial Structure," *Review of Economics and Statistics*, May 1957, pp. 162–171.

[6] See Jerome L. Stein, "The Productive Accuracy of the Marginal Productivity Theory of Wages," *Review of Economic Studies,* June 1958. Also see H. S. Perloff, E. S. Dunn, Jr., E. E. Lampard, R. F. Muth, *Regions, Resources and Economic Growth*, Baltimore, 1960, pp. 572–588.

[7] See my paper, "The Equalization of Returns and Regional Economic Growth," *American Economic Review,* June 1960, pp. 319–347. Also, see Muth *et al., Regions, Resources.*

3. Still another application has been suggested by Paul Studenski. Knowledge of produced income may be used to evaluate the fiscal capacity of individual regions. This application is explained in his remarks below. A statistical study which explores this use of the data has been completed recently by Mushkin and Rivlin.[8]

Procedures of Estimation

The following procedure was used to estimate net entrepreneurial income in states and regions:

1. The national economy was divided into nine major sectors which originate all of the net entrepreneurial income domestically produced. These are: agriculture; mining; contract construction; manufacturing; wholesale and retail trade; finance, insurance, and real estate; transportation; communications and public utilities; and services. For each sector, a national control total is developed which yields the sector's total net entrepreneurial income generated.

2. Each of the nine sectors is divided into forty-eight state components. It is, of course, impossible on the basis of published data to make a direct allocation of a sector's net entrepreneurial income to each state. Instead, data sources for each sector were examined to find an indicator of net entrepreneurial income. These indicators were then adjusted to the national control totals.

This procedure might appear at first glance to yield imprecise results. In practice, the data sources were frequently available in sufficient detail to allow very good estimates. This was particularly true for those sectors for which federal censuses were available on a statewide breakdown, such that a value added figure might be derived for the sector in each state. Under these circumstances, wages and salaries were deducted from value added to provide a measure of gross entrepreneurial income. The gross entrepreneurial income must be reduced to yield the national control total. The measures employed are described in Appendix B. The concept of value added used in federal censuses is, of course, a grosser magnitude than that employed in national income ac-

[8] Selma Mushkin and Alice Rivlin, *Fiscal Capacity and Tax Effort*, Staff Report of the Advisory Commission on Intergovernmental Relations, Washington, 1962. This study carries out a state allocation of income reported for federal corporate income tax purposes. The authors use a multiple regression between corporate income subject to state taxation and the factors used in state allocation formulas. The most common factors used are: wages and salaries, sales at origin and destination, and the value of property.

counting. The major differences involve the treatment of supplements to wages and salaries, inventory accumulation, capital consumption charges, business transfer payments, indirect business taxes, and the purchase of business services. All of these are included in the Census concept and excluded from the national income concept. To give some idea of the distinction, the Bureau of the Census reported value added minus wages and salaries in manufacturing at $53.9 billion in 1954, while the National Income Division reported national income originating minus wages and salaries as $25 billion.

3. The national control totals employed in this study are larger than those shown by the National Income Division (NID). An adjustment was made, which substantially increased the interest income originating in each sector, because the treatment of interest income in national income accounting was not considered to be the most appropriate for use in regional accounts.

Appendix A shows in detail how and why the adjustments were carried out. Stated briefly, we wished to eliminate the distinction made in current practice between interest payments as a business service and as a final factor return. Accordingly, interest income has been adjusted upward by the amount of interest which NID imputes as a receipt to the business sector. The increases are $1,081 million for 1929 and $2,096 million for 1953. These increments represent 16.8 and 24.8 per cent of the original total interest income for the respective years.

The national control totals and their components are shown by sector in Tables 1 and 2 below.

4. The allocation of sectoral income to the different states was determined by the availability of published information. In Appendix B there is a full description of the allocation method and the underlying data sources. I shall only indicate here the degree of reliability which can be placed on these data on the basis of the sources and methods employed.

For 1929:

A. Census data were employed to provide an estimate by state of gross entrepreneurial income (i.e., Census value added minus wages and salaries) for the mining, manufacturing, and construction sectors. These were reduced to net entrepreneurial income in two stages. Data from the *Source Books* of the Internal Revenue Service (IRS) provided estimates of the ratio of net to gross

TABLE 1
INCOME ORIGINATING BY SECTOR, 1929
(million dollars)

	Agri-culture	Mining	Manufac-turing	Construc-tion	Transport and Public Utilities	Trade	Services	Finance	Total
National income	8,390	2,084	22,233	3,830	9,670	13,455	10,485	12,845	
Compensation of employees	1,706	1,539	16,243	2,540	6,362	9,374	5,538	2,989	
Net entrepreneurial income	6,984	545	5,990	1,290	3,308	4,081	4,947	9,856	37,001
Corporate profits before taxes	6	417	4,848	119	1,945	759	145	1,157	9,396
Rental income	—	—	—	—	—	—	—	5,425	5,425
Income of unincorporated enterprises	6,033	54	565	1,127	229	2,867	2,980	762	14,617
Inventory valuation adjustment	—	6	313	6	11	278	—	—	614
Net interest	945	68	264	38	1,123	177	1,822	2,512	6,949

TABLE 2
INCOME ORIGINATING BY SECTOR, 1953
(million dollars)

	Agri-culture	Mining	Manufac-turing	Construc-tion	Transport and Public Utilities	Trade	Services	Finance	Total
National income	17,013	5,551	98,317	15,237	26,326	52,580	29,027	26,679	
Compensation of employees	3,457	4,074	75,052	11,637	19,196	35,055	17,747	7,955	
Net entrepreneurial income	13,556	1,477	23,265	3,600	7,130	17,525	11,280	18,724	96,557
Corporate profits before taxes	74	1,254	21,798	550	5,266	5,156	613	3,572	38,283
Rental income	—	—	—	—	—	—	—	10,596	10,596
Income of unincorporated enterprises	12,560	207	1,172	2,984	828	12,391	7,418	1,079	38,639
Inventory valuation adjustment	—	−44	−625	−16	−66	−408	—	—	−1,159
Net interest	922	60	920	82	1,102	386	3,249	3,477	10,198

entrepreneurial income. After the application of these ratios, the state distributions were adjusted to the national control totals.

B. The IRS *Source Books* were used directly to provide estimates of NEI for public utilities and communications and for certain portions of the finance sector.

C. Census data were used to derive estimates of net sales and salaries and wages in wholesale and retail trade. The IRS *Source Book* was used to estimate the net entrepreneurial income as a proportion of these magnitudes.

D. Publications of the Interstate Commerce Commission provided data on the transport sector.

E. Arbitrary allocations were employed in the case of agriculture, services, and the rental income and interest components of the finance sector.

In general, the most reliable state distributions are those provided by Census data, by ICC data, and for agriculture which was distributed according to a measure of farm proprietors' income.

For 1953:

A. Census data were employed to provide an estimate of gross entrepreneurial income for mining and manufacturing. The reduction to a net basis was carried out much the same as for the earlier date.

B. Publications of the Interstate Commerce Commission, the Federal Power Commission, and the Federal Communications Commission were used to estimate net entrepreneurial income for the transport and public utility sector.

C. Census data were used to estimate the value of sales for wholesale and retail trade. The reduction to net entrepreneurial income was carried out by ratios derived from the IRS *Source Book*.

D. The IRS *Source Books* were used to provide estimates of net entrepreneurial income for a portion of the finance sector.

E. Arbitrary allocations were employed for agriculture, construction, services, and the rental income and interest components of the finance sector.

Again the most reliable distributions are those provided by Census sources, by the ICC, FCC, and FPC data, and for agriculture.

Comparisons of Produced and Received Income

Table 3 shows the computed estimates of net entrepreneurial income by state for 1929 and 1953. To provide a comparison, the

TABLE 3
NET ENTREPRENEURIAL INCOME BY STATE AND REGION ON A PRODUCED AND A RECEIVED BASIS, 1929 AND 1953
(million dollars)

	1929			*1953*		
States	Produced NEI	Received NEI	Ratio of Received to Produced (per cent)	Produced NEI	Received NEI	Ratio of Received to Produced (per cent)
New England	2,433.5	3,157.0	129.73	5,276.1	7,036.2	133.36
Maine	201.2	224.8	111.73	427.9	482.9	112.85
N.H.	108.9	129.5	118.92	265.9	363.6	136.76
Vt.	96.5	100.3	103.94	169.2	217.9	128.76
Mass.	1,301.6	1,729.6	132.88	2,661.9	3,471.6	130.42
R.I.	169.6	243.4	143.51	391.9	528.1	134.74
Conn.	555.7	729.4	131.26	1,359.2	1,972.1	145.09
Middle East	10,143.2	12,560.5	123.83	23,613.7	25,354.9	107.37
N.Y.	5,688.4	7,132.4	125.38	12,211.6	13,129.6	107.52
N.J.	1,356.2	1,498.2	110.47	3,553.5	3,544.6	99.75
Pa.	2,483.5	3,138.8	126.39	6,106.5	6,479.0	106.10
Del.	176.9	160.5	90.73	285.8	511.0	178.81
Md.	438.2	630.6	143.91	1,456.3	1,690.7	116.09
Great Lakes	8,250.4	8,078.1	97.91	22,653.3	19,961.2	88.12
Mich.	1,565.2	1,541.0	98.45	4,744.3	3,814.4	80.40
Ohio	2,049.8	1,962.8	95.76	5,786.7	5,106.4	88.24
Ind.	944.5	727.8	77.06	3,007.4	2,243.6	74.60
Ill.	2,893.3	2,967.1	102.55	6,942.0	6,548.6	94.33
Wis.	797.6	879.4	110.26	2,173.0	2,248.2	103.46
Plains	4,280.1	3,669.7	85.74	9,257.3	9,332.3	100.81
Minn.	810.8	695.8	85.82	1,905.3	1,997.2	104.82
Iowa	865.9	760.0	87.77	1,897.7	1,852.9	97.64
Mo.	1,109.5	982.8	88.58	2,422.8	2,690.6	111.05
N.Dak.	157.8	114.0	72.24	372.0	331.2	89.02
S.Dak.	215.9	168.1	77.86	455.0	425.0	93.40
Nebr.	543.8	456.4	83.93	930.2	909.0	97.72
Kans.	576.4	492.6	85.46	1,274.3	1,126.4	88.40
Southeast	5,597.2	4,709.5	84.14	15,905.9	14,657.1	92.15
Va.	544.5	463.1	85.05	1,583.4	1,452.9	91.76
W.Va.	345.8	269.0	77.79	881.8	622.8	70.63
Ky.	528.2	508.3	96.23	1,340.5	1,235.8	92.19
Tenn.	585.2	461.8	78.91	1,504.7	1,290.8	85.78
N.C.	690.3	506.2	73.33	1,950.6	1,718.7	88.11
S.C.	327.7	210.2	64.14	853.6	777.8	91.11
Ga.	543.2	465.8	85.75	1,667.0	1,491.3	89.46
Fla.	281.2	364.3	129.55	1,667.1	2,376.6	142.56
Ala.	454.0	390.5	86.01	1,316.4	999.9	75.96
Miss.	432.1	357.2	82.67	911.2	778.4	85.42
La.	463.0	403.9	87.24	1,419.6	1,190.1	83.83
Ark.	402.0	309.2	76.92	809.8	722.0	89.16

(continued)

TABLE 3 (concluded)

States	1929 Produced NEI	1929 Received NEI	1929 Ratio of Received to Produced (per cent)	1953 Produced NEI	1953 Received NEI	1953 Ratio of Received to Produced (per cent)
Southwest	2,526.3	2,065.1	81.74	7,151.2	6,593.7	92.20
Okla.	610.6	510.8	83.66	1,128.5	1,167.7	103.47
Tex.	1,674.6	1,376.0	82.17	5,115.6	4,550.6	88.96
N.Mex.	111.0	82.1	73.96	368.3	325.2	88.30
Ariz.	130.1	96.2	73.94	538.9	550.2	102.10
Rocky Mountain	763.9	662.5	86.73	2,256.7	2,284.1	101.21
Mont.	138.9	103.3	74.37	452.6	456.8	100.92
Idaho	128.7	103.1	80.11	369.0	339.6	92.04
Wyo.	75.5	56.0	74.17	233.7	181.1	77.48
Colo.	285.9	284.8	99.62	826.7	959.6	116.07
Utah	134.9	115.3	85.47	374.7	347.0	92.61
Far West	2,980.5	3,427.3	114.99	10,433.6	12,381.7	118.67
Wash.	443.5	451.1	101.71	1,437.9	1,538.5	107.00
Ore.	262.1	258.4	98.59	958.0	1,065.5	108.17
Nev.	36.5	28.0	76.71	182.3	168.2	92.22
Calif.	2,238.4	2,689.8	120.17	7,828.3	9,609.5	122.75

national net entrepreneurial income is also shown distributed on a received basis. The latter figure has been prepared by expanding the received income by state as shown in *Personal Income by States since 1929.*[9]

On a state-by-state basis, substantial differences appear between produced and received net entrepreneurial income. For 1929, the received exceeds the produced by as much as 43 per cent (Rhode Island) and falls short of it by as much as 28 per cent (North Dakota). For 1953, received exceeds produced by as much as 45 per cent (Connecticut) and falls short of it by as much as 30 per cent (West Virginia).

[9] The personal income concept includes property income and proprietors' income. These have been adjusted as follows: (1) the receipt of government interest has been eliminated; (2) dividends received have been increased proportionally so that the total now includes undistributed corporate profits, corporate inventory valuation adjustment, and corporate profit tax liability; and (3) imputed interest received now includes the adjustment to total interest income described in Appendix A.

The national total of net entrepreneurial income received is slightly larger than the produced figure because the former still includes income originating in the rest-of-the-world sector. This amounted to $809 million in 1929 and $1,480 million in 1953.

It is important to point out that there is a considerable degree of stability over time among the states in this regard. There were twenty-five states where produced exceeded received in both years, and thirteen states where produced fell short of received in both years.

The above comparisons are very close to the results which Easterlin achieved for 1920. He computed produced income in a different fashion from the one employed in this study. Indeed, his method cannot be used for later years because it relied upon data which are no longer collected. His method allocates property income to states and regions on the basis of the value of property. The data are found in the *Census of Wealth* which was discontinued.[10] Table 4 permits a comparison between Easterlin's data and the results of Table 3. It shows the excesses

TABLE 4
EXCESS OF INCOME RECEIVED OVER INCOME PRODUCED FOR CENSUS REGIONS, 1920, 1929, 1953
(per cent)

Region	1920	1929	1953
New England	4	10.4	9.3
Middle Atlantic	5	8.8	2.3
East North Central	−1	−5.8	−3.7
West North Central	−7	−7.5	+0.3
South Atlantic	−6	−4.8	−0.6
East South Central	−5	−8.0	−5.5
West South Central	1	−9.3	−3.6
Mountain	−7	−7.0	−0.1
Pacific	2	6.2	5.6
Average absolute percentage differences	4.2	7.5	3.4

and shortfalls between produced and received total income for 1920 and for the two subsequent years in this study. The transition from net entrepreneurial income in the previous tables to total income below is made simply by adding the compensation of employees on a where-worked basis. Accordingly, the only difference between produced and received total income in my data arise from differences between produced and received NEI. Note that the geographic distribution used below is the Census distribution and not the one employed in the above table. The change was made to conform to Easterlin's computations. With the excep-

[10] See Easterlin's comments on Hochwald's Paper in *Regional Income,* p. 28.

tion of the West South Central region, there is a very close correspondence between the behavior of the regions in 1920 and 1929. However, the measurement of produced income in this study seems to yield greater variance. This probably arises from Easterlin's assumption of regionally uniform rates of return on capital. In the present study, as described above, the return to capital is allowed to vary from two causes: variations in gross value added as reported by the census, and variations in the ratio of net to gross value added as estimated from the IRS *Source Book* data.

There are a number of notable differences between behavior in 1953 and the prior years. For one thing, the variance has apparently narrowed, as seen by the decline of the average absolute difference to a level below the other two. In addition, three regions have changed position very markedly, indicating an increase in received relative to produced income. These are the West North Central Region, the South Atlantic Region, and the Mountain Region. This change appears to be part of a pattern under which received income is becoming distributed more equally over time. This will be discussed below.

Table 4 might lead one to think that at present there is not too much difference between produced and received income, that it is not worth worrying about the produced concept when we have the received data readily at hand. However, the small differences shown actually mask much larger percentage differences in the components. Adding the compensation of employees to both numerator and denominator has reduced the apparent difference. Returning to net entrepreneurial income, we see the distribution of differences shown in Table 5.

While there is again a reduction over time in the average absolute magnitude of the differences, it is not as dramatic as the reduction shown previously. The reason is a decline in the relative importance of net entrepreneurial income as a proportion of national income. In 1929, net entrepreneurial income was 41.8 per cent of national income; in 1953, this ratio had declined to 31.4 per cent.

While there are sharp differences between produced and received NEI, it is conceivable that these are nevertheless not large enough to change the relative position of regions with regard to the importance of NEI in the states' income pattern. In fact, this is not borne out by an examination of the data. This will be

TABLE 5
EXCESS OF RECEIVED OVER PRODUCED NET ENTREPRENEURIAL INCOME FOR CENSUS REGIONS, 1929, 1953
(per cent)

Region	1929	1953
New England	23.7	33.4
Middle Atlantic	20.7	7.4
East North Central	−3.2	−11.8
West North Central	−16.9	+0.8
South Atlantic	−6.2	−2.9
East South Central	−14.1	−15.1
West South Central	−17.5	−9.8
Mountain	−20.2	−0.3
Pacific	+6.8	+19.1
Average absolute percentage differences	14.4	11.2

discussed below when we consider the effect of these differences on the distribution of income.

The Distribution of Income

A quick picture of the influence of produced entrepreneurial income on the distribution of income is revealed by the following tabulation. We have computed the per capita received income of all states in 1929 and 1953. We then divide the states into two groups: those where produced income exceeds received income, and the converse case. We may then examine the difference in the mean income of the two groups, as shown in the following tabulation:

	1929 No. of States	*Simple Mean Received Income Per Capita (dollars)*	*Weighted Mean (dollars)*	*1953 No. of States*	*Simple Mean Received Income Per Capita (dollars)*	*Weighted Mean (dollars)*
Produced exceeds received	33	666	532	25	1537	1677
Received exceeds produced	15	943	973	23	2003	2131

We see that where produced income exceeds received, the mean received income is lower than average. It is clear that, in both periods, produced income is more equally distributed per capita than received income. This suggests that the inequality in received income per capita overstates differences among states in the per capita value of their output. It also suggests the possibility that the returns to labor are less equally distributed among states than the produced returns to capital.

TABLE 6
ANALYSIS OF THE DISTRIBUTION OF COMPONENTS OF STATE INCOME PAYMENTS, 1929 AND 1953

	1929		*1953*	
	Mean (dollars)	Coefficient of Variation	Mean (dollars)	Coefficient of Variation
Income per capita				
Produced	659	.3370	1735	.2409
Received	639	.3829	1759	.2752
Income per employee				
Produced	1778	.3049	4823	.1831
Received	1724	.3340	4853	.2107
Nonagricultural income per employee				
Produced	2103	.2000	5500	.1073
Received	1963	.2682	5520	.1330
Nonagricultural NEI per employee				
Produced	839	.3037	1632	.1335
Received	695	.4660	1651	.2544
Nonagricultural wages and salaries per employee	1266	.2449	3461	.1196
Nonagricultural produced NEI per private employee	—	—	1942	.1484
Private nonagricultural wages and salaries per private employee	—	—	3496	.1234

In order to analyze this further, we must examine the characteristics of the various components of state income payments. In the following table the means are unweighted, and the coefficient of variation represents the ratio of the unweighted standard deviation to the unweighted mean. Each of the components will be examined in turn, and are shown in Table 6.

INCOME PER CAPITA

This is simply the ratio of total income payments to total population in the state, including members of the armed forces. For both years, it is clear that produced per capita income is more equally distributed than received, the coefficient of variation for produced income being 12 per cent less (1 — .3370/.3829) in 1929 and 12.5 per cent less in 1953. It is also clear that both produced and received income have become more equally distributed over time, the coefficient for produced declining by 29 per cent, and that for received declining by 28 per cent.

In order to assess further the differences between the distribution of produced and received income, it is necessary to eliminate influences which account for some of their variation. Accordingly we have computed the next component.

INCOME PER EMPLOYEE

This is the ratio of total income payments to total employment in each state.[11] We see that the change from a per capita to a per employee basis reduces the variation. This is to be expected from the work carried out by Hanna.[12] It is explained by the variation in labor force participation among states and the relatively high proportion of the population out of the labor force in low income states. Having eliminated this influence, the previous patterns emerge with equal or greater force. The coefficient of variation for produced income is 9 per cent less in 1929, and 13 per cent less in 1953, than the coefficient for received income. Further, the coefficient for produced income now declines by 40 per cent from 1929 to 1953, while that for received income declines by 37 per cent.

NONAGRICULTURAL INCOME PER EMPLOYEE

A further refinement in the distribution is produced by focusing on nonagricultural income per employee. Because produced in-

[11] Total employment for 1929 was taken from the *Census of Population*, which includes full- and part-time workers, as well as the self-employed. The employment data are corrected by estimation to eliminate the self-employed, by eliminating nonagricultural occupational categories in which the self-employed predominate. The self-employed in agriculture are not eliminated. Total employment for 1953 was taken from two sources: nonagricultural employment was derived from the *Monthly Labor Review*, 1956; agricultural employment was derived from *Agricultural Statistics, 1954*, U.S. Department of Agriculture, Washington, 1955. It should be noted that there are two discrepancies between the two definitions of employment. First, the Census definition for 1929 includes military employment, the nonagricultural employment definition for 1953 does not. Thus there is a source of variation in the 1953 income per employee and nonagricultural income per employee which is not removed until we reach wages and salaries per nonagricultural employee. For the 1953 wages and salaries are defined exclusive of military payrolls. Second, nonagricultural employment excludes the self-employed, while they are included in agricultural employment.

[12] Frank A. Hanna, "Age, Labor Force and State Per Capita Incomes," *Review of Economics and Statistics*, February 1955, pp. 63–69.

come per worker is lower in agriculture than in almost any other sector, the elimination of this element should reduce the variation in the distribution of the remainder; it will bring out more clearly the difference between produced and received property income in the nonagricultural sphere.[13]

Produced nonagricultural income is obtained by subtracting from total produced income compensation of employees and NEI in agriculture. Received nonagricultural income is obtained by subtracting from total received income compensation of employees and income of proprietors in agriculture. No adjustment has been made to either series to subtract the farm realty component of the net rental income of persons. This remains in the estimate of nonagricultural income, although ideally, if a state distribution were available, it could be removed.

As expected, the distribution of nonagricultural income per employee is more equal than the distribution of total income per employee. The removal of the agricultural sector brings out very clearly the greater equality in the distribution of produced income as well as the equalization over time in the distribution of produced and received income. The coefficient of variation of produced income is 25 per cent less in 1929, and 19 per cent less in 1953 than the coefficient for received income. The coefficient of variation for produced income declines by 46 per cent between 1929 and 1953, while the coefficient for received declines by 50 per cent.

NONAGRICULTURAL NEI PER EMPLOYEE

The two major components of nonagricultural income per employee may now be examined, the first of which is nonagricultural NEI per employee. We see that here produced NEI is more equally distributed than received NEI. Further, the greatest difference appears for the later date. The coefficient of variation of produced NEI is 35 per cent less in 1929, and 48 per cent less in 1953, than the coefficient for received NEI. As before, there are marked increases in the equality of distribution between 1929 and 1953. The coefficient of variation of produced NEI declines by 56 per cent, while that for received NEI declines by 46 per cent. For the second date, there is also shown a coefficient of variation for produced nonagricultural NEI per private employee. This is

[13] In 1929, total national income per employee was $1,807; in agriculture, it was $790. In 1953 total national income per employee was $5,243; in agriculture, it was $1,960.

the ratio of NEI to the number of nongovernment nonagricultural workers in each state. The purpose of making this computation is to provide a more direct comparison between NEI, which in fact comes out of the private sector, and the number of each state's employees in the private sector. This calculation was not carried out for 1929 because the census data are less reliable in identifying the number of government employees in each state. Government employment accounted for 10 per cent of the national total of compensation of employees in 1929, and if reliable data were at hand, it would be useful to make the calculation for the prior year. The nonagricultural NEI per private employee shows greater variation. The coefficient of variation is 11 per cent higher than for nonagricultural NEI per employee. It is not immediately clear why the presence of a large percentage of government employees should be associated with higher than average levels of NEI per private employee. For this is what is implied when the removal of government employees increases the variation of the second series. A possible explanation for this is the fact that government employees generate private NEI through their purchases from the private sector. This would be particularly true if their purchases generated NEI in those sectors where there is no obvious production function restraint which might yield a predetermined range of ratios of NEI to employment. For example, the presence of government employees would generate interest and rental payments on housing which could show up as a higher NEI per private employee. Whatever the explanation for the difference, however, the fact remains that the variation in produced NEI has declined over time, whichever way we choose to measure employment.

While it is true that produced NEI is distributed among states differently from received NEI, the possibility remains that these differences are too small to affect the relative position of the states with regard to the amount of NEI generated. In fact, however, this possibility is not borne out by the data. We have computed the produced and received nonagricultural NEI per employee for the two dates in Table 7. There is a substantial difference in the relative position of the regions under the produced and received NEI concepts. If we rank the regions by NEI per employee, then we obtain correlation coefficients of +.29 for both 1929 and 1953 between produced and received series; these low values indicate

TABLE 7
PRODUCED AND RECEIVED NONAGRICULTURAL NEI
PER EMPLOYEE, 1929 AND 1953
(dollars)

Region	*1929* *NEI Per Employee* Produced	Received	*1953* *NEI Per Employee* Produced	Received
New England	715	883	1,411	1,909
Middle East	1,149	1,289	1,807	1,944
Great Lakes	861	804	1,754	1,517
Plains	962	576	1,616	1,651
Southeast	662	427	1,504	1,358
Southwest	898	555	1,874	1,704
Rocky Mountain	840	578	1,637	1,673
Far West	874	837	1,734	2,117

the degree to which relative position alters under the two definitions.

NONAGRICULTURAL WAGES AND SALARIES PER EMPLOYEE

The variation in nonagricultural wages and salaries per employee has also declined over time, there being a decline of 51 per cent in its coefficient of variation. This decline becomes 50 per cent if we compute wages and salaries per private employee for the second date in the same manner described above.

It should be noted that the nonagricultural wages and salaries per total employee exclude military payrolls and employment for the second date, but not the first.

It is now possible to compare the equality of distribution of returns to labor (wages and salaries) and to capital (NEI) on a per worker basis. It appears that wages and salaries are distributed more equally than NEI on a per worker basis, although this difference has narrowed considerably. The coefficient of variation of wages and salaries is 19 per cent less in 1929, and 10 per cent less in 1953, than the coefficient for produced NEI. What this means is that the distribution of NEI and wages and salaries has over time come to share approximately the same degree of inequality. However, the above comparisons do not tell us whether the distribution of NEI reinforces or counteracts the inequality of wage income. If the two series were negatively correlated, we could see that inequality in the one series would offset inequality in the other to produce a more equal distribution of income than either series possessed by itself.

In order to investigate this interaction between the two components, it is necessary to examine first the behavior of the shares of national income going into NEI and wages and salaries. We shall then examine the possibility that positive correlation between the two components reinforces the degree of inequality in the distribution of state income.

Income Shares Within Regions

While it is true that the inequality in the distribution of wages and salaries and NEI has declined over time, we do not yet know whether the share of income going to these sectors has altered

TABLE 8
RATIO OF NEI TO WAGES AND SALARIES, 1929 AND 1953

	1929		*1953*	
Region	Ratio of NEI to Wages and Salaries	Deviations from U.S. Ratio (per cent)	Ratio of NEI to Wages and Salaries	Deviations from U.S. Ratio (per cent)
New England	.5323	−19.5	.4513	−8.7
Middle East	.6113	−7.5	.5242	0.6
Great Lakes	.5589	−15.5	.4748	−8.9
Plains	.7335	+10.9	.5517	5.9
Southeast	.6627	+0.2	.5819	11.6
Southwest	.8194	+23.9	.6503	24.7
Rocky Mountain	.6128	−7.3	.5814	11.6
Far West	.6345	−4.0	.5007	−3.9
U.S.	.6611		.5212	
Average of absolute differences		11.1		9.5

among regions. If the inequality in NEI per worker and in wages and salaries per worker were eliminated entirely, then income shares would be equalized. In view of the reduction in inequality, what effect has there been on income shares? The ratio of NEI to wages and salaries may be seen in Table 8. The numerator is the nonagricultural produced NEI; the denominator is the wages and salaries in the private nonagricultural sector. It can be seen that there is a pattern of distribution of this ratio which has not really altered between the two years. Ranking the two sets of ratios and computing a rank correlation yields a coefficient of +.83. While it is true that the differences from the U.S. average ratio have narrowed over time, they still remain roughly unchanged in the two periods. There appears to be a contradiction between these findings and the earlier results that the distribution of NEI and wages and salaries had both become more equal over time. What must have happened is that the equalization process we have described is an intraregional equalization which has narrowed the extremes of the income distributions. While there is also an interregional equalization process going on, it is not going rapidly enough to equalize the share distribution of wages and salaries and NEI among regions.[14] The preceding remarks are not concerned with whether in fact complete equalization is possible; this will be discussed later in the paper.

The next question is whether the inequality in the distribution of NEI exaggerates or cuts down the inequality in state income produced by wages and salaries. This may be seen through the correlations which have been computed between the two series. Simple regressions have been fitted by least squares between NEI per worker and wages and salaries per worker. The samples of observations consist of the two series in 1929 and 1953. The following regression lines are found:

1929

$$\underset{\text{per employee}}{\text{Nonagricultural NEI}} = \underset{(.1141)}{.3342} \times \begin{bmatrix} \text{nonagricultural wages} \\ \text{and salaries per} \\ \text{employee} \end{bmatrix} + \$378$$

$$r = .3931$$

1953

$$\underset{\text{per employee}}{\text{Nonagricultural NEI}} = \underset{(.0203)}{.2890} \times \begin{bmatrix} \text{nonagricultural wages} \\ \text{and salaries per} \\ \text{employee} \end{bmatrix} + \$632$$

$$r = .5488$$

[14] Evidence of this may be seen in that the lowest and highest produced nonagricultural NEI per employee in 1929 and 1953 were the following:

		1929	*Ratio L/H*	*1953*	*Ratio L/H*
Among states:	Low	$ 514	.229	$1181	.593
	High	2241		1993	
Among regions:	Low	662	.576	1411	.753
	High	1149		1874	

Similar results hold for wages and salaries per employee.

Written under the slope coefficient is the estimate of its standard error.

It can be seen that in each period there is a weak but significantly positive relation between NEI per employee and wages and salaries per employee. The correlation is stronger in the second period, although in the first period wages and salaries appear to have a more direct influence on NEI.[15] In the first period, an increase of one dollar in wages and salaries per employee is accompanied by an increase of 33 cents in NEI per employee. This compares with a sample average ratio in 1929 of 63 cents of NEI for every dollar of wages and salaries. For the second period, an increase of one dollar in wages and salaries per employee is accompanied by an increase of only 29 cents in NEI per employee, compared with a sample average ratio of 47 cents of NEI for every dollar of wages. These results indicate that the distribution of NEI does tend to increase the inequality of state income payments over that already produced by wages and salaries.

Growth of Income Components

We have now completed our analysis of the effects of produced entrepreneurial income on the distribution of income by state and region. However, there are further comparisons with received entrepreneurial income which might be made. While it is true that the distribution of the produced and received entities are dissimilar, the two series may be substitutes for each other in any analysis involving changes over time. In order to check this possibility, we compared the growth over time in the two series (Table 9). The growth is expressed as the ratio (in per cent) of the value at the later date to the value at the earlier date. Growth is computed for nonagricultural NEI, for nonagricultural NEI per employee, and for wages and salaries per employee. It can be seen that the growth of produced and received NEI has roughly the same pattern among regions. The received entity shows a

[15] If we eliminate government employment from the 1953 distributions, and take the regression of nonagricultural NEI per private employee on wages and salaries per private employee, we get a correlation coefficient of .3765 and a slope coefficient of .2514. The reduced correlation is due to the increased random dispersion of NEI per employee produced by eliminating government employment. Consequently, there is no reduction in the slope of the correlation. Because of the similar slopes and the higher correlation, it was decided to use the distribution including government employees for the regression described above.

TABLE 9
RATIOS OF PRODUCED AND RECEIVED NEI IN 1953 TO THAT IN 1929
(per cent)

Region	NEI Produced (1)	NEI Received (2)	NEI Per Employee Produced (3)	NEI Per Employee Received (4)	Wages and Salaries Per Employee (5)
New England	219.85	227.28	197.48	216.10	265.59
Middle East	235.48	204.02	157.32	150.80	265.55
Great Lakes	286.14	261.18	203.83	188.80	264.06
Plains	231.24	337.46	168.07	286.43	289.87
Southeast	350.16	475.39	227.16	317.96	346.37
Southwest	344.24	464.54	208.76	307.25	317.85
Rocky Mountain	305.35	410.50	195.00	289.35	265.92
Far West	357.24	378.44	198.44	252.84	314.41

higher rate of growth in the regions outside of the Northeast, undoubtedly because of the low levels of received income in these other regions in 1929. Nevertheless the relative position of the regions is roughly unaltered. If we rank the first two columns and compute a correlation coefficient, we obtain a value of +.74. The same conclusion holds when NEI is expressed per employee and the growth rates compared. We see again a much wider dispersion of growth rates of received NEI per employee. Nevertheless, the regional patterns are similar insofar as the relative position of each region is concerned. Ranking columns 3 and 4, we obtain a correlation of +.57. If we compare the growth of NEI per employee with the growth of wages and salaries per employee, both the produced and the received concepts appear related to the wage growth. The rank correlation between the growth of wages per employee (column 5) and the growth of produced NEI per employee is .55. The rank correlation between the growth of wages per employee and the growth of received NEI per employee is +.88.

Thus we see that the produced and received NEI, while differently distributed, bear the same relation to each other over time. This brings out a point mentioned at the beginning of this paper. For some purposes, the received NEI concept, which is readily available from NID publications, may serve as a proxy for the produced NEI variable. We now see that these purposes consist of measurements of relative change among regions over long periods of time. However, we have also seen that at any moment of time, the produced and received entities are not alike.

Structure of Regions

Attention will now be turned to the structure of the different regions. We wish to know the relation between the level and changes in produced NEI and the composition of regional activities. This question will be examined in two parts. In the first, we shall identify the rapidly and the slowly growing sectors in each region. In the second, we shall examine the relation at a point in time between NEI and the sectoral structure of the region.

REGIONAL SECTORS

Table 10 shows the growth of produced NEI in each regional sector. The growth is computed as the ratio of NEI in the later period to that in the earlier, expressed as a per cent. Marginal totals permit a comparison with the over-all growth in the region, on the one hand, and with the over-all growth of the national sector, on the other.

As an aid to interpreting these changes, it is useful to consider first the following hypothetical patterns of growth among the regions.

1. Each sector of a region grows at the same rate as its national counterpart. Under these circumstances, the region's growth is determined by the nature of the sectors it contains at the beginning of the period. A region containing a large share of sectors which grow rapidly at the national level will itself grow rapidly, and so on.

2. The sectoral composition of the region remains at the end of the period the same as at the beginning. This means that each sector grows at the regional average, and the growth of the region is completely unrelated to the types of sectors it contains initially.

Neither of these hypothetical patterns describes or even approximates what actually happened. The growth of each region was not dominated by industrial composition acting as a weighting mechanism for national growth patterns. This was determined by computing the growth rate of NEI which each region would enjoy were each sector to grow at the national rate. When these hypothetical regional growth rates were compared with the actual

TABLE 10
GROWTH RATES OF PRODUCED NEI, BY REGION AND SECTOR, 1929–53

	Agri-culture	Mining	Manufac-turing	Construc-tion	Trans. and Public Util.	Trade	Services	Finance	Total	Total Nonagri-cultural
New England	172.44	100.00	274.74	176.84	117.11	401.14	169.23	181.82	213.86	219.85
Middle East	178.01	86.15	297.06	187.04	199.56	381.24	197.20	187.95	231.18	235.48
Great Lakes	208.52	174.00	425.73	242.63	234.02	483.48	213.40	165.76	280.81	286.14
Plains	189.85	145.83	325.50	296.26	184.36	300.91	198.18	169.65	215.03	231.24
Southeast	173.44	372.60	468.76	456.10	274.59	483.17	290.71	244.77	282.86	350.16
Southwest	155.21	323.76	1054.50	707.94	216.07	363.38	298.98	225.12	283.54	344.24
Rocky Mountain	277.48	290.32	329.75	522.22	270.00	427.37	279.38	217.39	293.88	305.35
Far West	311.73	435.42	637.62	349.54	218.82	688.26	309.92	201.81	347.45	357.24
United States	194.05	271.01	388.40	279.07	215.54	429.43	229.55	189.98	261.18	276.82

growth rates, it appeared that the assumption could not be sustained.[16]

It is also clear from the examination of Table 10, that the sectors of each region are not growing at uniform rates within the region, and that the sectoral composition of the regions are apparently undergoing a uniform pattern of change.

If we look at the fastest growing sectors in each region a small group of sectors is identified. These are manufacturing, construction, and trade—all growing at the national level more rapidly than the average of all sectors. Out of twenty-four (eight regions and three sectors) possible cases, these sectors are growing more rapidly than the regional averages in twenty cases. Similarly we find that the slow-growing sectors in each region are agriculture, mining, transport and public utilities, and services and finance—all growing slowly at the national level. Out of forty possible cases, these sectors are growing less rapidly than the regional averages in thirty-eight cases. Thus all eight regions are changing internally, with a shift of composition toward the nationally growing sectors away from the declining sectors.

At the same time, the rate of this shift does not appear to be related to the rate of growth of the region. Within the four most rapidly growing regions, their thirty-two sectors are growing more rapidly than their national counterparts in twenty-seven cases; while within the four slowly growing regions, their thirty-two sectors are growing less rapidly than their national counterparts in twenty-seven cases. Thus the following pattern emerges: the rapidly growing national sectors are expanding in all regions relative to the slowly growing national sectors. At the same time, the rapidly growing sectors slow down sufficiently in certain slowly growing regions to offset their initially greater preponderance in these regions.

REGIONAL COMPOSITION AND SHARE DISTRIBUTION OF INCOME

At any moment in time the total produced NEI in a region may be thought of as influenced by four factors: (1) the composition of private activities requiring the use of capital; (2) the amount of capital invested in each activity; (3) the marginal physical product of capital; and (4) the prices of the products produced by capital.

[16] The hypothetical and actual growth rates of NEI for the eight regions were ranked, and a correlation coefficient of —.52 was computed. This indicates that regions with an initial preponderance of rapidly growing sectors in fact grew slower than regions with an initial dependence on slowly growing sectors.

We shall ignore any difficulties introduced by varying degrees of monopoly power, although they undoubtedly may influence the distribution of income. Approximately the same list of influences operates on wage payments in a region, except that we would list under (2) the amount of labor employed in each activity, and under (3) the marginal physical product of labor.

The object of analysis is to remove and isolate the effects of the above influences on the regional distribution of income. This is an important goal of inquiry in order to understand the meaning and consequences of the equalization process described above. We should like to know whether there is an economic process at work which will eventually eliminate all differences in income distribution among regions, and if not, what differences are likely to remain permanently. It seems clear, on theoretical grounds, that even if all differences were eliminated in wage payments per employee, and in NEI per unit of capital, the share of income going to wages and NEI would still vary among regions. The reason is that all regions are not likely to contain the same composition of activities. Some activities use more capital per worker than others even when they all face the same factor prices. Consequently, the regions with a heavy composition of capital-using sectors will produce more NEI per dollar of wages than other regions.

In order to produce evidence for or against this proposition, we have computed hypothetical values of produced NEI for each region in 1953. These hypothetical values were computed in two ways. First, it was assumed that each regional sector yields the same ratio of NEI to wages and salaries as the national sector. Second, it was assumed that each regional sector yields the same ratio of NEI per worker as the national sector.

We may compare the two hypothetical values by writing the following definitions: Within a given sector let NEI $\equiv C \times P \times MP_C$, where C is the physical quantity of capital, P the price of output, and MP_C the marginal physical productivity of capital. In addition, let wages and salaries $\equiv L \times P \times MP_L$, where L is the number of workers, P the price of output, and MP_L the marginal product of labor. The ratio of NEI to wages and salaries within sector j may then be written:

$$a_j: \qquad \frac{\text{NEI}}{\text{wages and salaries}} = \frac{C \times MP_C}{L \times MP_L}.$$

In addition, the NEI per worker within sector j may be written:

$$b_j: \qquad \frac{\text{NEI}}{\text{worker}} = \frac{C \times MP_C \times P}{L}$$

Assume for the moment that all regional components of the sector share the same production function, that production is carried on subject to constant returns to scale, and that each regional component faces the same factor and output prices. Then the a_j term would be identical among regions within sector j, and likewise the b_j term would be identical among regions within sector j. Assume, in addition, that wages and salaries per worker are the same among all sectors of a given region. Then the hypothetical NEI computed from the a_j terms would be the same as those computed from the b_j terms. Under these assumptions, the regions would differ in total NEI only through the composition of capital-using activities. Therefore, the hypothetical and actual NEI would be the same for each region.

In fact, these assumptions are not satisfied, as the following computations reveal. The tabulation below shows: (a) the produced NEI in each region; (b) the hypothetical NEI based on the assumption of uniformity in the ratio of NEI to wages; and (c) the hypothetical NEI based on the assumption of uniformity in the ratio of NEI per worker. All three concepts are expressed in dollars per private nonagricultural employee. For comparison, column (d) shows the region's nonagricultural wages and salaries per private employee. In comparing columns (a), (b), and (c), bear in mind that they are formed from common sets of weights for each region.

	(a)	(b)	(c)	(d)
New England	1,595	1,846	1,928	3,534
Middle East	2,036	2,137	2,024	3,883
Great Lakes	1,951	1,941	1,846	4,109
Plains	1,894	1,835	2,018	3,433
Southeast	1,781	1,623	1,884	3,061
Southwest	2,240	1,870	2,023	3,444
Rocky Mountain	2,063	1,890	2,013	3,550
Far West	2,087	2,225	2,009	4,169

They differ in the terms which are weighted to form the respective sums. Thus, the actual NEI per employee (a) for a region may be written:

$$\frac{\text{NEI}}{L} = \frac{1}{L}\sum_j \left(\frac{\text{NEI}_j}{L_j}\right) L_j$$

$$= \frac{1}{L}\sum_j \left[\left(\frac{\text{NEI}_j}{\text{wages and salaries}_j}\right)(\text{wages \& salaries})_j\right]$$

where the subscript j represents one of nine sectors.

The hypothetical NEI per employee (b) based on wages may be written:

$$\frac{\text{NEI}^b}{L} = \frac{1}{L}\sum_j \left[(\text{wages and salaries})_j \left(\frac{\text{NEI}}{\text{wages and salaries}}\right)_{\bar{j}}\right].$$

The weights consist of the wages and salaries in each of j sectors; the jth weighted term consists of the ratio of NEI to wages and salaries, which is the same for the jth sector in all regions.

The hypothetical NEI per employee (c) based on employment may be written:

$$\frac{\text{NEI}^c}{L} = \frac{1}{L}\sum_j \left[L_j \left(\frac{\text{NEI}}{L}\right)_{\bar{j}}\right].$$

The weights consist of the L_j, employment in each sector; the jth weighted term consists of the ratio NEI/worker which is the same for the jth sector in all regions.

Returning to the tabulation above, we see that the hypothetical NEI series each reproduce the ranking of the actual NEI series with a fair degree of similarity. The rank correlation between columns (a) and (b) is +.55; between (a) and (c) it is +.52. Despite this correspondence, the two hypothetical series are quite unlike each other, with a rank correlation between them of +.19. A possible explanation of this lack of correspondence is the variation among regions in the level of wages and salaries per private employee shown in column (d). The hypothetical NEI based on wages apparently exceeds that based on employment in high-wage states and falls short of that based on employment in low-wage states.[17]

We have seen that a portion of the inequality in the distri-

[17] For this reason it is not meaningful to use the above relations to conclude that high-wage regions are or are not capital intensive. On the basis of series (b) they appear highly capital intensive. The rank correlation between columns (b) and (d) is +.95. However, on the basis of column (c), they do not appear to be capital intensive: the rank correlation between columns (c) and (d) is —.07.

bution of NEI per employee is due to differences in the sectoral composition of capital-using activities among the regions. To this extent, these differences may well be permanent. We must now investigate the influence of industrial composition upon the shares of income. The following tabulation shows: (a) the ratio of produced NEI to private wages and salaries; (b) the ratio of hypothetical NEI (based on wages) to private wages and salaries; and (c) the ratio of hypothetical NEI (based on employment) to private wages and salaries.

	(a)	(b)	(c)
New England	.4409	.5102	.5329
Middle East	.5243	.5503	.5212
Great Lakes	.4748	.4724	.4444
Plains	.5517	.5345	.5878
Southeast	.5818	.5302	.6155
Southwest	.6504	.5430	.5874
Rocky Mountain	.5811	.5324	.5670
Far West	.5006	.5337	.4819

Here we see a sharp difference in the correspondence between the actual ratios (a) and the hypothetical ratios (b) and (c). The rank correlation between columns (a) and (b) is +.48, while that between columns (a) and (c) is +.74. Apparently the assumption of regional uniformity of the ratio of NEI per employee within each sector brings us closer to the actual distribution which has occurred.[18]

[18] It would be a mistake to infer from these findings that the capital-to-labor ratio is a constant among regions within each sector. In fact, the reverse is closer to the truth. Let us assume a production function which is homogeneous of the first degree such that the marginal physical products of capital (C) and labor (L) are each dependent on the ratio of capital to labor. Let P stand for price, MP for marginal product, and assume only one sector represented in each region. The ratio of NEI per worker may then be written as

$$\frac{\text{NEI}}{L} = \frac{P \times MP_C \times C}{L} = P \times F(C/L).$$

The ratio of NEI per dollar of wages may be written as

$$\frac{\text{NEI}}{\text{wages}} = \frac{P \times MP_C \times C}{P \times MP_1 \times L} = h(C/L).$$

If the ratio of NEI to wages is not a constant among regions within each sector, C/L must vary among regions, within each sector. The possibility that the ratio of NEI to L is constant does not imply C/L constant, for the price term may vary to offset variations in C/L.

Returns to Capital and Labor

We are now in a position to compare the hypothetical indexes for 1953 prepared here with the regression shown earlier between NEI per employee and wages and salaries per employee. It will be recalled that this regression was not a particularly good fit, having a correlation coefficient of +.5488. The most likely reason for the poor fit is the difference in sectoral composition of regions in capital intensity.

The regression may be regarded as the embodiment of the hypothesis that all regions are alike in their sectoral composition of capital-using activities. The regions differ in the amounts of capital employed per worker within each sector, and in prices of outputs produced. These differences in prices and capital-labor ratios yield the relation between NEI per employee and wage payments per employee.[19] If the major differences among regions were the sectoral composition of capital-using activities, we would not expect a relation between wage levels and NEI per employee.

The existence of fairly large residuals from the fitted regression may be regarded as evidence that the last assumption is not satisfied. There are differences among the regions in the sectoral composition of activities. Using the 1953 regression equation shown previously, we computed the residuals for the eight regions. These residuals are the differences between the actual NEI per employee and the values predicted by the equation. A positive residual indicates that the actual NEI was above the estimate. Our

[19] Write the NEI per worker and wages and salaries per worker in terms of their definitions under the marginal productivity theory:

$$\frac{\text{NEI}}{L} = \frac{P \times MP_C \times C}{L}$$

$$\frac{\text{wages and salaries}}{L} = \frac{P \times MP_L \times L}{L}$$

We immediately see the presence of a price term in both expressions. Therefore regional variation in prices will yield the above correlation. We also see the terms $MP_C \times C/L$ and MP_L. The relations between these terms depends upon the nature of the production function specified. For example, under a Cobb-Douglas production function, with constant returns to scale, the two terms bear a constant ratio to each other. With less restrictive production functions, they will not have a constant ratio, but ordinarily will be positively related. In fact, the following restriction may be imposed and is easily perceived, although it will not be proved here. Assume the production function is homogeneous of the first degree. Then the two terms will be positively related if a 1 per cent increase in the ratio of labor to capital produces a less than 1 per cent increase in the marginal physical productivity of capital.

explanation leads us to expect that the positive residuals would occur in regions with a more capital-intensive composition of industry, and the negative residuals in regions with less capital-intensive sectors. The following tabulation provides the information necessary to evaluate these explanations. Column (a) shows the residuals from regression; columns (b) and (c) show the hypothetical values of NEI per worker, (b) constructed under the assumption of constancy in the ratio of NEI per dollar of wages in each sector, and (c) under the assumption of constancy in the ratio of NEI per employee in each sector.

	(a)	(b)	(c)
New England	$−236	$1,846	$1,928
Middle East	+52	2,137	2,024
Great Lakes	+51	1,941	1,846
Plains	+13	1,835	2,018
Southeast	−19	1,623	1,884
Southwest	+258	1,870	2,023
Rocky Mountain	−11	1,890	2,013
Far West	−96	2,225	2,009

If we compare column (a) with columns (b) and (c), we see that the rank correlation between (a) and (b) is —.07, and between (a) and (c) +.79. On the basis of the size of these coefficients, I would conclude that the explanation receives strong support from the hypothetical series based on employment and no support from the hypothetical series based on wages. The residuals from the regression appear to be explained by the sectoral composition of the regions with regard to capital-using activities. However, the measure of capital intensity needed to support such an explanation is provided by the second hypothetical series. That is, capital intensity must be measured by the ratio NEI per worker.

Usefulness of Estimates of Produced Income

The previous sections have described the estimation of produced net entrepreneurial income, the comparison of produced with received NEI, the influence of produced NEI on the distribution of state income, and the components of the regional distribution of NEI and its growth.

It is necessary to return now to the questions posed at the beginning of the paper. Is it worthwhile for the National Income

Division to estimate produced NEI by state and region on a continuous basis? Should this be done frequently or only for census years? What changes in data collection methods would be required to expedite the construction of this series? In particular, is it necessary to provide a closer link between the income data of the Internal Revenue Service, which is collected on a company basis, and the data of the Bureau of the Census, which is collected on an establishment basis?

I think that there is a great deal to be said in favor of the preparation and publication of a produced NEI series by state and region. As indicated in the previous sections, the produced NEI series is not distributed in the same fashion as the received series. Its distribution is determined by the amount of capital and the return on capital employed in each state. In turn, these elements are influenced by the patterns of growth and decline in each state. It is true that the received and produced NEI appear to change in a similar fashion over long periods of time. But we do not know whether they would follow similar patterns during shorter periods or during business fluctuations. The information on produced NEI is useful for what it tells us of the productivity of resources employed in the region.

There are no clear grounds on which to decide the frequency with which such series should be produced. In the absence of information on short-run fluctuations of produced state NEI, we do not know whether the received NEI is a suitable proxy. On a priori grounds, I would think that produced NEI would fluctuate in a different fashion from received NEI over a business cycle since business fluctuations will be transmitted to some regions through sectors which do not influence immediately the received NEI of the region. The fact that received exceeds produced NEI in some regions means that received income is sensitive to fluctuations of produced income in other regions.

Other than the few speculative remarks made immediately above, there does not appear to be any ground on which the user of data can indicate the frequency with which such data should appear. The decision would appear to rest on what changes in data collection methods are needed to expedite construction of a produced income series, and whether such a series be prepared annually, like the received series.

The answers to these questions can be given in two parts.

First, are there refinements in the present study, which a government agency could undertake? Second, how can census data which appear infrequently be linked up with annual data such as those provided by the Internal Revenue Service?

It seems clear that refinements in the present study are called for in those areas where arbitrary allocations of produced NEI were made. As mentioned above, and detailed in Appendix B, the most important of these are services, the rental and interest components of the finance sector, and construction. In addition, it would be highly desirable to investigate on a current basis the characteristics of the income of unincorporated enterprises in order to impute the income which is earned by the provision of personal services by the entrepreneur. An attack on the problem of unincorporated enterprises, in general, and the services sector, in particular, could be made by a finer processing of personal income tax returns in order to obtain a breakdown by region and industry of the income earned by unincorporated enterprise, with perhaps a splitting out of the components of the income statement to identify interest and trading profits.

Refinements also may be called for in dealing with those sectors where the Census identifies the value of sales in a region, but does not provide a measure of gross entrepreneurial income. This problem arose with wholesale and retail trade. Again it might be tackled through improved information on the income of unincorporated enterprise.

The second question is that of tying Census information, which appears infrequently, with current information such as that produced by the IRS in order to develop short-run estimates which could then be corrected with the appearance of new Censuses. However, this poses questions which have not been dealt with previously. First of all, IRS information, while it appears annually, is not really current. Secondly, the use of IRS information raises the problem of the residence of the corporation or individual filing the return. In certain sectors of the economy, the return is likely to be filed in the region where business is transacted. This would be particularly true in agriculture, trade, and services—sectors in which unincorporated enterprise is likely to be important. Construction also has a high proportion of unincorporated enterprises, but we find in this sector that firms are likely to carry on business in areas outside the area of residence of the firm.

The residence problem becomes particularly acute for large firms operating in many states. In our use of IRS *Source Book* data, we tried to avoid the more serious errors which this would produce by dealing only with the larger states as individual units, and treating the smaller states as a residual to be characterized by an average. In addition, we tried wherever possible to use sources other than the IRS to identify the size of the industry in the state, relying on the *Source Book* to provide a ratio by which such a measure of size could be reduced to an estimate of NEI. There is, of course, no way of knowing how much error exists in the present study because of the residence problem.

It has been suggested that the measurement of produced NEI requires a link-up between census and Internal Revenue data to solve the residence problem. Under such a program, census returns would be identified with company tax returns, which would then permit a regional breakdown of the company's NEI.[20] If at the same time, the NEI could be related to over-all measures of the company's activities, then a procedure could be worked out to provide annual estimates of regional NEI for the company until the next census was taken. This type of activity should certainly be encouraged. One of its by-products would be an estimate of the error in using the returns of resident corporations as an indicator of the total produced NEI in a sector of a region, or as an indicator of the ratio of net to gross entrepreneurial income. The chief limitation of this procedure is that it is restricted to sectors where we are well on the way to getting good estimates of NEI, namely mining and manufacturing. For these are the two sectors where we are likely to be provided with data on gross entrepreneurial income in future Censuses. This procedure can, however, do very little to illuminate problems in the services sector. While it is true that the Census does cover receipts and payrolls for the services sector, it was not possible to derive here a meaningful estimate of other costs which would allow the derivation of state estimates of NEI. This is the reason for the eventual resort to proration, as described in Appendix B. It would seem that the progress of greater refinement in the estimation of produced income lies in the identification of the industrial and regional components of the income of unincorporated enterprise. For this is the wide

[20] Such a program is under way at the U.S. Bureau of the Census under the direction of Julius Shiskin.

unknown area which could be opened to exploration through detailed processing of IRS personal tax return data. Once the information in the personal returns is opened up, it would then be possible to attack the sectors such as trade, construction, and services, where unincorporated income is so important.

Finally, we must say a word about rental income and the interest income components of the finance and services sectors. A more accurate breakdown of rental income by functional and regional source would be desirable. The farm realty component of rental income should be identified on a state basis and returned to the agricultural sector. In addition, for nonagricultural rents, the rent on commercial, industrial, and residential property should be identified by state.

The interest income component of the finance sector represents the net interest payments by individuals and firms in this sector after imputation of the interest received by this sector from nonfinancial sectors as a manager of capital. The latter aspect is discussed below in Appendix A. The chief source of interest originating in the finance sector is interest paid on real estate mortgages by real estate firms including private householders. The regional origin of these payments should be identified more accurately than we have done in this study. Again a possible source is the finer processing of itemized deductions in personal income tax returns.

The interest component of the services sector is very largely composed of private household interest on personal debt. Some objection has been voiced to including this payment as a part of the national income. It might be regarded, for example, as payment for a consumer service rather than an ultimate income payment for the use of capital. This objection might be expanded in a regional income study. For consumer interest reveals not the production of income in a region but the pattern of household expenditure. I feel this is too narrow a construction to place on consumer interest. It is a payment for the use of capital; and it would require a stretching of the ordinary economic meaning of utility to argue that this is a less useful employment for capital than others. As a consequence, the chief problem in the treatment of consumer interest is to identify its geographic origin. I feel that this task could be accomplished better than it has been here. There are data on new and outstanding consumer debt contracts. If these could be extended to a geographic breakdown, then an identification of the regional sources of consumer interest might be made.

Appendix A
The Treatment of Interest Payments as a Final Return to Resources

As indicated in the text, the national control totals have been adjusted upward to reflect a different treatment of interest income from that used by the National Income Division.

In order to explain the procedure followed in this paper, it is necessary to review the method currently employed by the NID to measure interest income. Due to inadequate data, the interest income is measured as a residual of total private interest payments (payments by business, individuals, and foreigners to U.S. sectors) less receipts by businesses and foreigners.[21] Although this simple definition would appear to allow unambiguous measurement, several difficulties arise. Interest income may in fact be produced, but never leave the private business sector in the form of payments to individuals. There are two reasons for this. First, interest payments received by insurance companies and certain financial intermediaries may be reinvested for their clients without actually having been paid out to them. Second, interest payments received by financial intermediaries may be used to pay their operating expenses and may be paid out in the form of dividends or may be retained.

In order to adjust the data for these deficiencies, the NID has correctly introduced processes of imputation.[22] The effect of these is to treat the interest correctly, in the sense that it is shown as originating in the nonfinancial sector. This produces the same result as would occur if the nonfinancial sector made interest payments directly to households, and the households then hired the financial sector as portfolio managers.

[21] The NID employs the following identity:

Interest payments are made by (a) business, (b) foreigners to U.S. sectors, (c) individuals, and (d) government. Interest is received by (e) business, (f) foreigners from U.S. sectors, (g) individuals and (h) government.

By definition, the interest paid by (a)–(d) is equivalent to the interest received by (e)–(h). The interest component of national income is defined as (g) interest received by individuals and (h) interest received by government minus (d) interest paid by government. This definition follows from the concept of interest as a contractual payment for the use of capital used in current production which is ultimately controlled by individuals or the government. For a discussion of these definitions, see *National Income*, 1954 ed., pp. 97–98.

[22] See *ibid.*, pp. 99–102.

The procedures described above do not pose real difficulties for the conversion of national income totals into regional components. The difficulties arise because the NID treats some interest payments as a business expense, and therefore not part of the value added of the nonfinancial sector.[23]

If interest payments are regarded as a business service much as transport charges, then the value added of the nonfinancial sector is reduced by the amount of interest in the same way that it is reduced by a transport charge. On the other hand, interest might be regarded as an ultimate income payment, with the financial intermediary acting as a cloak for an underlying group of property holders. In this case the value added of the nonfinancial sector is not reduced, as interest is truly a factor cost. In either of the above cases, the value added of the financial sector is largely equal to its receipts of interest payments. Thus the two treatments imply a different total national income. The NID would have shown an additional $1,485 million of net interest income in 1950 if it had adhered entirely to the second concept.

The NID has, in fact, chosen a compromise between the two views of interest. They have regarded the financial sector as the cloak for household portfolios in proportion to household ownership of the liabilities of certain financial intermediaries. Of the $2,994 million of interest paid in 1950 by commercial and Federal Reserve banks, $1,205 million are allocated to households on the basis of their ownership of funds "by use of which financial intermediaries obtained property income." In similar fashion, $1,485 million are imputed to businesses, and consequently are subtracted from gross interest payments to arrive at net interest income. Thus, the $1,485 million is regarded as the portion of business interest payments which represent a service charge by financial institutions to the nonfinancial sector. This amount is therefore subtracted from the value added of the nonfinancial sector.[24]

[23] A thorough discussion of interest as an intermediate or final payment will be found in *A Critique of the United States Income and Product Accounts*, Studies in Income and Wealth, 22, Princeton for NBER, 1958. See papers and discussion by G. Jaszi, R. Easterlin, and C. Warburton.

[24] A different procedure was chosen by Simon Kuznets although for the same purpose. He regarded short-term interest payments by the nonfinancial sector as the "service to business" portion of interest. This portion is then deducted from gross interest payments to arrive at the net interest income. Consistent with this, Kuznets regarded the net long-term interest payments of the nonfinancial sector as payments to households. See his *National Income and Its Composition, 1919–1938,* New York, NBER, 1941, pp. 408–409.

The procedure which I have followed in this paper is to treat all interest payments as part of value added. This implies adding back to the net interest income the NID portion of imputed interest received by the business sector. There are two reasons for taking this position. First, in a regional allocation of produced income, it is impossible to determine which firms are predominantly employing their own funds, which have borrowed in the long-term bond market, and which in the short-term market. Since we cannot determine the regional location of these characteristics, it is impossible to carry out the imputation of interest received even if we wished to. Second, and more important, there are strong grounds for treating all interest payments alike, no matter what the institutional arrangements under which they arise. It appears arbitrary and inconsistent to reduce the value added of any sector or firm because of the method of financing which it employs.

The procedure followed in this paper increases the net interest income by $1,081 million in 1929 and by $2,096 million in 1953. These increments represent 16.8 and 24.8 per cent, respectively, of the total interest income in those years.

The sectoral allocation of these increments was carried out in two steps. First, making use of the IRS Statistics of Income, the net interest paid by corporations in each nonfinancial sector was computed. Where this interest exceeded the NID figure for interest income generated in the sector, the IRS figure was employed. On this basis we were able to account for $679 million out of $1,081 million that we wish to add for 1929.

Second, the remainder, or $402 million in 1929, was attributed to the nonfinancial unincorporated enterprises in each sector and to the finance sector. The share of the residue going to the financial sector was determined by the relative importance of firms in this sector in the distribution of imputed interest received.[25] The remainder, or the share going to the proprietorships and partnerships, was allocated to the various sectors according to their relative share of income generated by unincorporated enterprise. Tables 11 and 12 show the original NID determination of interest income in each sector, the Kuznets figures for 1929, the IRS corporate net interest by nonfinancial sector, the adjustment of the remainder to the financial sector and to proprietorships, and finally the interest income figure included in the national

[25] See *National Income*, 1954 ed., p. 102, Exh. 6.

control totals. Note that the national control totals exclude the interest originating in the rest of the world. This came to $577 million in 1929 and $333 million in 1953. Also note that most of the interest originating in the services sector arises from personal

TABLE 11
DEVELOPMENT OF INTEREST INCOME BY SECTOR, 1929
(million dollars)

Sector	NID	IRS Corporate Returns	Kuznets	Finan. Sector Adjust.	Proprietorship Adjustment	Final Figure
Agriculture	833	20.9	436	—	112	945
Mining	32	66.4	45	—	2	68
Manufacturing	−81	253.4	209	—	11	264
Construction	16	17.4	13	—	21	38
Transport and public utilities	953	1,118.7	970	—	4	1,123
Wholesale and retail trade	80	123.9	56	—	53	177
Services	1,675	92.1	87	—	55	1,822
Finance	2,360	—	2,266	152	—	2,512
Total domestic interest	5,868					6,949

TABLE 12
DEVELOPMENT OF INTEREST INCOME BY SECTOR, 1953
(million dollars)

Sector	NID	IRS Corporate Returns	Finan. Sector Adjust.	Proprietorship Adjustment	Final Figure
Agriculture	730	17.6	—	192	922
Mining	16	55.7	—	4	60
Manufacturing	−74	902.5	—	18	920
Construction	44	38.6	—	38	82
Transport and public utilities	979	1,093.1	—	9	1,102
Wholesale and retail trade	156	248.1	—	138	386
Services	3,069	91.3	—	89	3,249
Finance	3,182	—	295	—	3,477
Total domestic interest	8,102				10,198

debt of households. For this reason the IRS figure and the proprietorship adjustment were both added to the original NID figure to yield the entry in the last column. The entries in the final figure column are carried into the interest originating columns of Tables 11 and 12 in the text showing net entrepreneurial income by sector.

Appendix B
Sources of Data and Methods of Allocating Sectoral Income to the States and Regions

In the following description of allocation methods, reference is made to the *Source Book of Corporate Income Tax Returns* which is maintained by the U.S. Internal Revenue Service. This provides data for 1929 on a state basis. For 1954, we were not able to use the *Source Book*. However, the IRS supplied a sample study of the returns of the 10,000 largest corporations for 1957. Profit rates and estimates of the ratio of net to gross entrepreneurial income were derived from these sources for sectors and states. In all cases, the estimates of NEI which these sources yielded were then adjusted to national control totals. In the description which follows, both types of Internal Revenue Service information are referred to as the *Source Book*.

AGRICULTURE

Net entrepreneurial income in agriculture was allocated according to the states' share of farm proprietor's income as shown in *Personal Income by States since 1929*. This series appears in the main to be on a produced basis already. While it does include certain government payments to farmers, no attempt was made to eliminate this component prior to carrying out the allocation.

MINING

Net entrepreneurial income in mining was allocated to the states in three steps.

First, the U.S. Censuses for 1929 and 1954 were used to develop by state the gross value added minus wages and salaries for each sector of the mining industry.[26] Henceforth the gross value added minus wages and salaries as reported by the Census will be referred to as the gross entrepreneurial income.

Second, the gross entrepreneurial income was reduced to an estimate of national income through the use of data on a state basis from the *Source Book*. The reduction was carried out individually for the major mineral-producing states and on an average basis

[26] *Fifteenth Census of the United States, Mines and Quarries, 1929,* U.S. Bureau of Census, Washington, 1933. *Census of Mineral Industries, 1954,* Volume II, U.S. Bureau of Census, Washington, 1956.

for the remainder. It was based on separate experience in metal mining, anthracite, bituminous coal, and oil and gas. The reduction factor in each case was an estimate of the ratio of net to gross entrepreneurial income. This ratio was formed from the income statement entries shown in the IRS *Source Book*.

Third, a final adjustment to the national control total of entrepreneurial income was carried out on a proportional basis.

MANUFACTURING

Net entrepreneurial income in manufacturing was allocated in three steps similar to those used for mining.

First, the Census of Manufactures for 1929 and 1954[27] was used to provide an estimate of gross entrepreneurial income by state for each two-digit industry group. Note that manufactured gas was not included with manufacturing in the first year, but incorporated into the public utility sector.

Second, the gross entrepreneurial income was reduced to an estimate of net entrepreneurial income through IRS *Source Book* data. The reduction was carried out for individual industries and states.

Third, a final adjustment to the national control total was carried out on a proportional basis.

CONSTRUCTION

Two different methods were used to allocate net entrepreneurial income in construction.

In the first one, for the year 1929, the Census of Construction was used to derive state estimates of gross entrepreneurial income.[28] This was reduced individually for the largest states by a net-to-gross ratio derived from the *Source Book*. For the other states, the reduction was on an average basis. The total was then adjusted to the national control proportionately to each state's share of the reduced entrepreneurial income.

In the second one, for the year 1953, net entrepreneurial income in construction was directly allocated on the basis of a state distri-

[27] *Fifteenth Census of the United States, Manufacturers, 1929*, Volume III, Reports by States, U.S. Bureau of the Census, 1933; *Census of Manufacturers, 1954*, Volumes II and III, Statistics by States, U.S. Bureau of Census, 1956.

[28] *Fifteenth Census of the United States, 1930*, Construction Industry, Reports by States, U.S. Bureau of Census, 1933.

bution of engineering construction contracts awarded in 1952, 1953, and 1954.[29] There is no recent Census of Construction to allow an allocation similar to that carried out for the earlier year.

TRANSPORTATION AND PUBLIC UTILITIES

A number of different methods were employed for the various industries in this sector.

Railways

The publications of the Interstate Commerce Commission were used for railway income.[30] For each region of the country, we derived the net entrepreneurial income of steam and electric railways of all classes. The regional income was then allocated to the states within the region according to the type and proportion of track mileage in the state. That is, the income of switching companies was allocated according to the state's proportion of the mileage of switching companies, and so on.

Pipe Lines

Again publications of the ICC were used for this industry.[31] For 1929 and 1953, the net entrepreneurial income was allocated to the regions in which the respective companies operated. It was then allocated to the states on the basis of an estimate of the state distribution of pipe-line mileage.

Air Lines

No allocation was made of air-line net entrepreneurial income. It amounted to $107 million in 1953, or 3.6 per cent of the national total in the transport sector. In 1929, it was negligible.

Highway Transport

Two different methods were employed to estimate NEI for this sector. For 1929, the *Source Book of Corporate Income Tax Returns* was employed to provide the NEI on a state basis. This was then adjusted to the national control total. For 1953, a pub-

[29] These series, as prepared by the *Engineering News Record*, are reported in the *Statistical Abstract of the United States*, for 1953, 1954, and 1955.

[30] *Statistics of Railways in the United States*, for the years ending December 31, 1929 and 1953, U.S. Interstate Commerce Commission; *Selected Financial and Operating Statistics from Annual Reports of Electric Railways*, 1953, U.S. ICC.

[31] *Statistics of Railways, 1929; Statistics of Oil Pipe Line Companies, 1953*, U.S. Interstate Commerce Commission.

lication of the Interstate Commerce Commission was employed.[32] The estimate of net entrepreneurial income was furnished on a regional basis. The income within the region was allocated to the states by using the mileage of the federal-aid highway system within each state. The latter figure was taken from the *Statistical Abstract of the U.S.* The allocation was then adjusted to the national control total.

Water Transportation

For 1929 and 1953, the state allocation of NEI for this sector was made by using the *Source Book of Corporate Tax Returns.* The totals were then adjusted to the national control totals.

COMMUNICATIONS AND PUBLIC UTILITIES

Telephones

Two methods were employed. For 1929, the *Source Book* was employed for the allocation. For 1953, a publication of the FCC was used.[33] Where it could be determined that a company operated in a single state, the company was assigned to that state. The remainder were allocated on the basis of the number of telephones in each state, and by a process of elimination all companies were assigned. In the case of Bell System companies, the total net revenue of the American Telephone and Telegraph Company was added back on a proportionate basis.

Radio Broadcasting and Television

Allocations were made from the *Source Book.*

Utilities, Electric and Gas, and Public Services

Electric utilities were allocated through the *Source Book* for 1929. For 1953, a publication of the Federal Power Commission was employed.[34] This provided information by company and state.

Gas utilities were allocated through the manufactured gas entry of the Census of Manufactures in 1929 although included in the

[32] *Statistics of Class I Motor Carriers, 1953,* U.S. Interstate Commerce Commission.

[33] *Statistics of the Communications Industry in the United States, 1953,* U.S. Federal Communications Commission.

[34] *Statistics of Electric Utilities in the United States, 1953,* Federal Power Commission.

public utility total. For 1953, the gas utilities were handled in the same fashion as the electric.

WHOLESALE AND RETAIL TRADE

For 1929, the Census of Business was used to provide the value of retail and wholesale sales in each state.[35]

Salaries and wages were also provided by this source. An estimate of cost of goods sold was then derived from the *Source Book* in conjunction with the above data. The *Source Book* data were then used to develop the value of net entrepreneurial income. This method has been mentioned previously when *Source Book* data are used in conjunction with the Census estimate of gross entrepreneurial income. It is somewhat more complicated in this case, because the *Source Book* is also used to estimate the cost of goods sold. In the other cases, the following procedure is used:

Let GEI, gross entrepreneurial income, stand for the difference between value added and wages and salaries as shown in the Census.

Then we must find an α such that α GEI is the net entrepreneurial income. Using IRS categories, our α is estimated by the following ratio:

$$\alpha = 1 - \left[\frac{G + H}{A + B - E - F - K}\right]$$

where A = gross sales, B = gross profits from other operations, E = cost of goods sold, F = compensation of officers, K = miscellaneous deductions, G = taxes paid other than income tax, and H = depreciation and depletion.

α may be interpreted as the estimated ratio of net to gross entrepreneurial income, where the net is the NID concept and the gross is the Census concept.

In the case of trade, it was necessary to use the *Source Book* first to estimate the gross entrepreneurial income.

Let X = net sales as reported in the census, and Y = salaries and wages, excluding proprietors, as reported in the census.

Then estimate

$$Z = \text{cost of goods sold} = \left[\frac{E + K}{A + B} - \frac{Y}{X}\right] \cdot X.$$

[35] *Fifteenth Census of the United States: 1930*, Volume II, Wholesale Distribution, State Reports, Volume I, Retail Distribution, State Reports, U.S. Bureau of Census, 1934.

Our estimate of gross entrepreneurial income is then $X - Y - Z$, and we apply the ratio to this expression to obtain NEI.

For 1953, a similar procedure is followed. The value of sales by state is given in the Census.[36] In this year, however, salaries and wages are not provided. Accordingly, *Source Book* data were used to provide an estimate of the ratio of net entrepreneurial income to sales. This ratio was then applied to derive an estimate of NEI. For 1929, we distinguished retail from wholesale trade, but did not split either sector. For 1953, the retail and wholesale sectors were each broken into components: food trade, eating and drinking, etc.

SERVICES

Allocation of the services sector was carried out in a more arbitrary fashion than the other sectors shown. *Source Book* data were not found useful in this case because of the small importance of corporate income in the services total. It will be recalled from Tables 1 and 2 that most of the NEI in services is accounted for either by unincorporated enterprises or by household interest payments. While there are a number of possible reasons for altering the NID treatment of household interest, it was finally decided to retain the existing usage. In the absence of a satisfactory breakdown by state for this sector, the NEI of services was allocated on a proportional basis to the nonagricultural proprietary income as shown in *Personal Income by States Since 1929.*

FINANCE, INSURANCE, AND REAL ESTATE

The NEI was allocated in two stages. The corporate profits and unincorporated income of firms in this sector were allocated according to the corporate profit distribution of the *Source Book.* The interest and rental income were allocated according to the estimated value of tenant-occupied buildings. This distribution follows an allocation supplied by the NID. The underlying distribution of housing value comes from the Census of Housing. While it would appear arbitrary to allocate interest payments in this sector in the same fashion as rental payments, there are two reasons which suggest this procedure. Information from the NID reveals that most of the net interest generated by this sector represents interest payments by personal landlords. Thus a possible

[36] *Census of Business, 1954,* U.S. Bureau of Census, 1954.

allocator is the state distribution of value of all real estate. Since this allocator is not available for the two study years, it was decided to allocate on the basis of the value of tenant-occupied buildings.

SUMMARY

Table 13 shows the relation between the estimates of gross entrepreneurial income after adjustment by *Source Book* information on the net-to-gross ratio and the actual national control totals for the sectors where such estimates are made. In the case of the finance sector, estimates were made only for the sum of corporate profits and income of unincorporated enterprise.

TABLE 13
ADJUSTED GROSS AND NET ENTREPRENEURIAL INCOME, 1929 AND 1953
(million dollars)

	1953		*1929*	
Sector	Adjusted GEI	NEI	Adjusted GEI	NEI
Mining	3,245	1,477	880	545
Manufacturing	24,527	23,265	7,986	5,990
Construction	—	—	1,123	1,290
Transport and public utilities	6,299	7,130	2,847	3,308
Trade	12,050	17,525	1,965	4,081
Finance	4,854	4,651	1,206	1,919

Most of the estimates are within 20 per cent of the national control totals. In those cases where the errors are larger, it is explained by the likelihood that the ratio of net to gross entrepreneurial income as reported in the IRS data are unrepresentative of the whole population. This would be true in the case of trade where the IRS data were used to estimate the ratios of net entrepreneurial income to sales, or used to estimate the cost of goods sold. The errors would arise because the IRS data represent the corporate sector only in 1929, and represent only the largest part of the corporate sector for the later years.

Another explanation is possible in those cases where *Source Book* data were used to provide an estimate of the over-all size of an industry—for example, public utilities in 1929. It is possible that the net entrepreneurial income is understated at the very start. In this industry, on the basis of the NEI definition I have used, the

Statistics of Income reveals a figure of $2,402 million, which is below the $3,308 million used in this study.

COMMENT

DANIEL CREAMER, National Industrial Conference Board

Despite the fact that George Borts' estimates of income produced by states are central to his paper, it seems to me that too little attention is given to the details of the derivation and the limitations of the estimates. Without a full understanding of the weaknesses of the estimates, one cannot judge whether the uses made of them are defensible and the results valid. For this reason, I have restricted my comments to the estimating procedures.

The heart of the problem is the estimation of property income by the state in which it is produced. The official estimates of personal income by state are by the state of residence of the recipient. However, the wage and salary component, being based on establishment data, is, in the first instance, estimated on a "where-produced" basis. It is transformed onto a "where-received" basis by correcting for interstate commuting. On the other hand, the property income component of personal income by state has two major defects for Borts' purposes. It excludes retained corporate profits, and individuals' receipts of distributed property income are estimated on a where-received basis. Thus, much the larger part of labor income is already available on a where-produced basis, but estimates of property income on this basis must be developed. The newly developed estimates account for about 30 per cent of his national control total, which is net domestic income produced, slightly modified to exclude imputed interest payments of the nonfinancial business sectors entered in the national accounts as an offset for financial services.

Borts develops the property income estimates for two benchmarks, 1929 and 1953. His national control total is divided into nine industrial sectors and each sector control total is allocated to the forty-eight states. The quality of the estimates then depends on the quality of his state allocation procedures.

Borts concludes that: "In general, the most reliable state distributions are those provided by Census data, ICC data, and for agriculture which was distributed according to a measure of farm proprietors' income." As a basis for judging how reliable the most reliable sector estimates are, I have concentrated on the agricultural sector and on manufacturing which is based on Census data.

The factor returns to capital—interest, net rent, and net profit before income tax—Borts calls net entrepreneurial income (NEI). The control total for the agricultural sector is allocated among the states by the relative state distribution of farm proprietors' income as shown in the official personal income estimates by state. Borts notes that this treatment ignores the consideration that some part of NEI in farm proprietors' income is actually a factor return to the farm proprietors' labor service. Perhaps more serious for his interstate and interregional comparisons is the large regional variation in the percentage of his NEI that must be a property return. This can be inferred from the large regional range in the ratio of physical farm capital to gross farm income in constant prices as estimated by Alvin Tostlebe.[1]

The estimate for the manufacturing sector is carried out in three stages. Remember that the objective is to derive some factors for allocating NEI by states for 1929 and 1953. For the 1929 estimate, Borts starts with a state distribution of value added for all manufacturing from the U.S. Census of Manufactures for 1929. This, of course, is much grosser than NEI. The first adjustment to approximate NEI is to subtract from Census value added wages and salaries reported by Census. The remainder Borts calls gross entrepreneurial income—GEI. This exceeds NEI, the factor returns to capital, by the inclusion of inventory accumulation, supplements to wages and salaries, capital consumption, taxes other than those on income, and purchases from enterprises other than materials, supplies, containers, fuel, purchased energy, and contract work. Borts sought for a reduction ratio, a separate one for each state, that would purge these items from GEI and leave NEI. He found such a ratio in the *Source Book* tabulations of the *Statistics of Income.*

The denominator of this ratio in terms of *Statistics of Income* entries must equal or closely approximate GEI from the Census of Manufactures. Borts states that this equivalence can be achieved by subtracting from the sum of gross sales and gross profits from operations (1) the cost of goods sold, (2) compensation of officers,

[1] *Capital in Agriculture: Its Formation and Financing since 1870*, Princeton for NBER, 1957, pp. 108–109.

and (3) miscellaneous deductions. The subtraction of this last item, as I read the evidence, introduces a significant error into the ratio. With the minor exception of repairs, miscellaneous deductions are not composed of expenditures for materials, supplies, containers, fuels, purchased energy, and contract work. Much the largest part relates to expenditures for business services, including rental on property, business transfer payments, and supplements to wages and salaries, such as they were in 1929. Such expenditures, conceptually, are part of gross entrepreneurial income.

Miscellaneous deductions, moreover, are not trivial in amount. For all corporate manufacturing in the forty-eight states in 1929, they represent 19 per cent of the sum of the cost of goods sold and compensation of officers; in mining, 26 per cent; and in contract construction, 29 per cent.

In the numerator of his reduction ratio, Borts enters only two items, taxes other than income taxes and depreciation and depletion. If my characterization of miscellaneous deductions is correct, these also should be part of the numerator. Moreover, it is a misconception to include depletion in the numerator. The NEI control total includes the estimate of net profit before income taxes prepared by the National Income Division. This estimate is gross of depletion. Therefore the reduction ratio should be so constructed as to yield NEI gross of depletion. Borts' ratio produces NEI net of depletion.

A statistical test supports this criticism of the Borts reduction ratio. The test consists simply of comparing GEI for total manufacturing according to Borts' specifications of the use of IRS data and according to my specifications with GEI based on the 1929 Census of Manufactures. Census value added less wages and salaries for corporations only (based on the data in *Historical Statistics*) amounted to \$15.1 billion. The comparable total based on IRS data for 1929 and Borts' specifications is only \$6.6 billion. If my specifications are used, the total is \$16.8 billion, only 11 per cent larger than the Census-derived total. The direction of this difference is expected since IRS data are company based and therefore include some nonmanufacturing operations, which is not the case with the establishment-based data of the Census.

If GEI for all firms in manufacturing based on Census data is \$16.3 billion in 1929 and the NEI control total is \$6.0 billion (Borts' Table 1), the perfect reduction percentage is 63. According to Borts' prescription, his reduction percentage is 40 and, according to my prescription, 76. In short, the level of his reduction ratio is very wide of the mark nationally. My computations suggest that his ratio would account for only 57 per cent of his control total. However, a more careful use of the available data would produce a much closer approximation to the required ratio. I am unable to perceive why its performance would be more accurate at the state level, even if we assume there are acceptable state data for the construction of the reduction ratio.

What are the state data? Borts relies on the state tabulations of data from corporate income tax returns presented in the *Source Book.* From *Statistics of Income, 1929*[2] we learn that:

> the data for States and minor civil divisions, although compiled from returns filed in each locality, do not represent what may be called the geographical distribution of income, there being no way of ascertaining from the income-tax returns the amount of income originating in the respective States as income reported by a corporation in one State may have been derived from sources in other States . . . a corporation files its income-tax return in the collection district in which its principal place of business or the principal office or agency is situated, excepting closely affiliated concerns filing a consolidated return. In the latter case the consolidated return is frequently filed in a State other than the State in which the principal place of business or principal office or agency of the subsidiary is located.

Borts is aware of this deficiency, but expresses his concern only in the last few pages devoted to a discussion of improving the estimates. That is, no mention of this deficiency is made in the technical appendix describing the estimates nor in the introductory pages of the paper where the derivation of the estimates is briefly described. At that early point, it seems to me, it would have been helpful to discuss this difficulty and to speculate on the direction and extent of bias created by the discrepancy between the state in which a corporate income tax return is filed and the state in which the manufacturing activity is located.

My own guess is that this data defect understates NEI produced in the older manufacturing states. My reasoning and assumptions are as follows: (1) The companies that have processing operations in more than one state are the larger firms. (2) The

[2] *Statistics of Income for 1929,* Washington, 1931, p. 3.

larger firms have a higher capital-output ratio than smaller firms. (3) Therefore, Borts' reduction ratio, which includes depreciation in the numerator, is too high and NEI too low in states in which the principal offices of companies with multistate operations are located. (4) The latter states, I assume, are the older manufacturing centers in the New England, Middle Atlantic, and Great Lake states.

If this reasoning is correct, the differences Borts finds in these states between NEI received and produced is overstated.

Thus far we have been concerned with the estimates of NEI for manufacturing by states for 1929. I have suggested that the formulation of the reduction ratio used to convert GEI to NEI is much too crude and that this defect is compounded by the use of state corporate income tax tabulations based on the state of the principal office.

The estimates for the manufacturing sector in 1953, also subject to these "data defects," suffer from additional deficiencies—the data used relate not to 1953 but to other years. For example, the initial allocation of the national control total for 1953 among the states is based on the state distribution of GEI from the Census of Manufactures for 1954. That, of course, was a recession year. And we know from Borts' earlier researches that there are regional variations in cyclical movements. One would not expect the state distribution of manufacturing in a recession year (even a relatively mild recession) to be an accurate proxy for the state distribution at the peak level of 1953.

Even less acceptable are the data for the reduction ratios by states. Because of the limited uses of state tabulations of corporate income tax returns, the Internal Revenue Service prepares state tabulations only at infrequent intervals and primarily for administrative purposes. Closest in point of time to 1953 were the state tabulations of a sample of large corporations for 1957. Borts reports a sample of 10,000 companies for all industries—the number classified as manufacturing is not given. The reduction ratios then have a large company bias, which further accentuates the basic defect of these state tabulations, and they relate not to 1953 but to 1957 when the fixed-capital-to-output ratio for all manufacturing had risen by nearly 10 per cent.

Now I come to my main point. Borts states that his estimates for manufacturing are among his most reliable. For the reasons just developed, I have grave doubts whether his estimates for the manufacturing sector attain a level of accuracy that can sustain the analytic burden he places on them. If this is true for manufacturing, it applies with even greater force to those sectors regarded by Borts as less reliably estimated.

This concentration on the negative aspects does not do full justice to the paper. We are indebted to Borts for showing us in a practical way what the difficulties are in preparing estimates of income produced by states and for showing us some of the imaginative analytical uses to which such estimates could be put once their margin of error is reduced to more tolerable limits.

Werner Z. Hirsch, University of California, Los Angeles

There can be no doubt that George Borts has presented us with a pioneering study in an area in which few economists before him have had the courage to rove. It opens a host of new questions and challenges at a time when economists, inside and outside government, are becoming increasingly aware of the usefulness of knowledge about regional economic activity. In his careful manner, Borts has kept the ratio of heroic assumptions to painstaking labor as low as possible and has achieved for the first time comprehensive estimates of produced income for forty-eight states in 1929 and 1953.

I will first attempt to raise a few questions about the methodology and data employed and suggest some possible answers. Thereafter, I will explore short-run applications of information on produced income to supplement Borts' presentation of its application to long-run situations.

I

Profit rates and the ratio of net to gross entrepreneurial income for sectors and states were estimated by Borts with the aid of the *Source Book of Corporate Income Tax Return* of the U.S. Internal Revenue Service. The use of these data can be justified on the grounds that at present no better ones are available. However, since these data occupy such a pivotal position in the income computations, an awareness of their main shortcomings is essential. Borts mentions the fact that they are based on corporation reports. Before they are applied to all legal forms of organization, adjustments using sole proprietorship and partnership data, meager as they are, could improve the estimates of net entrepreneurial income.

Secondly, the "miscellaneous deductions" category of the Internal Revenue Service used by Borts in his equation in Appendix B is designed precisely for tax purposes. It would have been desirable to modify the data to make them more consistent with the economic definition given them in this paper. For example, depreciation claimed on the tax return may not be the same as depreciation charged in accounting for profits to stockholders. Net entrepreneurial income may thus be understated.

In addition to these issues, the 1929 and 1953 data are not entirely comparable. While the IRS *Source Book* offered reasonably complete data for 1929, no such data are available for 1953. Instead, Borts uses an IRS sample of returns of the 10,000 largest corporations for 1957, which raises a number of questions. What is the nature of the bias introduced by this procedure? Specifically, what bias is introduced by using 1957 relationships for 1954? Also, what bias is introduced by using the 10,000 largest corporations instead of all corporations?

II

A corollary question pertains to the growth analysis. For example, the claim is made that "the received and produced NEI appear to change in a similar fashion over long periods of time." The basis for this assertion is a comparison of rather poor and only partially comparable entrepreneurial income data for two years—1929 and 1953. Much of the growth discussion appears somewhat tenuous because of the paucity of data, general statistical difficulties with time series data, and absence of statistical significance texts. Borts' enthusiasm appears to run away with him here.

III

One of the most interesting pieces of information offered by Borts is his Table 3, which shows net entrepreneurial income data by states on both a produced and received basis for 1929 and 1953. While the absolute data are intriguing, the ratios between received and produced NEI are even more so. In 1929 the ratio was highest for Maryland and lowest for South Carolina, i.e., 144 versus 64. The New England states exhibited the highest ratio. They were followed by the Middle Eastern states. The Plains,

Southeast, Southwest, and Rocky Mountain states had ratios below 100.

By 1953 the picture had changed greatly. Delaware had taken the place of Maryland, and West Virginia that of South Carolina. The ratios were 179 and 71, respectively. The ratios of the New England, Plains, Southeast, Southwest, Rocky Mountain, and Far West states had increased over 1929. Those for the Middle Eastern and Great Lakes states had declined.

Two major questions suggest themselves: On the assumption that the data are by and large accurate, what can explain the differences between the ratios of different states in either year, and what can account for the changes in the ratios of a given state from 1929 to 1953? Borts makes little effort to provide an answer to either question; and yet until good explanations are offered, further doubt is cast on the quality of the estimates.

A number of hypotheses suggest themselves as possible explanations—for example, older states have had more time to establish a substantial resource base and, therefore, their produced income should exceed that of newer ones. The data do not appear to support this hypothesis. While the ratios in the New England states are high, those in the Southeast are low, and both regions are about equally old.

Other hypotheses are that industrial structure can affect the ratio and that the age distribution of population has a major bearing. As to the latter hypothesis, Florida, Arizona, and California should have about similar ratios. All three states have attracted many retired persons with means. Received income should exceed produced income. It does so, but the differences between the ratios of the three states are major: 130, 74, and 120 in 1929, and 143, 102, and 123 in 1953, respectively.

Turning next to changes over time, no ready explanation suggests itself for the doubling in Delaware's ratio from 91 to 179, within a span of fourteen years. Why did the New York ratio drop during this period from 125 to 108 and that of Maryland from 144 to 116? On the other hand, why was only the ratio of Massachusetts virtually the same in 1929 and 1953?

A comparison of ratios over time may be more instructive if data are expressed on a per capita basis. In this manner, the general effect of population changes can be isolated.

Borts offers sound and at the same time challenging proposals to increase the availability of relevant data. Whether the Internal Revenue Service can be a major source for further data depends on the presence of the required information on the tax returns, a sufficiently large budget, and lead-time to build up the analytical resources necessary to plan and produce such data. For example, the sole proprietorship return for 1960 does not include information on interest income. In addition, a finer functional and regional breakdown would require a substantial increase in the size of the sample presently drawn by the Internal Revenue Service.

The Census link study opens the way for obtaining much improved data. However, it must be realized that this study, which attempts to link U.S. Census and Internal Revenue Service data, is merely in a pilot stage. The present main objective is to show industry subdivisions of the corporation data, and even in this connection only tentative findings can be expected. Ultimately, it can prove an important data source.

IV

I would like to turn next to a brief examination of the application for impact analysis of produced income estimates by states in general and the Borts paper in particular. Borts' main interest in produced income data appears to stem from his concern with long-run growth comparisons. But short-run impact analysis also often prefers produced income to received income data. It usually inquires into the impact various autonomous forces have on returns to resources employed in a state, rather than on returns attributable to factors supplied by residents of a given state. For example, a state government faced with prevalently low incomes might want to estimate the potential impact of alternative development policies. Its main criterion for evaluating the desirability of alternatives would be income to resources employed in the state.

To study such issues, state input-output accounts, centered around commodity and service flows rather than payment transactions, can be constructed. In this manner, the effect of autonomous forces on the state's resources and their returns can be appraised.

Borts' work can provide basic information for the development of the household row of such a state input-output transaction matrix. For many purposes, however, further disaggregation of the nine industry sectors is necessary. Especially, more detail is needed for the manufacturing, services, and trade sectors. Impact analysis points to the need for up-to-date information, which however is unlikely to be produced from Internal Revenue Service data. For many years to come, they will tend to be about two years late. Even Census data will not be ready much earlier.

V

In conclusion, I hope that my remarks in no way detract from the contribution made by George Borts. He deserves our gratitude for having opened up a significant new area of income analysis.

ROBERT E. GRAHAM, JR., National Income Division, U.S. Department of Commerce

George Borts' effort is a path-breaking one. The state estimates of income produced which he has presented here constitute the first such measure to be developed in a comprehensive and systematic fashion, and it is obvious that much imagination and statistical ingenuity have been marshaled to meet problems that stem basically from a lack of essential data. However, the measure which Borts has prepared does not appear to provide "a means of interpreting capital accumulation . . . and changes in the capital intensity of different sectors of the region's economy"; nor does it permit an examination of the respective roles played by the stock of capital and the rate of return on such capital employed in each state as determinants of the geographic distribution of the returns to property. The real contributions of this paper are that it focuses attention on the difficulties inherent in measuring monetary returns to capital on a geographic basis and outlines the dimensions of the problem.

Daniel Creamer and Werner Hirsch have commented extensively on the statistical aspects of the income produced measure, and I shall make only two points in this regard. First, in large degree the estimates reflect the geographic distribution of the volume of business activity as measured by sales, value added, miles of track, number of telephones, etc., with only rough adjustments for geographic differences in profit ratios. Secondly, there is a lack of comparability over time as illustrated by the construction industry. For 1929, net entrepreneurial income was estimated by applying profit ratios derived from corporate returns to value added less wages. For 1953, the value of contract awards by states was used to allocate the national total. Quite apart from any errors in the estimates for each individual year, two instances of lack of comparability stand out: (1) The distribution of value added (underlying 1929) reflects construction activity by the state of the home office of the company, while contract awards (underlying 1953) measure construction activity by the state of the location of the work. (2) The 1929 state estimates reflect profit differentials among the states as derived from IRS returns, while the 1953 distribution assumes equal profit ratios state by state.

On balance, the lack of temporal comparability, the absence of profit differentials in the estimates for a number of industries, and the potential error in the industries which the author terms "good" would seem to combine so as to blunt, if not actually distort, the over-all measure of NEI.

Borts' presentation would have been strengthened had more consideration been given the concept of income produced on a geographic basis. For example, what is the meaning of corporate profits in relation to their geographic origin? Do profits originate where a company's capital equipment is located, where its sales are made, or where entrepreneurial decisions are formulated? Take the case of a stock life insurance company with headquarters in one state, solicitors writing insurance in each of the fifty states; and the company's premium income invested in company-managed real estate or loans in a half dozen states. Where do the profits of this corporation originate? Or consider an integrated petroleum company with oil wells in one state, pipelines crossing several states to its refineries concentrated elsewhere, wholesale bulk plants in a number of states, and leased filling stations scattered even more widely. Does the "value-added" approach form the basis of the profits measure that is sought and so yield estimates which mirror state differences in the return to capital, or does it merely reflect the company's accounting practices?

It seems to me that much thinking along definitional lines remains to be done in order to formulate a satisfactory set of concepts before we get into the measurement phase of the geographic distribution of income produced. A primary consideration in such thinking should be the needs which the measure is intended to serve. Certain uses may permit the adoption of specific conventions in the measurement of property returns. For example, in revenue estimation or the analysis of fiscal capacity by states, the generally accepted formulae now in use in determining corporate state tax liability may be entirely acceptable as a means of allocating property returns. Similarly, other conventions, though lacking the theoretical basis, may well cut through the difficulties of statistical measurement and, at the same time, yield a useful measure of net entrepreneurial income produced.

REPLY by George H. Borts

In this section I shall examine alternative methods of estimating net entrepreneurial income. New estimates have been made for the manufacturing sector and the resulting changes incorporated into total NEI. One set of changes was investigated at the suggestion of Daniel Creamer for the reasons given in his comments above. The second set of changes was made in response to the appearance of new data in the 1958 Census of Manufactures. These data were made available after the first draft of this paper was written.

Comments by Daniel Creamer

Creamer questioned the validity of the formula shown in Appendix B, which was designed to convert gross to net entrepreneurial income by using regional data available in the Internal Revenue *Source Book*. The formula was written:

$$\frac{\text{NEI}}{\text{GEI}} = 1 - \left[\frac{G + H}{A + B - E - F - K}\right].$$

(For definition of the terms, see Appendix B.)

Creamer argues that the denominator of the expression is too small, by virtue of the subtraction of miscellaneous deductions. In 1929, for all manufacturing, the denominator I used would come to $6.6 billion for gross entrepreneurial income; if miscellaneous deductions were added back in, the estimate would be $16.8 billion. The actual census figure for GEI was $16.7 billion. Creamer does not object to the procedure used to arrive at net entrepreneurial income from Internal Revenue sources. Both his procedure and mine yield an estimate of NEI of $4 billion, compared with the National Income Division control total of $5.99 billion. The crux of Creamer's objection is that the reduction formula I use places too much emphasis on depreciation and therefore penalizes regions where depreciation is likely to play an important role. The formula Creamer prefers is

$$\frac{\text{NEI}}{\text{GEI}} = 1 - \left[\frac{G + H + K}{A + B - E - F}\right].$$

I have attempted to evaluate at the national level the importance of Creamer's very reasonable suggestion. I recomputed the reduction formulae for each manufacturing industry sector for 1929 and compared it with two other formulae, all of which are shown in Table A. Column 1 shows the national average reduction ratios based on Creamer's formula; column 2 shows the national average reduction ratios used in my study. Column 3 shows the national average reduction ratios implied by proceeding directly from Census GEI to the NEI measured by the National Income Division. Bear in mind that my study uses regional formulae which when averaged equal those shown in column 2. Also note that the ratios in column 2 have been adjusted equiproportionately for the shortfall of GEI which my procedure implies.

Asterisks are used in columns 1 and 2 to show which of the estimates is closer to the figure in column 3. It can be seen that Creamer's proposal, while reasonable, does not necessarily improve the estimate of the ratio of gross to net entrepreneurial income.

A second method of evaluating Creamer's proposal is to compute the net entrepreneurial income using the reduction formula he suggests. In order to carry out such a test thoroughly, it would be necessary to recompute the reduction formulae for each region. However, as a first approximation, I used the national ratios in column 1 of Table A and applied them to the manufacturing gross entrepreneurial income of each state. As a check I also used the national ratios in column 3 of Table A. The results are summarized by region in Table B. Column 1 shows the value of manufacturing NEI as derived from the reduction formulae in column 1 of Table A. Column 2 shows the manufacturing NEI derived from my study. Column 3 shows the manufacturing NEI derived from the ratios in column 3 in Table A. Also shown in Table B are the effects of these changes on total NEI in the regions. The total NEI of the regions were corrected by addition or subtraction for the changes in manufacturing NEI implied in columns 1 and 3. Columns 4 and 6 show the ratio of the total received NEI to the corrected total produced NEI.

TABLE A
Ratio of Gross to Net Entrepreneurial Income, 1929

	Creamer (1)	Borts (2)	Census NID (3)
Food products, beverages, tobacco	.309*	.367	.229
Textiles and textile products	.219	.291*	.266
Leather and leather products	.248	.354*	.323
Rubber and related products	.203	.293*	.254
Lumber and wood products	.243	.234*	.230
Paper, pulp, and products	.405	.334*	.305
Printing and publishing	.328*	.394	.271
Chemicals and allied substances	.402*	.324	.536
Stone, clay, and glass	.339*	.326	.341
Metal, metal prod., machinery, and transport equip.	.431*	.382	.416

TABLE B
Net Entrepreneurial Income for Manufacturing, 1929

	1929 Manufacturing NEI (million dollars)			*1929 Ratio of Received to Produced Total NEI*		
Region	Creamer (1)	Borts (2)	Census-NID (3)	Creamer (4)	Borts (5)	Census-NID (6)
New England	539.3	552.7	532.5	130.4	129.7	130.8
Middle East	2,055.5	2,067.7	1,989.4	124.1	123.8	125.4
Great Lakes	1,909.8	1,769.6	1,930.8	96.3	97.9	96.0
Plains	367.6	413.4	383.3	86.7	85.7	86.3
Southeast	589.0	651.7	625.2	85.4	84.1	84.5
Southwest	113.0	111.0	107.6	81.7	81.7	81.9
Rocky Mountain	55.5	63.2	59.7	87.6	86.7	87.1
Far West	356.5	359.3	356.8	115.0	115.0	115.0

If we examine columns 1, 2, and 3, we see that Creamer's procedure penalizes the following regions: New England, Middle East, Plains, Southeast, Rocky Mountain, and Far West. It favors the Great Lakes and Southwest regions. Thus it is not correct to say that my procedure favors newer as opposed to older regions.

If we examine columns 4, 5, and 6, we see that the changes in manufacturing NEI are not by themselves strong enough to offset the original regional patterns of divergences between received and produced income. This is, of course, an incomplete test of Creamer's proposal, for it is not applied to nonmanufacturing sectors. If it were, there would undoubtedly be additional changes in the patterns of produced NEI. Nevertheless enough has been done to indicate that, while Creamer's suggestion would lead to different results, they would not necessarily alter the basic findings of this study.

To determine the possibility that changes in NEI in other sectors might alter the regional patterns, the following computation was performed. The percentage change from column 2 to 1 in Table B was applied to the total produced NEI of the region. That is, I assumed that the percentage change implied by column 1 would apply to NEI in all categories. The ratio of received to adjusted produced NEI was then computed. These are shown in Table C.

TABLE C
RATIO OF RECEIVED TO PRODUCED NEI, 1929

Region	Manufacturing NEI Ratios of Column 1 to Column 2 (1)	*Ratio of Received to Produced Total NEI* Borts (2)	Adjusted (3)
New England	.976	129.7	132.9
Middle East	.994	123.8	124.6
Great Lakes	1.079	97.9	90.8
Plains	.889	85.7	96.4
Southeast	.904	84.1	93.1
Southwest	1.018	81.7	80.3
Rocky Mountain	.878	86.7	98.8
Far West	.992	115.0	115.9

The only region experiencing a significant alteration of position is the Rocky Mountain region. The relation of received to produced income remains roughly the same for the other regions.

New Data in 1958 Census of Manufactures

A special Census tabulation for 1957 permits finer approximations to net entrepreneurial income than those made previously.[1] The new data consist of state estimates for 1957 of supplementary employment costs, expenditures for maintenance and repairs, insurance premiums, rental payments, property taxes paid, and depreciation

[1] *Supplementary Employment Costs, Cost of Maintenance and Repair, Insurance, Rent, Taxes, and Depreciation and Book Value of Depreciable Assets: 1957;* Industry and Industry Groups, State by Industry Groups, 1958 Census of Manufactures. This report is also published as Chapter IX, Volume I, *Summary Statistics of the 1958 Census of Manufactures.*

and depletion charges. With the exception of maintenance and repairs, all of the above items should be subtracted from gross entrepreneurial income in order to approach net entrepreneurial income. Only that portion of maintenance and repairs should be subtracted which represents purchases from other firms. I have estimated the subtractable portion to be the amount charged for maintenance and repair over and above that paid to the firms' own employees.[2] Table D shows the magnitudes of gross entrepreneurial income, net entrepreneurial income, and the relevant cost items.

TABLE D
U.S. TOTALS OF GROSS AND NET ENTREPRENEURIAL INCOME, 1957
(million dollars)

Value added in manufacturing, Census		147,928
Payrolls		−76,379
Gross entrepreneurial income		71,549
Maintenance and repair	4,472	
Insurance	667	
Rental payments	1,411	
Property taxes	1,450	
Depreciation	7,295	
Supplements to payrolls	5,974	
	21,269	−21,269
Census approximation to NEI		50,280
National income originating in manufacturing, NID		112,517
Compensation of employees		−87,671
		24,846
Discrepancy		+25,434
		50,280

It may be seen that, without the new data, the Census GEI of $71.5 billion is over $50 billion greater than the NEI of $24.8 billion. The new data permit the allocation of $21.3 billion, so that the discrepancy is reduced to $25 billion. In the absence of additional information, reduction formulae must again be used. An alternative, not explored here, is to blow up the totals of the cost items, so that they equal the amounts shown in the IRS *Statistics of Income*.

A check of the new data was carried out through a crude

[2] In 1957 total maintenance and repair in manufacturing is shown as $9 billion; while $4.5 billion is paid to employees of the same firm. Thus $4.5 billion are assumed to be purchases from other firms.

reduction formula. The resulting distribution of NEI was then compared with the state manufacturing NEI prepared in my study. There are many reasons why the two series should not agree, so that the purpose of comparison is to give only a rough idea of the changes the new data imply.

The reduction formula employed is the following: For each state, the Census approximation to NEI was computed. The state entries were then reduced proportionately so that they totaled $23,265 billion, the NEI in 1953. No attempt was made to correct for state industry mix, although the data permit such correction. Undoubtedly such corrections will be made in later studies. The distribution of manufacturing NEI is shown in Table E. Column 1 shows the estimates made with the new data; column 2 shows the estimates made in the original study.

TABLE E
MANUFACTURING NET ENTREPRENEURIAL INCOME, 1953
(million dollars)

Region	Census (1)	Borts (2)	Ratio of Col. 1 to Col. 2 (3)
New England	1501.9	1518.5	.989
Middle East	6259.5	6142.3	1.019
Great Lakes	6876.3	7533.7	.913
Plains	1507.3	1345.5	1.120
Southeast	3444.9	3055.0	1.128
Southwest	1115.7	1170.5	.953
Rocky Mountain	285.8	208.4	1.371
Far West	2274.5	2291.0	.993

It can be seen that the new data do depart somewhat from the earlier estimates. While NEI is not reduced anywhere by more than 8 per cent, it is increased by 37 per cent for the Rocky Mountain area. It is curious that Creamer's ratios penalize the Rocky Mountain area, while the above data reward it quite heavily. Again referring back to a comment of Creamer's, there is no indication from this comparison that my method penalizes older areas and rewards newer areas. The same conclusion holds when the above changes are added to change the produced income for each region. Table F shows the original ratios of received to produced income, and those which are derived from the above changes in manufacturing.

TABLE F
Ratios of Received to Produced Income, 1953

Region	Census (1)	Borts (2)
New England	133.8	133.4
Middle East	106.8	107.4
Great Lakes	90.7	88.1
Plains	99.1	100.8
Southeast	90.0	92.1
Southwest	92.9	92.2
Rocky Mountain	97.9	101.2
Far West	118.9	118.7

It is to be hoped that further refinements of GEI will be made possible in the future. This will require additional special studies by the Census and some attempt at reconciliation of Census and NID estimates of national income generated in manufacturing. Presently available data do not permit such a reconciliation.

General Comment

A. ROSS ECKLER
BUREAU OF THE CENSUS

In listening to the discussions of the relationships among various economic series as presented in a number of papers, I have been impressed with the extent to which changes in the concepts and definitions used in the preparation of the basic series, as well as changes in industrial composition, can affect the interpretation of the relationships. This leads me to raise the question whether more disaggregation is not needed and whether the tools may not now be at hand which will make possible new and better measures of the relationships among factors. Specifically, the availability of modern electronic equipment makes possible the calculation of ratios for individual establishments to an extent not possible hitherto. Furthermore, the Census Bureau's company statistics program, combining data relating to companies and establishments and tying them to corporation reports in the Internal Revenue Service files, opens the way to much more effective studies of economic development.

It may be noted that as part of the editing program of our last two censuses of manufactures, many ratios for individual establishments were computed and placed on electronic tapes. This file of detailed ratios could be a rich source of research for students concerned with changes in the shares of different factors. Thus far, the only members of the Conference known to have taken advantage of the research possibilities are Richard and Nancy Ruggles and Karl Kaysen. We hope that many others will follow and, like them, will become familiar with our electronic equipment. It is not too much to hope that through such studies, there may be expected a real breakthrough in the analysis of economic processes and relationships.

Index